A Soldier's Story:

Forever Changed

A Soldier's Story:
Forever Changed

An Infantryman's Saga
of Life and Death in Vietnam

RICHARD F. HOGUE

A Soldier's Story: Forever Changed
An Infantryman's Saga of Life and Death in Vietman
by Richard F. Hogue

Editing – Dr. Gerald Grunska
Cover and interior design – Nick Zelinger, NZ Graphics

Hogue, Richard F.
A Soldier's Story: Forever Changed: "An Infantryman's Saga of Life and Death in Vietnam." / by Richard F. Hogue.
    p. cm.

Includes bibliographical references and table of contents.

ISBN: 978-0-9722264-1-7 (print)
LCCN: 2016914386

1. Vietnamese Conflict, 1961-1975—personal narratives, American. 2. Hogue, Richard F. I. Title.

DS559.5H64 2003 959.704'3'092
                QBI33-1291

First Edition

Published and printed in the United States of America

Table of Contents

Dedication and Tribute

**Hold your head high when Old Glory you see,
and remember those who fought so we could be free.**

A Soldier's Story: Forever Changed is dedicated to every American who honorably served in the U.S. military during the Vietnam War, with sincere gratitude to those who were wounded in action and supreme respect for those who died as a result of their service.

Most specifically this book is my personal tribute to fourteen brave comrades who served with me in Vietnam and were killed in action. I am proud to have briefly known each of you and to have served with you. You will never be forgotten. Although your families have endured the tremendous sorrow of your loss for many years, they should be proud of your honorable and courageous service to our country.

In memory of all who have given their lives in defense of the precious freedom we enjoy; I ask everyone to honor and respect those comrades for their courageous sacrifice, speak respectfully on their behalf and remember their families in your prayers.

*77% of the military personnel killed in Vietnam
held the enlisted rank of E-5 or below.*

*"We were expected to perform like men,
while most of us were still boys."*

Introduction

Although Vietnam was one of America's longest wars, a declaration of war was never invoked. Even though we prevailed in every significant battle, many Americans believe we lost the war. In reality, the American public and our political leaders lost the will to continue the war and a peace settlement was negotiated in January 1973 and American combat forces left Vietnam in March 1973. The fall of Saigon occurred on April 30, 1975, two years after American troops withdrew.

We battled with sophisticated weaponry, while the enemy used simple weapons like punji pits and booby traps and often fought from camouflaged spider holes and tunnels. Over 58,000 American lives were lost in Vietnam; however, an estimated 1.1 million North Vietnamese Army/Viet Cong troops were killed during the war. Searches continue to find and identify Americans missing in action in Vietnam.

The Vietnam War was unique because it was opposed by many Americans and was the most divisive event in America since the Civil War. There were nationwide anti-war demonstrations, the most notable of which was at Kent State University where four students were killed by National Guard troops on May 4, 1970. Emotions for many Americans were very intense and there is frustration felt by some to this day regarding our commitment to the war in Vietnam. By writing this book I share my experience and personal feelings about the war with the hope that my views will provide an improved understanding to others and calm tender emotions that may remain.

Although debate continues regarding our involvement in Vietnam, America's commitment resulted in a turning point for Communism. While South Vietnam was overtaken by communist North Vietnam in 1975, and Laos fell to Communism later that year, Communism has not spread to any other nation since the Vietnam War.

While historians debate which American war had the greatest impact upon our country, the war in Vietnam obviously had the greatest impact upon my life.

Our lives back in *the World* and even our intense infantry training did not prepare us for the experience of walking near a friend one minute and frantically watching him die the next, or losing half our platoon in a matter of minutes. Although the experience of each infantryman who served in Vietnam was different, we share one common sentiment. It changed our lives forever. We saw comrades maimed by the weapons of war and shed tears for friends who died in our arms. I will introduce the men with whom I proudly served and detail the dramatic events I experienced during my tour of duty in Vietnam. We lost our innocence in Vietnam and many will carry the physical and emotional scars of their combat experience to their graves.

It was emotionally difficult to relive my experiences in Vietnam. I sat at my computer on several occasions with tears in my eyes while I recounted the fond memories of friends who were killed over forty years ago. I thank God for my survival. My story is one that relatively few people know, but a story that should be shared. Because every American should understand what was asked of young men thrown into combat in Vietnam. This book shares the lifelong emotional impact of those of us who faced combat in America's most controversial war.

Although I detail many tragic events, this book is not intended to renew painful memories for anyone. Rather, I hope to convey the sense of pride I have attempted to instill as my tribute to those who honorably served their country during the Vietnam War.

The events in *A Soldier's Story: Forever Changed* are described as accurately as possible based upon the recollections of myself, my family and friends and comrades. A few names have been changed to avoid a negative depiction of anyone, and in a few cases, the actual names have long been forgotten.

A Soldier's Story: Forever Changed is a sequel to my previous book entitled *We Were The Third Herd*. I again describe my transition from a peaceful life in a small Iowa town to fighting as an infantryman in Vietnam. I share my thoughts about being drafted and tell how my family and friends were affected when I anxiously marched off to war. An added chapter includes my feelings about the war forty-six years later and describes how that experience drastically reshaped my life and continues to impact me to this day. The final chapter details my return visit to Vietnam in 2013 to share that very meaningful experience.

"... to care for him who shall have borne the battle and for his widow and his orphan."
~ Abraham Lincoln

Acknowledgments

I have many individuals to thank for their valuable assistance provided to enable me to write *A Soldier's Story: Forever Changed.* Several of my comrades helped to recall names, places and events, enabling me to accurately piece together our experience in Vietnam. Family members and friends helped me remember many details that surrounded my two years in the Army, and fellow writing associates provided expert advice and contributed time to review draft versions and make recommendations. I thank you all for your contributions and assistance, and especially for your friendship.

To my lovely wife Marilyn, thank you for your loving support and allowing me to spend endless hours writing and editing while I ignored you and many other tasks at home. And to my devoted editor Jerry Grunska, I thank you for your expert guidance and friendship.

Without the valuable assistance, encouragement and support from many individuals this book would not have become a reality. I am proud of my military service and am proud to be the author of *A Soldier's Story: Forever Changed.*

The first American casualties in Vietnam were suffered long before our significant involvement there. Army Lieutenant Colonel A. Peter Dewey was killed in an ambush in Saigon on September 26, 1945. Two civilian pilots, James McGovern and Wallace Buford were killed, on May 6, 1954, when their plane was struck by enemy fire and crashed, while delivering equipment to a French garrison during the French Indochina War.

The first known military casualty listed on the Vietnam Memorial in Washington, DC is Air Force Sergeant Richard B. Fitzgibbon, killed on June 8, 1956. His name is listed on the Wall with that of his son, Marine Corps Lance Corporal Richard B Fitzgibbon III, who was killed on September 7, 1965.

Chapter 1

The Peaceful Times

Sweat streaked down the side of my face on a stifling afternoon in the remote countryside of South Vietnam. I walked near the middle of a single-file column as the members of my infantry platoon quietly walked through knee high grass and dense brush with scattered lush green hedgerows. The twenty-pound load of ammunition and other gear I carried seemed to weigh a ton. We had been out on a patrol since 8:00 a.m. There was no breeze and we were all hot and tired.

Suddenly, a loud BOOM erupted in front of me!

One man was blown in the air from the force of the explosion as the deafening sound of more explosions and enemy rifle and machine gun fire sent the rest of us diving for cover. I grabbed my rifle with both hands while I desperately tried to determine where the enemy fire was coming from.

We immediately began spraying the area around us with rifle fire, and then BOOM, BOOM. Two enemy hand grenades exploded behind me with a thunderous sound that sent several of us scrambling and left a buddy screaming in pain, blood gushing from his lower left leg that was partially blown into shreds.

He frantically yelled, "Oh God, help me!"

I yelled, "Doc, get over here!"

I could tell by the looks on their faces, that everyone was scared. And so was I. We were receiving heavy enemy fire and suffering serious casualties. Every man struggled to find cover, wishing he could miraculously dig a hole to seek protection from the barrage of enemy fire while trying to return as much firepower as he could.

"What the hell's going on?" Someone yelled.

"We walked into an ambush. Throw some hand grenades into that hedgerow!" I shouted as I pointed to the eight-foot-high hedgerow in front of us.

"Lay down some fire!" I yelled to our machine gun team who began firing hundreds of deadly rounds through the smoking gun barrel.

I rose above a small mound of dirt that was the only protection I could find, as I fired my M-16 on automatic, quickly emptying the rounds in my ammo magazine into the hedgerow. I couldn't see any enemy troops, but I saw the smoke and flashes from their weapons when they fired from their concealed positions. After I grabbed a hand grenade from my pistol belt, I rose to my knees and threw it with all my might at the hedgerow 100 feet in front of me. The sound of the nearly constant rifle and machine gun fire and the exploding hand grenades was deafening. Men were yelling, but I couldn't understand most of what they were saying. I knew we were in trouble. We had been hit hard and the enemy was putting up one hell of a fight.

The man next to me rose to his knees to return fire and was immediately struck in the chest by a volley of enemy machine gun fire. His rifle fell from his hands as he collapsed to the ground.

I yelled, "Doc, I need you!"

I watched the man's green fatigue shirt turn red, soaked with blood from gaping wounds in his chest. Doc crawled up and frantically tried to stop the gushing blood by applying a large field dressing. A moment later I stood on my knees to open fire at the hedgerow, and then I felt my own body jump. Everything went dark.

I opened my eyes and saw a dim shadow of light across my bedroom walls. I felt my heart pounding and realized I had awakened from a frightening dream. I was in the Army fighting for my life in Vietnam. I had never had a dream like that before. I rolled on my side and slowly went back to sleep.

I woke up the next morning and walked through the cold morning air from my apartment to my first class of the day. It was January 1968. I had begun the final semester of my senior year at Wayne State College, a small college in Wayne, Nebraska. While most college guys had student deferments exempting them from the draft, upon graduation those deferments would end. With the war in Vietnam going strong, being drafted was becoming a likely proposition for many of us.

During my nearly four years of college, the war in Vietnam had escalated to the point where American casualties were nearing three hundred weekly. Several guys from my hometown had been drafted or joined the service and had survived a tour in Vietnam or were over there at that time. Realizing that friends I had known all my life were serving in Vietnam brought the war a little closer.

A group of us who lived in Sac County, Iowa received notices for military physicals in March 1968. If a man passed, he was eligible to be drafted. If he didn't pass, he received a 4-F medical deferment exempting him from the draft. Because the physicals were scheduled midweek, I rode home the night before with twin brothers Dean and Dennis Christiansen. The three of us had grown up in Schaller, a small northwest Iowa town. We had graduated from high school there and were attending college together. We caught a bus the next morning at Sac City, the county seat, for a two-hour ride to Omaha, Nebraska. After we arrived at the Induction Center in Omaha, we caught our first glimpse of the military style of business.

A sergeant yelled, "All right you guys, get off the bus and get in line – now!" As he pointed toward the Induction Center entrance. Many of us looked at each other with puzzled expressions on our faces as we were herded along like farm animals not knowing what to expect next. Once inside, the sergeant barked out directions for us to follow a blue line painted on the floor that led into a large room.

The physical started with each of us providing a urine sample and then continued by our proceeding through a series of stations to check our physical wellbeing. The physical ended with a large group of guys standing in a line wearing only under shorts. As a doctor moved down the line to check for hernias, each man dropped his drawers and coughed while the doctor completed his examination.

Most of us didn't take that day too seriously. The majority of guys I knew planned to wait it out and take their chances with the draft. Being drafted into the Army meant you only had a two-year tour, but it also meant you didn't have your choice of duty assignment. With the Army providing the majority of the infantrymen in Vietnam, draftees could end up there as infantrymen.

Although the war in Vietnam was on the opposite side of the World, it directly impacted me when I began interviewing for jobs prior to graduation. Each year, recruiters conducted interviews on campus with students anticipating graduation.

One of the first questions the recruiter asked during my first interview was, "What's your draft status?"

I said, "It's 2-S" (student deferment).

The recruiters knew that upon graduation we would lose our student deferment and were subject to being drafted. After the recruiter learned my draft status, he politely proceeded through a brief interview and then told me he would hold my résumé and contact me if they had a job opportunity. What he really meant was that they didn't want to hire potential draftees. It may not have been fair but that's the way it was. After getting the identical reaction during a second interview and hearing other guys tell the same story, I gave up trying to find a decent job and didn't schedule any more interviews. Some of the guys who planned to be teachers were getting job offers, but even teachers were subject to being drafted.

I could have avoided the draft by enlisting but didn't seriously consider that option. Enlisting in the Army or Marine Corps required a three-year enlistment, and the Navy and Air Force required a four-year enlistment. I finally decided I would go back home after graduation, find a job locally and wait to be drafted. It was a very disappointing way to end four years of college.

My only consolation was that I wasn't alone. Most every other male, eighteen years of age or older, who hadn't been in the service or didn't have a physical deferment was facing the same situation. In fact, during the last month of my final college semester, one of my professors came to class and said his Air Force Reserve unit had been called to active duty and he was going to Vietnam in two weeks.

During the first week of April I took final exams and passed them all. After everyone learned they had passed their finals, the "Gang" gathered at Little Bill's bar in downtown Wayne to celebrate. After four long years of attending classes, writing term papers and taking exams, it was finally over. Several of us would receive our bachelor's degree the next afternoon.

The following morning I welcomed my parents and two sisters who arrived just before noon for the graduation ceremony, which was held outdoors on campus. It was a pleasant day with bright sunshine and a gentle warm breeze swaying the trees. When my name was read on the afternoon of April 10, 1968, I joyfully walked forward and accepted my Bachelor of Science degree with a major in business administration.

The next morning I drove northeast into Iowa and arrived home early that afternoon. I talked with my mom for a while regarding my very uncertain future and then unpacked my car and carried my clothes and few belongings upstairs to my room. I reclined on my bed and thought about how I had gotten to that point in my life.

Except during college, I had lived my entire life in Schaller, Iowa with my parents Charlie and Jean and two sisters, Marilyn, four years older, and Jan, three years younger. My mother had lived her entire life in or near Schaller. She worked part time at the school cafeteria and provided piano lessons to kids at home. My dad was born and raised in southern Iowa and had moved to Schaller in the late 1930s. He had worked on my granddad's (mom's dad) farm and married Mom in 1940. Dad later began working for the P. A. G. Seed Corn Company near town and had worked there ever since.

Schaller was a small town of about 850 people much like hundreds of other farming communities that dotted the Midwest. The major industry was the Central and American Popcorn Companies, who processed and distributed Bango and Jolly Time popcorn worldwide. Schaller had identified itself as the "Popcorn Capital of the World" and held a weekend "Pop Corn Days" celebration each July.

Although Schaller was a very small town, it had been a great place to grow up. As youngsters, my friends and I spent the summers playing baseball, riding bikes, going on Boy Scout camping trips and, now and then, getting into a little trouble. As teenagers, we hunted rabbits, squirrels or pheasants in farmer's groves or fields. Little did I know, during those hunting excursions, that some of us would someday be hunting enemy soldiers in the rice paddies and jungles of South Vietnam.

High school sporting events and other school activities dominated the social life for many people around Schaller. Growing up it seemed like I would live with my parents and go to school forever. But when high school graduation day arrived on May 27, 1964, I knew I would finally be moving on.

After high school graduation I arrived home one evening during the first week of August and found Mom in the kitchen cooking supper and Dad in the living room reading the *Des Moines Register* while Walter Cronkite was broadcasting the evening news. Cronkite said the North Vietnamese had attacked U.S. Navy ships earlier that week and Congress had passed the Gulf of Tonkin Resolution giving President Johnson the power to take further action against North Vietnam, including the use of armed forces.

Mom said, "It sounds like they're getting us into another war – supper is ready, you guys."

"Oh, I don't think North Vietnam wants to take us on. They'll back off," I said as Dad and I sat down at the kitchen table. Our conversation soon turned to our day's activities.

In September 1964 I started college at Ellsworth Junior College in Iowa Falls, Iowa. After our sophomore year at Ellsworth, Dean and Dennis Christiansen and I transferred to Wayne State.

Although I was extremely proud about college graduation, I didn't have a job and I was unsure about what the Army had in store for me. For the first time in my life, my future was totally uncertain.

A few days later, I found a job with Roy Zofka who had a small construction business in Schaller. Transitioning from my relatively soft college life to performing hard physical labor was a shock to my body. The worst job was shingling. Working on an asphalt shingled roof on a hot and humid Iowa summer afternoon was miserable and was worth a lot more than the two dollars an hour I was paid.

Another good friend, Allan Schwab, returned home from college the end of May. Allan and I had grown up together and were high school classmates. He was attending the University of Northern Iowa and had one more semester to complete before graduating.

One morning during early June, Allan and I drove to the Selective Service Office in Sac City. We gave the clerk our names and asked about our options regarding the draft. She had been notified I graduated from college and my draft status had been changed to 1-A, which meant I was eligible to be drafted. Although Allan could have gone back to college that fall to finish his final semester he decided to get the service behind him. We both volunteered for the draft. We would likely receive our draft notices in July.

During the first week of July, I was eating lunch at home when my mother handed me a letter from the draft board. Neither of us said a word, we both knew what it was. Although that letter was certainly the most important letter I had ever received, I laid it on the table while I finished my lunch. I finally opened it to see when I had to report, August 5, 1968. Allan Schwab also received his draft notice that day. We drank a few beers that night knowing our fate had been sealed for the next two years.

That spring I had met Jan Griffin at a party in Omaha where she was attending nursing school. I called Jan to tell her I had been drafted and invited her to Schaller for Pop Corn Days the third weekend of July. Each year the Chamber of Commerce sponsored the celebration with activities including a parade, carnival rides and special festivities. For many small Midwestern towns, those summer celebrations were one of the highlights of the year.

It was soon the week of the Pop Corn Days celebration. The streets of Schaller that were normally relatively quiet most evenings were full of cars driving around while people ran errands in preparation for the big celebration. By Friday afternoon, two blocks of Main Street were completely full of concession stands and carnival rides waiting for the crowds to arrive.

Jan Griffin drove up from Omaha Friday evening to join me for what would be my last fling before joining the Army. We eventually joined some friends who were enjoying themselves at a party hosted by Kenny and Marlys Kroese. Marlys was the sister of my high school and college buddies Dean and Dennis Christiansen.

Saturday was the big day of the weekend celebration starting with a parade at ten o'clock. Mom yelled, "Hey, you guys better get up." We all got up and enjoyed a glass of milk and freshly made cinnamon rolls before the parade. My mother was well known around town for her cinnamon rolls. When I was a kid, if friends came by when she had a batch of rolls cooling on the back porch, we stopped whatever we were doing to eat a fresh cinnamon roll.

Jan and I joined my folks in a shady spot along the parade route amongst the crowd who were gathering for the parade. The VFW Hup-Tu Squad led the parade carrying rifles and the American flag. The parade continued for an hour with floats, antique cars and farm equipment, clowns, horses and fire engines.

I woke up on Sunday morning when Mom yelled, "It's time to get ready for church." She expected me to go to church unless I had a very good excuse, and staying out late on Saturday night wasn't a good excuse. After church Mom fixed one of her great Sunday noon meals. Granddad (mom's dad) joined us as we shared a relaxing afternoon.

It was soon Friday, August 2nd. I drove to Omaha to spend time with my girlfriend Jan that evening and shared our goodbyes Saturday morning. It wasn't a teary moment, but it was sad. She was the first girl I had considered a girlfriend and the Army was breaking us up just as we had started to get to know each other. We held each other tightly for a moment and said nothing. We then shared one final kiss.

After arriving home I enjoyed a delicious supper with my parents, younger sister Jan and older sister Marilyn and husband Gary who had driven from Sioux City to join us. That evening I went out for my final night on the town. Although I was looking forward to going out, it meant spending my last few hours with hometown friends and saying goodbye. Marlys and Kenny Kroese hosted a farewell party for Allan and me where we enjoyed many toasts made in our honor. I also spent some quiet moments saying goodbye to friends and sharing farewell hugs and handshakes with people as the evening quickly passed.

The next thing I knew it was time for church. I took a moment during the service to give thanks for what I had accomplished during my life and said a little prayer for the Lord to watch over me for the next two years. The reality of being drafted had arrived.

- ➤ Walter Lee Nutt III was a fellow student at Ellsworth Junior College. He served in the U.S. Army and arrived in Vietnam on March 22, 1969. He was killed in action on April 28, 1969, at the age of twenty-two. He was posthumously awarded the Distinguished Service Cross (the second highest military medal) for his gallant actions on that day.

- ➤ Albert Du Ward Benson was a fellow student at Wayne State College. He served in the U.S. Marine Corps and arrived in Vietnam on March 15, 1969. He was killed in action on July 6, 1969, at the age of twenty-three.

- ➤ Steven Eugene Backhaus was another fellow student at Wayne State College. He served in the U.S. Marine Corps and arrived in Vietnam on December 11, 1969. He was killed in action ten days later on December 21, 1969, at the age of twenty-two.

On January 20, 1968, the siege at Marine outpost Khe Sanh began. Two North Vietnamese Army (NVA) Divisions surrounded the out-post and launched repeated fierce attacks until the siege ended on April 8, 1968, when additional U.S. Marine and Army Air Cavalry troops reached Khe Sanh. The Marines suffered 205 casualties during the siege. However, an estimated 10,000 NVA soldiers were killed. Ironically, U.S. forces abandoned Khe Sanh in June 1968.

Chapter 2

You're in the Army Now

Tears formed in Mom's eyes as I shared goodbye hugs with my parents and reluctantly left home to join the Army on Monday August 5, 1968. Later that morning a busload of us draftees arrived at the Induction Center in Omaha.

We proceeded through a series of stations where they gathered personal information and double-checked our medical records. My buddy Allan Schwab and I became separated during the process and I didn't see him the rest of the day. That afternoon I was led into a room filled with about twenty-five other men to take our oath of induction into the United States Army. I raised my right hand and said:

"I Richard Hogue, do solemnly swear that I will support and defend the Constitution of the United States against all enemies, foreign and domestic; that I will bear true faith and allegiance to the same; and that I will obey the orders of the President of the United States and the orders of the officers appointed over me, according to regulations and the Uniform Code of Military Justice, so help me God."

We were then asked to take one step forward to represent our official Army induction. Man! I was in the Army. With that ceremonial step, I, along with thousands of my fellow Americans put my civilian life on hold to begin serving my country.

Later that afternoon we were taken by bus to Eppley Field in Omaha to board a flight to Seattle, Washington. We would undertake our basic training at Fort Lewis, about forty miles south of Seattle.

Most of us inductees enjoyed the flight except for a guy sitting in front of me who barfed in a bag shortly after takeoff.

I asked him, "How do you like the Army so far?" He just chuckled.

After landing in Seattle we were bussed to Fort Lewis, arriving about 9:00 p.m., where we were directed to an old two-story wooden barracks and told to find a bunk. It had been a long day and I was tired. I crawled under a green Army blanket and soon fell asleep.

About 6:30 the next morning a sergeant came into the barracks and startled everyone by yelling, "Get your butts out of bed! Your civilian life is over!"

We were a tired and raggedy looking group as we gathered outside to be marched to breakfast. Most of us still wore the same civilian clothes we had arrived in and slept in. We were in an induction holding area where we would complete preliminary activities before being taken to a basic training company.

The forty men in the barracks would become a platoon during our eight weeks of basic training. A platoon is the basic-level Army organizational unit. Three platoons would form our basic training company, the next level in the Army's organizational structure. Normally four or five companies were organized under a battalion. Above the battalion was a brigade or regiment and then an Army Division.

After breakfast we received a free haircut, Army style. When I sat down in a chair the barber wrapped a cover around my neck, and in about one minute he gave me a total buzz cut, leaving nothing but stubble on my head. Afterwards, some of us almost didn't recognize each other. We were then issued military clothing including fatigues, dress uniforms, hats, boots and shoes. We were told to leave on a pair of fatigues and boots and pack everything else into the olive drab (OD) green duffel bag we had been issued. We were also given a cardboard box and told to label it with our home address and place our civilian clothes inside. The boxes were mailed home at the Army's expense.

During my second day at Fort Lewis we were marching past a barracks when someone yelled from a window, "Hey, Hogue!" I looked up and saw my hometown friend Allan Schwab waving at me. I waved back, but couldn't stop to talk. I tracked him down that evening and learned his platoon was waiting to be joined with two other platoons for basic training. Although we had been separated for a couple of days it appeared we might be going through basic training together.

On the third day, we were loaded onto buses for a short ride to the basic training company. When we got off our bus all hell broke loose as the drill sergeants began yelling at the top of their lungs.

"Get your asses off that bus!"

"Hurry up and find your duffel bag, trainee!"

"Get into formation you lazy maggots!"

Anyone who wasn't hustling caught the wrath of a drill sergeant.

"Get your butt in gear before I kick it between your shoulders."

If we hadn't all been so startled, we would have laughed at each other as we scurried around, bumping into one another while we attempted to get into formation. A few minutes later the company commander (commanding officer/CO) walked out from the headquarters building. We were called to attention as he stopped in front of the platoon formations. The CO was a Captain and appeared to be in his late twenties. Although we had only been in the Army for three days, we believed that anyone with three or more stripes on their arm was someone we should respect. If we encountered an officer with bars or other insignia on their collar, we had best snap-to and salute.

The first thing the CO told us was that we were restricted to the company area unless we left as a group for training or if we were specifically authorized to leave. There would be no weekend passes and no trips to the clubs on post. After listening to the CO we were guided to our barracks.

The company area consisted of a two-story brick building with each platoon assigned a large open bay area on the second floor with bunks lined along each side and a metal wall locker and wooden footlocker for each trainee. On the first floor was a large mess hall, the headquarters area containing the CO's office, the company clerk and other offices. There was also an area called the Day Room with a pool table, television and other games we could use only at designated times, normally on weekends.

As we unpacked our belongings, we were shown how to store our clothes and personal items. Yes, our fatigues and uniforms had to be hung in a certain order and evenly spaced in the wall locker. Our socks and underwear had to be rolled up and placed in a specific location in our footlocker, and other personal items had to be stored in an assigned spot. We would be subject to periodic inspections throughout basic training. Most of us were generally stunned after leaving the comforts of our homes and being thrown into a barracks with over one hundred other men, and then, having our every move dictated by someone else.

We were issued clean sheets and blankets and shown how to make up our bunks. Wow, my mom had still made my bed when I was home. Unless you were sleeping in your bunk, it had to be made with the corners folded under and no wrinkles in the OD-green blanket. I soon learned that much of basic training was simply regimentation and uniformity. We spent hours shining the brass insignias for our uniforms, polishing our boots and shoes, cleaning the tile barracks floor and completing many other tasks to make sure we kept ourselves and the company area spit and polished.

Allan Schwab was in another platoon down the hall from mine, making it easy to keep in touch. We didn't talk every day but it was comforting knowing a friend was close by.

Basic training began with general orientations about the Army and completing tests to judge our general aptitude, personality traits and mechanical skills. The tests would also determine our eligibility for Officer Candidate School (OCS). Although some of us had college degrees the majority of the men didn't. In fact, several guys hadn't graduated from high school.

After the first week we settled into the basic training routine and soon learned the realities of how the Army determined permanent duty assignments. During the last week of basic training many of us would be assigned a Military Occupational Specialty (MOS). The men who had enlisted for three years had chosen an MOS. But over half of us were draftees who would serve only a two-year tour, but we didn't have the option to choose our MOS. Naturally, enlistees rarely choose hazardous infantry duty; however, there was a continual need for infantrymen because of the high casualty rates in Vietnam. Many of us draftees would likely be assigned to the infantry.

On August 14, 1968 I quietly observed my 22nd birthday as just another day. There was no party, no birthday cake, no gifts, not even a cold beer to celebrate. I did receive birthday cards from Jan Griffin and my family saying, "Enjoy your birthday." Oh sure.

Each of us ultimately experienced serving on kitchen police (KP) duty in the mess hall. The cooks used the KP guys mostly for the chores they didn't want to do, like cleaning garbage cans, washing dishes, mopping the floor, and of course, peeling potatoes. KP was a long day, starting at 5:00 a.m. and continued until the mess hall was cleaned after the evening meal.

We also shared fire watch on rotating shifts from lights out at 10:00 p.m. until we got up around six o'clock each morning. One man would roam the barracks for an hour and then wake up the man in the next bunk for his one-hour shift. Obviously a fire could have started somewhere in the barracks, but they were made of brick and concrete, nearly fireproof. Although the duty was called fire watch, it was really training for guard duty that many of us would be pulling in Vietnam.

One of the Army's primary basic training objectives was to get us in good physical condition. An hour of physical training (PT) was scheduled nearly every day. We did sit-ups, push-ups, jumping jacks, etc., and we would run and run and run. We went on many double-time runs that seemed to last forever while we sang cadences like, "I want to be an Airborne Ranger, I want to live a life of danger, Airborne! Ranger!" And on and on. We would run until my boots felt like they weighed a ton and my legs felt almost numb.

The men in the company were of all shapes and sizes. One man was too tall to join the Air Force, but the Army took him. A few guys were even shorter than me (5'6") and some guys were way overweight. One man who struggled with running was thirty-six-year-old Sam Pierce. He had been in the Army years earlier but had gotten out.

He had reenlisted and was going through basic training with the rest of us. Sam really wasn't that old, but compared to the rest of us who were eighteen to twenty-two, Sam was old. We soon nicknamed him the "Old man." Sam smoked and was out of shape. Guys often had to help him along to finish those torturous double-time runs.

The day we went to the hand grenade range we learned that a trainee had been killed a month earlier when a grenade with a short fuse detonated almost immediately after he threw it. Hand grenades were designed to explode about four seconds after the handle was released. After an orientation session we formed lines to take our turn throwing a grenade over a three-foot-high concrete wall.

When it was my turn, I walked up to the wall and took a grenade from the instructor who stood beside me ready to kick the grenade in a trench in case I dropped it or didn't throw it over the wall. I firmly held the grenade in my left hand chest high. I put my right index finger through the ring attached to the safety pin that held the handle in place and pulled the pin out. With a tight grip on the grenade I leaned back and threw it over the wall with all my might. I heard a ping and saw the handle fly away from the grenade after I released it. The grenade flew through the air while the instructor and I quickly ducked behind the wall. I felt the ground vibrate slightly as the grenade exploded in front of us. Throwing my first live grenade was an exciting experience. Everyone threw a hand grenade that day without an incident.

Basic training was limited to eight hours per day. We were up early each morning to eat a hearty breakfast of eggs or pancakes and bacon or sausage, or the good old Army's SOS (slop-on-a-shingle, aye). We also had to make sure the barracks were spic-and-span before we left. Training started about eight o'clock each morning and finished around five o'clock that afternoon. If we had night training, we got time off during the day to stay within the eight-hour per day training restriction. We normally marched to the nearby training sites or would be transported to remote sites by buses, deuce-and-a-halfs (2½ ton military cargo trucks) or in what we called "cattle cars." The cattle cars were tractor-trailer vehicles with a canvas-covered trailer with wooden benches along each side. We were packed into those trailers like cattle, with guys sitting on the benches and the floor.

Saturday was normally a light day with PT and cleanup details around the company area in the morning and then time off that afternoon. Sundays were totally ours with no training. Guys normally spent Sundays writing letters, playing cards or pool in the Day Room or just sleeping. I went to church a few times on Sunday with some of the guys and enjoyed a rare hour of personal freedom.

During basic training we held the lowest military rank of Private E-1. We were paid $102 per month in cash on the first day of each month. The only good thing about not making much money was that we didn't need much money. Our meals, our clothes and laundry were provided at no cost. We were normally marched to the Post Exchange (PX) once a week to stock up on personal items and snacks we craved, that weren't available in the barracks. If someone got hungry at night he couldn't just go to the mess hall and raid the refrigerator.

As basic training progressed we learned to read topographical maps and use a compass to navigate. One night we were sent off in pairs with a compass, a map and a flashlight to navigate through a remote heavily wooded area to an established destination. Navigating at night was difficult, but my partner and I ultimately reached the correct destination.

Another unique challenge was gas mask training that concluded with a test. It started with our low crawling through an open area without a mask on. Unannounced, canisters of 2-chlorobenzal-malononitrile (CS) gas were detonated, which was similar to tear gas but much more potent. A small whiff would immediately burn your nose and throat. A heavy dose of CS gas would choke you and make it nearly impossible to breathe. It wasn't lethal, but it could make you wish you were dead. When I got my first whiff of CS gas I held my breath until I pulled my mask over my face and tightened the rubber straps. I then low-crawled through the gas cloud while the mask filtered the gas.

The weather was pleasant during basic training, not too hot and only periodic rain. We appreciated nice weather because we spent much of our time outside. During week seven we took the qualifying test with our M-14 rifles. We then completed the PT test that included a low-crawl drill, an obstacle course, parallel bars, one-man carry (where we carried another man about thirty yards) and a one-mile run. Although I was in good shape, I was far from the fastest or strongest man in the company. But I passed the PT test with no problems.

It was interesting to watch the men as we completed our final testing. Although none of us were excited about being in the Army, a natural competitive instinct came out in most guys. We strived to score the highest on the rifle range and to complete each PT event as fast as we could, if for nothing else, a little self-pride. Amazingly, the Army actually had us enjoying busting our butts.

Allan and I spent time together talking about alternatives for dealing with our future that included the likelihood of being assigned to the infantry. Although they offered us the opportunity to re-up for a three-year enlistment, which would have given us the choice of a non-combat assignment, Allan and I agreed to take our chances and let the Army choose our duty assignment. I had a college degree and Allan was only one semester away from graduation. Surely the Army wouldn't assign us to the infantry. We could have pursued Officer Candidate School (OCS), but the only openings were in the infantry and required a four-year enlistment. We both passed on OCS.

It was finally the first week of October 1968, the last week of basic training that included a three-day bivouac (camping Army style). We hoped for good weather, because we knew the almost daily autumn rains would soon begin. Bivouac started by navigating through terrain during the first day and simulating taking an enemy position by slowly moving up a hill and overtaking the enemy. We carried our rifles but of course weren't issued ammunition. At night we established a defensive position and rotated guard duty. The bivouac wasn't as bad as I had expected. The maneuvers each day weren't too demanding, and we got a few hours of sleep at night in between guard shifts. Training bivouacs were traditionally concluded with a *forced march* back to the company area. The intent wasn't to have us run but to walk as fast as we could without taking a break. There were also bragging rights at stake for the CO and drill sergeants for the company that completed the forced march in the shortest time.

On the afternoon of the third day of bivouac we headed down a gravel road in two columns carrying our backpacks and rifles for nearly a ten-mile march back to the company area. The first few miles weren't too bad for me but then my 5′ 6″ body and proportionately short legs started to take their toll. I had learned the Army had no sympathy for someone who may not be as big or strong as other men, or if someone wasn't as intelligent and had more difficulty completing a particular training exercise. We were all expected to *suck it up* and somehow do what we were told.

As the march continued the columns spread out. The taller men and those who were in the best condition moved forward while others including several of us short guys fell behind. Although I was in good physical shape, I was becoming as exhausted as I had ever been in my life. But I kept forcing one foot in front of the other, determined not to quit. The drill sergeants and company officers moved up and down the columns and gave words of encouragement to those who needed it rather than yelling and cussing as they often had.

One drill sergeant, Staff Sergeant Trotten, settled in and chatted with a few of us during the last couple miles of the march. Although the drill sergeants had yelled and cussed at us during most of basic training, we got to know some of them and found their bark was louder than their bite. Most of the drill sergeants were Vietnam veterans with good intentions, trying to teach us the discipline associated with Army life and learning to take orders whether we liked it or not.

After a march that I thought would never end, we found a reward waiting for us in the company area; cold beer and soda. I grabbed a can and began drinking the first beer I had seen in eight weeks. I was almost too tired to enjoy it, but it tasted great. Most of us drank a couple beers while we relaxed and toasted the near completion of basic training.

The next day we were called to the Day Room to receive our orders stating our MOS and when and where to report for our next assignment. The mood for most of us was somber. When I stepped forward and stated my name a sergeant pulled my orders and said, "11 Bravo, Light Weapons Infantryman." I would be staying at Fort Lewis for Advanced Infantry Training (AIT).

He handed me copies of my orders and I turned and walked away feeling a little stunned. Although I knew the majority of us draftees would be assigned to the infantry, I had held out some hope I would be one of the few who would be assigned elsewhere. But it wasn't to be. I reluctantly accepted my assignment like dozens of other men did that day. One of the men in my platoon had been a high school music teacher and was assigned to an Army band. I should have told the Army I had played the baritone in my high school band.

I walked down the hall to see Allan Schwab. "Infantry," he said as I walked up to him.

I said, "Me, too." While we both shook our heads in disbelief.

We were both staying at Fort Lewis for AIT but Allan was assigned to another training company. We both accepted our fate that day and hoped for the best. That afternoon I packed most of my clothes in my duffel bag and went to the Day Room to relax for a while. When I walked in I noticed a banner on a bulletin board that read:

"For those who have fought for it, life has a meaning others will never know."

I read the words twice as though they were meant for me.

The final day of basic training began with a graduation ceremony at a nearby parade ground. Our company joined two other basic training companies to march in front of a reviewing stand of Army officers. We then stood in formation and listened to a speech from our battalion commander who said he was proud of us and we would be an important part of the Army's future. He also spent a few moments talking about Vietnam and stated that many of us would be seeing duty there. "Thanks for the good news," I thought.

After the graduation ceremony the men who were flying to other Army posts for further training grabbed their duffel bags and boarded buses taking them to the airport in Seattle. We quickly exchanged goodbyes as men left and wished each other the best of luck. Although we had been together for only eight weeks, good friendships had been formed. While everyone was happy to be moving on, it was also sad. Many of us would never see each other again.

Early that afternoon, those of us who had been assigned to the infantry boarded buses taking us to our AIT Company on Fort Lewis.

Richard Nixon was elected President on November 5, 1968. He committed to withdrawing troops from Vietnam. During 1968 the U.S. military force level in Vietnam was 536,000. That year 16,511 Americans were killed in Vietnam, making it the worst year for American casualties during the Vietnam War.

Chapter 3

Advanced Infantry Training and NCO School

A fter a short bus ride, we arrived at our AIT Company and were again greeted with drill sergeants yelling at us while we rushed into formation. The company area was comprised of wood frame World War II-era buildings, three two-story barracks, a one-story headquarters building containing the Day Room, and a mess hall. The cool and cloudy weather combined with old and drab surroundings made for a dismal welcome to AIT.

Many of us who had gone through basic training together at Fort Lewis were assigned to the third platoon along with other men who had just completed basic training at Army posts around the country and would be arriving later that afternoon. Despite being assigned to the infantry and finding our new living quarters old and cramped, there was finally some good news. During a brief orientation we were told we had the rest of the weekend off and we could go off post on future weekends. Finally, some freedom.

However, there was also some bad news. The eight-hour-per-day training restriction no longer applied. If we were out training until midnight, we still had to get up early the following morning for more training. We would still have rotating KP duty but we wouldn't have fire watch. What was going on? We were in an old wooden barracks that would quickly go up in flames. But no one complained. It sounded like we would need all the sleep we could get.

Before long I joined a group of guys walking to the nearby Enlisted Club to enjoy our first taste of freedom in eight weeks. We laughed and joked about basic training and the unique experiences we encountered as we enjoyed cold beers. We also talked about how our outlook on the Army had changed. Officers really didn't need to be feared, and although drill sergeants yelled and cussed at us, most of them were decent men just doing their job. We also knew another piece of our military future was in place. Whether we liked it or not, we were beginning nine weeks of training to become light weapons infantrymen, likely to serve as combatants in Vietnam.

Monday morning rolled around way too quickly as we were up at 6:00 a.m. to begin the day. Later that day we were issued M-16 rifles, the rifles used in Vietnam. The M-16 was much lighter than the M-14 rifles we used in basic training and fired a smaller round. However, the M-16 round traveled at such an extremely high velocity it caused serious damage when striking someone, often leaving a huge exit wound. M-16s could fire on semi-automatic or automatic simply by flipping a lever on the left side of the firing chamber. You could empty a twenty-round magazine in a few seconds.

Much of AIT was field training that included firing M-16s, M-60 machine guns, M-79 grenade launchers, and again, throwing hand grenades. The M-60 machine gun vibrated your whole body when you fired it. Firing those weapons was fun so long as no one was firing back at us. Physical training continued almost daily and included extremely challenging obstacle courses. We received survival training, continued navigation training across the wooded Fort Lewis terrain, and completed hand-to-hand combat and bayonet training.

During the month of October the weather got cooler and it began to rain frequently. Although much of our training was conducted outside, nothing was cancelled because of the rain. We began spending many long, cold and miserable days in the rain. We wore ponchos over our field jackets to keep us dry, but after spending a long day in the cold rain, my whole body felt numb.

We all looked forward to mail call when we returned from each busy day of training. A letter from a family member or friend provided a few minutes of escape from our controlled Army existence. Although most of us had been away from our families and friends for longer than we had ever been in the past, we had little time to get depressed about our circumstance. Each of us was just one of thousands of men who were enduring the same training across the country. Besides, with forty men crammed into a small barracks, it was difficult to feel too lonely.

I kept in touch with Jan Griffin by letter every few days. I had called her during the first week of AIT and told her I had been assigned to the infantry and that my prospects of going to Vietnam had dramatically increased. Although I told her about some of our training, it was nearly impossible for anyone to imagine what it was like without actually being there. We would complete AIT a week before Christmas, which was great. I would be home on leave over the holidays.

What helped keep us going week after week was knowing we could get away from it all each weekend and experience some of the outside world. I had asked my folks to send some civilian clothes. The weekend after my clothes arrived I joined a group of guys and went to Seattle for a party that a friend of one of the guys was having. Four of us shared a cab and arrived near downtown Seattle not knowing for sure where we were. We started bar hopping and asking directions to the address we were given for the party, which we never found.

After my first experience in Seattle, I wasn't too excited about going back. I spent the next few weekends on post going to the club, the movie theater or just relaxing around the barracks. Sometimes a little peace and quiet was more enjoyable than anything else.

Midway through AIT I learned about a four-month Noncommissioned Officer (NCO) Candidate Course at Fort Benning, Georgia. Upon graduation from what was referred to as "NCO School" I would be promoted to the rank of Sergeant E-5. The training had been established because there was a shortage of infantry NCOs in Vietnam. Rather than promoting a man to replace an NCO who was killed or wounded, the Army decided to provide additional training to those attending NCO School. New NCOs would be assigned as infantry squad leaders and platoon sergeants in Vietnam.

A recent NCO School graduate was assigned as our AIT platoon sergeant for his on-the-job-training (OJT). He told me I was likely going to Vietnam anyway, therefore I might as well take advantage of the additional training at NCO School. We had been promoted to Private E-2 after basic training and would be promoted to Private First Class E-3 upon arrival in Vietnam. I decided why not, if I was going to Vietnam, go as sergeant. I volunteered for NCO School.

A few other guys in my platoon also volunteered for NCO School, including the "Old man," Sam Pierce. Although Sam reenlisted in the Army he had volunteered for the infantry. While he knew it meant possibly risking his life in Vietnam, he also knew it was the fastest way to earn rank. He was willing to take the chance.

The final weeks of AIT became more intense. One night we were split into two-man teams to navigate through a wooded area where men identified as the enemy would attempt to capture us. My partner and I made it part way through the area when we heard a noise in front of us. Thinking it might be one of the enemy we lay down by a tree. A guy snuck up behind us and said, "You're captured." He grabbed us and took us to a mock POW camp where they yelled at us, put us through a mock interrogation and then locked us in a cage.

Another exciting night was the *live fire* exercise. It was completely dark when we began low-crawling through a fifty-yard long course with barbed wire strung a couple feet above the ground while two M-60 machine guns fired over our heads. That was the first time they exposed us to live rounds being fired toward us. Every fifth M-60 round was a tracer that glowed orange as it zipped through the air. The glowing tracers raced above our heads as hundreds of rounds per minute were fired and explosive charges were detonated around us simulating mortar and hand grenade explosions. I had no trouble low-crawling below the barbed wire that night.

We had to pass another PT test and a firing test for both the M-16 rifles and M-60 machine guns. Although we were being trained for the most dangerous job in the world, most of the guys maintained enough personal pride and determination to do the best they could.

Sure, there were a few slackers, but with the drill sergeants and instructors cussing them out and some of us trainees getting on their case from time to time, most everyone came around. We reluctantly accepted the fact that our lives might later depend upon what we learned during AIT. That in itself provided an incentive for most of us to pay attention and learn everything we could during those nine weeks. While most of us focused on learning as the training became more intense with each day, it was easy to forget what our lives before the Army had been like.

Unfortunately, the weather got colder and wetter in December. I was getting to the point I didn't care what was in store for me next. All I wanted to do was to leave that lousy weather and head home for the holidays. It was finally the last week of AIT as we headed out for another bivouac. It began raining during the first afternoon while we played war games in the muddy Fort Lewis terrain. That evening we arrived at a site with bunkers built in a circular perimeter, which we thought would protect us from the rain. However, the bunkers were partially underground and almost useless because water was leaking inside. "Son-of-a-bitch," was the general response when the guys found puddles of water in each bunker.

The drill sergeants relaxed the rules and let us start bonfires to help dry out our clothes and warm up a little. To make things worse, the rain later turned to snow. I knew it rained in Vietnam, but I also knew it didn't snow. It was a long and miserable night, as our soggy sleeping bags provided little warmth. Although bivouac was intended for us to apply our infantry skills, with the lousy weather, we were mostly focused on trying to stay dry and warm.

The weather finally cleared up on the third day and warmed up enough to help us slowly dry out. Just like basic training, AIT bivouac concluded with another grueling forced march carrying our back-packs and rifles. A group of us short guys eventually formed toward the rear of the two columns and we laughed because many of us had been in the same spot during basic training. The "Old man," Sam Pierce, was one of the last men to finish with one man on each side helping him enter the company area. Sam grabbed a cold beer that someone handed to him while he sat on the ground looking like he was about to die.

Those of us who volunteered for NCO School knew we would spend the next four months at Fort Benning, Georgia. The few men who volunteered for OCS would spend the next six months in training and graduate as second lieutenants. But for most of the men it was time to learn what the Army had in store for them.

I had very little opportunity during AIT to watch television or read newspaper accounts of what was happening in Vietnam. Newspaper accounts of the war had moved from the back pages to the front pages and radio and television news programs provided the weekly American death toll and accounts of war protests across the country.

But I knew peace talks between the United States and North Vietnam had commenced that past summer, and newly elected President Nixon had committed to withdrawal of American troops. However, I also knew hundreds of GIs (Government Issue) were being killed and wounded every week and they were still sending men to Vietnam. That told me the end of the war was still a long way off.

Each of us knew we could become a casualty in Vietnam, but we rarely discussed it. Most of the men tried to be macho and not expose their fears about what they might face. During AIT the drill sergeants yelled at us if we did something wrong saying things like, "If you screw up like that in Nam, Charlie will kill you," or "You better pay attention, you dumb shit, or you'll die in Vietnam."

Most of the AIT drill sergeants had served as infantrymen in Vietnam and they shared stories of men being killed or wounded because they made a foolish mistake. Their yelling and cussing was their way of getting our attention and trying to help us survive our time in combat.

When the day of reckoning arrived, the majority of the guys who weren't going to OCS or NCO School received orders for Vietnam, just as everyone had expected. A couple of men in our platoon received orders for Korea but everyone else was on their way to

Vietnam after the holidays. Although going to Vietnam certainly wasn't how anyone wanted to begin the new year, most of the men looked forward to spending the holidays with family and friends rather than dwelling on what would happen in January.

It was Thursday, December 12, 1968. After AIT graduation the following day, I had three weeks of leave. We all packed our personal belongings into our duffel bags except our Class-A uniform, which we would wear for graduation and while we traveled. Anything that didn't fit into a guy's duffel bag was offered to someone else or left behind. The priority for all of us was getting away from Fort Lewis.

After I packed my belongings I walked over to Allan Schwab's company to see what his orders were. He hadn't volunteered for NCO School. I walked up to his bunk, and without my asking, he said, "I'm going to Nam."

We both chuckled, thinking our strategy of volunteering for the draft and not reenlisting to get our choice of an MOS was working out pretty well. We were both in the infantry with Allan headed for Vietnam in three weeks and I was likely only a few months behind him. We had plane reservations to fly back to Omaha together, so we agreed to meet by my barracks after graduation and grab a cab to the airport.

After we cleaned up our barracks that afternoon, most of the men headed to the club to relax during our final night of AIT. I had been with some of those men since we met at the Induction Center in Omaha and had formed good friendships. That would be our last night together and likely the last time many of us would ever see each other. We enjoyed recalling the screw ups some of us had made and chuckled when we recounted the hours of PT, spending hours training in the rain, the snow during bivouac and the exhausting forced marches. We talked about the drill sergeants, most who were decent men and a couple who were just plain jerks.

The next morning we walked outside the barracks in our green Class-A uniforms and acknowledged we all looked a little more handsome since we had been allowed to grow our hair a little longer. As

Private E-2s, we wore one bright, yellow stripe on each arm and proudly wore the shiny brass crossed-rifle insignia with a light blue plastic trim signifying we were infantrymen. I had endured some of the most difficult training the Army offered including the most extreme physical demands of my life. I had passed every challenge they gave me and felt proud of my accomplishments.

Graduation day was cool and cloudy, but fortunately it wasn't raining. We again paraded in front of a reviewing stand and then listened while a senior officer provided a short speech. After we marched back to the barracks we all quickly shared hugs and handshakes with our buddies and then hustled to get away from Fort Lewis and forget about the Army for a while.

I shared the holidays with my family and friends in the familiar surroundings I had grown so accustomed to before I was drafted. And yes, Mom spoiled me by making my bed every morning. Unfortunately, those three weeks passed all too quickly. I also knew I probably wouldn't be spending the next holiday season at home. I anticipated going to Vietnam that following July to begin my one-year tour of duty.

It was soon Saturday morning, January 4, 1969. I was going to Omaha that afternoon to see Jan Griffin before I left Sunday morning. Allan Schwab was also leaving that weekend for Fort Lewis and then on to Vietnam. I stopped by Allan's house to say good-bye. We both ignored the possibility we might not see each other again as we shared a difficult farewell with a hug and handshake.

During the two-hour drive to Omaha, Mom told me she was already worrying about me going to Vietnam. I told my folks not to worry; I was just leaving for more training. But that was mostly wasted breath. They were going to worry until I was out of the Army.

After arriving at Jan's dorm, I shared farewell hugs with my parents. Jan had borrowed a friend's car and we drove to Paul and Jane Alesch's apartment where we planned to spend the night. Paul was a college friend who had married his girlfriend Jane that past September.

Later that night Jan and I settled in together on a sofa bed. After spending the past four months sleeping by myself in an Army bunk or on the ground, it was great snuggling with Jan and playing around under the covers until we finally fell asleep.

Sunday morning Jan and I drove across town to Eppley Field. The airport was filled with GIs, many likely headed for Vietnam. Several men were huddled with family and friends, quietly sharing their last few precious minutes together.

After they announced my flight I gave Jan a hug and kiss and said, "Good-bye, good-looking, I'll keep in touch."

I settled in and took a nap during the flight to Atlanta and then transferred to a flight to Columbus, Georgia. Fort Benning was about 15 miles southeast of Columbus.

It was dark when I arrived at Fort Benning and settled into another old wooden barracks in the NCO School company area. The next morning the full realization of my new surroundings hit me. The condition of those barracks made the AIT barracks at Fort Lewis appear like castles. The buildings at our NCO Company must have been pre-World War II. Paint was peeling from the wooden siding and the barracks had coal-fired furnaces and hot water heaters. Those buildings hadn't been used for years, but had been reopened when an NCO School training site was needed. It was the most depressing site I had seen on an Army post. I thought, "What have I done to myself?"

Inside the barracks we each had a desk and chair in addition to a wall locker and footlocker. We again had nightly fire watch, which finally made sense. An important duty while on fire watch was to keep the fires in the furnace and hot water heater burning by tossing in a scoop or two of coal every hour. We also learned that when we blew our nose it turned our handkerchief black from the coal dust in the air.

We had learned the training was jokingly referred to as *shake'n bake* school after the Shake'n Bake coating for fried chicken. We were promoted to the rank of Corporal E-4 upon our arrival and would be promoted to Sergeant E-5 upon graduation. There were some who thought graduates didn't deserve being promoted to the rank of sergeant with less than a year in the Army and no combat experience. Most infantrymen would have to spend most of their tour in Vietnam before they might be promoted to sergeant. Being called a *shake'n bake* was the least of my concerns. From what I had been told, NCO School would make basic and AIT seem like grade school.

We again were normally up at the crack of dawn for chow and off to training by 8:00 a.m. The classroom training covered many of the same subjects addressed during AIT but went into considerably more detail. We would have to pass both written and practical tests on most subjects. If you didn't maintain passing scores, you would be washed out and likely sent to Vietnam as a corporal. Physical training was a big part of NCO School. In addition to the double-time runs and the normal exercises, we went through demanding obstacle courses like I had never seen before. We would have to roll over a log suspended horizontally six feet high, jump ditches filled with water, climb rope ladders, and crawl over ten-foot-high wooden walls and more. I was in the best shape of my life, but those obstacle courses were tough on me. I was repeatedly pushed to my physical limit, but I never gave up.

Although the training was more difficult, some of it continued to be fun. I rode in a UH-1 (Huey) helicopter during a simulated combat mission and rode in an Armored Personnel Carrier (APC) that went on a lake. Yes, those things floated. I fired a M-72 Light Anti-Tank Weapon (LAW) for the first time. The LAW was an OD-green tube three inches in diameter containing a rocket designed to penetrate the side of a tank. We each took a turn shooting at old tanks. I don't remember if I hit a tank or just blew a big hole in the ground. We also learned how to call in a *fire mission* for artillery and mortar fire. It was an exhilarating experience to have rounds exploding a couple hundred yards away while we watched from the protection of a bunker.

NCO School concluded with a week-long bivouac. Fortunately, it was early April and the weather in Georgia was mild. We were given blank M-16 rounds and each platoon was issued an M-60 machine gun with blank ammunition to use in mock firefights. We would have to find an enemy position identified on our map and tactically maneuver forward while encountering simulated enemy fire. We would return fire until we had taken the position or had been wiped out ourselves. Instructors served as referees to determine who won the battle.

There were also trip-wired booby traps (actually trip flares) to watch for. If someone tripped a simulated booby trap, they were considered killed in action (KIA) for the remainder of that exercise. The training instructors also used smoke grenades and other small explosives to simulate mortar rounds to make the environment as close to real combat action as they could. Each night we established a perimeter and pulled guard duty. We also rotated setting up ambushes and simulated opening fire when *enemy* troops passed by.

By the end of the week we were dirty and tired and ready to get back to our rickety old barracks. However, there was one more forced march ahead of us. That twelve-mile forced march ended much differently than we expected. We weren't back at our company area, and there wasn't any cold beer awaiting us. Instead, we stopped near a lake to complete a confidence course. We were to climb a twenty-foot wooden pole that was set at the edge of the lake. We would then walk over the water along a twenty-foot-long plank that was attached to another pole set into the lake. The foot-wide plank had two steps in the middle. At the far end of the plank was a rope leading back to a pole at another edge of the lake. We would crawl along the rope for twelve feet to a little sign that said "Rangers." At that point we would hang from the rope with our hands and drop twenty feet into the water.

We weren't forced to complete the course but were strongly encouraged to prove we had the guts to do it. Several guys had completed the course and were standing nearby dripping wet when I began climbing the pole. That was the easy part. I then stood up and began walking slowly along the plank. I focused on the plank and not the water far below with my arms held out to keep my balance. When

I reached the steps I slowly took two steps up and back down and then, cautiously walked to the end of the plank. Whew! It wasn't as difficult as it looked from the ground.

I then grabbed the rope connected to the pole at the far end of the plank with my hands, crossed my legs up over the rope and pulled myself away headfirst. I was dangling twenty feet above the water. I kept a firm grip on the rope and pulled myself along until I reached the Ranger sign. I released my legs and hung from the rope by my hands for a couple seconds. I looked skyward, then released my hands. It seemed to take forever to descend, but finally, I splashed feet-first into the cold water. I took a couple of strokes to a ladder and climbed out of the water. A roaring cheer greeted each of us when we reached the top of the ladder. I walked away from the lake with a big smile on my face and gathered with my fellow platoon members to congratulate each other while we stood together in our soaking wet fatigues.

Yes, that is me dropping into the lake, completing the confidence course during NCO School.

During the last couple of days of NCO School everyone was in great spirits. We had completed four months of intense military training and were looking forward to a short breather. After graduation we would be assigned to an AIT Company for two months of on-the-job training (OJT). I was going back to Fort Lewis.

Seven candidates were designated as honor graduates for earning the highest test scores and were promoted to the rank of Staff Sergeant E-6. One of the honor graduates was the "Old man," Sam Pierce. I congratulated Sam the next time I saw him and told him there were many days I thought he would never make it. While Sam planned to make the Army his career, I told him I hoped to survive my two years and get out. We shook hands and shared a "Good luck" with each other.

The big event before graduation was to have our new stripes sewn on to our uniforms. On graduation day we each proudly wore our khaki uniforms with three yellow sergeant stripes on each sleeve. Sergeant E-5 was the lowest NCO rank, sometimes referred to as "Buck Sergeant." But I was proud of what I had accomplished and was happy to have a little status as I continued through my first year in the Army.

The afternoon following graduation I flew to Seattle and caught a shuttle bus to Fort Lewis. I soon found my assigned AIT Company that consisted of another group of World War II era buildings not far from where I had completed AIT that past fall.

The barracks were empty when I walked up to my second-floor private room and dropped my duffel bag on the bed. I thought, "Hey, this isn't too bad for Army life." Six of us new *shake'n bakes* were assigned to the AIT Company, including John Jarvis who had been in my platoon during NCO School. It was nice to have a familiar face around to start my OJT. Later that afternoon we used our new status and went to the NCO club for a couple of beers.

Two NCOs were assigned to each AIT platoon composed of men fresh out of basic training. Those trainees would be undergoing the same infantry training I had gone through the previous fall at Fort Lewis. However, this time I would be giving some of the orders and supervising while those men worked their butts off for nine weeks. We were expected to assist with some of the training, conduct the PT drills, keep the trainees in line, and discipline them when necessary. Permanently assigned to the company were three drill sergeants, a first sergeant and a captain, serving as Commanding Officer. Two second lieutenants, who were recent OCS graduates, were also going through OJT before their probable assignment to Vietnam. The permanent staff went home most evenings leaving the company in our hands each night. The trainees would be graduating from basic training that Saturday morning and arriving to begin their AIT that afternoon.

When the trainees arrived, we exercised our newfound authority by yelling at them until they finally got into platoon formation for an initial briefing. Those guys had just graduated from basic training and were very respectful of anyone who had three stripes or more on their arm. They didn't know the six of us NCOs had just sewn the stripes on our uniforms a few days earlier. For the majority of my nine-month Army career I had been yelled at and been given orders by someone else. It was a strange feeling to be the one giving orders for a change.

During OJT we were up early each morning to make sure our platoon got to the mess hall for breakfast, had the barracks cleaned and were ready to move out for training on schedule. It was somewhat like baby-sitting forty guys for nine weeks. Some trainees refused to wear a watch and were often late. Also, a few trainees caught the wrath of the first sergeant when they failed an inspection for not being clean-shaven or not having their boots shined. The rules weren't difficult, but most of the men had never been subjected to so much discipline and rules governing most everything they did. It took more than eight weeks of basic training for some guys to adjust to Army life.

Part of our job as NCOs was to set a good example for the trainees. We were expected to be clean-shaven and wear clean and starched fatigues. I had learned to spit-shine my boots in basic training using a cotton ball and water. During NCO school I also learned a light coat of Glow Coat floor wax made the toes of my boots even shiner.

One night midway through OJT, some men on the first floor of our barracks started a pillow fight after lights out. I yelled at them to knock it off, but they continued. I was tired and after a few more minutes I was mad. I ran downstairs and told the trainees that if they had so damn much energy, we would get up early and go for a run. The trainees knew I was pissed. They all climbed in their bunks without saying a word. I woke the entire platoon up at five o'clock the next morning and led them on a thirty-minute double time run before breakfast. There were no more late-night pillow fights in the third platoon.

Fortunately, the early summer days at Fort Lewis were normally sunny and mild with only an occasional rain shower, and just as I had anticipated, OJT wasn't overly demanding duty. We had to get up early but didn't have to directly participate in most of the training. We spent a lot of time watching over and assisting the trainees while they went through training exercises. We rotated leading the PT drills and double-time runs to get the guys in shape for their PT test. I was in the best shape of my life and could lead a double-time run almost forever without getting tired.

In early June I received a letter from Larry Dolish, one of the Wayne State gang, saying he and his fiancée Cheryl wanted me to be in their wedding on June 28th. I called Larry and said I would just make it. I planned to fly into Omaha on the 27th to start my leave.

I had received a couple of letters from Allan Schwab during NCO School. He was serving in the northern highlands of South Vietnam. I also got a letter from Allan in late June saying he had been home on emergency leave to get married because his girlfriend Vicki was due to have a baby in September. I wrote Allan back to say congratulations and also jokingly told him that was good planning to miss a couple of weeks of combat duty.

With OJT quickly winding down, I would soon learn my fate regarding going to Vietnam. The trainees had been advised about NCO School, and I encouraged those who I felt would make good

NCOs to go. Now and then a trainee would call one of us a *shake'n bake* in a derogatory manner and would find himself pulling an unpleasant detail for his comment. However, as the weeks passed, a mutual respect developed between most of the trainees and us new NCOs and between the drill sergeants and new NCOs. We often ignored ranks and just talked man to man. The trainees and we *shake'n bakes* knew that nearly all of us were headed for Vietnam. We were just trying to work together to prepare ourselves for that eventuality.

Our OJT concluded with the traditional AIT bivouac. While on bivouac we assisted the trainees on assault and tactical exercises and led them on simulated ambushes. It was interesting to see how they reacted to the simulated combat exercises designed to create new and challenging experiences for them. One night I took a group of trainees out to set up an ambush along a trail. An *enemy* patrol was to come by and we would simulate ambushing them. By the time the patrol walked by most of the trainees had fallen asleep. If it had been the real thing, they all could have been killed.

It was finally the last day of bivouac. We guided the trainees through their final drills and then started one more forced march, with us NCOs expected to set an example for the trainees. I pushed on as hard as I ever had on a forced march, encouraging the laggers to keep up and not give up until they reached the company area. I tried not to show my true fatigue when I walked into our company area. But I was beat. The trainees enjoyed the beer and soda that awaited them, and us *shake'n bakes* joined them in celebrating their completion of AIT.

The next day the trainees and we new NCOs picked up our orders. After all the trainees in the third platoon received their orders, I stepped up to receive mine. My orders read as I anticipated, "Vietnam." I was given three weeks leave and was to report back to Fort Lewis on Sunday, July 20, 1969. All us new NCOs and most of the trainees received orders for Vietnam.

When the trainees finished their details around the barracks, they were given the remainder of the day off. The men in my platoon wanted me to join them at a nearby club. I bought the first round of beer for some of them and relaxed for a while before returning to the barracks to hit the sack. It was almost dark when I was awakened by a group of trainees who barged into my room, pulled me out of bed, and carried me outside and around the barracks with me wearing only a pair of boxer shorts while they laughed and cheered. I let them have their fun and then crawled back into bed and fell asleep, ignoring the noise they were making.

Friday, June 27th was graduation day. Our next assignment would be the real thing with real ammunition and men being wounded and killed. I listened closely to the speaker during the graduation ceremony, hoping to hear words of wisdom or advice to take with me to Vietnam. Unfortunately, it was the same old, "Be proud and brave soldiers" with an expression of best wishes as we moved on.

After graduation many of the men in the third platoon shared a good-bye handshake with me while they grabbed their duffel bags and ran to catch a ride to the airport. They had enjoyed having me as their platoon sergeant and wished me well in Vietnam.

I checked in my duffel bag after arriving at the Seattle airport and eagerly walked on to the gate to board my flight to Omaha. It was great to be going home for my final fling before going to Vietnam.

---

159 men graduated with me from NCO School Class No. 27-69. The following members of that class were killed in action in Vietnam.

Name	Age	Date Killed in Action
*SSG Samuel H. Pierce, Jr.	37	August 16, 1969
SSG David P. Henry	19	September 25, 1969
SGT John H. Wilson	19	November 3, 1969
SGT Norris R. Borgman	21	January 6, 1970
SGT Charles M. Shumpert	21	February 11, 1970
SGT James A. Barnes	21	February 16, 1970
SSG Calvin W. Kolb	20	March 14, 1970

*Samuel H. Pierce, Jr. was the "Old man" who went through training with me. He arrived in Vietnam on August 4, 1969. Sadly, Sam's dream of making the Army his career ended when he was killed in action twelve days later. "Sam, thank you for your loyal and fearless service to your country."

> *An infantryman in Vietnam had an approximate 50% chance of either being wounded or killed in action. Infantrymen sustained over 53% of the U.S. Army casualties in Vietnam, meaning 20,460 Army infantrymen were killed in action.*
>
> *(National Archives, Combat Area Casualty file 11/93)*

Chapter 4

Home on Leave

I walked into the Omaha terminal and happily found Jan Griffin who greeted me with open arms and a smile. We shared a long kiss while I put my arms around her and held her tight. It was a relief getting away from the Army again. Jan knew I was going to Vietnam because I had called her after receiving my orders. But I put that in the back of my mind and looked forward to spending time with Jan plus my family and friends. I planned to stay in Omaha until Sunday when my folks would drive down to pick me up and return to Schaller.

That evening I joined many of my Wayne State friends for Larry Dolish's bachelor party. One of the first questions asked was, "Are you going to Vietnam?" A brief silence interrupted the celebration after I said, "Yes." That night was like the good old days, sharing fun and laughter with my college buddies. For those few hours I forgot about what awaited me on the other side of the world.

Larry and Cheryl had a big wedding followed by a reception at a private hall. It was an afternoon I wanted to last forever as I danced with Jan and talked and laughed with good friends. But I reluctantly made the rounds saying good-bye as Jan and I prepared to leave. It had been an enjoyable day, but it ended way too quickly.

Jan and I went to Paul and Jane Alesch's apartment and hit the sack early that night. I snuggled near her and enjoyed her warmth and comfort next to me all night long.

My folks arrived in Omaha about noon that Sunday to pick me up. While driving home I told my folks about my fairly pleasant past two months at Fort Lewis. We talked a little about my going to Vietnam, but I didn't share any details concerning humping through the rice paddies and jungles carrying an M-16 and hand grenades, or that enemy soldiers would be trying to kill me.

In years past there were normally several guys around town during summer evenings, but it was strangely much quieter that summer. Over a dozen men from Schaller were in the service, several in Vietnam. In a big city they wouldn't have been missed except by their families and a few friends. But in a town of only 850 people, the entire town missed every man who was gone.

One of those missing was my friend Dean Christiansen. He had been drafted that spring and was arriving home on leave July 11th. A welcome home party was planned for Dean by his sister Marlys for the evening he arrived home. When I found Dean, we shared handshakes and a hug. I then asked him where he was going. He said, "'Nam," with a serious look on his face. He would be leaving a week later than me. We had attended grade school, high school and college together. Now we were going to Vietnam together. It was hard to believe. Dean's twin brother Dennis wasn't at the party. He had been drafted that June and was in basic training at Fort Leonard Wood, Missouri.

After church the following Sunday, I spent the remainder of the day with my family who had gathered for another farewell. Although I wasn't leaving until the following weekend, it worked best for everyone to gather a week early. Mom fixed another one of her delicious Sunday noon meals that I especially enjoyed. Not only had I been living on Army chow for most of the past year, but I would be eating a lot of C-rations in the near future.

I didn't go into much detail about what I expected to be doing in Vietnam, but they all knew that it possibly meant that I could be killed. I shared a good-bye hug with my sister Marilyn and my little nephew Tim when she and her husband Gary left. It was the most difficult good-bye that I had ever shared with my sister.

Almost before I realized Pop Corn Days weekend arrived. My leave was almost over. I would leave Saturday afternoon July 19th for Omaha as my first step toward Vietnam. I soon stopped counting the days I had left and started counting the hours.

That Friday night Schaller was bustling with activities and filled with people as the weekend celebration began. Dean and I both put Vietnam in the back of our minds while we enjoyed a farewell party that I wanted never to end. People that I had known for years stopped by during the evening to say hi, and then later good-bye.

After enjoying the Saturday morning parade with my parents I packed a khaki Army uniform, my shaving kit and a few personal items in my duffel bag and was soon ready to leave. I would be issued new jungle fatigues and boots and most everything else I would need when I arrived at Fort Lewis and later in Vietnam. I had talked with Jan Griffin during the week and had arranged for us to spend Saturday night together in Omaha.

I had shared good-byes with several friends earlier in the day and my duffel bag was packed. It was finally time to go. My sister Jan wasn't going to ride to Omaha with us so I gave her a hug and she said, "Be careful, and write me." In a shaky voice I said, "Yeah, I will," and gave her a forced smile.

Driving away from our house that day was one of the hardest experiences of my life to that point. Although leaving for the Army a year earlier was difficult, that day was completely different. I didn't necessarily think I would be killed in Vietnam, but I knew my life as I had known it for twenty-two years would never be the same. Friends and family had been saying "Be careful over there," and "Take care of yourself," which I planned to do. But I also knew my welfare might be determined by events that were totally beyond my control.

While I drove the few blocks to the edge of town, I desperately wanted to reach out and grab something or someone to take with me as part of my past. I was leaving that peaceful little world in northwest Iowa and going to a strange place where Americans were being killed every day. I didn't want to go, but it was my duty to accept my assignment to serve in Vietnam.

The 120-mile drive to Omaha was fairly quiet. I knew my parents were worried, but there wasn't much more that I could tell them until after I got to Vietnam. Jan Griffin spent a few minutes talking with my parents after we arrived at her dorm, and then it was time to say good-bye. Mom made it quick as she put her arms around me to share a hug as tears formed in her eyes. She said a quiet, "Good-bye, I love you."

I shook my dad's hand while he said, "Don't try to be a hero."

I smiled and said in a quivering voice, "I won't. Good-bye." I had tears in my eyes and couldn't say anything else. I was going off to war, and we all had to accept it. I stood with my arm around Jan until my parents drove out of sight.

The one thought that kept me going during that last week of leave was spending my last night with Jan. My last few days in Schaller had been fun but were also somewhat sad. But I found that my mood changed after I arrived in Omaha. I had released my sadness about leaving home and was ready to spend an enjoyable evening with Jan.

We again stayed with my Wayne State friend Paul Alesch and his wife Jane. After Jan and I crawled in bed together we talked for a few minutes and then embraced with a long kiss. Our passions rose as I pulled her warm body close while we kissed and caressed each other in the darkness. Our bodies were ready to unite in the heat of passion when Jan hesitated and said, "Let's not let it happen like this."

We weren't madly in love and to make love because I was going to Vietnam wasn't the way she wanted it to happen. Making love because I was going to Vietnam certainly seemed like a perfectly good reason to me, but I respected her wishes. I held her close until I fell asleep.

The next thing I knew, Jane was saying, "Hogie, it's time to get up." It was 7:30 Sunday morning, July 20, 1969. I put on my Army uniform for the first time in three weeks and then gave Jane a hug and shook Paul's hand while saying reluctant good-bye.

Jan was my only remaining connection with home. In a couple of hours, I would be leaving her too. All the conversations, the parties, the good-byes, were a memory. I was facing the biggest unknown of my life and the greatest danger that anyone could ever imagine. What would it be like in Vietnam?

Jan and I shared a Coke while waiting for my flight to Seattle. Although I had openly told her what I would be doing, I'm not sure if Jan truly understood. A year earlier, I might not have understood either. When they announced the boarding for my flight, I stood up, put my arms around Jan and told her I would miss her. "Be careful. I'll be thinking about you," Jan said before we shared a final, long hug and good-bye kiss.

I turned and walked toward the walkway. I looked back with tears in my eyes and forced a smile. We waved at each other one last time. I then turned and walked down the walkway and onto the plane.

My final tie with the world that I had known for twenty-two years was broken. I sat down in my seat and stared out the window, trying to think about something other than the fact I was leaving for Vietnam. That moment was the saddest and loneliest moment of my life. Shortly after takeoff I settled into my seat and fell asleep.

In what became a turning point of the war, in May 1969, U.S. forces located enemy bunkers atop Hill 937 in the Highlands of South Vietnam. For over a week, four American infantry battalions attacked the hill. On May 20, 1969, they reached the summit to find the bunkers empty. During the battle for "Hamburger Hill," 72 Americans were killed, while nearly 700 enemy troops were killed. U.S. forces occupied Hamburger Hill for only two days and then abandoned the site, as it was deemed to have no tactical value.

Chapter 5

Welcome to Vietnam

I climbed aboard a shuttle bus at the Seattle airport for a ride to the Debarkation Center at Fort Lewis. After standing in line with dozens of other GIs I checked in and then claimed a bunk in a nearby barracks. I hadn't eaten anything except a portion of the meal served on the plane, so I found the mess hall. Even Army food sounded good.

The next morning I joined several hundred men, and a few women, to begin the clearance activities. We were given a final medical check to ensure we had all our shots and were approved to go medically. We were then issued jungle fatigues, jungle boots and a bush hat. We normally wore a baseball-style cap during the past year of training, but in Vietnam, when GIs weren't wearing a helmet they wore a casual-looking bush hat with a floppy brim all around. I would be issued more gear once I was assigned to a unit in Vietnam. I spent much of my day standing in line waiting to process through each checkpoint. The final action was to be scheduled for a flight to Vietnam.

I didn't sleep well during my last night on American soil. I wasn't afraid of going to Vietnam, but the anticipation of the unknown remained in the back of my mind. I woke up early to shave and take a shower in relative peace while most of the guys were still sleeping. When I started shaving I thought, "Now I can start growing a mustache." I had wanted to grow a mustache, but I wasn't allowed to while I was in training. I didn't shave my upper lip that morning and started growing what became a brown bushy mustache that I have worn to this day, although it has turned mostly gray.

After I dressed, I walked to the bulletin board and saw my name listed under a flight departing at 11:00 a.m., July 22, 1969. In four hours I would be leaving the United States for the first time in my life headed for Vietnam. Although I knew it wasn't a dream, it remained somewhat unbelievable that I would soon be facing combat.

When I walked into the terminal, it was filled with GIs, each carrying their duffel bag. The terminal was a large warehouse type building with signs indicating check-in points for each flight. Men, and a few women, were sitting on the few available chairs or on the floor quietly awaiting their flight.

After checking in for my flight, I stood in line to call home. I told Mom I was leaving for Vietnam in less than an hour, and got a quiet, "OK," as her response. I asked her to call Jan Griffin that night to tell her I was leaving, and I told her I would write when I had a permanent address for her to send mail.

Around 10:30 a.m. we began boarding a civilian plane chartered by the military. Shortly after eleven o'clock we taxied down the runway and quickly rose into the sky, heading for the blue Pacific Ocean. Our first stop was Honolulu about five hours later. After landing we deplaned and I walked around the terminal during our layover. I don't know if anyone had made a run for it in the past, but it certainly was tempting with palm trees swaying in the breeze. An hour later we were off to Guam, a U.S. territory in the western Pacific Ocean. After another layover at an Air Force base, we were off to South Vietnam.

After a five-hour flight, we neared Cam Ranh Bay on the eastern coast of South Vietnam. I couldn't see anything as we descended in the darkness as there were no lights visible from the air, except a few lights near the runway when we landed. After we deplaned and found our duffel bags, a sergeant gathered us together. He told us that we would complete more in-processing there and then be shipped off to one of the U.S. military's base camps scattered throughout South Vietnam for a permanent assignment. The sergeant tried to march us to a barracks, but most of us didn't attempt to stay in step with the cadence he was calling. We simply didn't care.

I looked off in the distance as we walked and saw three strings of red tracers flowing from the sky toward the nearby countryside. It was a C-130 Hercules aircraft firing 2,000 to 6,000 rounds a minute from each of the three Gatling style mini guns mounted on one side of the plane. When they fired, it literally looked like it was raining bullets. Those planes were nicknamed "Puff the Magic Dragon." If you were their target, "Puff" – you were a goner. I had arrived at the war.

Wars and resistance against foreign powers had dominated Vietnam's history for more than 1,000 years. During more recent times, the French battled communist forces for years after World War II with little success. The 1954 Geneva Accord established a settlement whereby a Demilitarized Zone was created between North and South Vietnam. Unfortunately, the Geneva Accord did not bring peace. North Vietnam was governed by a communist regime and received Soviet and Chinese support, while the U.S.-backed South Vietnam continued to fight the spread of communism into the South. The United States initially supported South Vietnam with money and supplies and then provided military advisors. However, as the fighting escalated, American military forces gradually assumed an active combat role. America's involvement reached a peak in 1968 when over 530,000 military personnel served in South Vietnam. That number had been reduced to approximately 475,000 when I arrived in July 1969.

Our enemy in Vietnam consisted of the North Vietnamese Army (NVA) who were organized and trained in communist North Vietnam and traveled to South Vietnam to fight. Additionally, Viet Cong (VC) troops were organized in South Vietnam and fought in support of North Vietnam. The VC were generally less well trained and often consisted of local citizens who volunteered or were forced to join.

The Vietnam War was considered a *guerrilla* war, meaning there were no front lines or battles involving thousands of troops on both sides. Rather, guerrilla tactics were a form of warfare where often a small group of combatants use military tactics including ambushes, sabotage, hit-and-run tactics, booby traps, and employ their mobility to fight larger and less-mobile U.S. military forces. Consequently, enemy troops could be encountered most anywhere in Vietnam.

While walking to our barracks I noticed a strange odor. It didn't smell like an Iowa barnyard; it was more like the unpleasant combination of odors near a garbage dump. I asked the sergeant who had led us what that odor was. He said, "It's just what this place smells like."

The next day I processed into Vietnam. They called it processing in-country. A clerk took my orders and annotated my arrival. He told me my name would appear on a nearby bulletin board when my permanent orders were ready in a day or two.

The Cam Ranh military base camp was built near Cam Ranh Bay on the South China Sea 200 miles northeast of Saigon, the Capital of South Vietnam. Cam Ranh had a natural harbor that was developed into one of the largest seaports in South Vietnam to supply American forces. During the 1960s the United States built numerous military base camps in South Vietnam. Many of the base camps were built near small towns and had the same name as the nearby town. The American base camps were well fortified and had restricted access by Vietnamese civilians.

Everything appeared peaceful around Cam Ranh. I hadn't been issued a weapon and I would only occasionally see someone carrying a rifle. Surprisingly, I felt safe. But there was one depressing sight for us new arrivals. While we were processing in country, there were also hundreds of men who had completed their one-year tour who were processing out of South Vietnam. Some of those men noticed our new jungle fatigues and shiny-toed jungle boots and knew we had just arrived. They chuckled and told us how sorry we soon would be about being there. "Watch out for Charlie," they jokingly said. *Charlie or Charlie Cong"* was slang for the Viet Cong (VC, meaning Vietnamese Communist) enemy troops.

As I walked around, I saw the distant peaceful looking hills covered with thick green vegetation. But that was also where I had seen the gunship firing its mini-guns the past night. It wasn't as friendly as it appeared out there. I also noticed little plumes of smoke around the base and learned the smoke was from burning trash and human waste in steel barrels. No wonder the place had an unpleasant smell.

On July 24th I was issued orders assigning me to the Army's 25th Infantry Division. Early that afternoon I boarded a camouflage-painted propeller-driven C-123 aircraft that would take several of us to Cu Chi, the 25th Division Headquarters Base Camp.

I slid near one of the small windows to view the countryside, which was mostly dense green vegetation, flooded rice paddies and a dirt road now and then. After a forty-five-minute flight we landed at Cu Chi, about twenty miles northwest of Saigon. After a short bus ride I arrived at the 25th Division receiving area for another brief stay.

The base camp was like a small city where the Division Head-quarters, the 12th Evacuation Hospital (12th Evac) and many infantry, logistical and support units were located. The main roads were paved with asphalt and the rest were covered with gravel. Numerous buildings of various sizes were scattered throughout the base.

The Cu Chi base camp covered about three square miles and was surrounded by sandbag bunkers built into a six-foot-high earthen berm called the perimeter. Personnel manned the bunkers to keep the base secure. Outside the row of bunkers were coils of concertina wire. The concertina wire was similar to the miles of barbed wire that surround Iowa farm fields, except concertina wire had little razor-like blades with pointed tips woven into the wire. Those blades would snag on an intruder's clothing or cut them if they tried to crawl through the wire.

The 25th Division Base Camp was named after the small town of Cu Chi, just outside the main gate. The area had once been a peanut plantation because the immediate area was well above the water table. That location had been selected for the base camp because the ground would hold the weight of planes, tanks and other heavy vehicles.

Shortly after the base camp was built in 1966, Viet Cong troops blew up an ammunition dump and then disappeared without a trace. The Army finally realized the base was sitting directly over a major tunnel complex built by the North Vietnamese Army (NVA) and VC. Sneak attacks from those tunnels continued for months until the tunnels were ultimately destroyed. Unfortunately, those attacks damaged numerous facilities, vehicles and aircraft and killed 50 GIs.

Amazingly, as the war continued, new tunnels were constructed completely surrounding the base camp, with some of them again leading inside base, from where enemy forces periodically launched attacks damaging facilities and vehicles and inflicting GI casualties. Enemy troops would periodically fire mortar rounds into American military bases intending to destroy equipment or property or wound or kill GIs and then quickly drop inside a tunnel, out of sight. When discovered, tunnels in or around the base camp were destroyed.

The NVA and VC effectively used tunnels throughout the war to hide in and sleep and store supplies and equipment. They actually built underground hospitals in some tunnels.

After two days of orientation that included explaining the rules of existence in Cu Chi and how the military operated in the area, three of us were taken by jeep to an infantry company as our permanent assignment. The jeep driver yelled at a man standing in front of the company headquarters, "Hey, Tom, I have some FNGs for you."

I looked at the two other men in the jeep and we shrugged our shoulders wondering, what are FNGs? I soon learned FNGs were *f---ing new guys*. The military had hundreds of acronyms, but I doubted that one was in any official manual. We three FNGs hopped off the jeep and walked toward the company headquarters to meet Specialist Fourth Class (Spec 4) Tom Powers. He took our orders and checked us into the company. It was late afternoon. Tom said he would issue our weapons and gear and finalize processing us in the next day.

I settled into the little hooch across the street by claiming a bunk and tossing my duffel bag underneath. There were about a dozen bunks in the hooch used by men who were temporarily in Cu Chi. The men permanently assigned to our company in Cu Chi stayed in other nearby buildings or hooches. I had been assigned to Company A, 2nd Battalion, 14th Infantry Regiment, 25th Infantry Division. My final assignment would be to one of the three rifle platoons in Company A or Alpha Company as it was commonly called.

I had adjusted to the slowly deteriorating conditions since I arrived in Vietnam, but I knew there was much more in store for me when I went to the field. There were many large warehouse type structures in Cu Chi for storing equipment and supplies; however, most of the smaller of the buildings were simple wood frame buildings with corrugated metal roofs and large screen-covered openings on the sides to allow for ventilation. A four-foot-high sandbag wall surrounded most of the buildings to protect anyone inside from shrapnel should an incoming mortar round land nearby. Unfortunately, if a round landed directly on a building, those inside were likely out of luck.

The latrines were similar to outhouses I had seen on Iowa farms. They were hot and smelly. There was also a nearby building with sinks and showers with water supplied from a large tank on the roof. Later that afternoon several of us walked to the mess hall. At the end of the chow line were two bowls containing malaria pills. One pill was to be taken daily, and the other pill was to be taken weekly to prevent our getting malaria from the mosquitoes that thrived in Vietnam.

That evening I found a fringe benefit of being in Vietnam. Adjacent to our company area was a little club that opened at 5:00 p.m. daily. It wasn't anything fancy, but they served cold beer for fifteen cents a can. I walked inside and met some of the other guys assigned to our company. Many of those men had previously served in the field and had been reassigned to the rear (meaning Cu Chi). Tom Powers was a big, husky guy who had been a machine gunner with the second platoon. He had recently been assigned to the rear and was in charge of the company's weapons. When replacement troops were assigned to platoons in the field they would often rotate the *old timers* (men who had been in the field the longest) back to the rear for the remainder of their tour. A couple of other men were returning from a week of rest and relaxation (R&R) in Bangkok, Thailand.

Some of the *old timers* told me about the loss of sleep, lousy food, getting soaked by the monsoon rain, and the rats and snakes I would encounter in the field. And they also solemnly told me about their friends who had been seriously wounded or killed. I quickly learned that the peacefulness of that evening was only a brief pause on my way to facing the realities of the war.

I made several new acquaintances that night. Regardless of who you were or where you were from, just being in Vietnam instantly made you one of the guys. The sad good-byes to my family and friends back home were being replaced by the pleasure of meeting new friends in the relatively crude existence of Cu Chi.

During the next couple days, I attended orientation and training sessions about serving in Vietnam. We were also told it was the philosophy of the 25th Division to use firepower rather than manpower. That meant, rather than engaging the enemy in a long firefight with rifles and machine guns and increasing the likelihood of numerous American casualties, we would, when possible, withdraw from direct enemy contact and call-in artillery or air support to knock out the enemy with the artillery shells, helicopter gunships, and bombs.

An instructor also explained a key American military philosophy regarding the grim reality of war. It was the tradition of the U.S. military to make every attempt to evacuate men from the battleground who were wounded or killed. He solemnly said, "All of you will want to be evacuated if you are wounded or killed. You'll be expected to do the same for your buddies. Any questions?" There were none.

My indoctrination wasn't too demanding, leaving me time to check out Cu Chi. The Post Exchange (PX), other little shops and a bank were near the center of the base camp. There was an NCO Club, Officer's Club, a chapel and two bathhouses where you could take a steam bath and get a massage. There were also other little clubs scattered around like the one near our company area. Some clubs served mixed drinks for a quarter and others showed free movies at night. There was also a Special Services Club with pool tables and games to play and books to read. There was even a swimming pool.

I soon learned there was a relaxed protocol in Vietnam regarding saluting officers. Normally, when meeting an officer outdoors, we were expected to render a hand salute and the officer would return the salute. But in Cu Chi I noticed most enlisted men didn't salute when they met an officer. Most officers followed a more relaxed practice and didn't expect a salute, except for some higher ranking officer who would give us a blunt reminder to salute him if we failed to do so.

It was also the rule not to salute an officer when in the field in Vietnam. A salute seen by an enemy soldier would identify that man as an officer, and possibly make the officer a prime enemy target.

After I was issued my M-16 rifle and ammunition I went to a rifle range to test-fire it and adjust the sights. I was also issued a helmet, a backpack, a pistol belt and web gear (shoulder harness), ammunition pouches, a gas mask, a canteen and everything else I would need, including a flak jacket, which was a thick, heavy vest to protect our upper body from shrapnel. I completed my final day of the orientation and training on August 3rd and was told I was ready for the *field*, the countryside of South Vietnam. Tom Powers told me Alpha Company had encountered an enemy bunker complex the previous day. One man in the first platoon had been killed and several men in the third platoon had been wounded during a firefight, and earlier that day; another man in the third platoon had been killed by a booby trap. I was being assigned to the third platoon, because they needed more men.

After lunch the next day, a convoy of a jeep and two deuce-and-a-half trucks loaded with supplies was assembled along the gravel road that led through the company area. I put on my helmet, grabbed my gear and my rifle and climbed on the back of a deuce-and-a-half, ready for my first trip to the field along with three other men. There were no traditional front lines in South Vietnam like there had been in most previous wars. Our company operated out of smaller complexes called fire support bases and patrol bases and normally went into the countryside on patrols during the day and set up remote ambushes at night.

When we reached the main gate of Base Camp Cu Chi and passed the guards at the gate, we *locked and loaded*, by locking in an ammunition magazine and loaded a round into the chamber of our rifles.

We traveled through the village of Cu Chi and then turned west on Highway 1 that started in Saigon and led northwest to Tay Ninh near a mountain we could see in the distance called Nui Ba Den

"Black Virgin" Mountain. Further west was Cambodia. Many civilians were riding along the highway on bicycles or motor scooters, and the kids and adults walking near the roadside moved aside as we roared past.

We drove a few miles on Highway 1 then turned northeast on a gravel road, known as 7 Alpha. We passed through the village of Bau Dieu that consisted of primitive huts/hooches with corrugated metal or thatched roofs. I saw no sign of modern civilization. I hadn't seen an automobile since we left Cu Chi. After continuing on for less than a mile we stopped at a small compound occupied by a group of GIs.

Tom Powers who was riding in the lead jeep, turned around and yelled, "Sergeant Hogue, this is where you get off." I had finally found my new home. I grabbed my gear and jumped down from the truck and waved to Tom as the convoy moved up the road.

———————

On July 1, 1964, Army medical evacuation helicopter pilot Major James Kelly was killed in action in South Vietnam. Thereafter, his call sign, "Dustoff," became the nickname for a medical evacuation helicopter (medevac).

The Army UH-1 (Huey) helicopters accumulated over 7.5 million flight hours in Vietnam. 4,643 Hueys were lost in action in Vietnam.

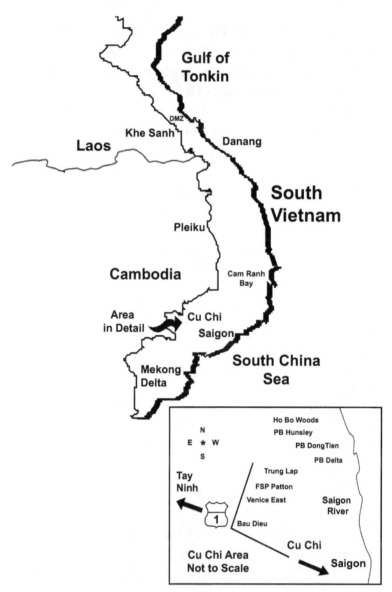

Map of South Vietnam

Gulf of
Tonkin

Laos

DMZ

Khe Sanh

Danang

South
Vietnam

Pleiku

Cambodia

Cam Ranh
Bay

Area
in Detail

Cu Chi

Saigon

Mekong
Delta

South China
Sea

Ho Bo Woods

PB Hunsley

N

E ✳ W

S

PB DongTien

PB Delta

Trung Lap

FSP Patton

Venice East

Saigon
River

Tay
Ninh

1

Bau Dieu

Cu Chi

Cu Chi Area
Not to Scale

Saigon

Chapter 6

Meeting the Third Herd

———————————

I was met alongside the road by a man who introduced himself as the platoon sergeant, Tom Brown. Staff Sergeant Brown was a fairly tall guy with sandy brown hair.

He reached out to shake my hand and said, "Hi, welcome to the third platoon. They call us the Third Herd."

I looked at the compound for a few seconds and then asked, "What's this?" I saw a group of four sandbag bunkers on the east side of the road surrounded by rice paddies on the remaining three sides.

"It's Venice East," Sergeant Brown replied. It was an outpost to guard the road at night intended to prevent the enemy from setting land mines as they had done in the past. Sergeant Brown said the road was used daily by military vehicles traveling to and from "Patton," our battalion fire support base (firebase). I could see the outline of bunkers that formed the perimeter of the firebase a half-mile to the northeast. He said we would be heading there in several days after a few more men, like me, were assigned to replace the men they had lost two days earlier in the Ho Bo Woods.

I didn't understand exactly what was going on, but assumed I would soon learn. Sergeant Brown and I walked from the road onto a metal walkway that covered the muddy ground leading through the entrance to the compound, a small gateway built into a ten-foot-high chain link fence that surrounded the compound. Sergeant Brown walked to one of the bunkers to introduce me to our platoon leader.

He leaned into the bunker entrance and said, "Hey, 3-6, I want you to meet a new NCO."

Platoon leaders were nicknamed after their radio call sign. The third platoon leader's call sign was "3-6." The second platoon leader was "2-6" and so on. "6" was the call sign for the Company Commander (CO) who was the next in the line of command above the platoon leaders. Our CO was a Captain in charge of the four platoons in Alpha Company. The first, second and third platoons were rifle platoons armed with M-16 rifles, M-60 machine guns and M-79 grenade launchers. The mortar platoon provided support with 81MM mortars.

A few seconds later, a man my size and wearing glasses stepped from the bunker. He reached out to shake my hand and said, "Hi, I'm Steve Donaldson, platoon leader. Glad to have you with us."

First Lieutenant Donaldson served as the platoon leader in command of the platoon and delegated duties to the platoon sergeant and squad leaders, as he desired. If anything happened to him, the platoon sergeant would take command.

After talking with Lieutenant Donaldson, Sergeant Brown and I walked to a bunker facing the road that would be my home. He then introduced me to Larry Jackson, the platoon's medic. "Doc" was a tall thin guy with a bushy mustache who had been in country for several months. Men were often assigned as medics if they refused to carry a weapon because of religious or personal beliefs. But Doc Jackson carried an M-16 along with the rest of us.

I was also introduced to Sergeant Jim Overbey. He was a slender guy from Kentucky with light brown hair and spoke with a strong southern drawl. Jim was another *shake'n bake* who had arrived a week earlier. Sergeant Brown told me that Jim and I would be his squad leaders. I would have the first squad and Jim Overbey had the second squad.

I set my gear inside the bunker and claimed a small area as my home where I would be sleeping on an air mattress that night. The bunkers were made of dark green sandbags with a plastic fiber woven into the cloth to make them less susceptible to deterioration from constant exposure to the sun and rain. Large wood beams provided a framework and support for the bunkers. 4' x 8' sheets of perforated steel planking (PSP) supported the layers of sandbags and plastic sheeting that formed the top of each bunker. Bunkers provided protection from small arms (rifle and machine gun) fire and shrapnel from incoming rockets or mortar rounds. Whether a bunker could withstand a direct mortar round hit depended upon how well it was built and how many sandbags were used. I hoped never to find out for sure.

The name Venice East sounded like an exotic place, but it was actually another big step away from the modern world. The 120-foot square compound sat in the middle of an abandoned rice paddy and was surrounded on three sides by other rice paddies flooded with two feet of water. With all the water around us, I understood how the place had earned its name.

Four sandbag bunkers inside the compound were elevated on 55 gallon steel barrels filled with dirt. Wooden walkways between the bunkers enabled us to move around inside without walking through the muddy water directly below. In the center of the compound was a fifteen-foot-high wooden tower with a platform atop that housed a .50 caliber machine gun and radar equipment used at night to spot enemy movement in the area. Sandbags and wooden ammunition crates filled with dirt were placed along the outer edge of the platform to offer protection when men pulled guard duty at night. The chain link fence surrounding the compound would detonate an incoming enemy B-40 rocket (rocket-propelled grenade (RPG)). The RPG would detonate when it struck the fence rather than detonating when it hit a bunker or something inside.

Dave Hardy was one of the men in my squad who had been in country for a couple months. I spent much of my time talking with him during my first few days in the field and asking questions about what I should be doing. Hardy was a slender (most all of us were slender then) twenty-year-old from Wisconsin who was friendly and very willing to answer my questions and share his experiences. I appreciated that. Although I had spent most of the past year in training to serve as an infantryman in Vietnam, I hadn't expected anything like Venice East.

Hardy told me about the company running into the enemy bunkers on August 2nd. One man in the first platoon was killed by machine gun fire and nearly half the men in the third platoon received shrapnel wounds when the VC popped out of tunnels and began throwing hand grenades during the firefight. Hardy then went on to tell me that they had lost George Conrad earlier that same day when a huge explosion literally tore his body into pieces. Dave said they picked up body parts and put them in a body bag. I could tell by the sad tone of his voice that it was difficult talking about losing a friend.

The company normally walked in two single columns when on a patrol (search-and-destroy mission) or Reconnaissance in Force (RIF), as the Army called them. They also would normally have one man walk roughly thirty meters to the side of each column for expanded vision over the countryside. That man was the *flank man* and it was called *walking flank*. It was a dangerous place to be. George Conrad was walking flank when a booby-trapped land mine killed him instantly.

Thousands of American artillery and mortar rounds were fired in South Vietnam every day. However, a few of those rounds were duds and didn't explode. If the enemy found a dud round, they often made a booby trap[1] by connecting a firing mechanism that was activated by stepping on it or tripping a wire attached to the firing mechanism which would detonate the round, often with deadly consequences. The NVA and VC used a variety of devices as booby traps, including land mines that contained enough explosives to destroy a vehicle, and "Bouncing Betty" mines, which would pop out of the ground and detonate when it was two to four feet in the air.

The platoon sergeant, the medic and two radio/telephone operators (RTOs) were assigned directly under the platoon leader. Each RTO carried a PRC-25 two-way radio that was (naturally) OD-green and had an antenna that extended several feet into the air. Chuck Gorman and Dennis Schultz were our RTOs who carried the nearly twenty pound radios on their backs with a shoulder harness. We used a Phonetic Alphabet intended to ensure clear radio communication. Each letter of the alphabet was assigned a word. We would say Alpha

---

[1] I will normally use the term "booby trap" throughout the book because that was the term used in Vietnam. During more recent years the military has used the term improvised explosive device (IED).

for A, Bravo for B, and Charlie for C and so on. If an RTO radioed that we saw some VC he would say, "We saw some Victor Charlie."

The remaining men in the platoon were divided into two squads of six to ten men each, depending upon the actual number of men in the platoon. Each squad had a two-man M-60 machine gun team consisting of a *gunner* who carried the weapon and 400 to 500 rounds of ammunition and the *assistant gunner* who also carried about 500 rounds of M-60 ammunition in addition to his M-16 and ammunition magazines. An M-60 machine gun could fire nearly 500 rounds a minute by connecting 100-round belts of ammunition together with the black clips attached to each shell casing. The assistant gunner would feed the ammunition into the machine gun while the gunner fired the weapon. The rest of us each carried a 100-round belt of M-60 ammunition that we could pass on to the team if needed. One man in each squad also carried an M-79 grenade launcher and the remaining men carried M-16 rifles. The two squads were pre-designated and normally had an NCO in charge for tactical maneuvers in combat situations or other duty that didn't require the entire platoon. The two squads also normally rotated ambush duty assignments. Each squad also carried a Light Anti-Tank Weapon (LAW). The NVA and VC didn't have tanks, but the LAWs could destroy bunkers or other targets.

Each platoon was also assigned a Vietnamese soldier called a Chieu Hoi, which meant open arms. They were former VC or NVA soldiers who had either surrendered or were captured and then volunteered to support the South Vietnamese cause. Our Chieu Hoi was named Hue and served as our scout. Although the idea of having a former enemy soldier working with us sounded unwise, the guys said Hue was trustworthy. He carried an M-16 just like most of us. Hue's job was to help search for signs of the enemy during our daily RIFs and help communicate with Vietnamese people. Hue of course spoke Vietnamese and spoke enough English to communicate with us.

Platoons were normally assigned to Venice East on a rotating basis for about a week at a time. The third platoon was there as a reprieve after the firefight in the Ho Bo Woods. The platoon was slowly growing back to a normal strength of about twenty-five men.

The atmosphere at Venice East was relaxed during the day. We didn't carry our weapons and guys often hung out along the road. But when darkness fell, we got serious.

Our first task each evening was to arm the many claymore mines (claymores) which were placed around the perimeter. The blasting caps were removed from the claymores each morning to prevent an accidental detonation and were reinserted each night. Claymores were rectangular antipersonnel mines an inch thick. There was a layer of BBs in front of a layer of C-4 plastic explosive. The claymore was detonated by a blasting cap that was connected to an electric wire leading to a detonator kept inside the bunkers. When the detonator handle was squeezed it sent an electrical charge that fired the claymore. The claymores fired a huge shotgun-like blast of hundreds of BBs in a convex pattern. We often connected two or three claymores in a series, using blasting caps and detonation (det) cord. One detonator could fire several claymores blasting a deadly wall of BBs.

After we closed the gate, we were barricaded inside Venice East for the night. We placed our ammunition and weapons in a convenient location in case we might need them. Since there were no lights, except for a few flashlights, the men started to settle in when darkness fell, while we set up guard duty assignments.

Two radar operators not assigned to our platoon, rotated nightly duty in the tower to monitor the radar for enemy movement around us. The rest of us rotated one-hour guard shifts along with one of the radar operators. After dark I crawled inside my bunker and curled up on an air mattress and covered myself with a poncho liner (a light blanket with camouflage design). It was a strange feeling lying inside a bunker with sandbag walls over a foot thick. Although I was in the middle of a war, that bunker gave me a feeling of security. I soon fell asleep as the monsoon rain poured outside. That night passed without incident. Shortly after sunrise men began crawling out of their bunkers and taking a stretch while looking around at clear morning skies.

Lieutenant Donaldson stepped out from his bunker and said, "Sergeant Hogue, your squad has road detail today." I replied, "OK sir," but I didn't know exactly what I was supposed to do. While I was putting on my gear, I asked Dave Hardy, "What are we doing?"

He said it would be easy. We would escort two mine sweepers as they cleared the road and hope nothing happened. I thought, "I can handle that."

Two men carrying mine detectors led us in separate columns as we walked along the road. They slowly moved their detectors back and forth over the road to detect any metal objects. It took over half an hour to sweep the road from Venice East to the entrance of Firebase Patton. We then turned around and swept the road southwest through the village of Bau Dieu. The total distance was over a mile. When we neared Bau Dieu I noticed a little compound north of the village. I asked the guys what it was.

"It's an ARVN compound," someone replied. ARVN was the acronym for the Army of the Republic of South Vietnam. They were on our side. After we completed the sweep without detecting any mines, we radioed the Alpha Company Command Post (CP) at Patton to inform them the road was clear. The local civilians also waited until after we had cleared the road before they began their travels by walking or riding along on scooters or wooden carts pulled by cows or water buffalo. We walked back into Venice East and I took off my gear, wondering what was next. The rest of the platoon had disarmed the claymores and cleaned up the compound while we were gone.

A deuce-and-a-half arrived a short while later and dropped off a hot breakfast from the mess hall at Patton in several insulated food containers. A hot breakfast and evening meal were normally delivered to Venice East every day.

We organized a chow line in a tent set up along the side of the road and loaded up on scrambled eggs and bacon on paper plates. They also delivered two cases of C-rations that we could rummage through if we got hungry during the day. Each case of C-rations contained a dozen smaller boxes that each contained a meal like potatoes and beef, spaghetti and meatballs, or scrambled eggs and ham. There was also canned fruit, peanut butter and jelly, crackers, and everyone's favorite treat, sponge cake. Additionally, there were plastic utensils, packets of coffee and hot chocolate mix, and most importantly, there were small P-38 can openers and packets of toilet paper.

After the road was cleared and the compound was cleaned up, we could relax for the rest of the day and do mostly whatever we chose. Men would catch up on letter writing, take a nap, play poker or hang out along the road and talk with kids and adults who were walking past often trying to sell them something. During my first full day there I joined a friendly quarter-limit poker game. But rather than using American money, we used Military Payment Certificates (MPC). After we arrived in country, we exchanged our American money for MPC to control inflation and corruption in South Vietnam.

South Vietnam was approximately 1,000 miles north of the equator. Spring and summer were the rainy season, normally called the monsoon season. The mornings were usually sunny and dry, but during the hot and humid afternoons, the skies would turn cloudy and it would begin to rain. We were fortunate at Venice East because we could seek shelter in the bunkers. The layers of plastic sheeting on the top of each bunker normally kept the rain from leaking inside. Because the monsoon season would continue through October, we would have to put up with the daily rain and flooded countryside for a couple more months.

During my third day at Venice East they delivered what was called a Sundry Pack (SP). The men acted like it was Christmas. The SPs that contained nearly everything we needed in the way of personal items and goodies were delivered weekly to each platoon. In addition to shaving cream and razors, toothpaste and soap, there were cartons of cigarettes, two boxes of little Crooks cigars, candy bars and stationery. Someone would control the dispensing of items to ensure everyone got his fair share from each pack. I didn't smoke cigarettes, but I did take a couple Crooks cigars and stashed them to enjoy later.

I soon learned there wasn't much I needed in the field that the

Army didn't provide. Along with hot meals and C-rations, they often delivered sodas. We could chip in and have beer delivered but the men stuck to an unwritten rule of generally not drinking in the field. It was more important to have a clear head out there and drink liquor in the relative safety of Cu Chi.

My first couple days at Venice East passed peacefully. I spent a lot of time getting to know the men and learning as much as I could from the *old timers*. One of our RTOs, Chuck Gorman, was one of those *old timers* who had been with the Third Herd since that past May. He told me about a man in the first platoon who had been killed a couple months earlier when shrapnel struck and detonated a white phosphorous grenade he was carrying. The man was literally burned to death by the tremendous heat generated from the burning white phosphorous. None of us knew exactly what might happen next. But I knew one thing for sure, the relative peacefulness of Venice East wouldn't continue forever, and the day would come when we would suffer more casualties.

It was soon August 14th my birthday. I had spent my past birthday in basic training, without any celebration. It appeared my twenty-third birthday would be just another day in South Vietnam. But, late that afternoon Sergeant Brown told me the CO wanted two men to pull guard that night at the ARVN compound south of Venice East.

I looked at him and said, "And I bet one of them will be me?"

Tom Brown smiled and put a hand on my shoulder, "Yep. Pick someone to go with you and grab your gear."

When I walked to my bunker Dave Hardy asked, "What's up?"

I said, "Grab your gear, you're coming with me."

"What for?"

I smiled like Tom Brown had smiled at me and said, "We're spending the night at the ARVN compound."

"Oh, you're kidding, Sarge," Hardy replied.

"I'm not kidding, grab your gear."

Hardy wasn't happy that I had picked him to join me, but he grabbed his gear without saying anything else. Neither of us knew exactly what we would be doing, and we definitely weren't excited about being the only two GIs spending the night with the ARVN troops (ARVNs). It sounded like a night of OJT for me.

We each took our M-16s, several hand grenades, a starlight scope and a radio to communicate with Venice East and our company command post (CP) at Firebase Patton. A short while later a deuce-and-a-half with a few men riding in the back stopped in front of the compound. Company Commander Captain William Branch was riding in the front seat and stepped out. Lieutenant Donaldson walked out to the road with Dave Hardy and me and introduced me to our CO.

Captain Branch said, "Sergeant, welcome to Alpha Company, I'm glad to have you with us," as we shook hands.

The CO explained to Lieutenant Donaldson and me that the ARVNs had observed enemy activity around the village the past night and the VC had fired RPGs into their compound. The ARVNs asked to have GIs pull guard in their tower and call-in mortar fire if needed. It sounded like they should be sending an entire platoon to provide reinforced support rather than sending two GIs. But I wasn't given the opportunity to recommend that option. After talking with Captain Branch for a couple more minutes he said, "Hop aboard." Hardy and I climbed in the back of the deuce-and-a-half.

With Venice East fading in the distance, I asked Hardy, "What the hell are they getting us into?"

"I don't know Sarge," was his reply as he shook his head.

A minute later we were at the ARVN compound just north of the village of Bau Dieu. After Hardy and I jumped to the ground we walked with Captain Branch toward the entrance and were met by two ARVN officers. The CO told the ARVNs that Hardy and I would spend the night at their compound.

Captain Branch pointed to a wooden tower in the center of the compound and told Hardy and me that was where we would pull guard. He told us to call the command post (CP) for a radio check when we were settled in. The Alpha Company's CP at Patton was where Captain Branch and his staff were located. Hardy asked the CO what call sign we should use. The CO told us to use "Alpha Papa 3."

When a squad or platoon set up a nightly ambush, Alpha Papa was the phonetic radio term for Ambush Patrol. "3" was the third platoon's designation. Hardy and I were "Alpha Papa 3" for that night.

Captain Branch said he would send a truck to pick us up in the morning. We waved to the guys in the back of the truck who were providing an escort guard as the driver turned it around and headed north towards Firebase Patton. Hardy and I walked through the main gate with the two ARVN officers.

When Dave Hardy and I stopped when we reached the tower, the ARVNs kept walking on without saying a word. We never saw them the rest of the night. After Hardy and I climbed up the tower, we looked around and saw several wooden shacks and sandbag bunkers scattered around the compound. Coils of concertina wire were strung around the perimeter, and I saw one machine gun sitting on top of a bunker. There were also several women and children running around.

While I looked around I asked Hardy, "What kind of an Army compound is this?

Hardy replied, "The ARVNs are a pretty loose outfit."

And it looked like it. I began to see why they need us to help fight their war.

The wooden tower was about fifteen feet high with a small platform at the top. There was just enough room for one of us to curl up and sleep on one side while the other man sat up and pulled guard. There was a two-foot wall of sandbags built around the edge of the tower floor, giving us some protection. But it looked like we were sitting ducks if enemy troops wanted to take a shot at us. RPGs had been fired into the compound the past night. Heaven help Hardy and me if a rocket hit the tower. Fortunately, there was a solid roof to protect us from the rain that would certainly fall during the night.

We did a radio check to establish communications with our command post. I also looked over the nearby countryside to identify the pre-established locations that had been coordinated with our mortar platoon. If we needed their support, we would first call in mortar fire to one of those pre-established locations that were marked on my map and adjust the fire from there.

There was also a twist to the rules of engagement in the inhabited areas of South Vietnam. Those areas were considered *no-fire* zones during the day. That meant we weren't supposed to fire on anyone unless we were fired upon first. If we saw someone with a weapon or if it was otherwise obvious he or she was an enemy soldier, we could fire, but otherwise the civilians were free to move around in the *no-fire* zones without their lives being threatened by American fire.

The radar operators at Venice East frequently observed movement in and out of nearby villages and hamlets at night. We had to assume they were enemy soldiers. But because most of the Vietnamese people looked the same when we saw them during the day, we had no idea who were truly friendly civilians and who were VC who had hidden their weapons. However, at night the rules changed. Anyone moving outside a village was considered to be the enemy and could be fired upon, with no questions asked.

It was five o'clock in the afternoon. There wasn't anything for us to do except wait a couple of hours until darkness. I sat in the tower looking over the compound and noticed a young woman walk to an open area near one of the hooches. She pulled down her pants and squatted over a small hole in the ground.

I said, "Hey, Hardy," as I pointed to the woman, "Don't they have outhouses?"

He said no, they just dig a hole in the ground. He told me if I listened closely when I walked by one of those holes I might hear the buzzing sound of maggots. The hole was in the open with no walls or anything to provide privacy. The people who walked near her paid no attention. After a few seconds the lady quickly pulled up her pants as she stood up and walked away.

I then thought of a way I might celebrate my birthday. The kids in the compound had stopped by periodically and held their hands out hoping we would give them something to eat. I had learned the kids and adults who had stopped by Venice East were always trying to sell us watches, jewelry, clothes, and yes, girls in exchange for money, cigarettes or C-rations. Hardy and I had brought some C-rations with us, but neither of us was very hungry. I took two cans of C-rations and climbed down the tower hoping to make a deal with the kids.

I said, "Two beers," holding up two fingers.

I held out the C-rations indicating I would trade them for two beers. The kids understood and returned a short while later with two cans of beer. I gave the kids the C-rations and climbed up the tower with the two beers.

After we opened our beers Hardy said, "Happy Birthday," as we tapped our cans together.

We laid back on the sandbag wall and talked while we drank a beer, and I quietly commemorated my twenty-third birthday in a way that I could never have imagined.

As darkness slowly arrived the ARVNs closed the main gate, and activity along the road ceased. Many civilians traveled along the roads and across the countryside during the day, but they knew it wasn't safe to be outside the scattered villages or hamlets at night.

It was finally completely dark, and I mean dark. There were no porch lights or streetlights in the nearby village of Bau Dieu; in fact, there was no electric power in any of those villages. I saw a few flickers of light from cooking fires or lanterns, but for the most part, it was totally dark. It wasn't raining, but the clouds had moved in just before dark. We couldn't see anything beyond the perimeter. There was a little movement inside the compound, and I could see a few ARVNs standing guard by their bunkers, that was good.

Hardy offered to take the first one-hour guard shift. I wrapped up in my poncho liner and settled in for an hour of sleep. We had rotated the one-hour guard duty in the tower at Venice East among all the men in the platoon. But this night, it would be one-hour on and one-hour off duty for the entire night for Hardy and me.

I didn't sleep much during my first hour off guard. Eventually, Hardy shook me and said it was my turn for watch. As I sat up, Hardy said there was nothing happening. I moved next to the radio while Hardy curled up for his first hour of sleep. I turned on the starlight scope and scanned the countryside but saw no movement. The starlight scope was a battery-powered night vision device that increased available starlight and/or moonlight, enabling the viewer to see in the darkness. It looked like a fat eighteen-inch-long telescope. Objects appeared as a slightly-fuzzy green image. The clouds obscured most of the moon and starlight, but I could still see the faint outlines of a few objects as I scanned the nearby countryside. I observed a few ARVNs moving inside the compound periodically, but for the most part, it was totally quiet while I sat in the tower with Hardy sleeping beside me. One of the company RTOs at the command post checked in with us every hour, on the hour, to make sure we were awake and OK.

He would say, "Alpha Papa 3, Alpha Papa 3, radio check."

We would simply acknowledge everything was fine by clicking the handset switch twice to avoid the noise of talking. Clicking the handset switch would *break squelch* and cause static that the RTO could hear. Maintaining silence wasn't critical that night, but when on an ambush in the countryside, being quiet was very important. I also had a watch with hands that glowed in the dark, eliminating the need to use my flashlight to see the time. Even if we had a flashlight, there were times when we didn't want to use it for fear of disclosing our position. That night I didn't want to shine any light in the tower to give the enemy a target to shoot at.

As each hour passed with no activity, I became more comfortable with our situation and was tired enough when I ended each guard shift that I quickly fell asleep. With everything being quiet, it was sometimes a struggle to stay awake while staring into the darkness for an hour at a time. Around midnight, it started to rain. Although we had ponchos to keep most of the blowing rain off us, it quickly became a wet and miserable night in that little tower. As the morning light began to appear on the eastern horizon, it seemed we would safely survive our remote duty. The sun rose, bringing welcome daylight and a sense of semi-security as the countryside became visible, minimizing the likelihood of enemy activity. The enemy often used the cover of darkness when they attacked U.S. or ARVN compounds.

Hardy and I gathered our gear, climbed down the tower and stretched out the kinks after spending the night in that confinement. After the ARVNs opened the front gate we walked to the road to wait for a ride back to Venice East. A short while later we noticed the mine sweeping team walking down the road toward us. Hardy and I decided we would walk back with them. I radioed the CP and told them not to send anyone to pick us up.

The following evening Bill Casey, a new guy from South Carolina, and one of the *old timers*, Zeke Weil, were selected to spend the night with the ARVNs. I was pulling guard in the tower at Venice East shortly after midnight when I heard explosions and small arms fire directly to our southwest. I couldn't see anything in the darkness, but assumed it was coming from the ARVN compound.

I soon heard Casey on the radio, saying, "This is Alpha Papa 3. We have incoming RPGs. We need a fire mission, over!"

The VC had fired RPGs into the ARVN compound again and Casey was calling for mortar support. Our mortar platoon at Patton fired several rounds east of the compound where the RPGs had been fired from while Casey and Weil and the ARVNs sprayed the surrounding countryside with M-16 and M-60 machine gun fire. One of the RPGs wounded two ARVNs, fortunately Casey and Weil were uninjured.

The next morning we were told to pack up our gear in preparation to move to Firebase Patton. Two deuce-and-a-halfs brought another platoon to Venice East. While the new platoon moved in the Third Herd boarded the trucks and we were soon riding towards Patton.

➤ George D. Conrad, Jr. was from Plantation, FL. He arrived in Vietnam on June 17, 1969. He was killed in action on August 2, 1969 at the age of twenty-six.

➤ The first platoon member killed on August 2, 1969 was twenty-year-old Venancio Vera. He had arrived in Vietnam on June 7, 1969.

The youngest American serviceman to die in Vietnam was PFC Dan Bullock from New York City. He altered his birth certificate to join the Marine Corps. Dan Bullock was killed by enemy gunfire on June 7, 1969, at the age of fifteen.

Standing in front of Venice East shortly after I joined the Third Herd with the elevated bunkers and guard tower in the background.

Chapter 7

Welcome to the Woods

O ur little convoy pulled into the firebase which I had seen in the distance from Venice East. Fire Support Base (FSB) Patton was the 2nd Battalion headquarters for the 2/14th Infantry Regiment and was manned by the five infantry companies (A, B, C, D & E) in the battalion on a rotating basis. These companies and companies from other battalions also operated from other smaller patrol bases scattered around the countryside. We were headed for one of them, Patrol Base Hunsley near the Ho Bo Woods. Unfortunately, I had heard nothing good about the Ho Bo Woods.

Patton was huge compared to Venice East. The firebase had been built during the early summer of 1969 as a state-of-the-art replacement for the original Firebase Patton located a quarter mile north, just outside the village of Trung Lap, which I could see in the distance. After we hopped off the trucks we stood by while Lieutenant Donaldson checked to find out when we would be leaving.

He soon returned and told us to be on the landing zone (LZ)[1] in thirty minutes. We would gather on the LZ on the east side of Patton and hop aboard Hueys which would fly us to Patrol Base Hunsley to join the rest of our company. The Huey was the military utility helicopter designed to transport troops and supplies in Vietnam and was also used to evacuate those wounded or killed in action.

I took a few minutes to check out the firebase before we left. Patton's circular perimeter was about 250 meters in diameter, consisting

---

[1] The term *pick-up zone* (PZ) was often used for the location designated for helicopters to pick up troops while the term landing zone (LZ) was used for the location designated for helicopters to drop off troops. For the sake of simplicity, the term landing zone or LZ will be used throughout the book when referring to those sites.

of a continuous six-foot-high dirt berm with twenty-four large sand-bag bunkers built into the berm forty meters apart. There was a gravel road circling the interior of the firebase just inside the row of bunkers, and a few other roadways leading into the center of the firebase.

There were 81MM and 4.2 inch mortar positions, and six 155MM artillery howitzers (called an artillery battery) spaced around the interior along with very large bunkers for the battalion headquarters staff and company CP groups. There were also two ammunition dumps, a mess hall and a medical aid station. A wood-framed tower rose twenty feet in the air, where men kept watch over the surrounding countryside.

Three rows of coiled concertina wire attached to steel posts surrounded the entire firebase. There were two coils spread along the ground, one behind the other, with the third coil lying on top to make it difficult for someone to jump over the coils. There were also trip flares and claymore mines spaced around the entire perimeter. The trip flares were set into the ground with a stake or attached to a solid object. A small wire (tripwire) attached to a cotter pin was then stretched tight and attached to another object. If someone tripped the wire, it would pull the pin and release a spring-loaded cap, igniting the flare and lighting up the surrounding area.

The five companies in our battalion were normally rotated from Patton and other smaller patrol bases every couple of weeks. The living conditions and hazards of the duty varied among the various patrol bases. I guess the Army wanted to be fair and let everyone share in the good and bad experiences. After taking a few minutes to check out Patton, I walked through the eastern perimeter to a flat grassy area used for landing choppers. I was looking forward to my first chopper ride in Vietnam but wasn't too excited about what might be waiting for us at the end of the ride.

Most of the men were sitting on the ground or milling around smoking cigarettes and talking while they waited near the LZ that peaceful sunny morning. When we heard the sound of Hueys in the distance we lined up in groups on each side of the LZ enabling us to quickly load from both sides of each chopper when it landed.

Someone *popped* a smoke grenade that spewed colored smoke into the air to mark a landing spot for the lead chopper. When the choppers neared, one man in each group walked to the center of the LZ and held his rifle horizontally over his head to mark the location for each chopper to land and pick up their men. The normal load for a Huey was six or seven men. Three choppers landed to carry twenty-one of us who were going out to Hunsley that day to join the remainder of our company which had left earlier.

There were two pilots in the front of each Huey and a door gunner on each side with an M-60 machine gun. Four men sat on the canvas-covered bench seat that ran through the center of the chopper while the rest sat on the floor. The side doors were always kept open enabling men to make a quick entrance or exit. However, with the doors open you couldn't hear much over the sound of the swirling chopper blades.

After nearly a fifteen-minute flight, the pilot began descending into the landing zone (LZ) outside Patrol Base Hunsley. I had become accustomed to the small villages and many civilians around Patton. But when I looked from the chopper I could see nothing but grass, trees, bushes and water as we descended near the patrol base. The base looked like a circle carved out in the middle of nowhere. Normally two companies were assigned to defend it.

The Ho Bo Woods was a former French owned rubber plantation used by the NVA and VC during the war as a base area. It was laced with tunnels and underground complexes, well-concealed bunker complexes and fortified small base camps. The area consisted of sparse to dense woods with scattered vegetation covering open areas and abandoned rice paddies. It was a remote enemy controlled area with no civilians. The Army had been trying to chase the enemy troops out of there for years and it was the scene of some of the bloodiest and deadliest firefights that had occurred around Cu Chi. Unfortunately, it had been mostly a losing battle. On top of all that, the Ho Bo Woods was heavily infested with booby traps and land mines to discourage us from going out there.

After we landed outside the perimeter of Hunsley I walked toward the main gate thinking, "What is this?" The patrol base was 100 meters in diameter with bunkers built into a three-foot-high berm surrounding the compound. I quickly found out why the berm was only three feet high. We were in the middle of *Charlie's* country and more susceptible to enemy ground attacks. The 105MM artillery pieces at Hunsley could be lowered to fire at point-blank range over the berm to repel a ground attack. Those howitzers could fire a beehive round containing 8,000 flechettes (two-inch darts). At 150 yards the beehive round would kill anything in a path fifty yards wide. I hoped we wouldn't have to call on those beehive rounds to save our butts while I was there.

There was a wooden guard tower in the center of the patrol base and a few tents and other bunkers scattered around the interior. There were also circular mortar pits ten to twelve feet in diameter. An approximate three-foot-high sandbag wall surrounded each pit to protect the men inside from incoming mortar-round explosions. Our mortar platoon set up one mortar tube in the middle of each pit.

The third platoon was assigned a group of bunkers along the northeast perimeter. The bunkers were small, making it a cozy fit for us. We left most of our gear outside to leave enough room inside the bunkers to sleep. Fortunately, we would only be out there a few days.

The mood of the men became more serious after our arrival at Hunsley. There was little laughter or horsing around like I had seen at Venice East. For the first time in Vietnam, although not scared, I definitely felt uneasy. Lieutenant Donaldson gathered the platoon to brief us on the plan for the night. Captain Branch had planned to send out two ambush patrols, but the intelligence reports indicated there had been a recent buildup of NVA troops in the Ho Bo Woods. It was recommended we keep everyone inside the base and be prepared for incoming mortars and to defend against a possible ground attack.

My heart almost stopped when I heard the words *ground attack.* "Take me back to peaceful Venice East," I thought to myself. Lieutenant Donaldson told us to double check our weapons and set up a guard rotation.

As it started to get dark several of us were outside our bunker organizing our gear while two men had started pulling guard duty.

Suddenly, someone yelled from a nearby bunker, "INCOMING!" Almost immediately there was a loud BOOM, with more explosions quickly following. I saw the flash of a mortar round when it exploded near a bunker to our south as I instinctively turned and dove for our bunker entrance. I don't know how we all made it through a bunker entrance that was about four feet high and two feet wide in the matter of a few seconds without crunching each other, but we did.

More incoming mortar rounds continued to rain in on Hunsley while we huddled inside the bunker. Fortunately, someone must have heard the whistling sound of one of the first incoming rounds and had given us a little warning. The enemy would fire mortar rounds into a patrol base assuming we would all jump inside our bunkers, and then try to sneak through our perimeter and launch an attack before we could establish a defense. We waited inside the bunker while a series of fifteen to twenty incoming mortar rounds seemed to walk across the base. We needed to get outside to grab our weapons and stand guard along the perimeter, but we didn't want to get nailed by more incoming mortar rounds either.

While we were inside the bunker two men watched through two sight holes built into the front wall of the bunker. If they spotted any movement near the perimeter they would detonate the claymore mines in front of our bunker using the detonators which were near each site hole. The incoming rounds stopped after a couple minutes.

I said, "Let's go, guys."

We quickly moved outside, put on our helmets and flak jackets, grabbed our weapons and ammunition and spread along the berm on each side of our bunker watching for any movement. Other men were popping out from nearby bunkers and setting up along the berm.

Our mortar platoon and the artillerymen were firing outgoing rounds. The pops from the mortars being fired and the louder booms from the firing 105MM artillery rounds were almost constant. Whenever we received incoming mortar fire our mortar and artillery crews would start firing outgoing rounds in all directions, even if that meant exposing themselves to the incoming rounds.

If someone heard the pop of the enemy mortar or could identify the general location of the incoming rounds, they would get word to the mortar platoon and artillerymen to direct their fire in that direction. If they didn't know where the enemy mortar fire came from, they sprayed a pattern of rounds all around the surrounding countryside. The 82MM mortars normally used by the enemy had a maximum range of nearly three miles; however, with the accuracy of the incoming rounds that night, they were likely firing from a much closer range.

I looked toward the south side of the patrol base when I heard someone yell, "Doc Jackson, we need you!"

I told the men to stay along the berm while I went to see what happened. None of the men near our bunker had been hit but when I reached the south side of the patrol base along with Doc Jackson, we found a disaster. The mortar rounds had clobbered several men in the second platoon. Men were screaming in pain and yelling, "Doc! I need help!" Men were scattered, lying or sitting on the ground.

Captain Branch walked up to me and told me to get more guys to help the injured men. I ran back and grabbed several men and told the rest of the guys to spread out along the berm.

Someone asked, "What happened?"

I said, "Second platoon got hit."

I told the men with me to spread out among the wounded men and help the medics treat their wounds, ranging from minor shrapnel wounds to life-threatening injuries. It was agonizing to hear one man scream while I helped Doc Jackson put a large bandage on his mangled shoulder. Two men had serious leg wounds but hopefully the doctors in Cu Chi could save their limbs. Another man had received a blast of shrapnel in the stomach and was in terrible pain.

When Sidney Morrison, our company medic, gave us the OK, we loaded the most seriously wounded men onto litters that were stored at the patrol base and carried them toward the northern perimeter where the medical evacuation helicopters (medevacs) would be landing to evacuate them. Two choppers were soon circling Hunsley. An RTO directed them to the landing zone that was marked with a strobe light. As the medevacs landed we quickly loaded the first group of wounded men aboard. We then took the litters that had been delivered by the medevacs and returned for the rest of the injured men. A third medevac soon arrived and flew the last of the eleven wounded men from the second platoon to the 12th Evac hospital in Cu Chi.

Those men were all alive when they left Hunsley but several men were in serious condition. The first few rounds had detonated near bunkers along the southern perimeter of the patrol base and wounded the men before they could run for cover. Unfortunately for us, *Charlie* had been a good marksman that evening.

We stood on 100% guard for about an hour but everything remained quiet. When we went back to our normal one-hour guard rotation I quietly stood beside our bunker and thought how lucky the Third Herd had been that night. If we had been assigned to those southern bunkers, we would have been the ones getting nailed. There was a higher power than all of us that determined our destiny that night.

I got up the next morning, put on my boots and walked outside the bunker to find a nice sunny day. Although we had air mattresses and hammocks to provide some comfort while we slept, believe me, it wasn't that comfortable night after night. My breakfast consisted of canned ham and eggs that I doctored up with some grape jelly to make them a little more palatable. I also learned that if we had time, we could burn a little piece of C-4 explosive to heat up a can of C-rations.

I couldn't believe it until I saw someone do it one day. C-4 was a powerful white plastic explosive that looked like modeling clay kids might play with. A blasting cap would be pushed into a stick of C-4 to detonate it. An exploding stick of C-4 would cause serious damage, when it detonated, but amazingly you could burn it without it exploding. It was probably expensive cooking fuel but, it was readily available. We used C-4 to heat C-rations whenever we could.

After my cold breakfast Lieutenant Donaldson briefed us NCOs about the day's RIF. We would fly to the northeastern edge of the Ho

Bo Woods then walk back to Hunsley looking for any signs of enemy activity, and for the mortar tube that had fired the rounds the past night.

I carried a topographical map covered in plastic to keep it dry. When I was briefed about our daily mission I would line out our route on the plastic cover with a grease pencil. It was important to know where we were at all times in case we needed to call in mortar or artillery fire, or an air strike, or if we had casualties and needed a medevac. The maps had numbered horizontal and vertical grid lines that formed one thousand-meter squares. If we needed any type of support we could identify our location by referring to those numbered grid lines.

When I returned to brief the men in my squad, their first question was, "How many klicks is it?" A "Klick" was 1,000 meters or about .6 miles. The military referred to distances in meters rather than miles. We would be covering about fourteen klicks (eight miles). There were a lot of "Oh shits" and "Damn its" when the guys heard the news.

Before I put on my gear I took off the OD-green boxer shorts I had been wearing under my fatigue pants and put them into my backpack. GIs in the field in Vietnam had learned if they wore boxer shorts under their fatigue pants, they often developed chafing or a rash in their crotch from the moisture and from underwear rubbing while they walked. However, a simple solution was discovered: don't wear underwear. Sort of an *open-air* approach. It worked for me.

I put on my web harness and pistol belt which were designed to carry our gear, like my canteen, a pouch for my compass, and a canvas ammunition pouch I used to carry my camera. I then threw on the two bandoleers of M-16 ammunition and a 100-round belt of machine gun ammunition. I also carried two smoke grenades and four hand grenades. The M-26 fragmentation grenade was oval-shaped with a flat bottom, it weighed 1.7 pounds. They also made what we called baseball grenades, but which were actually about the size of a tennis ball. Some men carried M-26s because they were more powerful while others liked the baseball grenades because they were lighter and could be thrown farther. I normally carried two of each type.

I put my map in the side-leg pocket of my fatigue pants, slapped on my helmet and was ready for action. Well, almost. I had seen several guys sorting through a box of C-rations and taking a can or two with them. I walked to the box to see what was left. Ham and eggs? No way. Crackers? No, too dry. And then I found a can of fruit cocktail; perfect, I thought. I put the can in my pocket along with a plastic spoon. I carried my trusty little P-38 can opener that came with the C-rations and I was set for lunch.

We gathered in an open area outside Hunsley's main gate that was used as the landing zone (LZ). A group of choppers would fly us out and drop us off in the boonies. Most of the company was going on the RIF, requiring two lifts (a lift was a group of four to six Hueys) to carry everyone out. The twelve remaining members of the second platoon stayed back at the patrol base. The third platoon was on the first lift and we were soon aboard and flying high above the Ho Bo Woods.

We flew over the countryside for a few minutes to allow time for the artillery batteries at Hunsley to soften the LZ. "Soften" meant firing several artillery rounds near the LZ, hoping to scare off any enemy troops who might happen to be in the area. They would pepper two or three locations to confuse the enemy and not telegraph our actual landing site. When the artillery gunners had finished their job, they notified the pilots it was safe to drop us off.

The door gunner near me opened fire with his M-60 when we neared the LZ. It scared the hell out of me. What did he see? What was he shooting at? It didn't appear we were taking enemy fire and I didn't see any movement on the ground.

Chuck Gorman noticed the shocked look on my face and leaned toward me and yelled, "They're just spraying the area, no problem."

I gave him a thumbs-up while the chopper descended into the LZ. The machine gun fire was another precautionary measure intended to force any enemy personnel in the area to head for cover, hopefully letting us land safely and allowing the choppers to fly off without being fired upon.

The LZ that morning was an open area covered with tall grass. I had been told that when we were dropped in a remote LZ that exposed the choppers to enemy fire, we wouldn't wait until the chopper was on the ground to hop off. Because the choppers were easy targets when they were moving slowly near the ground, most pilots would hover a foot or two off the ground while men hopped off in the boonies.

I was sitting on the floor next to the door so I swung my legs outside the chopper and placed my feet on top of the round landing skid as we neared the ground. I was the first to jump. And boy was I surprised. The grass was a lot taller than it appeared. When I jumped I thought we were a couple feet off the ground, but we were actually about four feet in the air. I wasn't ready for that kind of a fall and stumbled and fell when I hit the ground. I quickly picked up my helmet that had fallen off, stood up and hurried away as the chopper roared off.

We spread out and established a defensive perimeter around the landing zone. Setting up a perimeter meant placing men normally in a circular formation, facing outward, to establish a secure area inside the formation. The choppers flew back to Hunsley to fly in the rest of the company. We sat tight until they returned.

A couple of the men who saw me jump from the chopper chuckled after we settled into our perimeter. One of them said, "Jumped a little early didn't you, Sarge?"

I smiled and said. "Yeah, I think so," as I shook my head in disbelief at what I had done. A combination of adrenalin from my first drop in a remote LZ and poor judgment about our distance from the ground made me look pretty silly that morning. We all had to be quick learners while we began serving as infantrymen in Vietnam. My little mistake had no consequences, but other mistakes could cost someone's life.

About twenty minutes later the rest of the company arrived on a second lift of choppers, including Captain Branch who took charge.

We lined up in two parallel columns about twenty or twenty-five meters apart and started moving south along our designated route.

First platoon led the RIF, followed by the CO and his CP group while the third platoon brought up the rear. Each day the order of the platoons on the RIF changed. Obviously, leading the RIF was the most dangerous duty, especially for the first man in each column who was the *point man*. His job was called *walking point*. He was not only the first to be exposed to enemy fire but was also the one most likely to trip a booby trap should they be in our path. And they were.

We normally had the FNGs rotate walking point until another new guy arrived to assume the duty. Walking point wasn't a friendly welcome to the field but it had become a fair way to assign and rotate point duty. I didn't walk point because I was a sergeant. I normally was the third or fourth man in the column, near the middle of my squad, to take control if something happened. Lieutenant Donaldson and Sergeant Brown normally walked near the center of one of the columns, enabling them to give directions to the entire platoon when necessary.

We kept ourselves spaced about twenty feet apart to avoid presenting a group target for the enemy and to minimize the extent of casualties from booby traps, land mines or hand grenades. The saying we heard often during training, "One grenade will get you all," began to make a lot of sense.

One of my responsibilities while on RIFs was keeping an eye on the men to make sure they remained spread out and paid attention to what was going on around them. We kept our eyes moving all the time. We not only watched where we were stepping but also glanced out over the countryside for any movement or anything that looked suspicious. The NVA and VC were clever soldiers. They could conceal themselves in the vegetation, becoming virtually invisible until we were nearly upon them. They also had tunnels under much of the countryside from where they could pop up, fire a few rounds at us and quickly drop out of sight before we could return fire.

I had a sling connected to my M-16. Being left handed I placed the sling over my left shoulder and rested my left hand on my rifle as we walked across the countryside. We didn't hold our rifles ready to fire unless we spotted something or expected to be walking up on enemy troops. We didn't talk too much while conducting a RIF unless we had something of note to say to someone, we often used hand signals to communicate. We tried to move across the countryside as quietly as sixty to seventy-five men could.

The first hour of the RIF was uneventful. I walked along not quite sure what to expect. If we stopped for a break we would sit or kneel down with the two columns of men facing outward watching out over the countryside. Anytime we were *outside the wire*, which meant outside of a patrol/firebase, we were always on the defensive, even when we took a break. I took my helmet off and took a drink of water and then poured a little water on the OD-green towel I carried around my neck and wiped the sweat from my face. Carrying a towel around my neck during RIFs was one of the little infantryman's *tricks of the trade* which helped me deal with the sweat caused by the constant heat and humidity of Vietnam.

We had been resting for only a couple of minutes when I heard the sound of gunfire coming from the front of our column. I immediately grabbed my rifle and looked across the countryside around me. The gunfire continued but we weren't taking any incoming fire near me.

I then heard Lieutenant Donaldson yell, "Sergeant Hogue, take your machine gun team up front."

"What are we getting into?" I thought as I waved at my machine gun team, Bob Emery and Mike Stark, who were right behind me. We quickly moved to the front of the column where the first platoon's machine gun teams were laying down fire along a hedgerow about 100 meters to the northeast.

Captain Branch said, "Set your team up and spray those hedgerows. There's NVA out there." As he pointed to a line of hedgerows.

Bob set his machine gun on a little mound, resting it on the two legs that folded down from the barrel. Mike quickly attached a long belt of ammunition to the small string of ammunition Bob always kept loaded in the gun. Bob opened fire. The loud firing of three machine guns was nearly deafening. Every fifth machine gun round was a tracer so the gunner could see where his rounds were going and could adjust his fire accordingly. I crouched beside Bob Emery and watched the orange glow of the tracers from the three machine guns fill the air as they raced into the distant hedgerow.

Two men were also firing M-79 grenade rounds into the area exploding with a "KA-BAM" when they landed. The M-79 grenade launchers looked like a fat sawed-off shotgun and fired a golf ball sized grenade to over 300 meters. It was nice to have a weapon that could fire an explosive round that far, but the M-79 grenades didn't have near the destructive force of a hand grenade. We probably scared the enemy more often with the M-79s than we injured them. The M-79 could also fire a shotgun-like pellet round at short-range targets.

Someone had spotted two enemy troops moving into the hedgerow in front of us while we were taking a break. Anyone spotted in that remote area was considered to be the enemy. Our men had opened fire on them before they had a chance to do the same to us. We weren't taking any return fire and after spraying the area with machine gun rounds for a couple of minutes, the CO yelled, "Cease fire!"

Captain Branch had called in a Cobra gunship to *pepper* the area before we moved through to search for the enemy troops. Cobras were sleekly-designed heavily armed helicopter gunships that could deliver awesome firepower from the air. They were armed with a 7.62MM machine gun, 20MM and 40MM grenade launchers and rocket launchers. The pilot sat in the front seat of the Cobra and the co-pilot, who was the gunner, sat directly behind the pilot.

Many of the Cobras had huge shark-like teeth painted on the nose of the chopper. The Cobras would scare the hell out of a lot of enemy troops when they looked up and saw a chopper with shark's teeth coming at them and unleashing its weaponry. The Cobra arrived and fired several rockets and grenades into the hedgerow and surrounding area and then remained overhead on standby while we moved into the area.

We cautiously walked in two columns toward the hedgerow with every man holding his weapon ready to open fire at any movement. We spent nearly an hour searching the area but didn't find any bodies, blood trails or signs of enemy troops. It appeared that by some miracle they hadn't been hit by our gunfire. They were long gone or may have slipped into a concealed tunnel that we were unable to find. Captain Branch finally decided we should move on. We didn't get those gooks that day, but I bet we scared the heck out of them.

We normally didn't walk too fast during a RIF. The point team moved cautiously while they watched for booby traps and signs of enemy activity. The point man had a compass and would be given a heading to follow or a target landmark to move toward. The second man in the column, called the *pace man*, was responsible for looking over the terrain in front of him to observe for any movement. The pace man was also responsible for tracking the distance by counting his footsteps. When we were on Company size RIFs, we walked in two columns; therefore, there were two point teams (point man and pace man) each tracking our direction and distance. With the point teams leading the way and several of us checking our topographical maps to monitor our travel, we could closely keep track of our location as we moved along the designated route.

We continued along the route and stopped only to check out anything that looked suspicious or unusual, or to take a short break. It was a hot and dry afternoon with no clouds in sight. I was getting beat. The lack of physical exercise during the past few weeks caught up with me. In one sense it was nice not to have encountered an afternoon rain, but that afternoon, I would have actually enjoyed a shower from Mother Nature. Some of the other new guys had tired looks on their faces while we made our way back toward Hunsley. After a couple more hours of uneventful walking through three-foot-tall grass, crossing a small stream and abandoned rice paddies, we pulled into Hunsley at about four o'clock that afternoon.

Even happier than I to see Hunsley were Bob Emery and Mike Stark, my machine gun team. They were also on their first RIF. Bob had been lugging the twenty-three-pound M-60 and ammunition all day long. Mike had been carrying about 500 rounds of machine gun ammunition plus his M-16 ammunition. They were both beat. Their only salvation was that they had fired a few hundred rounds of ammunition during the day which lightened their load a little. I chugged most of my canteen of warm water when we got back to Hunsley. A shower would have felt great about then, but we didn't have water to spare for showers out there. I had to settle for pouring a little water over my head to wash off some of the sweat and dirt.

That evening we learned that all the men in the second platoon who were wounded by the mortar fire during our first night at Hunsley had survived. But most of them had serious injuries and would be flown back to *the World* to recover. When in Vietnam, we referred to the United States as *the World* because Vietnam was so strange and different from the life we had all previously known. It sometimes felt like we were on another planet.

We spent the next couple of days going on RIFs around Hunsley. We saw lots of footprints and trampled grass indicating that enemy troops had been moving through the area, but we didn't see any enemy troops and didn't find any of their bunker complexes we knew were out there someplace.

There were likely many well concealed tunnels because the area was mostly high ground covered with thick vegetation. If enemy troops had spotted us, they could have slipped into a tunnel, not wanting to take us on. We were also fortunate and hadn't tripped any booby traps. The *old timers* said it was amazing we didn't run into some enemy troops out there. But that was fine with me.

On our third day at Hunsley we returned from a short RIF just after noon. We were then told to pack up our gear because we were flying back to Firebase Patton. With sighs of relief, we quickly packed up and stood by on the LZ for the welcome flight back to Patton.

Patrol Base Hunsley was named after First Lieutenant Dennis Hunsley who served in the 25th Infantry Division and was killed in action on March 15, 1969. He had been awarded the Silver Star for gallantry two weeks before his death.

Patrol Base Hunsley was established to draw out the enemy and provoke a ground assault. However, "Charlie" never took the bait for a ground assault at Hunsley while we were there. The NVA and VC had previously initiated ground assaults at other remote patrol bases and suffered heavy casualties from Cobra gunships, artillery and mortar fire and air strikes.

Sitting on a sandbag bunker left to right – Larry "Doc" Jackson and Bill Casey
Middle left to right – Dennis Schultz and Staff Sergeant Tom Brown
In front – First Lieutenant Steve Donaldson

Chapter 8

Glad to be a Ground-Pounder

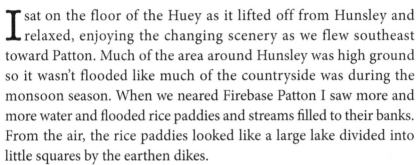

I sat on the floor of the Huey as it lifted off from Hunsley and relaxed, enjoying the changing scenery as we flew southeast toward Patton. Much of the area around Hunsley was high ground so it wasn't flooded like much of the countryside was during the monsoon season. When we neared Firebase Patton I saw more and more water and flooded rice paddies and streams filled to their banks. From the air, the rice paddies looked like a large lake divided into little squares by the earthen dikes.

The scars on the countryside left by years of fighting were clearly visible. The ground was dotted with large and small craters from exploding artillery shells and bombs. Clusters of ten or twenty craters could be seen where a firefight had occurred and artillery shells or air strikes had bombarded the area. Those craters, filled with water from the monsoon rains, created a pretty scene from the air; however, there was likely a tragic story associated with each of those clusters of craters scattered across the south Vietnamese countryside.

After landing on the east side of Patton we entered the perimeter and settled into a group of bunkers along the west side. The large bunkers at Patton provided ample space to sleep and to store our gear and personal items. Captain Branch and his staff settled into their Command Post, a small group of bunkers near the interior of the firebase. His staff (CP Group) included a medic, two demolitions experts, a forward observer to call in mortars, artillery or air strikes, three RTOs and First Sergeant William Seavey, who kept us in line, or at least tried to.

Most first sergeants were nicknamed "Top." Top was close to fifty years old and had served in World War II, Korea and Vietnam.

Like many first sergeants he sometimes got carried away with enforcing some of the Army's rules. Top kept an eye on us, making sure guys shaved every few days, that our hair didn't get too long and that we kept the area around our bunkers clean. Yes, even in the middle of Vietnam, we had to keep things clean. But it wasn't just because of Top. There were many rats, mice, snakes and flies that were attracted to trash, especially any food left around. So, it was important to keep our so-called living quarters clean to keep the critters away. The flies were around during the day; the mosquitoes came out at night. The rats and mice were around all the time.

That afternoon mail and other supplies were delivered from Cu Chi. Just like in the movies, someone would take the bundle of mail for our platoon and call out the name written on each letter or package. The men receiving a letter would find a quiet spot to read about what was happening back in *the World*.

I received a letter from Mom dated August 17, 1969. She started the letter by saying that Steven Crum had been killed in Vietnam on August 13th. I stopped reading. Steven had grown up on a farm near Schaller and graduated from high school one year after I did. The realities of the war in Vietnam had finally hit Schaller, Iowa by taking the life of one of their own. It was a shock knowing Steven had been killed likely not far from me in Vietnam. Mom's letter went on to say President Nixon had briefly stopped sending troops to Vietnam the day my friend Dean Christiansen was to leave. Dean had been reassigned to Fort Ord, California. What a lucky break for him.

After mail call, most of us cleaned our weapons. We normally cleaned our rifles every couple of days whether we used them or not. Our lives depended upon them. The M-16 was a good rifle but had the reputation of jamming if not kept clean. The two machine gun teams worked together to clean the machine guns, which was more effort than cleaning an M-16.

Because our machine gunners had the most physically demanding job in the platoon, the husky guys were often chosen to be machine gunners. Bob Emery was a well-built eighteen-year-old, good looking guy from Michigan who had been assigned to the third platoon a few days after I arrived. After completing AIT Bob had been sent to Germany since he was only seventeen at the time, but he volunteered for Vietnam when he turned eighteen. Bob came to me on his first day with the platoon and volunteered to be my machine gunner when he learned that we needed a permanent gunner in the first squad. After taking one look at Bob's physique I said, "The job is yours." Michael Stark had arrived with Bob. I assigned Mike as Bob's assistant gunner.

The routine at Patton was more relaxed than at Patrol Base Hunsley. I didn't notice anyone peeking over the berm to see what was happening outside. Historically, there had been no enemy assaults at Patton but there had been several mortar attacks. We didn't carry our rifles with us when we were inside the perimeter and didn't pull guard at our bunkers during the day. Men rotated lookout from the guard tower at the center of the firebase both day and night. That didn't seem like much protection to me but I was told rarely did anything serious happen during the day around Patton, so I shouldn't worry about it.

It was always hot during the afternoons, unless it was raining; therefore, most of us would take off our fatigue shirts and just wear trousers when we were inside a firebase or patrol base. Some of us would run around in our OD-green boxer shorts or other shorts and take off our jungle boots and wear rubber thongs or sandals. At about four o'clock during my first afternoon at Patton I saw three of the guys grab their towels and begin walking toward the center of the firebase.

One of the guys said, "Hey, Sarge, want a shower?"

"Shower?" I said, "Where?" No one had told me about showers at Patton. I grabbed my towel as the guys waved for me to follow them.

I hadn't had a real shower since I had taken a quick shower in the makeshift shower at Venice East, which was a small barrel elevated on wooden framework with a showerhead attached at the bottom. I quickly caught up with the guys who were walking toward the interior of the firebase, and I looked in amazement when I saw several showerheads spraying water on guys who were lathering up to clean off the dirt and grime. In a minute I stripped off my pants and joined the others under the showers. The water was cool but on that hot afternoon it felt great as I washed several days of dirt off my body.

There weren't walls around the showers, which made us visible by anyone in the area (not that we cared). I chuckled to myself thinking we looked like a little nudist colony showering under blue skies in the middle of the firebase. A well had been drilled at Patton shortly after it was constructed. About four o'clock every afternoon a pump was turned on that fed the showers for an hour or so. Believe me, even a cool shower was a luxury in the field in Vietnam.

The mess hall at Patton was another luxury. They served a hot breakfast every morning, and evening meal starting about five o'clock each afternoon. After my shower, I joined the chow line that formed at one end of the mess hall. In a few minutes I walked out the far end of the mess hall with a plate of food that looked much better than the C-rations I had been living on the past few days. We walked back to our bunkers to eat, because the mess hall didn't have tables and chairs inside like the mess hall back in Cu Chi. They served the meals on paper plates and we used plastic utensils. We tossed everything into a nearby trash barrel when we were through.

The schedule for the daily assignments (normally a reconnaissance-in-force {RIF}) was determined by the battalion headquarters staff, based upon observations by U.S. troops in the field, aerial observations or intelligence reports about enemy activity. The orders would be passed down to our CO who would then brief the platoon leaders each evening for our mission the following day. If the area to be patrolled was a long distance from the firebase or patrol base, we would be flown out on choppers early in the morning to search the designated area and normally would be flown back that afternoon. If the RIF covered an area closer to the firebase or patrol base we would walk out and back.

After Lieutenant Donaldson was briefed about the RIF he briefed us NCOs, who in turn briefed the remainder of the platoon. We thought we would be working out of Firebase Patton for a while, but Lieutenant Donaldson informed us that plans had suddenly changed.

The third platoon would be operating with a mechanized unit for a few days. Mechanized units were infantry companies who used armored personnel carriers (APCs) and tanks to travel across the countryside. Alpha Company was a traditional infantry Company. We were nicknamed *ground-pounders*, meaning we walked most of the time. But riding rather than walking appeared to be a pleasant alternative.

We settled in for our one-night's stay at Patton and set up a guard schedule. Two men pulled one-hour guard shifts at each bunker from dusk to dawn. We established a rotation for guard duty early each evening so everyone knew who followed who and knew where his relief man was sleeping. The rule was, you made sure your relief man was on guard before you went back to sleep. We had air mattresses to sleep on inside the dirt or wooden-floored bunkers, and most of us had a hammock we could tie to the huge wooden rafters that supported each bunker. I preferred sleeping in a hammock. My towel served as my pillow and I covered myself with a poncho liner. I soon learned to sleep like a baby, rocking in my hammock.

I took first watch on guard that night wearing my helmet and flak jacket. Although our flak jackets offered good protection, we often didn't wear them while on guard because they were heavy, uncomfortable and extremely hot. If Top caught us on guard without a flak jacket he would yell and cuss until we put one on. I had my rifle and a couple hand grenades by my side. We also often set a machine gun on the top of the bunker with a few hundred rounds of ammunition ready, just in case someone tried to surprise us. There were little walkways on each side of the bunkers to provide access through the berm to the front of each bunker. One man would stand in each walkway while on guard.

I pulled my first hour of guard without incident and woke up the next man, who got up and took his place beside the bunker. I then took off my boots, rolled into my hammock and fell asleep. The night passed quickly without incident. I woke up and after putting on my boots, I walked to the mess hall and enjoyed a warm breakfast of pancakes and sausage. About nine o'clock that morning we boarded a convoy of deuce-and-a-halfs, traveling several miles west on Highway 1 and then turning north where we met up with the mechanized units along a gravel road. I had no idea where we were.

I hopped off the truck and walked toward a group of armored personnel carriers (APCs) when I heard, "Hey, Hogue, what the hell are you doing out here?"

I looked around and saw a man hop off an APC, waving at me. It was John Jarvis who went through NCO School and OJT with me. We smiled when we met and shook hands, both glad to see a familiar face. He was in charge of one of the APCs. We shared a conversation about our brief time in Vietnam for a few minutes and then mounted up on the APCs to move out.

The APCs were track-driven vehicles made of thick metal. They were smaller than a tank and didn't have an artillery gun like a tank. They normally had a .50 caliber and M-60 machine gun mounted on top. APCs were as their name implied, armored vehicles designed to carry personnel in the battlefield. There was a large open space inside where personnel could ride, with a large rear door that lowered to the ground to enter and exit. There were also two circular hatches on top you could crawl through to enter or exit.

However, the APCs had weaknesses. Although the sides were made of heavy aluminum, an enemy rocket propelled grenade (RPG) round could penetrate the side and detonate inside. If a round penetrated the side of an APC, it meant serious injury or more likely death to those riding inside. Additionally, the bottom of the APC wasn't thick enough to withstand most land mine explosions. But the solution was simple: we rode on the flat top of the APC. Although that meant being exposed to enemy fire, it was considered safer than riding inside.

Five or six men hopped on each APC and we were off. We held on for dear life while the driver maneuvered through abandoned rice paddies and across the rugged terrain. We would travel on the APCs for a while and then hop off to search certain areas on foot while the mechanized units stood by. After hours of riding and walking, riding and walking, the process didn't make much sense to me. Although we obviously had a huge number of personnel and tremendous firepower, unless we ran into a large number of well-fortified enemy troops, they would likely run away or hide unnoticed when they heard us coming. I doubted a small number of NVA or VC would take us on.

We had traveled on high ground during most of the morning, making it easy for the tanks and APCs to maneuver. But after noon we ran into mushy terrain that was flooded from the monsoon rains. The APCs and tanks struggled to travel through the mud and muck. About mid-afternoon one of the APCs became stuck in a muddy abandoned rice paddy. They attached a cable and tried to pull it out with another APC, and almost buried the second vehicle. After spending most of an hour trying to get the APC unstuck, they gave up. They would have to bring out an armored recovery vehicle with a huge boom and winches to pull out the APC the following morning.

Since it was getting late, we established a perimeter around the stuck APC in a *night logger* position. Establishing a logger position meant setting up a defensive position in the boonies with no bunkers or other pre-established defenses. We attempted to dig foxholes but it was a hopeless because the ground was saturated. When we started digging holes they quickly filled with water. We ultimately arranged ourselves using rice paddy dikes for cover. After working with the mechanized units only one day it became evident that it wasn't as easy of duty as I had imagined it would be.

Our night logger looked like a wagon train in the 1800's circling their wagons at night. Only we had considerably more firepower than the cowboys had against the Indians. The APCs were stocked with C-rations. I ate part of a can of cold potatoes and beef that evening and threw the rest away. It tasted lousy. I did luck out and find some sponge cake to treat myself with desert.

As darkness fell we settled into rotating guard duty, but sleep in between guard shifts was extremely difficult because rain continued for much of the night. That night passed without any action but I woke up cold and wet. Most of us moved on that morning while two APCs and a dozen men stayed behind until help arrived to free the stuck APC. The mechanized unit CO finally made a smart move and headed toward higher ground. I thought they would have learned long ago it was impractical to move tanks and APCs through the soggy countryside and let us *ground-pounders* search those areas.

We slowly moved away from any inhabited areas and were out in the boonies by afternoon. The mechanized guys said they had been in that area and lost several men during a firefight with the VC a couple weeks earlier. We were southeast of the Ho Bo Woods. The North Vietnamese Army (NVA) and Viet Cong (VC) mostly traveled across the country in the uninhabited areas and maintained larger concentrations of personnel in base camps in those remote locations. We stopped several times and found trails that had recently been used, but we didn't have any enemy contact.

We finally stopped in an open area called a hard spot to rendezvous with another mechanized unit for the night. A hard spot was a designated remote location used periodically by American units to establish a perimeter. The vegetation had been cleared away and there were foxholes or guard positions established around the perimeter. After we ensured the area was secure, we located guard positions where we would have good visibility across the countryside and established a perimeter with groups of men interspersed between the APCs and tanks.

Late that afternoon we received word that the second mechanized unit that was to join us had been ambushed about four klicks southwest of our location. They had sustained heavy casualties and needed help. Three APCs, one tank and their men were ordered to move out to help them make their way back to our position. The mechanized units headed out while the rest of us went on guard. It was believed an enemy unit was moving through the area and possibly headed our way. With all the noise from the tanks and APCs, we certainly had made our presence known if they were out there.

It had been dark for about an hour when the group of APCs and two tanks pulled into our perimeter. I was standing a short distance from one APC when they dropped the rear door. The men standing around me were speechless. We saw the bodies of twelve men lying inside, stacked on top of each other. It was a gruesome sight. Lieutenant Donaldson came to me and asked for three men to help unload the bodies from the APC. I hated to ask anyone to help move the bodies, but it had to be done.

I heard one of the men in the first platoon say, "I'm not going to touch those bodies."

His platoon sergeant grabbed his arm and said, "If that was your dead ass in there, we'd carry you out. Get over there and do your job." The man slowly walked toward the APC without saying a word.

Medevacs were on the way to first evacuate several wounded men and then the twelve American bodies. One by one the bodies were moved from the APC and laid on the ground nearby. Several of us found ponchos to cover the bodies of our fallen comrades until they were flown to Cu Chi. The men who had survived the ambush were in shock, some of them crying and consoling each other.

John Jarvis, my friend from NCO school, walked up to me after the bodies were removed from the APC. Neither of us had personally known any of those men but seeing the bodies of twelve fellow Americans was a shock for both of us. I couldn't imagine what it would be like losing twelve men in the Third Herd in one day.

Later that evening we learned the mechanized unit had been ambushed while traveling through an area a short distance west of where we had traveled earlier. A group of NVA troops suddenly popped up from holes in the ground covered with brush and vegetation (spider holes) and opened fire on the GIs. Although most of the enemy were ultimately killed, it was a devastating loss for the mechanized unit.

One of the men who survived said, "Those men dropped off the APCs like dead flies. They didn't have a chance." He then looked at me and said, "War is hell. Actual combat is a mother-f---er," and turned and walked away. I hadn't heard that crude description of combat before, but I couldn't disagree with it either.

During the rest of the night we periodically sprayed the surrounding countryside with machine gun and rifle fire to deter an enemy attack. We had made our presence known and took a better safe than sorry approach by blasting the countryside. After a long night the sun rose to reveal over 120 GIs, six APCs and three tanks circled around that hard spot. It was difficult to believe that only a few enemy soldiers had inflicted so many casualties while facing the awesome firepower of the mechanized unit. However, it was the mindset of most NVA and VC soldiers to sacrifice their lives knowing they would take some of us with them.

We spent the third day working our way back toward Firebase Patton, and fortunately, had no enemy contact. We drove through the small village of Trung Lap north of Patton and then headed south on 7 Alpha, the gravel road leading to Patton. The APCs stopped near the front gate on the west side of Patton to let us off that mid-afternoon.

I quickly found my *shake'n bake* buddy, John Jarvis. We shared a handshake while I said, "Take care. Hopefully, I'll see you again."

He said, "OK. You be careful out here."

We waved at each other while the APCs moved on, headed to Cu Chi for a *stand down*, two days of rest and relaxation.

I walked through the front gate of Firebase Patton thinking about what had happened the past three days. I then decided if I had to be in the infantry I was actually satisfied to be a *ground-pounder*. After watching the APCs struggle through the mud and one getting stuck, and then seeing the bodies of twelve men who had been picked off from the top of their APCs, I was comfortable taking my chances humping through the boonies on foot. Although being a ground pounder was certainly a dangerous job, I wasn't ready to trade my old buddy John Jarvis for his job assigned to that mechanized unit.

————————————

Some Vietnam veterans who served with mechanized units believe the APC wasn't intended to be used the way it was in Vietnam. They were designed to accompany tanks and protect troops after they dismounted and maneuvered. The APCs were often used like Cavalry units and ridden into battle in Vietnam. Unfortunately, infantry mechanized units often suffered higher casualty rates than infantry ground units in Vietnam.

Although over 58,000 Americans were killed in Vietnam, an estimated 1.1 million North Vietnamese Army and Viet Cong troops were killed during the war. An estimated 415,000 Vietnamese civilians were killed and 935,000 were wounded during the Vietnam War.

Pictured atop an armored personnel carrier (APC) (left to right) Mike Stark, David Hardy and me (my arm is resting in the turret of a .50 caliber machine gun). Bob Emery is standing beside the APC.

Chapter 9

Fire Support Base Patton

W̲e were all glad to be back at Patton. For the men who had been there for a while it was like being back home. I was just glad to be surrounded with a six-foot berm again and having a bunker to sleep in. Most of us soon headed for the showers and then enjoyed our first hot meal in three days. Ah, the comforts of Fire Support Base Patton.

That evening the second squad, led by Jim Overbey, gathered their gear and left Patton to pull an ambush. One or more squads from our company normally set up an ambush every night at designated sites approximately 1000 meters from our assigned firebase or patrol base. The ambush team would rotate guard duty all night and if enemy troops passed near them they would ambush those troops by opening fire. We called it *popping* the ambush. It appeared to be dangerous duty to me.

The first night at Patton passed without incident except for another night of monsoon rains. The men from second squad returned from their uneventful ambush the following morning. The ambush team normally received the day off following their ambush to catch up on sleep, since the men spent much of the previous night on guard duty. I headed for the mess hall for a warm breakfast to start my day before we headed out for another reconnaissance in force (RIF).

Our RIF that day took us west of Firebase Patton. We left through the front gate shortly after eight o'clock, first heading through a group of rice paddies and then open countryside. Because the rice paddies were still filled with a foot or two of water, we normally walked on the grassy earthen dikes that surrounded each paddy. I had been told during NCO School we shouldn't walk on the dikes because the enemy planted booby traps on them. However, Lieutenant Donaldson informed me the enemy rarely booby-trapped the dikes in inhabited areas because the local civilians worked in or around the rice paddies and walked along the dikes daily. If they did, those booby traps would likely kill or wound more civilians than GIs. However, he warned me if we were operating in uninhabited areas of the countryside we should be much more careful about walking on the dikes. And Lieutenant Donaldson was correct. During my tour in Vietnam, we never encountered a booby trap on a rice paddy dike in inhabited areas.

Rice paddies were built in squares or rectangles 150 to 200 feet square. The earthen dikes were two or three feet high and normally less than two feet wide at the top. During the springtime the civilians planted little rice plants in the paddies and then monsoon rains eventually flooded each paddy with a foot or two of water during the summer. Scattered openings in the dikes allowed water to flow among the paddies to ensure they all became flooded. The rice grew in the water until the monsoon season ended each fall. The paddies would then dry up and the rice was harvested.

As we continued our RIF that day we passed hamlets with four to six hooches clustered together. We didn't search the hooches, which consisted of clay walls and a corrugated metal or thatched roof. The plan for the day was to walk through the villages and hamlets to let the local civilians know we were keeping an eye on them. The VC and their sympathizers were out there, even if we didn't recognize them, often using violent measures to encourage civilians to support their cause. The VC would beat or torture civilians or threaten to kill family members to recruit their support. For many civilians it was either support the enemy or be killed.

The adults often stood around looking at us as we passed by, while the kids often begged for food or candy. One youngster, about ten-years old, came up to us on wooden crutches. His left leg had been amputated below his knee. He had likely tripped a booby trap, becoming one of the innocent civilian casualties of the war.

When we moved through a small cluster of hooches, a Vietnamese woman came running up to us carrying a young girl. The adult civilians normally kept their distance, so that woman running up to us created a concern. She could toss a hand grenade that could kill or injure a bunch of us. Several of us pointed our rifles at her, waiting to see what she might do. Someone yelled, "Dung lau!" (Vietnamese for *stop*.)

The woman ignored our rifles and commands to stop and continued to slowly walk toward us; frantically shouting in Vietnamese and pointing with one hand to the little girl she was carrying. The little girl was crying, and we soon saw the child was bleeding.

I asked Doc Jackson who was standing next to me if he wanted to help the little girl. He said, "Yeah, but let's be careful."

The woman finally stopped when she was a few feet away from our column and then placed the little girl on the ground. Doc Jackson and company medic Sid Morrison walked up to the little girl, who was crying in pain. Two men quickly searched the woman. She had nothing concealed under her clothing. The woman pointed to the ground as she talked frantically and then swung her arms outward, we thought, trying to indicate something had exploded.

Doc Morrison told the CO the little girl had serious shrapnel wounds and should be medevacked to Cu Chi.

Captain Branch told an RTO to radio for a chopper to fly the woman and girl Cu Chi. The woman would be interrogated to determine what actually happened. Did someone trip a booby trap injuring the girl or was someone making a device and it accidentally detonated? When a chopper landed the girl and woman were placed aboard along with one of Captain Branch's staff to escort them to Cu Chi.

Later that day Steve Robinson, a Third Herd member yelled, "Fire in the hole!" As we walked along.

He pulled the pin from a hand grenade and dropped it down a well. After about four seconds the grenade exploded, sending a gush of water about eight feet in the air. The enemy sometimes used the water wells scattered around the countryside to hide supplies or ammunition. They would seal items in plastic to keep them dry and drop them in a well. The package would sink to the bottom and they would come by later and fish it out. A grenade exploding in the well might destroy anything hidden in the well and send debris floating to the top. We didn't often find anything in the wells, but the men enjoyed dropping a hand grenade in a well and watching the water soar in the air for a little fun.

The morning had been sunny and hot but clouds moved in by early afternoon. In what seemed like only a few minutes, the clear skies clouded over, and the monsoon rain began falling. We worked our way back to Patton without finding any signs of enemy activity, but we got soaked. We settled into our bunkers about four o'clock. I put on dry fatigues after the rain stopped a short while later. Along with the mail and other supplies, they delivered sodas and blocks of ice. I took a can and laid it on its side on a block of ice and began rolling the can with my hands while the turning can melted an indentation in the ice. After rolling the can for a couple minutes the soda was ice cold. "Rolling a soda," was another infantryman's *trick of the trade* in Vietnam.

Another special treat for all of us was receiving care packages from home. Almost every day one of the guys in the platoon would receive a package, normally from their mom, containing homemade goodies. We would often gather around whoever received a package when they opened it, hoping they would share the goodies inside. My mom sent many care packages of homemade chocolate chip cookies that were normally devoured in minutes by the guys.

My squad had ambush duty that night, so after late afternoon chow it was time to get the men ready. Lieutenant Donaldson gave me our ambush site and I marked it on my map. We were going about 700 meters east of Patton. I would take eleven other men, including a machine gun team and an RTO. We would each take all the gear we normally carried, plus our poncho liner and a claymore mine. It was still daylight when we walked along the path through the concertina wire on the east side of Patton. I gave a compass reading to our point man Carlton Quick, which would lead us to our destination. Quick led the single column to our ambush site while Ed Leberski, walked second and counted paces.

When we neared our ambush site, I motioned for Quick to lead us into a group of trees a short distance south of the site, which would conceal us until darkness neared. I didn't want to set up the ambush with too much daylight to minimize the risk of being spotted by the enemy. Just before darkness fell, I walked directly behind Quick and guided everyone into the ambush site. We set up near a path that ran alongside a canal adjacent to a group of rice paddies. We would set up the ambush behind a rice paddy dike about ten meters to the side of the path, to give us concealment.

We set up the ambush with three groups of four men spaced a short distance apart, like the three points of a triangle. Two positions faced the path and the third position faced the rear to protect our backside. I designated *fields of fire* for each position, by identifying a target to their left and right as their primary responsibility to open fire, enabling us to protect ourselves in all directions. While we settled in, one or two men at a time placed their claymore mine in front of each position. The electrical wire attached to the blasting cap inside each claymore was then strung along the ground, back to the detonators we kept near each position. The men facing the trail placed their claymores beside the trail, enabling them to fire a blast across and down the trail. When finished, a dozen claymores surrounded our ambush site. If enemy personnel passed by we would first fire the claymores without revealing our exact position. We would then throw hand grenades, and, lastly, open fire with our rifles and machine gun.

It was nearly dark by the time we were settled in. I was in one of the positions facing the trail to call the shots if something happened. We assigned guard duty, with one man staying up at each of the three positions while the rest of us found a spot to sleep. The rice paddy had been abandoned, but there were scattered pools of water and the ground was damp and muddy, making it impossible to sleep in the paddy. So the men not on guard spaced themselves along the top of the dikes surrounding the rice paddy, hoping to catch a little sleep.

I didn't have my first guard shift for a couple of hours, but it was going to be tricky trying to sleep on a two-foot-wide dike. A turn too far one way or the other and I would be in the mud. Before I laid down, I rubbed mosquito repellant on my hands, neck and face. I had learned, during my first night in the boonies, you needed to put mosquito repellant on any exposed skin or the mosquitoes would eat you alive. And then I added one more defense against the mosquitoes. I placed my mosquito net over my head to cover my entire face.

With repellant on my skin and my mosquito net in place, I curled up in my poncho liner with my towel under my head and fell asleep to the hum of mosquitoes flying around my head. I was awakened about an hour later by the pitter-patter of rain on my poncho liner. Within minutes it began pouring. I was soon completely soaked. We had been issued waterproof ponchos, but we didn't carry them on ambushes because the rustle of the heavy plastic made too much noise. The rules while on an ambush were, no lights and minimal noise. When we communicated, we used hand signals or whispered.

The rice paddy soon became a watery mess. There was nothing I could do except wrap up in my soggy poncho and try to stay halfway warm. I didn't fall asleep again before it was my turn for guard duty. I sat there on guard with water dripping off my helmet, staring out into the darkness. When we pulled guard on an ambush we either held our M-16 or kept it by our side. We also kept the claymore detonators handy and had several hand grenades lying nearby. When we slept, we kept our weapons and gear nearby and ready if needed. Pulling guard seemed like a hopeless cause that night. The clouds obscured any light from the moon or stars and the rain made it impossible to see more than a few feet in any direction. Someone could have walked along the trail and I wouldn't have seen them. I looked around with the starlight scope but it was useless. I hoped Charlie was as miserable as we were and was holed up somewhere rather than roaming the countryside.

The rain had stopped during the early morning hours and after what seemed like an endless night, the sky brightened as the sun began to rise in the eastern horizon. We hadn't seen any movement during the night, although a dozen enemy troops could have passed by during the heavy rain without our seeing them. When daylight arrived we gathered up our claymores, loaded up our gear and headed back to Patton to dry out and relax during our day off.

On the morning of August 24, 1969, we left Patton for an enjoyable chopper ride, except they dropped us in the middle of a swamp east of the always-dangerous Ho Bo Woods. Lieutenant Donaldson was the first to hop out of the chopper I was riding on and landed in waist-deep water. The rest of us had no choice but to join him with a splash. We would have been in trouble if the enemy wanted to hit us as we slowly sloshed through deep water for almost 50 meters, until we reached shallow water and finally worked our way onto dry ground.

Fortunately, it was a warm, clear morning. We would dry out soon. We organized ourselves with the first platoon leading the RIF, followed by Captain Branch and his CP group, the third platoon behind them and second platoon bringing up the rear. Everyone was pretty serious. The stories about working in or near the Ho Bo Woods seemed to get worse every time I heard one. Several companies, including Alpha Company on August 2nd, had taken heavy casualties when they ran into heavily fortified NVA bunker complexes out there. Our job was to try to find one of those bunker complexes.

We had been walking straight north from our LZ through mostly flat terrain with trees and hedgerows growing everywhere. About mid-morning a signal came from the front of the columns for everyone to get down. I passed the signal on back and kneeled to the ground holding my rifle in my hands while I looked around for movement. There was no rifle fire or explosions indicating a firefight.

Someone asked, "What's going on?"

Lieutenant Donaldson waved for me to join him. He told me there was a bunker complex in front of us and we were moving up on the right flank.

The third platoon slowly maneuvered forward and to the right and set up on-line to the right of the bunkers that were about forty meters away. Second platoon was doing the same on the left side. I expected all hell to break loose at any moment. Captain Branch had each platoon slowly move closer and closer to the bunkers, with the first platoon and the CP group in the center. Amazingly, nothing happened. We hadn't encountered any enemy fire and hadn't seen any movement around the bunkers. First platoon's Chieu Hoi then walked up to a bunker and peeked inside. It was empty. We slowly moved in and checked two other bunkers, which were also empty. But where were the NVA?

Whew! That was a relief. I had prepared myself for a nasty battle. Captain Branch, Lieutenant Tom Cannava (our Artillery Forward Observer (FO)) and other members of the command post (CP) group were standing near the first bunker when the Chieu Hoi from the first platoon walked toward them. Suddenly, BOOM! An explosion threw dirt and debris in the air and sent everyone to the ground.

I thought, "This is it, they're around here somewhere." But it was quiet except for someone screaming for help.

Then someone else yelled, "We need medics up here!"

It must have been a booby trap, a surprise left by the NVA. The NVA were very inspired soldiers, and despite our superior firepower, were a formidable enemy. They would randomly place booby traps across the countryside, which included booby trapped mortar or artillery rounds, hand grenades and land mines. Unfortunately for us GIs, many of those devices would be detonated when someone stepped on the trigger mechanism or tripped a wire, normally causing serious injuries or death to anyone nearby.

Everyone in the third platoon was okay since none of us had been near the booby trap. Lieutenant Donaldson motioned for the third platoon to stay in place while he moved forward to see what had happened. I soon heard chatter over the radio that the Chieu Hoi and some men in the CP group had been wounded. Lieutenant Donaldson (3-6) called for Tom Brown, Jim Overbey and me to join him.

He said Captain Branch received a shrapnel wounded in his arm but would be OK. 3-6 went on saying the Chieu Hoi and a couple other men had also been wounded. Lieutenant Donaldson was taking command of the company for Captain Branch and told SSgt. Brown to take charge of the platoon.

The wounded men, Captain Branch, Lieutenant Cannava, an RTO from the first platoon and the Chieu Hoi, were soon helped away from the bunkers and the entire company pulled back to set up a landing zone for a medevac. The NVA often planted several booby traps around their bunker complexes, and since we had tripped one Lieutenant Donaldson wisely decided to cautiously pull back from the bunkers to avoid any other booby traps that might have been near the bunkers. We had been lucky that only one booby trap had been triggered, with so many of us stomping around while we searched the area.

A medevac soon landed in the middle of our perimeter and evacuated the four wounded men to Cu Chi. Fortunately, none of the injuries sounded life-threatening. After we pulled back, an air strike was called in and destroyed those bunkers.

As the air strike began, we learned one of our sister companies, Delta Company, had also found a bunker complex several klicks northwest of us; however, they found the NVA at home and had taken heavy casualties during a firefight. We hurried south until we found a clearing to use as a landing zone and waited to be flown over to help them. A group of Hueys arrived a while later to shuttle us over to help Delta Company. We were told to expect a *hot* LZ, meaning expect to receive enemy fire as we landed. The door gunners on the choppers sprayed the nearby countryside while we descended into another small clearing. We quickly hopped off the choppers and spread out to find cover. As the choppers flew off, we heard rifle fire just to our east.

After our entire company arrived we moved out and found Delta Company, who had been involved in a two-hour firefight. They had run into a bunker complex occupied by several NVA troops. Delta Company had finally withdrawn and called in artillery and an air strike to demolish the area. Unfortunately, three members of Delta Company had been killed and nearly a dozen others wounded.

We joined Delta Company in a clearing preparing to sweep through the demolished area. Surprisingly, an NVA soldier walked out from the middle of the rubble with his hands in the air to surrender.

Some men from Delta Company began yelling, "Shoot him! Shoot the bastard!"

Most everyone was pointing his rifle at the enemy soldier. I was surprised someone didn't shoot him.

Lieutenant Donaldson quickly walked forward yelling, "Hold your fire! Hold your fire!"

The NVA soldier stopped near the center of the clearing.

Suddenly, two men from Delta Company ran toward him. When the two GIs reached the NVA soldier one of them pointed his M-16 and appeared ready to shoot him.

Lieutenant Donaldson pointed at the GI and shouted, "Don't even think about pulling the trigger."

The man kept his rifle pointed at the NVA's head for a few seconds and then lowered his weapon. I thought it was over. But then, the same GI took the butt of his M-16 and smacked the enemy soldier as hard as he could on the side of his head and yelled, "You f---ing gook bastard!"

The NVA soldier slumped to the ground while other men restrained the angry GI and pulled him away. I thought the enemy soldier was dead. Obviously the man from Delta Company was distraught after losing several friends and was in no mood to accept a peaceful enemy surrender. Amazingly, the NVA soldier survived the head blow and was flown to Cu Chi for interrogation.

We finally moved cautiously through the area where the enemy bunkers had been located. I saw for the first time the awesome destructive force of artillery shells, bombs and napalm. I hadn't seen the area previously but there wasn't much left as we searched. The smell of thousands of pounds of explosives filled the air while smoke and steam rose from bomb craters twenty feet wide and six to eight feet deep. Hedgerows and trees had been blown into splinters and napalm had scorched much of what remained. We found the remains of what appeared to be three enemy log bunkers. They would cover the log framework of the bunkers with branches and dirt and after a while the grass and vegetation would grow over them making them look like part of the natural landscape. From a distance what might appear to be natural mound was really an enemy bunker.

We saw several enemy bodies and body parts, along with several weapons that had been partially destroyed. The men in Delta Company estimated they engaged thirty to forty NVA troops in the firefight that day. The actual number of NVA killed couldn't be determined after the destruction caused by the artillery and air strike, but the Delta Company CO claimed a body count of fifty. Regardless of the number of enemy troops killed, it had cost the lives of three men from Delta Company. For those three Americans the enemy body count was meaningless.

We landed back at Patton around six o'clock that evening and everyone was hungry and tired. We had humped through the Ho Bo Woods for nearly ten hours. All I had eaten during the day was my trusty can of fruit cocktail while we waited to be flown over to help Delta Company. I headed for the mess hall and enjoyed a warm meal along with a quart of chocolate milk served in wax-coated paper containers.

While we settled back in at Patton, we learned that Captain Branch's shrapnel wound was minor and he would return in a few days. The first platoon's Chieu Hoi had a serious abdominal wound and we would likely never see him again. An RTO lost a testicle and would be flown back to *the World* to recover. Lieutenant Tom Cannava, our Artillery Forward Observer (FO), was hit in the hand with shrapnel but would recover.

The 155MM howitzers (artillery guns) at Patton fired periodically day and night. They could receive a fire mission from the field any time twenty-four hours a day. They also fired harassment and interdiction (H & I) fire at night. They would select targets where friendly troops weren't located and fire rounds periodically in the hopes of hitting enemy personnel who may happen to be in the area. The 155MM howitzers were mounted on self-propelled tank-like vehicles, but they remained in place at Patton. We would often hear the engines fire up to move the gun turret, which gave us a warning before they fired with a tremendously loud boom. Often, the artillerymen would yell, "Fire in the hole," to warn everyone nearby they were about to fire a round. If we knew they were about to fire a round, we could cover our ears to lessen the noise. We somehow learned to sleep through most of their firings unless they fired directly over us and the concussion would shake the dust from the ceiling of our bunker.

Several new men had joined the Third Herd since I arrived in early August and many of the *old-timers*, including Dave Holt, Zeke Weil, Bill Tally and Dan Darling, gladly packed up their gear when they received an assignment in the relative safety of the rear in CU Chi. Staff Sergeant Tom Brown moved on and Sergeant Rick Shields, who had recovered from being shot in his leg on August 2nd, returned to take over as platoon sergeant. Rick was a dark-haired twenty-year-old from Los Angeles. He had been drafted and was a *shake'n bake* like me with no plans for making the Army his career.

Most of the FNGs were Private First Class (PFCs) directly out of Advanced Infantry Training. Bill Casey was an easygoing guy from South Carolina, who became one of our RTOs, replacing Chuck Gorman who moved to the Command Post group. David Debiasio was a carefree Italian from Providence, Rhode Island and was quickly nicknamed "Wop." Carlton Quick was a little guy with a southern accent, from Griffin, Georgia. Bob Ryken, from California, arrived carrying his guitar, and Ed Leberski, was a tall and slender guy from Pennsylvania. Danial Heiderich was a good old boy from Overbrook, Oklahoma, and was soon nicknamed "Whitey" because of his light blond hair, while red-haired James Mincey, from Conway, South Carolina was naturally nicknamed "Red." Fellow Iowan Mike Myers, from Marshalltown, Iowa, was nicknamed "Babysan" (Vietnamese slang for baby) because he didn't look old enough to be in the Army. Glennon Haywood, Terry Thornton, Vic Ortega, Robert Draughn and Junior Houchens (Houch) had also joined the Third Herd since I arrived.

A few men had been in the platoon longer than I, including Hal Harris, Steve Robinson, David Hardy and Randal Johnson. Each had been in the field for a few months along with Verney Prettyhip, an Indian from South Dakota, who was nicknamed "Chief."

My time as a new guy was short-lived with all the new men assigned to our platoon. After just over a month, I wasn't quite one of the old guys, but I laughed when we referred to others as FNGs. We normally called each other by our last name or nickname. I soon earned the nickname of "Hound Dog." While many of the men had little or no body hair, I had lots of hair on my chest and back. Wop thought I was as hairy as a hound dog and that soon became my nickname.

The most recent new arrival was Ron Peterson. The first morning after he arrived I told him to be on the landing zone (LZ) and ready to fly out at eight o'clock. Peterson didn't show up and we left without him. When we returned that afternoon I found Peterson sitting by his bunker. He said he had gone to the latrine that morning and missed the choppers. I accepted his explanation, considering it was his first morning in the field. But the next day the same thing happened. Peterson didn't show up on the LZ and we left without him. I again found him by his bunker when we returned. Peterson's explanation that day was that he lost track of time and missed the choppers. I didn't believe him.

I took him aside and asked, "Peterson, what the hell's going on?"

He reluctantly admitted he was afraid to fly on a chopper. I told Peterson that flying in a chopper should be one of the least of his worries. If something was going to happen to him it was likely to happen on the ground, not on a chopper, "Do you understand?"

He replied, "Yes, Sergeant."

"I'll ensure you're on the LZ next time," I said as I walked away.

A couple mornings later several of us kept an eye on Peterson and I personally escorted him to the LZ. When the choppers neared, one man grabbed each arm and walked Peterson to a chopper. We sat him on the canvas seat in the center of the chopper, away from the doors.

Peterson tightly held the bottom rail of the seat while we lifted off. I looked at him and gave him a thumbs-up as we flew along but he sat there looking straight ahead and holding onto the seat.

I was normally one of the last men to board a chopper after I made sure everyone else was aboard. I usually sat on the floor and sometimes dangled my legs out the door and let them swing in the breeze while we flew high above the countryside. I couldn't imagine someone being afraid to fly on a chopper. I loved flying on Hueys. After a couple days of dragging Peterson onto a chopper, he overcame his fear and showed up with the rest of us on the LZ whenever we flew out on choppers, officially referred to as an air combat mission.

During the first week of September 1969, Lieutenant Donaldson was reassigned to our battalion headquarters. A new platoon leader, nineteen-year-old Second Lieutenant Craig Fielding, was soon assigned to the third platoon. He was a Mormon from Salt Lake City, Utah who said he didn't drink and didn't cuss, much. We did notice he was gung-ho, the John Wayne type. He wanted to see action every day. When we were on a RIF, he wanted to be near the front of the column rather than in the middle where the platoon leader should be. He volunteered to go on nightly ambushes with us, which the other platoon leaders rarely did. We all liked Lieutenant Fielding but couldn't understand how he could be so gung-ho about being in Vietnam.

One morning we were leading the RIF when we came across a cluster of trees and bushes that looked like it had been occupied recently. The grass was trampled and we found an abandoned cooking fire. We set up a defensive perimeter and searched the area that was on high and dry ground. Captain Branch, who had just returned to the company, suspected there might be tunnels or underground storage caches.

Someone soon found a tunnel and yelled "Fire in the hole!" before they dropped a hand grenade down the tunnel. It detonated, sending dirt flying up from the entrance. We normally dropped a grenade down any tunnel we found before we did anything else, intending to kill or injure anyone inside or to detonate a booby trap the enemy might have planted inside. We also dropped a smoke grenade inside the tunnel and then covered the entrance, hoping the smoke would come up elsewhere to reveal other entrances. We didn't see any other smoke.

Lieutenant Fielding was chomping at the bit to crawl inside, but when Captain Branch saw him kneeling nearby he yelled, "Hey, Fielding, you're not going in there." He didn't want his new platoon leader going inside a tunnel. Lieutenant Fielding's job was to command his platoon, not be a *tunnel rat*. Bob Ryken was small enough to squeeze through the entrance and volunteered to crawl inside with a .45 automatic pistol and flashlight. Bob popped up after a couple of minutes with a cloth bag filled with clothes.

We found two other small tunnels in the area and confiscated clothing, rice and weapons but didn't find any NVA or VC. After searching the tunnels we used bangalore torpedoes to destroy them. We often carried a few bangalore torpedoes, metal tubes about five feet long, filled with C-4. The bangalore torpedoes could be connected together to blow away hedgerows or destroy whatever else we chose to destroy.

The CO had two combat engineers on his staff who were responsible for setting explosives when needed. Captain Branch had nicknamed those two demolitions men "Poof" and "Puff" because they both had the last name of Brown. Poof and Puff helped us push one bangalore torpedo into each tunnel and then detonated them.

After destroying the tunnels we moved on without any enemy contact. The NVA, and more so the VC, normally moved around the countryside in small groups of six or less. If they saw up to one hundred GIs coming their way, they often found a hiding spot unless we saw them first. Although I wasn't looking for a firefight, I also knew that unless we inflicted enemy casualties, they would be back another day trying to inflict casualties upon us. It was like a game of hide-and-seek except it wasn't a game. We were facing deadly consequences in Vietnam.

Sergeant Rick Shields (standing) and Carlton Quick cleaning their
weapons at Fire Support Base Patton.

*The U.S. military dropped six million tons of bombs and fired
over fifteen million tons of artillery shells during the Vietnam
War.*

Chapter 10

In the Boonies

During the second week of September 1969, we moved from Patton to a small patrol base, simply named Delta, several miles northeast of Patton. I stored most of my personal items, and gear I wouldn't need on our daily RIFs, in a gray metal ammunition box that was about eighteen inches square. The lid had a waterproof seal to keep the contents dry. That morning I strapped the ammunition box to my backpack, slung the pack over my shoulder, grabbed my rifle and walked to the landing zone outside the wire at Patton, ready to move on.

A large Chinook helicopter would fly each platoon to Patrol Base Delta. Chinooks had twin engines and tandem rotor blades with a large fuselage to carry troops and large equipment. The twin rotor blades stirred up twice as much dirt and debris as a Huey, making it wise to keep our distance until the Chinook landed. Because our entire platoon could fit into a Chinook, we all quickly walked up the ramp that dropped down from the rear of the chopper. Most of us found a seat on the long canvas-covered benches while others sat on the floor. The pilot revved the engine and we slowly lifted off toward our new home. It was a fairly short but bumpy flight on the Chinook. The ride on a Huey was normally pretty smooth once we were in the air but the huge, rotating twin blades on the Chinook strongly vibrated the chopper the entire trip.

We landed outside the northern perimeter of Patrol Base Delta, which was slightly larger than Hunsley. Delta was over 100 meters in diameter with bunkers built into a three-foot berm. The interior of Delta was similar to other patrol bases with a few tents, scattered bunkers, mortar pits and three 105MM artillery guns. When I looked outside the perimeter I could see fairly open countryside but no villages or hooches. It looked like we were back in the boonies. We soon settled into another group of small bunkers and made ourselves at home for the duration.

Captain Branch wanted each platoon to go out for a couple hours that afternoon to make a sweep of the surrounding area, to see what we might find and to help many of us newer guys learn the area. Each platoon saddled up and took off in a different direction. During our route, that took us about two klicks east, then turned south and circled back west to the patrol base, I had my first close look at the effects of Agent Orange. Agent Orange (Dioxin) was a chemical defoliant used to kill the vegetation in Vietnam. Agent Orange was normally sprayed from specially equipped choppers or planes as they flew over an area. Engineers often came through after spraying an area and bulldozed most of what was left, leaving almost nothing for the enemy to use for concealment. That was fine for us, but it was an eerie feeling to walk through areas where there previously had been lush green vegetation. There was nothing left but dead vegetation lying in small clumps or flat on the ground, sometimes for hundreds of meters in any direction. We didn't find any signs of enemy activity during our sweep and walked back through the perimeter at Delta about four o'clock.

Ambushes started the first night at Delta with the first platoon. Early that evening, we checked the claymores and trip flares in front of our bunkers to make sure they were operational for the night. After we set up a schedule for guard duty we were prepared for another night in Vietnam. A few hours later I was standing guard by my bunker along with a new man, John Potts, who had joined the third platoon only a few days earlier. There was nothing but silence around the perimeter and darkness outside the patrol base.

Unexpectedly, I heard a dull *pop* sound in the distance directly in front of us. My eyes opened wide as I turned and shouted "INCOM-ING! INCOMING!" While I hurried for our bunker. When I reached the entrance I looked for Potts. He was frozen in place beside our bunker. I stepped back and peered out over the perimeter for an instant thinking he had spotted something. I didn't see anything.

I yelled, "Potts get in here!"

Potts jumped as though he had been in a trance and then turned and quickly followed me into the bunker just as a mortar round exploded outside the perimeter in front of our bunker. Several more rounds quickly followed. The men inside the bunker quickly woke up when I ran inside and they sat up when they heard the sound of the exploding mortar rounds. There was a brief silence and then our mortar platoon and the 105MM batteries began firing outgoing rounds.

I said, "We had incoming! Get out on guard while I run over to our mortar pits." I wanted to tell the guys the direction I thought the incoming rounds had come from. Wearing my helmet and flak jacket I ran over to the mortar pits and the artillery batteries and pointed northeast, the direction I believed the mortar rounds came from. They directed several rounds in that direction for a few minutes and then stopped firing. There was silence again.

When we checked around the patrol base it appeared only a couple of rounds had landed inside the perimeter and fortunately had caused no injuries or damage. We stayed on full guard duty for a while, but all remained quiet. We finally went back to our normal guard rotation for the remainder of the night. We were all tired the next morning, but Captain Branch had us up early to grab some chow so we could get an early start in hopes of finding that enemy mortar tube or any trace of the VC or NVA who had fired the mortars at us.

There wasn't a mess hall at Delta but there was a mess tent where they prepared some hot food or served the food delivered each day in insulated containers for the morning and evening meal. The food out there was better than surviving on C-rations but I soon learned the scrambled eggs they delivered were horrible. They were powdered eggs and actually had a slight greenish tint. They sure as heck didn't taste like eggs; in fact, they didn't have much of a taste at all. Even ketchup on them didn't help. Most of the guys would take a few bites and throw the rest away. In fact, the Third Herd had recently adopted a dog named Oliver and even he wouldn't eat those scrambled eggs.

The company headed toward the northeast before eight o'clock that morning to conduct our assigned RIF. We worked our way northeastward and ran into heavy vegetation with tall grass, trees and hedgerows. They hadn't sprayed Agent Orange out there and everything was growing wild, fed by the monsoon rains. We knew there had been enemy troops out there so we took our time walking through the area hoping to avoid walking into an ambush or tripping any booby traps they might have left behind. By mid-day, we hadn't found any signs of enemy activity. Captain Branch called for a Huey gunship to scout the area around us, that was about two klicks northeast of the patrol base.

The third platoon led the way as we started walking west in two columns. Our point men, Robert Draughn and Carlton Quick, were both having trouble finding a clear route and slowly weaved through and around hedgerows, trees and tall green grass. We all stayed closer to each other than normal to keep in sight of each other.

Suddenly, two bursts of gunfire erupted from a cluster of trees about sixty meters in front of us. Everyone immediately hit the ground. The vegetation was so thick I couldn't see more than a few feet in any direction when I crouched to the ground.

I yelled, "Is anybody hit?"

"No," was the reply as guys cautiously looked around for any movement, ready to duck if enemy fire erupted again. There was no more gunfire coming from the trees, but Captain Branch was on the radio telling the Huey gunship that was now overhead to check out the trees directly west of us. The gunship immediately flew in that direction and one of the door gunners began firing his M-60 machine gun as the chopper circled the trees.

We stepped up the pace as we closed in on the trees without receiving any more gunfire. The chopper pilot radioed they had seen two enemy personnel in the trees and had opened fire on them. They hadn't seen any other enemy troops in the area but we knew they could have quickly taken cover and might still be nearby.

The third platoon spread out when we reached the trees and maneuvered forward on line as we swept through the area with the chopper circling overhead. A door gunner dropped a smoke grenade to help guide us into where the enemy troops had been seen. We cautiously walked toward the purple smoke, ready to fire at any movement. We then came upon two VC lying on the ground, both dead. Their bodies were covered with blood and riddled with wounds caused by the M-60 rounds. They had climbed the trees and opened fire on us when we moved toward them. Unfortunately for them, they must not have seen or heard the Huey gunship until it was too late. They were sitting ducks when spotted by the door gunner.

The CO had the first and second platoon established a defensive perimeter around the cluster of trees while the third platoon continue to search the area and examined the two enemy bodies. We hoped to find a mortar tube or mortar rounds, but we found nothing except their AK-47 Russian-made rifles, some ammunition and a small bag of rice. We spent about twenty minutes searching the area without finding any more VC or a mortar tube. If there had been other enemy troops out there, they had managed to sneak away.

I picked up the AK-47 lying by one of the bodies. I had seen an AK-47 during training but wanted to hold one the enemy had actually used. I pulled out my camera and asked someone to take my picture holding the weapon. Some of the other guys quickly did the same to have a picture of the enemy bounty we captured. Although we hadn't found the mortar tube, the gunship eliminated two VC and stopped any plans they had for us. We took their weapons and supplies with us and left the bodies lying where they had fallen from the trees. We continued on by circling south back to Patrol Base Delta without spotting any other enemy movement.

Although we normally out-manned and out-gunned the enemy, they operated effectively in small groups that were much more mobile than we were. They could fire mortar rounds at us during the night or open fire on us like the two VC did that day, and then they were often gone. For all we knew, the enemy troops who had fired the mortar rounds toward Delta the past night were miles away ready to use the mortar tube elsewhere, or they could have crawled into a tunnel for the day, ready to pop out after dark and drop more rounds in on Delta.

When we returned to the patrol base about mid-afternoon I took off my gear to relax for a while before our scheduled ambush. To our surprise, a group of ARVNs (Army of the Republic of South Vietnam) had been assigned to Delta that afternoon to work with us. Although the United States military was leading the battle against the VC and NVA, the ARVNs were also fighting them. Part of our job was to work with the ARVNs in hopes they would assume a greater fighting role; thereby, enabling the United States to reduce their involvement, and eventually pull out of South Vietnam.

The process was called "Vietnamization." It was a good idea, but from what I had seen of the ARVNs they had a long way to go before they would be a formidable fighting force. President Nixon had initiated peace talks with the North Vietnamese that included the withdrawal of American troops from Vietnam. But until the fighting actually stopped and we were safely back in *the World*, those peace talks weren't helping any of us infantrymen who were serving all over South Vietnam.

We were told some of the ARVNs would be going with us to set up the ambush that night. I hadn't worked directly with the ARVNs and didn't know what to expect. Rick Shields, Jim Overbey and I were taking nine other GIs and six ARVNs with us on the ambush. After a quick meal, Lieutenant Fielding gave us our ambush assignment. We would head south of Delta, walk through a cluster of hooches and then establish an ambush one hundred meters beyond. We GIs were ready to leave the perimeter on schedule, but we had to wait for the ARVNs.

Rick yelled, "Hurry up," although they likely didn't understand him, and waved at a group of ARVNs who were slowly walking toward us.

Six ARVNs leisurely walked up to join us and we finally walked out through the perimeter wire and headed south toward our ambush site. The sun was setting low in the western horizon. We weren't going to make it to our ambush site before dark. Hal Harris was walking point and Carlton Quick was behind him, with John Potts walking third. Hal wasn't our designated point man but Rick, Jim and I wanted to have an experienced man walking point that evening. We had asked Hal to walk point and he agreed to lead us.

Rick Shields walked near the front of our column to help guide Harris while the rest of us followed in a single column intermixed with the ARVNs. I was walking near the rear of the column. It was almost completely dark when we neared the group of hooches about 600 meters south of the patrol base. I was about to walk through a hedgerow when suddenly, BOOM! BOOM!

Two explosions in front of me sent me to the ground. Bursts of rifle fire immediately followed and knocked some branches off the hedgerow directly over me. The rest of the column had disappeared. I looked around but I could only see the hedgerow directly in front of me. My heart pounded as I held my rifle with the safety turned to automatic while I tried to figure out what was happening and where the rest of the men were. Rifle fire and what sounded like hand grenade explosions continued in front of me.

I yelled, "Where are you guys?"

I couldn't hear anything over the noise of the gunfire and explosions. I needed to find somebody to determine what was going on. Intermittent rifle fire continued while I crawled through the hedgerow hoping to find one of the guys. When I reached the far side of the hedgerow I came face-to-face with a Vietnamese soldier. I froze! I didn't know if it was an ARVN or VC. It was too dark to see the man's clothes, but I could see that he wasn't wearing a helmet. Most of the ARVNs weren't wearing their helmets that night. I thought about shooting him for an instant, but since he hadn't already tried to kill me, he had to be one of the ARVNs. I tried to talk to him but he didn't understand a word I was saying. He just looked at me. I crawled to my right, with the ARVN behind me, and finally found Dennis Shultz and Mike Myers kneeling near one of the hooches. It was suddenly quiet. Dennis Shultz, our RTO, was talking with the command post at Delta.

I heard him say, "We have a KIA."

I couldn't believe what I heard. "What the hell happened?" I thought.

I asked Schultz, "Where's Rick?"

He pointed in front of the nearby hooch. I told Schultz and Myers to follow me while I led them forward. I soon found Rick Shields and the rest of our men.

Rick said, "We were ambushed," then hesitated a few seconds to catch his breath, "Harris is dead. Quick and Potts are wounded!"

I didn't have time to react to Rick's words. A Huey gunship had been called in and was circling overhead providing cover and dropping flares to light up the area, which helped us to quickly organize the men and account for everyone. Hal Harris' body had been carried back from where he had been killed instantly by a rocket propelled grenade (RPG) and laid on a poncho liner beside a nearby hooch. Quick and Potts could both walk, but they needed further medical attention. The rest of us were uninjured.

Rick, Jim Overbey and I briefly huddled together and agreed we should get out of there and get the wounded men back to Delta. We weren't going to surprise anyone with an ambush after all the action that had occurred. In fact, it had been the opposite. We had been on the wrong end of an ambush. Rick radioed Captain Branch and told him what happened. The CO agreed we should return to Delta. We spread the word that we were moving back to Delta.

Everyone knew it would be dangerous walking back to the patrol base in the darkness, but they also wanted to get out of there before something else happened. We somehow organized the ARVNs and got the message across that we were moving back to Delta.

We took a minute to make sure everyone was accounted for, and then Rick Shields and Dave Hardy led us north in a single column. I joined Doc Jackson, Jim Overbey and Mike Myers to carry Harris' body back to Delta. I hadn't closely seen his body and was shocked when I looked down to grab a corner of the poncho liner. Hal's body had literally been torn into pieces. His right leg had been completely severed and was lying grotesquely on the poncho liner. His lower right arm also had been mangled and there was a golf-ball-sized hole on the right side of his head. I didn't say a word. I took a deep breath and lifted my corner of the poncho liner as the four of us moved out.

No one knew for sure how many enemy troops we had run into or if any of them had been killed or wounded during the firefight. I hoped and prayed they weren't waiting for us somewhere in the darkness on our way back in. Hopefully, those night navigation training exercises would pay off for us. It was slow going as we cautiously walked through the darkness. The four of us carrying Harris had to stop periodically to take a short break and to switch arms. Harris was a good-sized man. After a while, it felt like the arm I was using to carry him would fall off.

After what seemed like forever, we neared the perimeter of Patrol Base Delta. We stopped while Schultz radioed the CP to alert the men on guard around the perimeter that we were coming in so they wouldn't fire on us thinking we were the enemy. It was warm night and the sweat was running down the faces of the four of us who had been carrying Hal Harris' body as we waited outside the perimeter. Someone fired a colored flair into the air to identify ourselves and when we knew it was safe, the column of men moved forward and soon walked through an opening in the concertina wire surrounding Delta. The four of us carried Harris' body into the mess tent and laid him inside. Someone found another poncho to cover him. I walked away in almost disbelief about what had happened.

We quickly checked to make sure the rest of the men were OK and then provided a report of what happened to Lieutenant Fielding and Captain Branch. Rick had been near the front of the column and provided most of the details.

Rick simply said, "We were ambushed."

He continued saying Hal Harris who had been walking point was hit by an RPG when he passed through a group of hooches. Enemy troops then threw hand grenades and opened fire with AKs. Our guys returned fire and threw several grenades and then it was over.

Rick concluded by saying, "It was too dark to see much, but I think they soon took off after hitting us."

Captain Branch asked if anyone else had been wounded. I told him that Carlton Quick and John Potts had minor wounds, but everyone else was OK.

After talking with Lieutenant Fielding and Captain Branch for a few minutes, Rick and I went back to see how the rest of the men were doing. Doc Jackson was checking Quick's wounds again. He had shrapnel wounds in his left shoulder and needed to be medevacked to the 12th Evac in Cu Chi. I then found John Potts. He hadn't been physically injured but he was in total emotional shock. He had been behind Harris and Quick and had been in the middle of the action. I tried to talk with Potts about what happened but he jabbered incoherently. He kept walking around staring off in the distance. He wouldn't make eye contact with anyone and didn't seem to comprehend what anyone said to him. I don't think he even knew where he was. Two men stayed with Potts while I found Doc Jackson.

I told Doc I thought Potts needed to be medevacked out. I said, "He's lost it."

Doc Jackson tried talking with Potts but had no better luck than the rest of us. Doc agreed Potts should be flown out with Quick on the medevac that was on its way. Potts had been with us for only a few days and that night's action was the first he had seen. All of us were in a degree of shock after being ambushed and losing Hal Harris, but the rest of the men appeared to be in control of themselves. The third platoon had lost George Conrad in early August, but for those of us who had arrived later, Hal Harris was the first casualty we had suffered. It was difficult to comprehend that he was dead.

A medevac soon landed outside Delta's main gate to fly the three men to Cu Chi. Quick was able to walk on his own but two of us guided Potts to the chopper. The chopper really scared him. We had to force Potts on board. If we had let go of him, I believe he might have taken off running out into the darkness, not realizing what he was doing. Doc Jackson told the medic on the chopper what was going on with Potts, advising him to keep a close eye on him. A litter carrying Hal Harris' body was then loaded on board the chopper. We backed away when the chopper lifted off and stood there for a moment to pay our brief respects and say good-bye to our friend and comrade Hal Harris as the medivac disappeared into the darkness. I assumed Quick would return to the platoon after he recovered from his injuries. But I didn't know if we would ever see John Potts again. Less than one week in the field in Vietnam may have destroyed him emotionally for life.

Hal Harris had walked point for a while after he joined the third platoon that past summer. He knew it would be dangerous to walk point that night but was willing to take the added risk to help the rest of the platoon. Rick Shields, Jim Overbey and I felt horrible that we had asked Hal Harris to walk point that night. It was a decision that cost Hal his life. That evening I realized the enormous responsibility I had as an NCO. My decisions could mean life or death for any one of us in the platoon. That scenario had certainly played out that evening.

Several of us lingered around our bunker a while talking about the ambush and exactly what had happened out there.

I overheard Jim Overbey tell someone, "I shot two of them."

I asked, "Jim, you shot two gooks?"

"No," he said, "I shot two water buffalo!"

Jim had been in front of me when we neared the hooches. When he crawled forward Jim saw something moving to his left and opened fire with his M-16. He didn't realize until later it had been two water buffalo tied up near one of the hooches.

What many of us thought would be another routine ambush patrol, turned out to be a first-hand taste of combat. That night truly brought the realities of war directly before my eyes. Hal had eaten chow with us earlier that evening. He put on his gear along with the rest of us and led us on the ambush without reservation. Less than an hour later, he was dead. That night I learned to no longer take anything for granted. We had walked through similar groups of hooches that I had considered to be safe. After that night I knew no place was truly safe over there.

It was almost midnight when I walked back to my bunker and crawled inside hoping to get a little sleep. I lay down on my air mattress and pulled my poncho liner over me. I tossed and turned, trying to get the thoughts of the past few hours out of my mind.

Early the following morning, the cook yelled for help after he walked into the mess tent. Several of us ran over and saw the shocked look on his face as he pointed inside.

The cook said, "What the hell is that? Get it out of here!"

When Hal Harris' body was carried from the mess tent to the medevac his severed leg had somehow been left behind. Finding Harris' leg was a gruesome way for the cook, and the rest of us, to start the day. A couple men took Hal's leg and buried it outside the perimeter at Delta.

After breakfast the third platoon led the rest of the company back to the site where we had been ambushed. The two water buffalo Jim Overbey had shot were lying on the ground east of the first hooch. We spread out and cautiously moved through the hooches. Although it was obvious people had been living there, no one was around. There was food, utensils, personal items and clothing inside the hooches. Either the VC forced the civilians out or the occupants were VC sympathizers who may have helped with the ambush.

We searched the area but didn't find any enemy bodies or weapons. Knowing the VC had been in the area we commenced to burn or destroy the food and clothing we had found. Captain Branch also called for explosive charges to be flown out. After they arrived, we helped our demolitions men Poof and Puff set a charge inside each hooch.

After we pulled back a safe distance, the charges were detonated with the huge explosions sending smoke and debris in the air, and leaving nothing but flattened hooches in a pile of smoking rubble. It may have been cruel to destroy someone's primitive home, but we frankly didn't give a damn. Hal Harris died in the middle of those hooches. We returned to Patrol Base Delta that afternoon with smoke rising to the sky behind us.

After we returned to Delta we learned one of our sister companies, Charlie Company, who we had replaced at Delta, had sent ambush patrols near those same hooches their last two nights at Delta. That meant the third platoon had unknowingly become sitting ducks, with the VC waiting for us when we again walked through the same group of hooches. An apparent lack of communication between Charlie Company and Alpha Company had cost Hal Harris his life.

The Third Herd didn't have much time to dwell on Hal Harris' death. The next morning Alpha Company and the ARVNs were told to pack our gear. We were moving to another patrol base. There was a lot of bitching and moaning from the men when they were told we had to pack up and fly to a patrol base with the strange name of Dong Tien, on the southeastern edge of the Ho Bo Woods. An hour later we hopped on a lift of Hueys and flew toward the Ho Bo Woods. The countryside near Dong Tien was covered with lush grass, hedgerows and trees, giving the enemy plenty of concealment. It would be difficult to spot anyone out there even from the air.

When I walked in from the LZ at Dong Tien I found another small patrol base with the traditional circle of bunkers built into a small berm and surrounded by rows of concertina wire. The first couple hundred meters surrounding the patrol base had been sprayed with Agent Orange and partially cleared to give us visibility, but beyond that there was nothing but thick green vegetation. Those little patrol bases were quickly starting to look about the same. When we returned after a short RIF with the ARVNs late that afternoon some of the men in the company were missing a radio or camera they had left behind. We normally left our personal gear in or around our bunkers when we went out on RIFs and rarely had a problem with anything missing.

Since most of the GIs had been on the RIF except our mortar platoon, we guessed the ARVNs had taken the missing items. The ARVNs were assigned bunkers along the opposite perimeter but the mortar guys said they noticed two of them wandering around our bunkers that afternoon and had told the ARVNs to move away. Some of our guys wanted to go search ARVN's bunkers for the missing items but Captain Branch didn't want to cause an uproar. He told the ARVN commander to keep his men on their side of the patrol base from then on. After that day we left one man behind to protect our possessions whenever ARVNs were in a patrol base with us. What a sad state of affairs. The ARVNs were stealing from us while we were risking our lives fighting their war.

The following morning, September 16th, we were organizing ourselves outside the perimeter of the patrol base before a RIF. Most of the ARVNs didn't intermingle with us often, but one of them came up that morning and asked to bum a cigarette from one of the guys. That man was a friendly little guy who tried to talk using the little English he knew. I noticed he was wearing sandals while all of us GIs and most of the ARVNs wore jungle boots. He carried an M-16 but carried no ammunition other than the single magazine of ammunition in his rifle. I looked around and noticed most of the ARVNs were carrying extra ammunition magazines but none of them carried as much ammunition as we did. They weren't prepared for any long battles.

The ARVNs led the RIF while we followed in two columns behind them. We had been walking most of the morning when the columns stopped. The word quickly came back the ARVNs had spotted an enemy bunker complex. We cautiously moved forward and formed a perimeter in front of the bunkers while the ARVNs and some members of the third platoon walked toward the hedgerow that partially concealed the bunkers. Amazingly we received no enemy fire as we closed in. Were they gone, or waiting for us to get even closer?

Captain Branch moved forward and laid out his plan. He had called for forty-pound explosive charges to be flown out. If we didn't run into any enemy troops, we would place the charges in the bunkers to destroy them. The CO wanted us to maintain a perimeter on the front side of the bunkers and watch for any enemy movement. Everyone held their places for about twenty minutes watching over the nearby countryside, but we didn't see any movement. When the charges arrived on a Huey, they were unloaded behind us.

Our company demolitions men, Poof and Puff, walked forward while other men helped carry the charges to the front of the column. We still hadn't seen any enemy movement and hadn't received any enemy fire. Jim Overbey, Mike Myers and RTO Dennis Schultz were with the point group for the third platoon, and moved toward the bunkers with the Poof and Puff and some of the ARVNs to stand guard and help place the charges. The men began to set the charges when BOOM! BOOM! All hell broke loose. Enemy RPGs exploded around them and enemy rifle fire came from NVA troops who had been concealed in another bunker complex, behind a hedgerow north of the original bunkers. Soon we all were receiving enemy fire.

We couldn't see the NVA because of the thick vegetation but the smoke and flashes from their weapons revealed their location. The ARVNs and our point group dove for cover and returned fire while the rest of the company sprayed the surrounding area with rifle and machine gun fire and fired M-79 grenades, directing as much firepower as we could toward the enemy. The continuous noise from the rifles and machine guns was deafening as I emptied several magazines of ammunition into the nearby hedgerow.

After the first RPGs were fired, the ARVNs who were with our point group and demolitions men returned fire but then quickly pulled back. I looked forward and saw the little ARVN guy, whom I had seen with only one magazine of ammunition, stand up and fire his M-16 into the bushes in front of him until his magazine was empty. He then ran back toward the rear of the column and sat down. I thought, "You son-of-a-bitch! Run behind us and hide while we fight the rest of the battle."

Unfortunately, the ARVNs had left about a half dozen of our men all alone by the original bunker complex taking enemy rifle and rocket fire. Dennis Schultz radioed Lieutenant Fielding saying they needed more cover fire so they could get out of there.

Lieutenant Fielding spread the word to direct our fire on the northwestern hedgerows where the initial enemy fire had come from. Additional men joined us along our northern perimeter and we bombarded the area with a barrage of M-16 fire along with four M-60 machine guns and four M-79 grenade launchers. After a few very long minutes, Jim Overbey and the rest of our men crawled back from the bunkers and rejoined the rest of the company who were spread out behind rice paddy dikes. Miraculously, we hadn't sustained a single casualty.

But the battle wasn't over yet. Just when we thought we had nailed all the NVA or they had made a run for it, a group of at least a dozen more were spotted moving behind another hedgerow and someone yelled, "There's more gooks on the right!"

Ed Leberski dropped one man with his M-16 and Wop hit two more with his M-60 machine gun. Rick Shields also dropped another enemy soldier with his rifle while the rest of us began firing where several of the NVA had hit the ground. Most of us couldn't tell if we were hitting any enemy troops while we continued to spray the area around where they had last been seen with rifle and machine gun rounds for several minutes, but we were making it nearly impossible for the NVA to survive or escape.

We had been taught "thou shall not kill;" however, when you face an enemy soldier who is trying to kill you, regardless of what the *good book* says, we would kill if necessary to survive.

Wop had fired hundreds of rounds during the firefight. His hot machine gun barrel was smoking, and it smoked even more, when he stopped firing for a minute and poured silicone lubricant on the barrel to cool it down, preventing it from warping.

Captain Branch then called for a cease-fire and ordered us to slowly pull back about 100 meters. His Forward Observer was calling in artillery to be followed by Cobra gunships and then an air strike. The Forward Observer's (FO's) job was to call in artillery fire or an air strike when the company encountered the enemy. We didn't know for sure what we had run into but the CO wasn't taking any more chances in fighting it out until he called in the heavy stuff. To sweep through the area and continue the firefight would likely result in American casualties like Delta Company incurred in a similar situation in the Ho Bo Woods a few weeks earlier. Pulling back and letting the big boys "sock-it-to 'em" sounded like a fantastic idea to the rest of us.

A couple of minutes after we had pulled back, the first 155MM artillery round from Patton landed near the bunkers with a deafening, crackling explosion. Over a dozen more rounds followed and landed across the area in front of us while we ducked for cover each time we heard the whistle of an incoming round. We had pulled back about 100 meters from the target area but we were getting peppered with debris after each round exploded. 155MM artillery rounds looked like huge bullets about two feet long and six inches in diameter and made a thunderous explosion when they detonated.

When the artillery stopped, two Cobra gunships began spraying the area with grenades, rockets and machine gun fire. The bunkers and surrounding area were slowly being demolished. Smoke filled the air and I could smell the explosives and smoldering debris. The Cobras continued their mission for several minutes while we scoured the surrounding countryside for movement and watched the awesome air show.

I then heard, "Air strikes are on the way." I looked over my shoulder and saw a jet swooping toward us, I yelled, "Take cover."

I peeked up and saw a huge bomb released while the jet was directly over us. It sailed through the air, heading toward its target in front of us. I ducked as the first bomb exploded and shook ground beneath me. A rain of dirt clods and debris began falling all around us. More jets followed dropping 500-and 1,000-pound bombs that literally leveled the countryside to our west and north while continuing to pelt debris upon us with each exploding bomb.

Some of the chunks of debris might have caused injuries if they landed directly on someone, but we all escaped with only close calls. We probably should have pulled back a little farther than we had but it was an awesome show of firepower from my vantage point, one I will never forget. I had watched a demonstration of the 25th Division's philosophy of using "Firepower rather than manpower," and I liked it.

After the last jet flew into the distance, there was silence. I looked toward the northwest and saw smoke and dust streaming from the ground. But there was one final weapon to employ. Flame baths of napalm in 55-gallon drums were dropped, from helicopters sending huge billows of flame into the air. We could feel the heat from the huge balls of orange flame while huge plums of black smoke rose into the air. Napalm was a flammable substance used in flamethrowers and aerial bombs. When the napalm exploded, it spewed a flaming jelled liquid that stuck to whatever or whoever was nearby. I couldn't imagine anyone surviving the barrage of artillery rounds, rockets, bombs and then napalm. If there had been any NVA troops in or near those bunkers when we withdrew, they were goners.

Lieutenant Fielding came by and told us we are moving out to sweep through the area.

We cautiously walked forward in two columns and weaved through the area that was totally decimated. There were again huge bomb craters and the hedgerows and trees in the area were totally destroyed. We couldn't even identify the original bunkers that were spotted. The napalm had scorched much of what little was left; however quite amazingly, Dennis Schultz found an undamaged NVA flag in a pile of rubble when we swept through the area. Schultz kept the flag as a souvenir of our encounter that day.

We found 10 bodies and several body parts in the remains of what was two bunker complexes, along with pieces of destroyed weapons. Although we believed there had been at least thirty NVA in the two groups who had put up a fight with us, most of their remains were either totally destroyed or buried under the dirt and debris. Captain Branch reported a body count of 36 later that day.

It was eerie when I walked through that destroyed area. About two hours earlier there had been two enemy bunker complexes filled with who knows how many NVA troops. Now there was nothing but wasteland. We walked on for another klick or two with no further enemy contact. The best news of that day was that amazingly we sustained no friendly (American) injuries or casualties. The NVA, with the protection and concealment of their bunkers, could have inflicted some significant casualties upon us, but they had failed.

When I took off my gear after we returned to the patrol base I finally felt like we had accomplished something for a change. It was a combination of good military tactics and the good Lord watching over us that helped us all survive that day. Although we had kicked the NVA's butt, the big picture still didn't make much sense to me. The NVA and more so the VC operated in small groups roaming the countryside, engaging in encounters with the American and ARVN forces.

Although there had been some major battles involving hundreds of enemy forces in areas closer to the Demilitarized Zone (DMZ), across much of South Vietnam the NVA often operated from isolated strongholds like the Ho Bo Woods. They deployed small groups to set booby traps and land mines, to build punji pits with sharp bamboo stakes, and to fire sporadic mortar rounds into U.S. bases. They tactfully used their mobility to avoid or elude American forces and would use their vast network of tunnels to avoid detection.

The NVA and VC had us fighting their kind of war, a *guerrilla* war, because they knew they would soon lose to our awesome firepower if they engaged in conventional warfare. Although the NVA and VC had suffered significantly more casualties than the Americans since the beginning of our involvement in Vietnam, we hadn't gained any significant advantage. If both sides continued to contribute personnel, equipment and supplies, that kind of war could go on forever. I had been going daily on RIFs for nearly two months and we hadn't accomplished anything except getting some of our guys killed and wounded.

But then we got some good news. Stand down!

———————————

➤ Private First Class Hal Harris was from Detroit, MI. Hal arrived in Vietnam on May 28, 1969. He was killed when the third platoon was ambushed on September 14, 1969. Hal was twenty-two years old and would have celebrated his 23rd birthday on September 18th. He was married with one child.

"Hal was a good man. When Hal was walking point in July 1969, he spotted a booby trap and prevented casualties that might have occurred had someone tripped it. He was wounded on August 2nd and I recommended him for a Bronze Star (for valor) for his actions that day." (Steve Donaldson, Hal Harris' platoon leader)

An estimated nineteen million gallons of Agent Orange chemical defoliant were sprayed on an estimated five million acres in South Vietnam between 1962 and 1971. The Department of Veterans Affairs ultimately acknowledged that exposure to Agent Orange is related to serious illnesses and deaths among Vietnam veterans and thousands of Vietnamese civilians.

Chapter 11

Stand Down

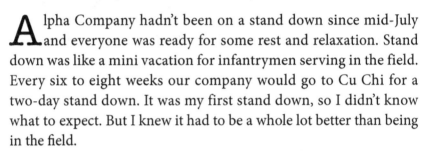

Alpha Company hadn't been on a stand down since mid-July and everyone was ready for some rest and relaxation. Stand down was like a mini vacation for infantrymen serving in the field. Every six to eight weeks our company would go to Cu Chi for a two-day stand down. It was my first stand down, so I didn't know what to expect. But I knew it had to be a whole lot better than being in the field.

The timing for a stand down couldn't have been any better for the Third Herd. We needed a couple days to refresh our minds and put the night of September 14th behind us. After one more night pulling guard at patrol base Dong Tien we were up early and packed our gear for a chopper ride to Cu Chi. Two Chinooks shuttled in a new company to take over the patrol base. After a Chinook landed to drop off a platoon of new men, one of our platoons loaded on board the waiting Chinook and relaxed during the bumpy ride. In about fifteen minutes we were dropped off on a landing pad not far from our company area in Cu Chi.

We walked to our company area and dropped our gear near the large metal storage container holding our personal possessions we hadn't taken to the field. During that morning we cleaned our weapons and took care of any problems we might have been having with them. We then checked in our weapons with Tom Powers who kept them locked inside the company headquarters building. Most of the men shaved and took a long shower, because we hadn't taken a shower since leaving Patton about a week earlier. We then put on brand new fatigues that made us all look like FNGs. It felt great to be clean and have fresh fatigues, but more so, it was a relief to be in the peaceful environment of Cu Chi without worrying about the hazards of combat. We had the rest of that day and the next to do mostly whatever we wanted.

There was an area in the middle of Cu Chi reserved for companies on stand down. It was called the Cu Chi Hilton. It wasn't exactly like a Hilton Hotel back in *the World*, but there were clean wooden barracks, showers and a mess hall. It would be our home for the next two days. After lunch I walked to the Post Exchange (PX) with several other men. The PX was like a department store with clothing, personal items, small appliances, cameras and film, radios and a host of other things GIs might need for their day-to-day living.

I left the PX and joined several guys at the Special Services Club. There were pool tables, Ping-Pong tables and other games as well as a small library inside. Some of us also enjoyed talking with two American Red Cross girls who worked there. I had seen lots of Vietnamese women in the villages around Firebase Patton and there were also many Vietnamese women working inside the division base camp. But it was nice to see a *round-eyed* American woman again. Most of the American women in Vietnam were Red Cross girls or military nurses.

I played a couple games of pool with the guys and then moved on to our stand down area. There would be a trailer full of cold beer arriving about five o'clock that afternoon and then at seven o'clock a band would entertain us for an hour or so. I claimed a bunk in our barracks and lay down to take a nap, something I rarely had an opportunity to do in the field. I woke up about an hour later and heard someone shout, "The beer is on the way."

"All right!" I thought. I hadn't had a beer since the one I drank with Dave Hardy on my birthday. I was ready for one, or two or three. I walked out to an open grassy space with scattered trees in the center of the stand down area, which made a peaceful spot to relax and enjoy ourselves. Most of the men in Alpha Company were mingling around and talking while they patiently waited for the beer trailer to arrive.

A few minutes after five o'clock, Tom Powers honked the horn of the jeep as he pulled a trailer full of iced-down beer into the stand down area to the cheers of Alpha Company. We mobbed the trailer in a semi-orderly fashion until everyone who wanted one had a cold beer in his hand. We smiled and toasted each other with our beers and talked, while not wandering too far from the trailer. It was great to enjoy a brief reprieve from the war that continued outside the perimeter of Cu Chi. For the first time in over six weeks, I could relax briefly and forget about fighting the war. The main objective for most of us at that moment was to simply enjoy the free beer.

Captain Branch mingled amongst us while he enjoyed a cold beer. He had been an infantry platoon leader during a previous tour of duty in Vietnam. He had begun his second tour that past June and became the Alpha Company CO shortly thereafter. Captain Branch was a friendly guy and laughed and joked along with the rest of us that afternoon. For the first time in my brief Army career his rank didn't matter. I wouldn't have felt comfortable back in *the World* drinking beer with a captain. But that afternoon, Captain Branch was just one of the guys.

I then saw our Battalion Chaplain. To my surprise, he also had a beer in his hand. I said, "Good afternoon, Chaplain."

He said, "Good afternoon, Sergeant. I see you're wearing the cross I gave you."

I had met Chaplain Wideman a few weeks earlier when he visited Patrol Base Delta and several of us gathered near a 105MM artillery position for a brief service. A little religion that day brought some comfort to me knowing that my dangerous combat duty would continue.

At the conclusion of the service, the Chaplin gave each of us a silver cross on a chain. I had also removed an M-16 round from its brass casing and heated it with C-4 to melt the lead enough to stick the ends of a small loop of wire into the backside of the round. I slipped the chain through the wire loop and wore the M-16 round along with the silver cross around my neck. Rick Shields had done the same thing with the AK-47 round they removed from his leg in July. Most of the men wore some type of necklace or bracelet to establish their own unique identity. Some of them were as simple as a braided bootlace.

I then ran into Verney Prettyhip (Chief) near the trailer. We smiled at each other as we reached in and pulled a cold beer from the trailer.

"How's it going, Chief?"

He replied, "Great. I hope we don't run out of beer for a while."

Lieutenant Fielding then walked up to Chief and me and said, "Hi, guys, where's the soda?"

"Soda," I said, "Have a beer."

"Oh no, I don't drink beer, just soda."

Fortunately, there were a few sodas in the trailer for the non-beer drinkers like Lieutenant Fielding.

I later found Carlton Quick standing with some of the guys from the Third Herd. I hadn't seen him since he had climbed aboard the medevac the night of September 14th.

I walked up and put my arm around Quick's good shoulder and said, "Hey, Quick, how're you doing?"

Quick smiled and replied. "I'm fine, Sarge," as he raised the beer in his right hand.

His left arm was in a sling after doctors had removed several pieces of shrapnel from his shoulder. He was still a little sore but they told him he shouldn't have any permanent damage. Quick was happy to see his Third Herd buddies again and it was great to see him, especially since he seemed to be doing fine both physically and emotionally.

We talked about the night we were ambushed.

He said, "It scared the hell out of me." Quick believed he was wounded by shrapnel from one of the grenades thrown by the VC.

"I didn't see a damn thing before I was hit," Quick said. "I fired my M-16 hoping to hit whoever was out there."

I then asked Quick if he knew anything about John Potts. He said Potts was still in the psych ward at the 12th Evac. Quick had walked over to visit him one day but the staff wouldn't let him in.

I said, "Potts was out of control at Delta. We'll probably never see him again."

And we didn't. John Potts never returned to the third platoon.

Our party in the middle of the Cu Chi Hilton continued, with most of the guys drinking beer until it was all gone. But that was probably for the best. Most of the men were feeling pretty good by then. If there had been more beer some of them would have been falling-down drunk before much longer. Many of the men were under twenty-one years old and were enjoying the freedom of drinking beer without someone checking their ID. Having recently turned twenty-three, I was the oldest man in the third platoon at that time.

After the beer was gone, most of us walked toward the grandstand where the band was preparing to entertain us. There was a covered stage where the band played, with wooden benches in front for us to sit and enjoy the show. A short while later four young Korean girls walked out on stage to a huge reception of cheers and whistles from the rowdy group of Alpha Company GIs who had gathered for the show. We had seen many Vietnamese women when we were operating around Firebase Patton but nothing like the girls in the band. Most of the women we saw in the field were working around their villages or carrying supplies along a road and weren't looking their Sunday best. For the past couple of weeks at the remote patrol bases, we hadn't seen a single female. Seeing those young ladies in short dresses revealing their curvy figures was an enjoyable treat on our first night of stand down.

The girls sang songs like "Tie a Yellow Ribbon Round the Old Oak Tree," "The Green Green Grass of Home" and "I Left my Heart in San Francisco" that reminded us of *the World* we left behind. Those songs could have easily made us sad and homesick, but for an hour or so we all forgot about being halfway around *the World* and the hazards we faced every day in the field and about Hal Harris dying a few days earlier. We enjoyed the music while we sang along and cheered the girls throughout the entire show. It was great.

After the show everyone scattered. Some of the men headed to a club to continue drinking, others were going to play poker, while some of the guys were drunk and were slowly working their way back to the barracks. Dave Hardy, a couple of other guys and I decided to walk back to the barracks to see what was happening. As we neared our barracks, Chief came staggering out of our barracks. After the beer ran out, he and a couple of other men had started on a fifth of whiskey. Chief saw us and waved with a .45 automatic pistol in his hand.

Bang! Chief fired a round into the air.

I yelled, "Chief, put the gun down!" He ignored me, of course.

He started walking away and fired another round into the air. We had to get it away from him before he shot himself or someone else. Dave Hardy and I ran up to Chief. Hardy wrapped his arms around him while I carefully reached for the pistol and pulled it from Chief's hand. Chief was so drunk he didn't put up much resistance.

He only said, "Hey, give me my gun."

"No way Chief," I said.

We helped Chief inside the barracks and laid him in a bunk. He tried to get up a couple of times hoping to get the pistol back. I told him to go to sleep and we would give him the pistol in the morning. After a couple minutes, Chief was out for the night.

I don't remember what happened to that pistol but I know we never gave it back to Chief. Someone said Chief had taken the pistol from a dead enemy soldier in July. After our little battle with Chief I decided it was too late to get involved in a poker game and I didn't need any more to drink. I took off my boots and crawled into a bunk to enjoy a comfortable night's sleep.

I slept in for much of the next morning. The only thing I had to do the second day of stand down was attend an awards ceremony that afternoon. When I finally walked outside, I ran into Rick Shields and a couple of the *old timers* from the Third Herd who had been assigned to the rear.

Rick said, "Come on, Hound Dog. We're going to the bathhouse"

They had also talked Lieutenant Fielding into going along as a friendly gesture towards our new platoon leader. As we walked toward the steam bathhouse, the guys told me what to expect. It cost a few bucks to get in of course. You could sit in a sauna or a steam machine and then get a massage from one of the young Vietnamese ladies. The military maintained control over the steam bath houses in Cu Chi and there weren't supposed to be any sexual favors available. But the guys said to ask for whatever you want when you're getting a massage and see what happens.

We paid a girl on our way in and were given a white towel. We walked to a changing room, took off our clothes and put them in a little basket that we checked in with another girl. We each wrapped a towel around us and walked into the bathhouse. I had never been in a steam bathhouse before. It was a totally new experience, thanks to good old Uncle Sam. I first sat down inside a sauna with a couple of the guys. Naturally, it was hot, but it soon became way too hot for me.

I said, "I'm out of here, guys."

Past the sauna was a row of one-man steam machines. The front of each machine opened to get in and out. I thought I might as well try one. There were several Vietnamese girls in the room to help us with whatever we needed. They spoke and understood some English, enabling us to communicate with them. When I walked toward one of the steam machines one of the girls walked over and opened the door. I stepped in and she held her hand out and said, "Towel?"

A GI in a steam machine down the line chuckled and said, "Just give her the towel."

I said, "Oh, yeah," and handed her my towel.

When I sat down in the steam machine, she closed the door and placed the towel around my neck. There I was sitting inside with my head sticking out the top, like I had seen in the movies. Now that felt good. It was warm but not too hot. The steam generated inside the machine rose around my neck while I relaxed and checked out the three Vietnamese girls as they helped other men in and out of the machines. After relaxing for a while in the steam machine I decided to move on to see what else they had to offer. I asked one of the girls to open the door. She pulled the towel from around my neck and unlatched the door. I took a couple steps outside the steam machine and smiled when I took the towel from the young lady.

I said, "Thank you," and wrapped the towel around my waist.

One of the girls told me to walk down a little hallway to my left if I wanted a massage. I walked along the hallway and was greeted by another young Vietnamese girl. She led me into a small private room, with a table in the middle covered with a foam mattress and a sheet. She patted her hand on the sheet with her hand and said, "Lie down."

I lay down on my stomach. Without saying another word she began to massage my body using pleasant smelling lotion. I just relaxed while she slowly massaged my shoulders, arms and back and then worked on my legs. She chuckled when I turned my head and smiled when she began giving me a quick little massage on my butt through the towel that was still covering me. It felt great. "What a way to go," I thought.

She then told me to roll onto my back and began massaging my chest and arms and again worked her way down to my legs. I didn't say much while she was massaging me. I simply relaxed and enjoyed her gentle touch. After she had massaged most of my body she stopped and appeared to be finished. Being a first-timer in the bathhouse I didn't know what would happen next.

The girl placed her hand on the towel that covered me, indicating there was one more place she could massage and said, "Five dollar."

I had learned when dealing with the civilians most everything was negotiable, so I automatically said, "Three dollars."

She came back saying, "Four dollar."

I quickly said, "OK." I wasn't exactly dealing with high finances. I gave her four dollars.

The young girl slowly reached under my towel and gently began a very *personal* conclusion to my massage. After receiving the first massage of my life, I got up and picked up my wallet and began walking out of the room.

The young Vietnamese girl said, "Thank you."

I looked back, smiling, and said, "And thank you." She gave me a little wave as I walked on to get my clothes.

When the rest of the men from the Third Herd began straggling in after their massage, we began exchanging our experiences. A couple of the men got a massage and that was it. And then there was Lieutenant Fielding.

Someone asked, "Hey 3-6, how was your massage?"

He smiled and said, "Oh, it was great," and paused for a second and then added, "My masseuse offered me sex. But I said no."

"What?" Was the reply, as several of the guys looked at Lieutenant Fielding.

He said, "I just couldn't do it. It's not right."

The rest of us looked at each other and shook our heads when we heard his tale. The one girl who was willing to have sex ended up with Lieutenant Fielding, who turned her down. While most of us may have accepted that girl's offer, we respected Lieutenant Fielding's beliefs.

Asking those girls for sexual favors may not have been the right thing for any of us to do, but there were a lot of things that weren't right in Vietnam. It wasn't right for Hal Harris to have died a few days earlier and it wasn't right that men were probably dying somewhere in Vietnam while we enjoyed ourselves in that steam bathhouse. We all knew that any day in Vietnam could be our last; accordingly, most GIs took the opportunity to enjoy themselves when they could. After our trip through the steam bathhouse we ate lunch in the mess hall and enjoyed rehashing our pleasant morning of rest and relaxation.

In addition to the girls in the bathhouse, there were hundreds of Vietnamese civilians working on the base. The military had conducted security screening of those civilians prior to their being allowed to work, and they were all searched when they entered through the main gate each day. However, as I was learning in the field, it was impossible to determine whether someone was an innocent civilian or a VC or a VC sympathizer. When some of those Vietnamese civilians were periodically interrogated, it was learned that they were relaying information gained while working in the base camp during the day to VC leaders at night. There had also been instances when a booby trap was detonated inside the base. Those devices were most certainly smuggled in by one of those civilians who really wasn't innocent.

I took an hour after lunch to get a quick letter off to my folks and to Jan Griffin. I tried to write a letter every few days to my folks and Jan. I wrote letters to other family and friends whenever I had time to respond to letters I had received from them. In my letters to my folks I only gave them general details about what I was doing, like going out on patrols every day and staying at a firebase at night. I definitely didn't tell them we had lost Hal Harris that past week. I'm sure my folks would have been worried sick if I had told them the truth about what really was happening. I was a little more open in my letters to Jan but asked her not to share any details with my folks if she happened to talk with them. I did mention that I had enjoyed my first steam bath but didn't share the details about my first massage with either my folks or Jan. Those were details about my tour of duty in Vietnam that they didn't need to know.

It was almost two o'clock when I finished writing the letters and dropped them in a nearby mailbox. One fringe benefit of serving in Vietnam was that we didn't have to pay postage. What a deal, risk your life for your country and they give you free postage.

I then found most of the company gathered with their platoons for the awards ceremony. The military's way of recognizing special or heroic achievements was to award medals based upon the nature of the achievement. Most of us weren't in Vietnam to become heroes or to see how many medals we might earn, but most men accepted their recognition with pride and proudly wore their medal(s) while they had their picture taken.

First Sergeant Seavey called the company to attention and then turned the ceremony over to Captain Branch. The CO asked for a moment of silence while Chaplain Wideman said a prayer for Venancio Vera, George Conrad and Hal Harris, who were the last three men in Alpha Company to be killed in action. Captain Branch expressed his personal sadness about the men we had lost but reminded us all it could have been worse considering what we had encountered the past couple of months.

The men receiving medals stood in a separate line to accept their due recognition. Captain Branch stood in front of each man while a citation for his medal was read. The CO pinned the medal on the man's fatigue shirt, said a few personal words and exchanged salutes. Several men received a Bronze Star for heroic action, three men received Purple Hearts for being wounded and others received Air Medals for completing twenty-five air combat missions (flying out in choppers).

After all the medals were awarded, we were dismissed. We congratulated the men who had received medals and I took pictures of Doc Jackson, Rick Shields, Dennis Schultz and a few other guys in the third platoon wearing their medals. There were no medals for those of us who had recently arrived in country, except for Carlton Quick who received a Purple Heart for being wounded the night we were ambushed.

The one award most infantrymen in Vietnam earned was the Combat Infantryman's Badge (CIB). The CIB was a rectangular metal badge with a silver musket centered on a light blue background and a silver wreath in the background. The CIB is awarded to Army infantrymen who serve in combat. Most of us in the third platoon who had been in the field the past month had earned our CIB and proudly wore the cloth replica insignia on our fatigue shirt.

After the awards ceremony, many of the men who had received medals wanted to celebrate, not so much because they received medals, but because they were alive to receive them. Many men never lived to see any of the medals they earned in combat. I joined a group of men at the club near our company area that had opened early because we were on stand down. A bond of comradeship quickly developed between most of the men in the company because we shared the most dangerous duty of anyone in Vietnam. Once a man showed he was willing to carry his own weight and fight alongside his comrades, he was welcomed into the family of fellow infantrymen. We shared a mutual respect for risking our lives every day. I was no longer a FNG and wasn't called a "shake'n bake" except in a joking manner.

I had many good friends in the Third Herd, with Dave Hardy and Rick Shields becoming very good buddies. It was great spending time together with several newfound friends while we relaxed during our last day on stand down, sharing a few cold beers together. We laughed while picking on each other about things we had done, like me jumping out of a chopper for the first time, or simply joked about where we were from. Rick Shields and Bob Ryken were from California; therefore, were accused of being gay. Guys like Whitey from the South were all hillbillies and men from Montana or Wyoming were accused of having more sex with sheep than women. Mike Myers and I were simply *dirt-busting* Iowa farmers. It was amazing how we got along and had fun as if we had known each other for years.

We enjoyed ourselves for a couple of hours and then went back to the stand down area to take advantage of another trailer load of free beer. Why pay fifteen cents a beer when you could drink free beer?

The second night of my first stand down progressed much like the first. Most of the men drank free beers as fast as they could, and later, we again cheered and sang along while another all-girl band played songs that reminded all of us of our world so far away back home. A bottle of whiskey was passed around during the concert and I took a couple swigs during the hour or so the girls were singing. By the end of the show I was feeling no pain. The beers I had drunk that afternoon and the sips of whiskey during the concert had done me in. For once I made a smart move and headed for my bunk to crash for the night.

Morning arrived way too soon. I woke up tired and hung over like many of the other guys. We had to literally pull some of the men out of their bunks to get them moving to make it to the convoy taking us back to the field at 10:30 that morning. We returned to our company area, got our rifles and gear, and reluctantly climbed aboard what we called the "Cu Chi Express," a convoy of deuce-and-a-halfs, for our journey back to the field.

While we rode toward the main gate of Cu Chi, men exchanged stories of what they had done for the past two days and laughed about the good time they had. Some of the men had smoked pot, others had found hookers, while a couple men bragged about how much money they won playing poker. But when we passed through the main gate and entered the countryside of Vietnam, we again *locked and loaded* our weapons and left the good times behind.

We headed back to Firebase Patton that was about an eight-mile ride from Cu Chi. I hoped we wouldn't be going out on a RIF that day. Most of us needed the day to recover from stand down. It had been fun, though.

Our First Sergeant William Seavey (Top) was one of the few men awarded the Combat Infantryman Badge (CIB) for service in World War II, Korea and Vietnam. He was therefore authorized to wear a CIB with two stars representing his third award (the first award does not have a star). William Seavey is listed on a registry of three-time CIB recipients at the National Infantry Museum, Fort Benning, Georgia.

The Medal of Honor, the nation's highest military decoration, was awarded to 241 men for their actions in Vietnam. 64% of those awards were made posthumously. Staff Sergeant Hammett Bowen was serving with Charlie Company (one of our sister companies) on June 27, 1969 when his platoon came under enemy fire. After returning fire, Sergeant Bowen ordered his men to fall back. As they moved back, an enemy grenade was thrown amid Sergeant Bowen and his men. Sergeant Bowen shouted a warning and hurled himself on the grenade, saving the lives of his fellow soldiers. Sergeant Bowen's extraordinary courage and concern for his men cost him his life. Staff Sergeant Bowen was posthumously awarded the Medal of Honor.

"There is a certain enthusiasm in liberty that makes human nature rise above itself, in acts of bravery and heroism."
— Alexander Hamilton, 1st U.S. Secretary of the Treasury

Left to right – Junior Houchens (Houch), Dave Holt, Bill Tally,
Sergeant Jim Overbey and Mike Myers (Babysan). This picture was
taken at one of the patrol bases. Behind the men is the dirt berm
and the coils of concertina wire that surrounded the entire perimeter.

Chapter 12

Back in the Field

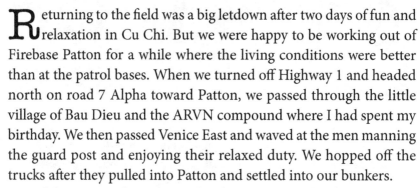

Returning to the field was a big letdown after two days of fun and relaxation in Cu Chi. But we were happy to be working out of Firebase Patton for a while where the living conditions were better than at the patrol bases. When we turned off Highway 1 and headed north on road 7 Alpha toward Patton, we passed through the little village of Bau Dieu and the ARVN compound where I had spent my birthday. We then passed Venice East and waved at the men manning the guard post and enjoying their relaxed duty. We hopped off the trucks after they pulled into Patton and settled into our bunkers.

While I was settling into my bunker I saw David Debiasio (Wop), one of the men in my squad, carrying a little gray monkey.

I asked, "Wop, what are you doing with a monkey?"

"I bought him in Cu Chi. He can be our mascot," Wop said and handed me the monkey.

The monkey was friendly and appeared harmless. He tugged at my fatigue shirt with his little hands and then hopped up on my shoulder and began playing with the hair on my head. Like Wop had said, the little monkey soon became the Third Herd's mascot.

Fortunately, there was no RIF assignment that afternoon, giving us time to recover from stand down. While I pulled guard by our bunker during that evening, I thought about my nearly two months in the field and how my outlook about my own future had changed.

Although I had completed considerable training to prepare me for serving as an infantryman in Vietnam, I arrived in country somewhat naïve about certain realities of war. However, after two months in the field I fully realized that on any given day one or more of us could be seriously wounded or killed. But I also had learned that the hazards of war should not be feared, but rather, must be respected because it was inherent in being an infantryman. I also knew regardless of our training or experience, there was an element of luck that might determine our fate. I had seen the peace and quiet of a day or night instantly change into terror most people could never imagine. The fate of an individual might be determined simply by where they were at a given moment. Unfortunately, there was little I could do to change my situation. I continued to hope and pray for the best.

After an uneventful night at Patton we were up early the following morning to prepare for a flight into the boonies near the Saigon River. One of the first things I did was to take a long drink of cool water from my canteen. The water they supplied us contained chlorine and tasted like swimming pool water. The water in my canteen would warm up during the day, and although it would still quench my thirst, drinking warm water wasn't very enjoyable. Shortly after I arrived in the field, I established a routine of enjoying the simple pleasure of a drink of cool water from my canteen each morning.

After eating a warm breakfast, I put on my gear, walked to the landing zone (LZ) just east of the perimeter and waited for choppers scheduled to arrive about eight o'clock. When the choppers arrived we climbed aboard for an early morning aerial tour of the Vietnamese countryside. I noticed a lot of water in the area while we descended into the remote LZ. Although it was nearing the end of the monsoon season there were still frequent rain showers. The rice paddies remained mostly full of water and much of the low-lying areas of the countryside were still flooded.

The LZ was on high and dry ground, but that didn't last long. As we moved north along our designated route, we soon began walking through a grassy swamp area about a klick west of the Saigon River. At times, the ground seemed to bounce when we walked, like walking on a trampoline. As we moved on, I would take one step in ankle-deep water; the next step, the water would be knee deep. We had been flown out there to look for enemy troops that supposedly had been spotted. If there were gooks out there, they had to be crazy to be maneuvering around all that water.

Before long, we were all soaked after crossing a waist deep channel of water. We hadn't seen any signs of enemy activity as we continued north into an area that had more water than I had ever seen before. We then came upon a stream about thirty meters wide. Our designated route took us across the stream and continued north where we would rendezvous with choppers at a LZ over two klicks away. Whoever had planned the RIF must not have known how much water was out there, or (more likely) they knew about all the water but didn't give a damn because they wouldn't be coming out with us. Regardless, we were surrounded by water.

Captain Branch wanted to try to cross the stream. A point team from the first platoon slowly walked into the water with more men following. Suddenly, the point man who was chest deep in the water, slipped and went under. His helmet fell off and floated away upside-down in the current, while the man behind him went to his rescue. They both struggled to keep their heads above the moving water while other men moved forward to help. The men struggled to maintain their footing as they yelled back, "The current's too fast, we can't stand up!"

The point man wasn't even halfway across the stream. It would have gotten worse if they continued. With all the gear, ammunition and weapons each man carried, it would be impossible to safely cross the stream. Captain Branch waved for the men to come back. The men in the stream helped each other struggle back from the swiftly moving water. They finally made it safely back to the edge of the stream but they were soaked to their heads.

The CO smartly altered our course, taking us parallel to the stream through more knee-and waist-deep water. If enemy troops had come through there, they probably thought what most of us were thinking: "Let's get out of here and find some dry land!" After another hour of sloshing through more swampland, we finally found high ground and made our way to a newly established LZ. The day proved to be a waste of time for us, because we didn't find any sign of enemy activity.

After reaching the LZ, we established a perimeter while waiting for the choppers which were scheduled to arrive in about twenty minutes. We took that time to check for leeches. Although we wore elastic bands around the bottom of our trouser legs to hold them tight, leeches often found a way to get inside and latch onto our skin. You normally couldn't feel a leech, making it necessary to always check ourselves after we had walked through water that was more than ankle deep.

When I pulled up my right pant leg, there was an ugly leech. It was small, about the size of the tip of my little finger. Those leeches were a brownish-gray color and slimy, like worms. They got bigger as they latched on to you and sucked your blood into their bodies. Some men had found leeches the size of their index finger in the past. If we touched the leech with the tip of a lit cigarette or put a drop or two of insect repellant on them, they would normally release their bite and fall off. We didn't want to just pull them off or their fangs might stick in our leg and cause an infection. Several of the guys found at least one leech on them before the choppers arrived that afternoon.

As we heard the distant sound of the choppers, we gathered our gear and organized to board. The wind blowing through the chopper during the fifteen-minute ride back to Patton began drying out our soaked fatigues and gear. When we arrived at our bunkers inside Patton, I immediately took off my boots and soggy socks and wet fatigues and found dry clothes. Most of us kept an extra set of fatigues and a couple pairs of socks in our personal gear to wear on those occasions.

After our evening meal we organized guard duty and settled in for another night in Vietnam. After I finished my first guard shift about ten o'clock and had rolled into my hammock inside our bunker, I soon heard several loud explosions outside.

The men who had been on guard came running inside, saying, "We have incoming."

I jumped up and scrambled to get my boots on while two men peered through the viewing holes in front of our bunker. There were several more explosions from incoming rounds and then there was silence. After a minute of silence we hurried outside, put on our flak jackets, grabbed our weapons and spread out along the berm near our bunker like we always did after receiving incoming rounds.

Someone then told me two of our men had been wounded. I rushed over to the bunker next to ours and found Doc Jackson and other guys tending to two men lying on the ground.

I leaned over Doc's shoulder and saw it was Chief. Chief was due for reassignment to the rear soon. It looked like he was going to the rear the hard way.

Doc looked at me and said, "He'll be OK."

I then heard Ron Peterson yelling nearby. I rushed over and I saw he had taken a blast of shrapnel in his right thigh. Two men were trying to stop the blood gushing from the wound, as Peterson yelled in panic for them to get away. He didn't want anyone other than Doc Jackson to treat him. I told Peterson, calm down and I would help him, but he shouted "No!" I frustratingly said I would bring Doc over.

I rushed back to Doc Jackson and said, "Peterson doesn't want anyone but you to treat him. I'll stay with Chief."

Doc left some bandages for me to cover Chief's wounds.

We were all trained in basic first aid and were prepared to help anyone who was wounded, but Peterson didn't want the rest of us to touch him. A medic from another platoon soon arrived to help Doc Jackson bandage Peterson's leg and help calm him down. Peterson had only been in country a couple of months but it looked like the war was already over for him. Chief was doing fine. He had been peppered with shrapnel and had wounds on his face, arms and legs, but none of the injuries looked too serious. I tightened the bandages Doc had put on. Although he was in pain, Chief quietly lay on the ground while I bandaged his wounds.

Immediately after the incoming rounds landed inside Patton three 81MM mortar platoons, two 4.2-inch mortar teams and six 155MM artillery guns began firing. It sounded like a loud Fourth of July while outgoing mortar and artillery rounds flew over our heads as we treated Chief and Peterson.

It would have been pure luck if one of our mortar rounds actually hit the culprits who had fired the mortars at us. They could have been anywhere in the surrounding countryside. After the outgoing firing stopped a few minutes later, I noticed a commotion a short distance away toward the center of the firebase. We soon learned our Battalion Sergeant Major had been seriously wounded. He was leisurely showering in a shower stall outside his bunker when a mortar round landed nearby. What bad luck. We put Chief and Peterson on litters and carried them to the nearby medical aid station. In a short while a medevac was on the aid station landing pad. We quickly loaded the Sergeant Major and our two wounded buddies onboard, and they were soon on their way to the 12th Evac in Cu Chi. So much for a quiet night at Patton.

We often went several days, or sometimes a week or two, without anything serious happening. During those times, some of the men started thinking that combat duty might not be quite so hazardous after all. But then BAM – something like that night's incoming mortar fire brought us back to reality. One moment there was peace and quiet, and the next, men were lying on the ground fighting to stay alive. Fortunately, there was no more incoming mortar fire and no other action the remainder of that night.

The following morning Alpha Company went out on a RIF near the firebase. Before we left, we heard that surgeons in Cu Chi were forced to amputate the Sergeant Major's leg. Ron Peterson's leg was a mess but they were able to save it. Chief was listed in fair condition with multiple shrapnel wounds. They would all be flown back to *the World* in a few days for further medical care.

Alpha Company headed north along the 7 Alpha toward the village of Trung Lap about a quarter mile away. As we neared the village, we were greeted by a group of kids with their hands out, hoping for anything we might give them. If we had candy, we would throw it in the air and watch the kids scramble for it. Although our primary task was to search the village for any signs of the enemy, we also performed public relations work in an effort to keep the civilians on our side. While we searched their hooches the medics took time to check children when a mother carried a child up and tried to explain what was wrong. Our medics treated the kids or adults for bumps and bruises but couldn't treat anything too serious. The U.S. military periodically sent medical teams into the villages to provide additional medical care for the civilians. They didn't want any serious disease to get out of control and spread to us GIs.

We normally used our Chieu Hoi Hue to communicate with the civilians. Most of us GIs knew a few words in Vietnamese but not enough to carry on a conversation. Hue would communicate with us as best he could about his conversations with the civilians. Hue was also helpful while we searched the village looking for anything unusual. He knew what to look for better than most of us.

As we worked our way through the village, I received further exposure to rural Vietnamese civilian life. Most of the hooches had clay walls about four inches thick and four to five feet high, with an open space between the top of the walls and the corrugated metal or thatched roof. There were usually no doors, just an open entrance. The floors were dirt, and sometimes covered with bamboo mats. The inside of the hooches were sometimes divided into two or three small rooms. There was normally a belowground storage area providing a cool place for food. Their homes were primitive, but they protected the people from the hot sun and monsoon rains.

There was no electricity, no indoor plumbing and no other modern conveniences. They carried water from nearby wells. There were also a few small shops in the village that sold food, clothing or personal and household items. There were no cars or trucks. Some of the civilians had a bicycle or motor scooter, but most people just walked everywhere. They often used oxen or water buffalo to pull a two-wheeled cart, transporting items too large or too heavy to carry themselves; however, I had not seen any horses. I later learned oxen/cattle and water buffalo were used because they were stronger than horses.

Although those people lived in the most primitive existence I had ever seen, they survived in relatively good health. They appeared to have enough food to eat, although it was mainly rice. The adults wore loose-fitting shirts and slacks or shorts; some wore sandals while others were bare-footed. Some of the babies and young children ran around naked but most of the kids wore shorts and were bare footed. After we entered the village and while we searched the hooches I noticed odors I hadn't smelled before. Some of the smells were from small cooking fires, but there were also other strange odors inside the hooches. Some of the guys swore they could smell a Vietnamese person because they had a different body odor than us GIs. Maybe that's what I smelled. Whatever those odors were, they were another new experience for me.

We spent over an hour searching through the village of Trung Lap that was only about 200 meters long. After we didn't find any weapons or other signs of enemy presence, Captain Branch decided to move on to our next checkpoint, which was a cluster of hooches a klick southeast of Trung Lap.

We found only four hooches there and only five or six people around when we arrived. It reminded me of the small group of hooches where we were ambushed on September 14th. We began searching the hooches, and then, Bingo!

In the first hooch we found medical supplies, syringes, medicine and bandages. In another hooch the men found AK-47 ammunition. We also found a stash of clothing that was more than just extra clothing for those few people. We soon gathered the inhabitants together and held them under guard. They were no longer considered innocent civilians. Hue and a Chieu Hoi from the first platoon helped Captain Branch and others interrogate the civilians, but they didn't reveal much information. Captain Branch radioed the Battalion CO about what we had found. The Battalion CO wanted the civilians taken to Cu Chi for further interrogation and ordered the hooches destroyed.

We established a perimeter around the hamlet and waited for a chopper to arrive with demolition charges, which Poof and Puff, our demolitions men, would set to destroy the hooches. An intelligence officer, who arrived on the chopper, tied the hands of the civilians and then loaded them on board the waiting Huey for a trip to Cu Chi. We helped to set a demolition charge inside each of the hooches and then pulled back. A few minutes later explosions leveled the hooches to the ground, spewing huge clouds of smoke and debris into the air.

It was difficult to imagine how it was for the Vietnamese civilians trying to live in the middle of that war. It appeared that some civilians supported us; however, we knew others sided with the Communist North Vietnam. Although we had destroyed several hooches and confiscated the medical supplies and ammunition, we didn't know if the people who lived there were VC sympathizers who willingly hid the supplies, or if the VC had forced them to hide the supplies under the threat of injury or death. Many Vietnamese civilians innocently lost their homes or their lives simply because they were stuck in the middle of that lousy war.

It was mid-afternoon when we headed towards Patton with the third platoon in the lead. Captain Branch stopped us after we had moved about a klick south and walked to the front of the columns. We were supposed to continue south and then circle northwest towards Patton.

But the CO said, "Head straight west towards Patton," pointing to the guard tower in the distance. He wanted to get back by four o'clock so he could listen to some country music that day. The Armed Forces Radio Network broadcasted music most of the day and played country music between four and five o'clock each afternoon.

Robert Draughn, one of our point men, smiled and said, "OK sir, let's go home."

We headed through mostly open countryside and rice paddies, and walked through the southeast path in the concertina wire that surrounded Patton a few minutes after four o'clock that afternoon. The CO was happy. As I took off my gear by our bunker, someone turned on a radio and several of us stomped our feet and clapped our hands to the beat of country music. Although I knew Captain Branch took his role as our CO seriously, it was nice to have a leader who gave us a little slack now and then. I soon headed for the showers.

A couple of nights later I took my squad out on an ambush. We had no difficulty in setting up the ambush and had an excellent site behind a little rise to view a trail that crossed the countryside. I took first watch that night, quietly sitting on the ground looking off into the darkness for any movement. Midway through my first hour on guard I heard the sound of a 155MM artillery gun firing from Patton. A couple seconds later I heard the whistle of the huge round flying through the air over our heads, and then, a few seconds later, I heard a distant boom as the round detonated on impact far to the east. We often heard artillery and mortar rounds whistling over our heads while we were on an ambush. We could only hope they kept going on to their intended target.

We quietly rotated guard during the night and I wrapped in my poncho liner while I slept. It was quiet, but for some reason I suddenly woke up in the middle of the night. I looked at the man who was supposed to be on guard at my position. He was slumped over, asleep. He jumped when I nudged him.

I whispered, "Wake up!"

I then moved to the other forward position and found everyone there also asleep. I couldn't believe it. The man who should have been on guard there was also sleeping. I shook him and said, "Stay awake."

When I moved to the rear position, I found one of the guys awake and on guard.

I whispered, "Everything's OK, I'm just checking."

I sat there for a minute thinking about the scary situation I had found. Two of the three men who were supposed to be on guard had fallen asleep. How many times had it happened before? Pulling guard on ambush and looking into the darkness for an hour at a time was a boring job. But you were expected to do whatever it took to stay awake. Enemy troops could have walked up on us and we all could have been history. Although I was pissed, I was more concerned about why those men fell asleep on guard. How could they doze off knowing everyone's life was on the line? I thought I knew why.

Fortunately, we made it through the remainder of the night without incident and without anyone else falling asleep on guard.

I didn't say anything to the men the next morning. I wanted to talk with Rick Shields and Jim Overbey about what happened rather than yell at the two men who had fallen asleep. During the past few weeks we three NCOs had noticed some men having trouble staying awake while on guard and we also noticed a couple of men dozing off during the day while we took breaks during recent RIFs.

The word was a few men in the Third Herd were smoking pot or taking speed. They would find a little hideout somewhere inside the firebase or patrol base and have a little party rather than getting some much needed sleep at night. The combination of drugs and lack of sleep was taking its toll on those guys. Even if those men stayed awake while on guard, they weren't as alert as they should be. We knew there were only a few guys who were putting everyone else at risk.

Rick, Jim and I proposed some new guidelines to Lieutenant Fielding. He agreed without question. We gathered the entire platoon later that afternoon and established new rules. The first rule wasn't new, but needed to be reemphasized. NO drugs in the field. Although the military didn't condone drug use, it was pretty difficult to control in Vietnam. Drugs were cheap and readily available most anywhere. We wanted to make sure drugs didn't create any more problems with the third platoon while we were in the field. Hopefully by bringing the drug issue out in the open, the rest of the platoon would put enough pressure on those few men to make them stay straight in the field.

The second new rule was there would be two men on guard at each position while we were on an ambush. We had been keeping only one man on guard at each of the three ambush positions so we all could get a little more sleep. But after the past night, we decided it was better to lose a little sleep than never to wake up again. The two men on guard at each ambush position could keep each other awake during their one-hour guard shift. We would rotate guard shifts, with two men on guard and two men sleeping at each position on ambushes. Everyone agreed to the new ambush guard rotation, or at least no one verbally disagreed.

Rick Shields and I had a private conversation with the two men who had fallen asleep on the ambush and with the other guys who we believed had been doing drugs. We simply told them to knock it off or we would go to the CO if the problem continued. They also knew the rest of the platoon wasn't happy with them. That problem ended.

A couple days later we pulled an all-night mission. During mid-afternoon a truck convoy took us to a firebase about twenty miles southwest of Patton where we had never worked before. From that firebase I could more clearly see Nui Ba Den, the 3,300-foot-high mountain to the west. We would work with another company to surround a small village with suspected VC living there. Sometime after midnight we would begin walking about three klicks from the patrol base across the countryside and surround the village before daylight. At dawn the other company would sweep through the village. We would be waiting outside the village to stop any VC who may try to escape. It seemed like a good plan, but I certainly wasn't looking forward to walking across the countryside at night.

We ate some chow and then relaxed and caught some sleep. Shortly before 2:00 a.m. we packed up and were on our way. We began walking down a dirt road, then turned east and walked through rice paddies that covered much of the countryside. We had to walk in the rice paddies because it was too dark to walk along the narrow dikes. The water in the rice paddies around Patton was receding but we must have been in some low-lying countryside because the water in those paddies was still over a foot deep. We moved through several rice paddies, through some hedgerows and then through more rice paddies. I had no idea where we were. That area was way off the map I had. Hopefully the CO had a map of the area and was keeping track of our location.

After walking for over an hour, we slowed down when we came upon a three-foot-high dirt berm. Dave Hardy directly in front of me suddenly dropped out of sight. He had slipped into a small bomb crater that couldn't be seen because of the water. He soon popped up out of the water and Carlton Quick and I grabbed him to help him out. Hardy was OK, but we were all a wet and muddy mess. It quickly became another long, miserable night in Vietnam. We were all tired, wet and muddy as we neared the village over two hours later. We stopped in a group of rice paddies and spread along the dikes, quietly watching for any movement in front of us. It was still dark and we couldn't see far, but apparently the village was out there somewhere.

After daylight arrived the other company swept through the village from the west. We had the other three sides of the village surrounded and could see anyone trying to leave. The third platoon was spread along the northeast side of the village. We would have to keep our fire low if any enemy personnel were spotted to avoid exposing the GIs inside or around the village to *friendly fire* (fire from American troops). After a few minutes RTO, Bill Casey, heard over his radio that some VC were making a run for it through the east side of the village. The men on our eastern perimeter opened up with M-16 and machine gun fire, dropping three VC in a muddy rice paddy. Anyone trying to escape the village had little chance of survival, with about 85 GIs waiting for them and probably that many other GIs sweeping through the village. We then heard gunfire coming from inside the village.

Casey listened to his radio and kept me informed of what was happening. The gunfire from inside the village killed two more VC who tried to escape. A couple more VC surrendered to the GIs sweeping through the village without putting up a fight. After about thirty minutes without any more action we headed south to check out other nearby hamlets. There were believed to be fifteen or twenty VC living in the village or nearby. When we moved out, we walked past the bullet-riddled and bloody bodies of the three VC who were lying where they had fallen in the rice paddy.

We took a break on some dry ground later that morning and most of us found a leech or two sucking on our legs. What a way to start the day. We spent the rest of the morning checking several hooches in two hamlets. We found no more signs of the enemy. After what happened earlier, any other VC were either well-hidden or, more likely, were long gone. We arrived back at the patrol base shortly after noon and then rode on another deuce-and-a-half convoy back to Patton.

We spent the next hour cleaning our weapons and gear, and then hit the showers to wash away the mud from our past night's escapade. While we were taking showers, someone noticed two Red Cross girls standing atop a large bunker near the center of the firebase with two GIs. Red Cross girls visited Patton periodically to talk with the men trying to boost our morale. We waved at the girls and motioned for them to join us for a shower. That would certainly have boosted our morale! The girls appeared to ignore us at first, but then one of them waved at us while the two GIs quickly escorted the girls down from the top of the bunker when they realized what was going on.

That night I was standing guard near our bunker, watching out over the perimeter and chatting with Vic Ortega who was on guard on the other side of the bunker. I heard footsteps behind me and turned to see First Sergeant "Top" Seavey walking in the darkness toward our bunker. Top started yelling, "Why in the hell aren't you men wearing your flak jackets?"

I said, "Sorry, Top, I forgot," while Vic scrambled to find his flak jacket.

"Oh bullshit, Hogue," Top replied. "Put your flak jacket on!"

"OK Top", I said as Top moved on, ready to check on the guys at the next bunker.

Top was right, I hadn't forgotten about wearing my flak jacket, I had been lax, thinking nothing would happen. I knew better.

Top was normally a decent guy and would often visit and joke around with us during the day. But Top liked to prowl around the perimeter bunkers at night and raise hell with us when he saw something he didn't like. We normally just took it in stride. After over twenty years in the Army, it was just his way of doing his job. If we knew Top was on the prowl, we would spread the word to be sure the men on guard had their flak jacket and helmet on before he came around.

The Third Herd's next assignment was to provide security for a group of engineers while they built a temporary bridge in a swampy area west of the Saigon River. That duty was pretty soft, but we stayed wet much of the time because a portion of the area was under water with scattered patches of high ground, and although the monsoon season was nearing its end, we got soaked during the periodic evening rains.

We set up a perimeter around the engineers each day while they built the bridge. Before dark, we pulled back onto higher ground, to dig in for the night. We set out claymore mines around us and prepared to pull guard all night. There was a small stream running along the back side of our position that could be used as an enemy infiltration route. We ordered a supply of concussion grenades that we dropped in the stream periodically all night long to deter anyone from trying to sneak up the stream. Other than walking through swampland and getting wet nearly every day our time guarding the engineers was uneventful.

Two weeks later we had more fairly easy duty. After spraying designated areas of the countryside with Agent Orange, bulldozers were used to plow down the vegetation. Our job was to pull guard for the bulldozer operators. We would establish a perimeter around the area to be leveled, and when finished with that area, we would move on to the next area and establish a new perimeter. Fortunately, we didn't encounter any enemy action while we provided guard for the bulldozers, but the days soon became long and boring.

It was during some of those relatively peaceful days that I had time to get to know some of the men better. I had time to talk with them while we were sitting in a daytime perimeter.

Terry Thornton was from Tulsa, Oklahoma. He was married and had a young daughter. Terry was genuinely concerned about his welfare and worried about leaving his wife and daughter without a husband and father. He was seriously considering reenlisting to get out of the infantry. He had joined the third platoon that past August and had seen what could happen in the field. I told Terry we would send him to Cu Chi to talk with the headquarters staff if he desired. He said he would let me know.

I also talked with James "Red" Mincey one day. Red told me his older brother was a Marine and had died of malaria in Vietnam in

1968. I then asked Red if the Army knew about his brother. He said he had talked with his CO in basic training and spoke with someone when he arrived in country. But nothing changed. I told Red I would talk with Captain Branch about getting him out of the field. His family had sacrificed enough for that damn war.

Red said he was willing to stay out there with the rest of us; but regardless, I planned to talk with the CO about Red's situation.

And then there was Bob Emery, the eighteen-year-old who had been sent to Germany, but volunteered for Vietnam. One day I asked what made him volunteer for Vietnam. Bob told me he decided if he was going to be in the Army he wanted to be in a real war. Bob had made a courageous decision and I was glad to have him in the Third Herd.

I noticed when I arrived in the field that none of us had been issued bayonets. The M-16 rifles were designed for a bayonet to snap on over the end of the barrel to use as a weapon in hand-to-hand combat. None of us ever wanted to experience hand-to-hand combat, but we all had received hours of bayonet training during basic and AIT. I never did get an answer about why we weren't issued bayonets.

As an alternative, most of the men acquired a knife. Some had a pocketknife but most of the guys had a hunting-type knife with a 4" to 6" blade. We didn't carry a knife so much to use as a weapon, but rather, as a handy tool. I had asked my parents to buy me a small hunting knife and they sent it to me after I arrived in the field. I carried my knife in a sheath attached to a loop on my fatigue pants, with a metal snap ring called a carabiner. Carabiners were used to loop the rope through when rappelling, or were used to attach cargo straps to choppers.

One of the challenges for many of us was sharpening our knives. Danial "Whitey" Heiderich had learned to sharpen knives back home and became the expert Third Herd knife sharpener. Whitey had shown me how to rub the knife blade against a sharpening stone just right to get the blade razor sharp. After a while I was able to sharpen my knife just like Whitey had shown me. But some of the guys gave up trying to sharpen their own knives and asked Whitey to do it.

Whitey enjoyed spending some of his spare time teaching guys to sharpen their knives or sharpening other guys' knives for them.

After pulling guard for the engineers, we returned to the duty of daily RIFs with the company. Late one morning the third platoon was leading the RIF southeast of the Ho Bo Woods. The area was covered with tall grass, scattered bushes and hedgerows. It had been a calm morning when I heard someone near the front of our column yelling for help. It likely wasn't a booby trap because there hadn't been an explosion. I walked through a small hedgerow and saw two men gathered around Junior "Houch" Houchens who was sitting on the ground.

"What happened?" I asked.

Someone said, "He stepped in a punji pit!"

I walked closer and looked at Houchen's leg that had plunged into the pit.

Houch looked at me and hesitantly said, "I think I'm OK."

I turned and yelled, "Doc, get up here!"

Lieutenant Fielding walked up. I told him what happened and said we needed to set up a perimeter while Doc Jackson checked on Houch. Houch had been lucky. He only had a few scrapes on his leg.

The NVA and VC built punji pits that were simply a hole dug into the ground with pointed bamboo stakes pushed into the bottom of the pit with the points up. They often dipped the stakes in human waste hoping to cause infections. The pit would be concealed with branches and vegetation. If someone stepped on the covering it would give way and they would plunge into the pit and be spiked with the pointed stakes, often causing serious injury. Houch had fallen into a pit in which some of the stakes had fallen over, creating a clear spot that Houch happened to hit just right. If his foot had gone a few inches in any direction we would be calling in a medevac for him.

Doc treated Houch's scrapes with two small bandages and said he would be OK. He could get checked out further at the aid station when we got back to Patton.

I gave Houch a pat on the back when he stood up and asked if he was OK. He took a deep breath and said, "I'm fine Sarge, but that scared the hell out of me." It would have scared me too.

We cleared away from the punji pit and let Houch throw a hand grenade into the pit to destroy the stakes and blow away the cover, to reveal it to any other friendly troops who might pass through the area another day. We continued moving on through the area which was mostly tall grass and scattered bushes.

A while later I heard someone yelling, "Ouch! Damn it! Ouch!"

I looked forward and saw Ed Leberski standing near a bush, jumping around in circles and slapping himself all over. I guessed he had run into a nest of fire ants, reddish-brown ants that lived in huge nests. We were in an area that was high and dry and prime land for fire ants. Ed had either stepped on a nest or they had been on a bush he brushed against on his way through.

I yelled, "Ed, move back here!" He needed to get away from the source of the ants. Ed took a few steps then threw his helmet on the ground, dropped his M-16 and began taking off his gear. The ants had gotten under his fatigues and were biting him all over. Ed continued to yell and cuss while frantically pulling off his gear. There wasn't anything the rest of us could do except watch. The red ants would continue to bite until they were knocked off his body. Ed soon had his shirt off and had dropped his trousers down to his ankles. Some of us chuckled as we watched Ed strip down in the middle of the boonies.

We helped Ed slap the ants off, using our towels. Finally, Ed thought we had gotten them all off.

Ed was nearly out of breath after his encounter with the red ants. He stood there for a moment and then slowly pulled up his pants, looking for more ants that might be still be there. He shook out his shirt and put it on. We shook his gear to knock off any fire ants that might be clinging on, waiting to attack again. Ed finally smiled when we told him how funny he looked jumping around and ripping off his gear and fatigues out there. He said, "They hurt like hell," and he pointed to the little red marks the fire ants had left with each bite.

The rest of us took another route to avoid the nest of fire ants Ed unfortunately had found. We finished the RIF without any more encounters with punji pits or fire ants.

Besides enemy troops, punji pits and booby traps, we faced a variety of natural obstacles including fire ants and snakes. There were several varieties of snakes, including constrictors, pythons, and deadly cobras. Cobras would try to bite anyone who walked upon them, and they could actually spit blinding venom up to six feet away. A cobra's bite was usually fatal.

We saw snakes everywhere and we normally dealt with them with a burst of M-16 fire. We didn't take any chances and didn't take the time to determine whether it might have been a harmless snake or a king cobra. Most of the men believed, "The only good snake is a dead snake." A cobra was killed inside Patrol Base Delta early one evening while we shared the patrol base with a group of ARVNs. The ARVNs took the dead snake and cooked it for dinner.

I received a letter from my hometown buddy Allan Schwab after I had been in the field a couple months. He was with the Americal Division which operated in the northern part of South Vietnam generally referred to as the *highlands*. A natural hazard they encountered up there were tigers. He mentioned that a tiger had killed a man in his company while the man sat on guard one night. We hadn't seen any tigers and hadn't even worried about tigers until I read Allan's letter. I wrote Allan back and said, "Thanks for telling me about the tiger. Now I have something else to worry about over here."

But so it was. Each day in Vietnam I learned something new. When I arrived in country I thought my only enemies were the NVA and VC. But I learned there were also many natural enemies in Vietnam. Even the malaria carried by the mosquitos could kill you.

Near the end of October we went back to Cu Chi for another stand down which was much like the first. I got new boots and a clean uniform, drank free beer and cheered the all-girl band that entertained us each evening. The two days on stand down flew by while I relaxed and enjoyed fun times with my friends in the Third Herd and Alpha Company.

When I arrived in Vietnam in July 1969 my monthly base pay as a Sergeant E-5 was $255. Military personnel serving in Vietnam also received $65 per month hazardous duty pay. In January 1970 my monthly base pay increased to $275. In reality we needed little money while serving in the field because the Army provided most everything we needed and there were few opportunities to spend money. I received only $40 a month in Vietnam with the balance sent to my bank account back home via an allotment. If I needed additional money, I could cash a personal check at the Post Exchange or bank in Cu Chi.

Left to right – Bob Emery, myself and David "Wop" Debiasio at
Fire Support Base Patton with M-60 machine guns. Bob and Wop
were the third platoon's machine gunners at the time.

Chapter 13

Dry Weather and Danger

While we were on stand down, Carl Seals, a little guy with reddish-brown hair joined the third platoon along with Chuck Merritt, another fellow Iowan from Runnels, Iowa. Two new NCOs Sergeants Mike Daniels and John Matson also joined us and were assigned as team leaders in charge of four or five men within each squad. Our platoon sergeant, Rick Shields, had arrived in country early that past summer and would soon be due for a job in the rear. We actually had more NCOs than we needed, but it would work out when Rick was reassigned to the rear.

Rick, Jim Overbey and I each spent time with the two new *shake'n bakes*, explaining how we operated and what we expected of them. Sergeant Matson began to assume his responsibilities but Daniels didn't seem to care about what we had to say. During the next few days several men complained to me about Sergeant Daniels, who was assigned to my squad. Guys said he was basically one of the laziest men they had ever seen. When we were out on RIFs, I noticed Daniels just walked along and didn't take any initiative to watch over his team. He was one of those men who could easily get someone else killed. I had a couple private talks with Daniels and told him he needed to shape up if he expected to survive out there. But I saw no change in his behavior.

We were working out of Patrol Base Delta when another group of ARVNs joined us one evening shortly after the first of November, to go out on an ambush. I vividly remembered what happened the last time we went on an ambush with the ARVNs. We lost Hal Harris. I was in charge of twelve GIs, and one of the ARVNs, who spoke some

English, identified himself as the leader of a dozen ARVNS. We GIs led the way and walked quietly toward the ambush site while keeping a watchful eye over the countryside. But the ARVNs leisurely moved along, not seeming to be concerned about much of anything. They talked and laughed like they were headed for a picnic. I told their leader to keep his men quiet. They finally quieted down.

It was nearly dark when we reached the ambush site along a dirt road. I told the ARVNs to set up on the south side of the road behind a hedgerow that provided concealment. I set up our position to their left where the road curved north. Like we normally did, we set up two four-man positions along the trail to observe in both directions and placed one position to our rear. We set out claymores in front of our positions, and within a few minutes, we quietly settled in.

But the ARVNs took forever to settle in. They mingled around alongside the road for several minutes and finally organized themselves behind the hedgerow. We began pulling guard with two men awake at each of our positions but the ARVNs took a totally different approach. All but one of them lay down and went to sleep. That single ARVN stayed on guard while, the rest of them slept and I guess they hoped he would stay awake. I didn't notice how often they rotated guard duty, but it was definitely a risky approach to pulling guard on an ambush.

I was in the right forward position along the trail with Sergeant Daniels and two other men. I had learned from one of the men in our CP group that Daniels had been assigned to us because he was kicked out of another company for being a loafer. We had someone else's dead wood and I wanted to keep an eye on him. Later that evening, Daniels and I were pulling guard during our second one-hour shift. It was quiet and we hadn't observed any enemy activity. Halfway through our shift I looked over and saw Daniels' head hanging down. He had fallen asleep! I nudged him so hard he nearly fell over.

I whispered, "Hey, wake up!" I could have slugged him.

He said, "I wasn't asleep."

"Bullshit," I whispered, "You were sleeping!"

That was it. I wasn't going to let Daniels mess up the Third Herd. He was worthless. After returning to the patrol base the next morning I went to Rick Shields and Lieutenant Fielding. I was mad.

I said, "I want that son-of-a-bitch Daniels out of the platoon. He's going to get someone killed out there."

Rick looked at me with a surprised expression; he hadn't seen me so angry before. Rick and Lieutenant Fielding both agreed with me. The three of us went to see Captain Branch. I explained to the CO about Daniel's lack of initiative since he arrived and repeated my story about his falling asleep on guard during our ambush the past night. I asked the CO to have Daniels reassigned.

Captain Branch said he understood and would take care of it.

I smiled and said, "Thank you, sir, I owe you one."

"Don't worry about it, Hound Dog. I don't want his kind in Alpha Company," Captain Branch replied as he gave me a friendly pat on my shoulder upon leaving his bunker.

Two days later there was good news and bad news. The good news was Sergeant Daniels was told to pack his gear. He was being reassigned, again. I'm sure he knew why but he didn't say a word to me or anyone else before he left. The bad news was Captain Branch was being reassigned to our battalion headquarters to gather intelligence information about enemy activity.

Captain Branch had been a great CO. He cared for the welfare of every man in the company. We all hated to see him go, but for his sake, his new duty would be safer than walking through the boonies every day with us. Our new CO was Captain Larry Dalton. No one knew too much about him except the word was he was gung ho. Maybe he and Lieutenant Fielding would hit it off together.

On November 6, 1969, Alpha Company was assigned to Patrol Base Hunsley. The last time we were there the second platoon lost eleven men the first night. A lot of the men grumbled about going back to Hunsley, but I knew complaining wouldn't change anything. After serving as an infantryman in South Vietnam three months I knew the living conditions were always lousy and we could encounter danger nearly everywhere. My biggest challenge was to stay alive for nine more months regardless of where I was assigned.

The third platoon was assigned ambush duty the first night after we arrived at Hunsley. Lieutenant Fielding planned to take the entire platoon because of the increased probability of encountering larger numbers of enemy troops roaming near the Ho Bo Woods. Rick Shields, Jim Overbey and I double-checked the men while we prepared for the ambush to make sure their weapons were clean and they had all their gear and plenty of ammunition.

Only Lieutenant Fielding was happy about being near the Ho Bo Woods. We had a lot of brave and dependable men in the third platoon but most of us didn't welcome enemy action. In fact, most of us were happy to see a day pass without any action because that meant we had one less day to survive before we could go home. While most of us weren't looking forward to going out on the ambush, Lieutenant Fielding couldn't wait to move out.

We left before five o'clock that afternoon and headed north toward a trail almost two klicks away that was supposedly heavily used by the NVA and VC. We moved cautiously through the heavy vegetation, continually looking around for movement and hoping to avoid walking into an enemy ambush. I didn't like what we were doing and was prepared for a long night.

We safely arrived near the ambush site well before dark and settled into a concealed area. Shortly before dark, we moved toward the trail to set up the ambush. We split into two groups with Lieutenant Fielding and Jim Overbey in charge of fourteen men who set up along the well-defined trail and Rick Shields and I in charge of eight men to cover the back side of the ambush site. We quietly settled into two half-circle positions to form a perimeter. Several men stayed on guard while we took off our gear and set out claymores. We placed one machine gun team at each end of the forward position to lay down fire in either direction along the trail.

While we settled into our positions and arranged our gear for the night, unbeknownst to anyone, Lieutenant Fielding had slipped away and boldly walked a short distance down the trail to the west to set up a trip flare. If someone came along the trail they would trip the wire and ignite the bright flare to expose themselves. It wasn't something we routinely did on ambushes. To make matters worse, Lieutenant Fielding hadn't told any of us he had gone out to set up the trip flare.

Rick Shields made a final check of our position and then walked toward the trail for a final observation before dark. Rick noticed Lieutenant Fielding kneeling beside the trail and then saw him get up and turn toward the forward position. Rick also noticed Lieutenant Fielding wasn't carrying his rifle. At the same instant Rick heard noises coming from the trail behind Lieutenant Fielding. Three VC were approaching with a dozen or more following behind. The VC hadn't seen Rick, but they had spotted Lieutenant Fielding and raised their weapons toward him. Lieutenant Fielding was defenseless and in a real predicament. The rest of third platoon still wasn't aware of Lieutenant Fielding on the trail or of the approaching VC.

Without hesitation, Rick Shields opened fire with his M-16 on automatic, spraying rounds and hitting three of the VC. He turned and yelled, "Blow some claymores! There's gooks down the trail!" As he started running back toward our ambush site.

When Rick opened fire, Lieutenant Fielding turned and saw the VC and immediately hit the ground. However, most of the men in the forward position hadn't seen Lieutenant Fielding and didn't know he was near the trail in front of them.

The sound of loud explosions filled the air as several men detonated their claymores spraying a hail of BBs toward the trail and stirring up a huge cloud of smoke and dust with each explosion. Rick was knocked to the ground by the back blast from one of the claymores. One of the guys helped Rick up and pulled him inside our perimeter. Rick was dazed but otherwise was uninjured.

I jumped when I heard Rick firing and immediately grabbed my M-16 while surveying the backside of our site looking for any signs of trouble. I didn't see any movement, but after I heard Rick yell, I told the men beside me to throw some hand grenades.

I yelled at Red, who was kneeling beside me, "Detonate some claymores!"

I ducked as two claymores blasted in front of us and then rose to my knees to throw a hand grenade into the near darkness. The men facing the trail were firing their weapons and throwing hand grenades at the enemy who were probably struggling to find cover as our machine gun team on the left opened fire, filling the air with orange tracers. We all scrambled for cover from the enemy rifle fire we were receiving while we unleashed everything we had on the VC. I could barely hear myself as I yelled to the men near me to continue spraying the area with M-16 fire and to throw more hand grenades.

When I saw Rick in the middle of our site, I crawled over to him and huddled together for a few seconds as the gunfire continued.

He yelled, "3- 6 is out near the trail!"

"What was he doing out there?" I yelled back.

Rick took a few seconds to catch his breath and then yelled, "I don't know, but we have to find him." Rick and I moved to the forward position and asked the men if they had seen 3-6. No one had.

Rick and I quickly told Jim Overbey and the rest of the men that Lieutenant Fielding was in front of them and to be careful with their fire. The firefight continued with the thunderous noise of rifles and machine guns and exploding hand grenades. We hadn't sustained any casualties, except possibly for Lieutenant Fielding. After a few minutes Rick yelled, "Cease fire!" and we held our breaths, waiting to see what might happen. There was silence.

Then someone heard moaning in the tall grass beside the trail. We believed it was Lieutenant Fielding. Rick looked at me and said he would go find him.

"All right," I said, "We'll give cover you."

Rick slowly crawled through the tall grass while the rest of us stood watch, our hearts pounding, and our weapons ready to fire. After a couple of very intense minutes, Rick found Lieutenant Fielding and pulled him back inside our ambush site with the aid of two other men. Lieutenant Fielding had been hit with BBs from our claymores and continued to groan in pain. Doc Jackson immediately checked the extent of his injuries. The front of Lieutenant Fielding's fatigue shirt was soaked with blood. He had serious chest and abdominal wounds.

Doc said if 3-6 (Lieutenant Fielding) was going to survive, we had to get him out of there ASAP. Bill Casey, one of our RTOs, spoke on the radio with Captain Dalton at Hunsley advising him of our situation. Casey told Doc Jackson a medevac was on the way.

While most of the men watched for movement around the perimeter, Rick, Jim Overbey and I huddled together and agreed that as soon as Lieutenant Fielding was evacuated we needed to get out of there. We were vulnerable if there were any VC still alive. Trying to make a sweep along the trail at night was too risky. Although we believed we had inflicted heavy casualties on the VC, more of them could be out there in the darkness planning their next move. We didn't want to stay any longer than we had to. We quickly spread the word for the men to start packing up to move out after we evacuated 3-6.

The men began retrieving the claymores that hadn't been fired by following the wire from each detonator to find the claymores, while others stood guard. We didn't want to leave any claymores out there to fall into enemy hands. The combination of the darkness and heavy vegetation made it impossible to see more than a few feet and made it scary as hell out there.

Doc continued to do all he could for Lieutenant Fielding, who was semi-conscious and having trouble breathing. Doc was anxious to get him on a medevac. The rest of us began gathering our gear while glancing into the darkness beyond our perimeter. Amazingly, no one else had been hit. We had been lucky.

The Cobra gunship our new CO Captain Dalton had called in began circling overhead. We identified the center of our site with a strobe light placed inside an upside-down helmet. Putting the strobe light in a helmet made it visible from the air but minimized the light directly around us to limit exposing ourselves to the enemy. After the pilot acknowledged our position, we took cover while the gunship fired several rockets around our position and then circled to unleash a barrage of machine gun fire before the medevac dropped in to pick up Lieutenant Fielding. With the Cobra gunship circling overhead we expanded our perimeter and the medevac landed on the back side of our ambush site. We carefully placed our badly injured leader on a litter and loaded him aboard the medevac.

While the medevac flew off toward Cu Chi, Rick Shields remained in touch with the CO at Hunsley. Captain Dalton wanted us to work our way back to the patrol base if we could. It would be another dangerous trip, but we had to move. The enemy knew where we were; the longer we stayed the more danger we could be in.

Rick asked our Chieu Hoi, Hue to help lead us back to Hunsley. Hue was more familiar with the area than the rest of us and was the best man to take the lead. In a few minutes everyone was ready. Hue, with Rick Shields right behind, led the column through the rear of the ambush site and away from the trail. We simply played the odds by moving away from where we knew the enemy had been and hoped any remaining VC hadn't circled around to our rear to wait for us.

Rick wanted me to bring up the rear of the column to keep guys moving and ensure we didn't lose anyone. He kept RTO Bill Casey with him and I had Dennis Schultz with me to maintain communications.

We were moving through heavy vegetation in strange territory, requiring us to walk slowly. We stayed close together to maintain contact with each other to prevent guys from getting lost, especially those of us at the rear of the column. I glanced behind me periodically but couldn't see anything. It would be my luck; some enemy soldiers would surprise us and start picking us off from the rear.

Rick stopped the column periodically to give us a short breather. Rick and I kept in touch by radio to make sure everyone was still together. He also had to work with Hue to determine where we were and adjust our course to keep us moving toward the patrol base. We were all hot, sweaty and dead tired, but willingly kept moving for nearly two hours until we finally reached Patrol Base Hunsley. We had taken a fairly direct route going out in the daylight, but I'm sure we weaved back and forth many times on our way back in. But we finally made it.

The first thing most of us did when we reached our bunkers was sit down, catch our breath and chug some water from our canteens. I took off my gear and breathed a sigh of relief that we had safely made it back to Hunsley.

Rick briefed the CO. Captain Dalton shook his head when Rick explained what Lieutenant Fielding did. The CO told Rick we would go back to the ambush site in the morning to see what we might find. Rick also learned that Lieutenant Fielding made it to the 12th Evac in Cu Chi alive, but he was in serious condition. While I settled into my bunker later that night, I thought about how lucky we had been. We had a firefight with over a dozen VC and our own claymores had caused our only casualty.

The next morning the entire company packed up and returned to the ambush site. The Third Herd led the RIF, because we knew the way and also wanted to be the first to see what was left out there. As we neared the trail, Captain Dalton had the other platoons fan out to our left and right while the third platoon walked through the ambush site and moved along the trail. It looked like we had won the battle. We spotted several VC bodies on or near the trail and eventually found a total of ten bodies grotesquely lying on the ground. We had obviously surprised them before they had time to react and return significant fire. We confiscated several weapons, ammunition and a few supplies.

We expanded our search and followed a couple of blood trails that turned into dead ends. The surviving VC likely pulled back shortly after we opened up on them and didn't stay around for a long battle. We spent the rest of the day moving west along the trail trying to trace the route we believed the VC may have taken, but found no more signs of the enemy and didn't encounter any enemy troops.

Serving as an infantryman in Vietnam, I knew casualties were inevitable. Lieutenant Fielding had only been with us for two months, but I felt a big void without him. He had become a good friend to many of us; it took a while for us to adjust to his absence. While there was a strong bond of comradeship among most of us in the Third Herd, I also saw a hesitation by some men to build too-strong a friendship with any one man because they knew on any day that person could be gone. About a week later we learned

Lieutenant Fielding was stable enough to be flown back to *the World* for further treatment and rehabilitation. We would probably never see him again.

The CO appointed Rick Shields as our acting platoon leader until a new lieutenant was assigned. Jim Overbey and I informally shared platoon sergeant duties in addition to leading our respective squads. We continued our daily RIFs and nightly ambushes out of Patrol Base Hunsley for a few more days without any significant encounters. We knew the VC had strongholds scattered across the area, but they were well concealed in areas with thick vegetation. They knew if their complexes were spotted from the air or by ground troops, they would be immediately destroyed by air strikes and artillery fire. Often those enemy fortresses were found simply by chance.

While my tour in Vietnam continued, I realized the decided advantage we had simply because we were resupplied almost daily. The NVA and VC normally had to live day-to-day to find food and water. They maintained some central supply locations, but most often stored food or supplies in tunnels, wells or other hiding spots, which they used when they came across their stashes. We often found small wire mesh cages with a spring-loaded door they used to trap rats to eat. I would have to be awfully hungry to eat one of those ugly, black rats that were the size of a small cat. When we found a rat trap we shot the rat, if there was one inside, and destroyed the trap.

One day we found a bag of supplies in a tunnel and I dumped the contents on the ground. There were some clothes and a green hammock. I stuffed the hammock into one of the big pockets on the side of my fatigue pants. I thought it would be fun knowing that the NVA or VC soldier who hid the hammock would return to find it missing. I slept in that hammock for a couple weeks until one of the ropes broke while I was sleeping. I dropped to the floor of our bunker with a thud, leaving me with a sore butt for a couple days. Maybe that enemy soldier got the last laugh after all?

We saw one good change in early November. The monsoon season that generally lasted from May through October was over. The daily rains had stopped and the countryside was slowly drying out. We could go out on an ambush at night and not get soaked and didn't have to worry any longer about a bunker springing a leak. That was the good news. The bad news was the enemy would be planting more booby-traps as the countryside dried out. Additionally, the skies were normally sunny all day long, making the afternoons hot and muggy and our daily RIFs even more uncomfortable. I normally wore my fatigue shirt with the sleeves rolled up to my biceps to stay as cool as possible and many of the guys started carrying a second canteen of water.

One afternoon in mid-November we were working our way across a fairly open area on our way back to Patrol Base Delta. Agent Orange had been sprayed across much of the surrounding country-side, making it desolate and dry. It had been an uneventful day while the third platoon led the RIF through a grassy area. I was the third man walking in the right column when Rick Shields, who was right behind me, suddenly yelled, "Everybody stop!" We all knelt down and looked around for signs of trouble.

Rick then shouted, "There's a booby trap here!" As he cautiously backed away from where he had been standing.

We all looked around for others. Where there was one booby trap there sometimes were more. Rick notified the CO by radio what he had found and wanted the demolitions guys to move up. Rick had spotted a shiny reflection from something on the ground. When he looked closer he realized it was a booby-trapped mortar round.

The men took watchful steps while we formed a defensive perimeter. After carefully surveying the device, Poof and Puff carefully placed a stick of C-4 explosive beside it. The exploding C-4 would detonate the mortar round. While the C-4 was being set, Rick and I talked.

The booby trap was alongside the path our point man, Vic Ortega, the second man, Jim "Red" Mincey and I had just taken. Each of us had stepped near that booby trap without seeing it, and fortunately, without detonating it. My heart pounded when I thought about the disaster that could have happened. That mortar round likely would have killed anyone who detonated it and wounded others nearby. If

Vic, Red and I were cats with nine lives, we had each used up one of those lives that afternoon. After the entire company moved forward, the fuse leading to the blasting cap was lit. A couple minutes later a loud explosion sent a cloud of dust and smoke into the air behind us. I kept walking, trying to forget I could have died back there.

We walked safely back into Delta later that afternoon. I took off my gear, feeling very thankful. I checked my M-16 before I hung it on a rack. It was still clean. Most of the guys were pretty diligent about keeping their weapons clean but I periodically checked their rifles to be sure. I looked at the M-16 hanging next to mine. It was filthy. The firing chamber was covered with dirt and sand. That rifle would likely have fired only a few rounds before it would have jammed.

I asked whose rifle it was. PFC Randal Johnson walked up and said it was his.

I said, "Look at your rifle, it's filthy. Clean it now and keep it clean."

Johnson wasn't the most ambitious guy in the platoon and bordered on being lazy. Johnson who was much bigger than I, said, "You can't make me clean it."

After my close encounter that afternoon, I was in no mood for his bull crap. If someone else's life had depended upon Johnson being able to fire his rifle, they would have been in trouble. I put my face close to his and said, "Listen, Johnson, if I can't make you, I know twenty other guys who will. Understand?"

Johnson understood. He grabbed his rifle and began cleaning it. He knew all I had to do was to show his filthy rifle to the rest of the guys. They would be all over him in an instant.

Although we had the most dangerous job in the military, the incident with Johnson's dirty rifle reminded me of how lax some men could get. We all knew the risks of falling asleep while pulling guard, but some guys still fell asleep. Some days were boring while drudging across the countryside, so we had to remind each other to stay alert, because in a careless moment any of us could trip a booby trap.

I am sure many GIs were either wounded or killed because someone failed to abide by the rules of combat they learned during their training and that were reinforced after they arrived in Vietnam.

I knew I couldn't prevent all casualties in the Third Herd, but I would do my best to ensure casualties were not caused by someone's negligence.

It had been nearly two weeks since we lost Lieutenant Fielding and we still hadn't been assigned a new platoon leader, but that wasn't a big deal. Everyone was comfortable with Rick Shields leading the platoon, while Jim Overbey and I worked with Rick to manage the men. We knew that most every man in the platoon could be relied upon to do his job when the bullets started flying without waiting for orders. The strong bond of comradeship that had developed among the men in the Third Herd made the job of running the platoon much easier.

A few days later, the third platoon was again leading the RIF on a hot and humid November afternoon as we walked along a path that led through a hedgerow. Sergeant John Matson, who was near the front of the right column, walked up to the opening in the hedgerow, and suddenly, BOOM! There was an explosion near him. Everyone hit the ground and looked around holding their weapons ready. I looked forward and saw a thick cloud of purple smoke rising from the ground by the opening in the hedgerow. What had happened?

I walked forward and saw Sergeant Matson lying on the ground. He had been wounded by what was likely a booby-trapped hand grenade. The dense cloud of smoke was coming from a smoke grenade he was carrying that had been hit by shrapnel and was spewing a purple fog into the air. Someone pulled the smoke grenade from Matson's gear and tossed it in the distance.

Doc Jackson ran forward and knelt at Matson's side. Doc was a gutsy medic who willingly put his butt on the line whenever one of the Third Herd went down. A booby trap had peppered Matson's body with shrapnel, but it looked like he would survive. Doc bandaged Matson's wounds and gave him a shot of morphine to ease his pain while he waited for a medevac. Jim Overbey and I told the men to keep a close eye out for other booby traps as we guided them to set up a perimeter around Doc Jackson and Sergeant Matson.

Bob Emery had also been hit in his right arm by a small piece of shrapnel, but it was a minor injury. Fortunately, no one else had been wounded because the men were well-spread-out when the booby trap exploded. The enemy often secured a hand grenade near the ground, attached a wire to the pin holding the handle, and then attached the trip wire to another object a few feet away. When someone snagged the trip wire with their foot, it would pull the pin releasing the handle from the grenade. In a few seconds it would detonate. One of the men in front of Matson had unknowingly tripped the wire, which would have been nearly impossible to see in the tall grass that covered the area.

RTO Dennis Schultz talked with the medevac pilot and then yelled "Pop smoke!" to help guide the Huey into our position. We hadn't seen any signs of the enemy, but we knew the sound of the exploding booby trap had drawn the attention of anyone in the area. Most medevac choppers had a big red cross painted on the nose and on each side and, theoretically, should have been off limits to the enemy. But the NVA and VC fought the war with no rules, and they would shoot a medevac down if they had a chance.

We kept a watchful eye around us as the medevac landed and John Matson was swiftly carried aboard on a litter. Bob Emery hopped aboard on his own. In less than a minute the chopper was off to Cu Chi. Just like that, we were down two men. I expected Bob Emery to return in a few days, but I doubted we would see John Matson again. He had been in the field just over a month and was already going home. It wasn't an easy way to get a trip home, but he was going home alive. As the chopper flew off into the distance we gathered Matson's and Emery's gear and cautiously moved on. Bob Emery was my machine gunner, so his assistant, Mike Stark, instantly became my gunner.

The following day we were flown from Patrol Base Delta back to Firebase Patton to again work out of there for a while. After we settled into our bunkers we were told we had to clean the place up because Vice President Agnew was flying out for a visit. He had traveled to Vietnam to discuss Peace Talk alternatives with the South

Vietnamese officials. The brass wanted to show him one of their newest state-of-the-art firebases. Patton was it. The vice president would fly out on a chopper the next morning.

We spent several hours on details around the firebase, picking up the trash (even cigarette butts) and fixing up anything that looked in need of repair. The brass wanted the firebase spic-and-span for the Vice President's arrival. Top was having a heyday. He was walking around barking out orders to fix this and pick up that and cussed up a storm at anyone who wasn't moving fast enough for his satisfaction.

Early on the morning of the Vice President's arrival we were each given a new helmet cover. We were told to put new covers on our helmets and to wear our helmets during Agnew's visit. A helmet cover was a camouflage cloth cover that fit over our steel helmets, to eliminate the glare from the metal helmet. Most of us wore the original helmet cover that we had been issued with our helmets when we arrived in country. Those covers had been dulled by constant exposure to the sun and many of the men had written slogans or drawn designs on them, many of which were derogatory or offensive. So, we all removed our old helmet covers and put on the new ones to look presentable for the occasion. We were to be clean-shaven and were told to wear the cleanest jungle fatigues we could find.

Shortly before eleven o'clock that morning one shiny, OD-green Huey landed on the landing pad near the aid station. Vice President Agnew stepped out, dressed in a suit, white shirt and tie. I hadn't seen anyone in a suit and tie since I left *the World*. Secret Service agents in suits and ties and a couple other military officers in jungle fatigues also hopped off the chopper.

Our battalion commander met Agnew at the landing pad and escorted his group to the headquarters bunker. While the Vice President was in the headquarters bunker we gathered around a small speaking platform that had been built early that morning. Fifteen minutes later Vice President Agnew and his entourage walked to the platform. The battalion commander introduced the Vice President and we gave him a hospitable round of applause, although many of the men weren't necessarily happy to see him. At least we weren't out on a RIF that morning, which was something to be pleased about.

The Vice President spoke for a few minutes saying how proud he was of us and what a great job we were doing in fighting the war. He concluded his speech with a statement I will never forget. He said, "And I wish I could take you all home with me."

That statement earned him a loud cheer from us GIs, although we all knew most of us were a long way from going home. After his speech he shook hands with every man who wanted to shake his hand. I slowly moved forward with the large group of men and eventually shook the hand of Vice President Spiro Agnew.

A short while later the pilot of the shiny Huey started the engine and the chopper carrying the Vice President lifted off the landing pad at Patton and flew off into the distance.

Vice President Agnew had taken a few minutes to walk around the interior of the firebase and checked out one of the artillery batteries, but he hadn't come near any of the perimeter bunkers. We had worked for hours and he didn't even notice. Oh, well, at least the place was cleaned up for us to enjoy. After the Vice President left most of us took off the new helmet cover issued that morning and put our old one back on. Many of the new helmet covers issued earlier that day ended up in the trash before nightfall. What a waste to look spit and polished for the Vice President, which was far from the reality of our daily lives.

The next morning we put on our gear and headed out the east side of Patton to begin a fairly short, and what turned out to be uneventful RIF. But we found a surprise when we returned. There had been a fire. One of the wooden latrines near our bunkers had burned down. The Army's way of dealing with the waste was to cut a metal drum in half and slide it under each hole in the outhouse. Each morning one or two men in the company would stay back in the firebase for latrine duty to pull out the drums filled with the smelly waste and burn it. They would pour diesel fuel into each drum, mix it in with the waste, light it and let it burn. The waste would burn down into a little pile that was then buried near the outskirts of the perimeter. Although it wasn't pleasant duty, guys knew latrine duty was safer than going out on a RIF.

One of the men who had latrine duty that day apparently hadn't pulled one barrel far enough away from the latrine. After lighting the fuel he moved on to another latrine. When he returned he found the latrine in flames. There was no fire department to call while the latrine continued to burn until there was nothing left but a pile of rubble. Fortunately, a few days later a supply of lumber was delivered. Several men from Alpha Company built a new latrine and were back in business.

During that stay at Patton, Alpha Company was assigned to a group of bunkers on the northeast side of Patton. In addition to entering and exiting through the main gate on the west side of Patton, we used two other paths. There was a path on the southeastern perimeter leading to the landing zone, and a second path near our bunkers on the northeast perimeter was used to leave or return from RIFs or ambushes in that direction. The two paths went through sections of the concertina wire that were opened during the day to make our way in and out. At night, we pulled the concertina wire across the path.

Early one evening we were standing outside our bunker when a group of men from another company walked by on their way to pull an ambush. We waved and said, "Be careful," as they passed by and walked toward the northeast perimeter path near our bunker. Suddenly, BOOM! An explosion near the edge of the perimeter destroyed the evening's peace and quiet. We were all startled and instinctively ducked down.

Some of the men started running into our bunker when someone yelled, "Incoming!"

I then heard someone yelling, "Medic!"

As some of the men from the other platoon walked back inside the perimeter one of them said one of their men hit a booby trap. I couldn't believe it.

Doc Jackson pushed men aside, trying to get to the wounded men who were near the last row of concertina wire on the outskirts of our perimeter where the explosion occurred. The two seriously wounded men were screaming in pain while Doc Jackson and the ambush patrol's medic attended to them. The seriously wounded men were soon carried inside the perimeter and placed on litters that had been brought over from the aid station. Two other men with less serious shrapnel wounds were helped back inside the perimeter. All the injured men were taken to the aid station and loaded onto a medevac that landed a few minutes later. While walking back toward our bunkers Doc Jackson told me he thought one of the men might lose his right leg. A booby-trapped hand grenade had detonated right next to him.

Most of us didn't think about looking for booby traps close to the perimeter of Patton. We had all walked that same path many times and thought nothing of it. Normally the only non-GIs who came near the perimeter at Patton were kids, who sometimes wandered around the perimeter playing or looking for whatever they could find. It was unlikely an adult civilian could have walked up unnoticed. That meant one of the kids who we often tossed candy to must have set the booby trap. We couldn't even trust the kids any longer.

Although I felt bad for the wounded men, I also knew that if those men hadn't used the path that night, one of us would have gone out there later to pull the concertina wire across the path and would likely have detonated that hand grenade.

The following morning we gathered on the LZ (landing zone) outside the eastern perimeter to wait for choppers to take us up north for a RIF. I noticed a lone chopper flying from the north and then suddenly turn east. I wasn't sure what the pilot was doing, but several of us watched him circle a cluster of trees 500 meters northeast of the LZ. Suddenly, a door gunner opened fire with his M-60 machine gun. The pilot radioed that two VC had been seen in those trees. While the lone chopper continued to circle the trees, the choppers scheduled to take us out on the RIF were arriving from the south. The CO yelled, "We're going over to those trees!"

The third platoon hopped the first lift of choppers, and in a matter of seconds were dropped near the cluster of trees. We quickly spread out to surround the trees, cautiously watching for any movement. If they were alive we didn't want them to escape. The rest of the company soon arrived on choppers to join us.

When we swept through the area we came upon two VC lying near the center of the cluster of trees. They were both dead. One soldier had an AK-47 and the other had a .45 automatic pistol and two American hand grenades. They had apparently climbed up a tree in an attempt to take a few shots at us while we were on the LZ, or shoot at the choppers when they flew near that cluster of trees. The choppers often came in directly from Cu Chi, which was southeast of Patton, to pick us up. That meant they took off to the north directly over or close to that cluster of trees. The pistol wouldn't have had long-range capability, but AK-47 rounds could have damaged a Huey as it flew above those trees. A Huey had been hit by rifle fire a couple of days earlier shortly after it took off from Patton. Fortunately, the pilot was able to maintain enough control of the chopper to return and make a safe emergency landing at Patton. Maybe those two dead VC were the culprits.

When I looked closely at the soldier with the pistol I noticed the long hair. One of the guys reached down and ripped open the soldier's shirt. It was a woman who appeared to be in her early twenties. She was wearing a white shirt, black slacks and sandals, and looked like many of the other women we saw walking up and down the roads and trails and in the villages. Except that young woman would have tried to kill us if she had the chance.

We checked the two bodies for anything that might provide useful information and swept the surrounding area for any other signs of enemy activity. We found nothing more. However, that little incident had disrupted the plans for our scheduled RIF. Captain Dalton split up the company to conduct sweeps to the north, east and south of Patton. Although the area around Patton normally appeared peaceful, the booby trap in the wire at Patton and the two gooks in the nearby trees proved the enemy worked everywhere.

The third platoon was assigned the southern sweep. We walked three klicks southeast and then turned west shortly after noon. As we moved through an open grassy area with a few scattered bushes, we began to smell a terrible odor. The odor became even stronger as we moved west. There had to be something dead or rotten around there. We slowed our pace, searching more closely for the source of the odor.

Finally, one of the guys yelled, "There's a body over here!"

And did it stink. Men were holding their towel or the sleeve of their fatigue shirt over their noses, trying to filter out the smell. When I walked closer I saw a Vietnamese man lying under a small bush. Maggots and other bugs were crawling over his skin that had turned almost black. There was no indication of a firefight in the area; in fact, we didn't find a weapon anywhere nearby. We didn't take the time to closely examine the body because of the smell but we thought he might have been wounded by harassment and interdiction (H & I) mortar fire and crawled under the bush and died. We quickly moved on and turned north towards Patton without finding anything else out of the ordinary.

We walked past one of the artillery batteries on our way to our bunkers and waved at the artillerymen standing nearby. The artillerymen rarely left the perimeter of Patton, but they worked long hours to clean and maintain their guns and perform fire missions any time, day or night. We didn't spend much time with those guys and never really got to know them. That day one of the artillerymen asked what had happened that morning east of Patton. A few of us stopped and told them about the two VC in the trees and that one was a woman.

One of the artillerymen then told us a story about one of his friends that involved a Vietnamese woman. The man had somehow found a girlfriend in Trung Lap, the village directly north of Patton. He would leave Patton during the day to visit her and return before dark. Two weeks earlier the man left to visit his girlfriend but didn't return that evening. The next day there was still no sign of him. His buddies knew something was wrong. They finally told their CO their friend was missing in Trung Lap. A company of men was sent to search the village for the missing GI. They eventually found him.

The artillerymen were told that their friend's body had been badly mutilated during what had to have been a painful and terrifying death. It was surmised the VC discovered the GI in the village and they tortured him to death. The VC knew we would ultimately find his body and that the brutality of his death would be very demoralizing. That story was another reminder that Firebase Patton and the nearby villages and countryside really weren't as safe as we often thought.

While we prepared for another air assault mission the following morning someone asked me what date it was. I looked at the little calendar in my wallet. November 21st. We often lost track of the date. We didn't get weekends off and most holidays were just another day. We had gone on a RIF on Labor Day, and although Veterans Day had become more meaningful for all of us, it was just another workday for us. Most days in Vietnam became much like every other day as we continued our routine of RIFs and ambushes; however, no two days were identical. Each day we patrolled different areas and faced new encounters, often with discrete hazards. Most of us simply hoped and prayed we would see the sun rise each morning.

We were to fly ten miles north of Patton for a RIF. I was again one of the last men to board the chopper after making sure everyone else was aboard before we lifted off. While I sat on the floor with my feet hanging out the door I noticed most of the bomb craters that had been filled with water during the monsoon season were drying up. As we neared our remote LZ we were startled by a loud *thud* coming from the tail section of the Huey. Some of the men glanced at each other with a startled look thinking the chopper had been hit by enemy fire.

One of the pilots yelled, "Hold on!" As the chopper swayed back and forth a couple times and then continued smoothly on our flight path. The door gunners both immediately opened fire spraying the countryside on both sides with M-60 fire. I quickly slid back toward the center of the chopper floor realizing I had made myself an easy target by sitting in the doorway. I guess it wasn't my time to go.

The huge main rotor blade of each Huey that swirled directly over our heads provided the lift to get the chopper in the air. The turbine-powered engine sat overhead, just behind the main body of the chopper. The tail section led to a smaller rotor blade that rotated vertically and guided the chopper in a straight path or through turns. Bullets striking the tail section could damage the controls leading to the tail rotor and impact the pilot's ability to control the chopper. Fortunately, we descended into the LZ and landed without any difficulties.

Although we were in the boonies, the pilot kept the chopper on the ground while the door gunner behind me quickly stepped out to check the tail section of the Huey. I stayed near the chopper while the gunner walked along the tail section and then pointed to a bullet hole only a few feet back from the main section of the chopper. The door gunner gave a thumbs-up and quickly boarded the chopper. The chopper was soon back in the air with no apparent serious damage.

The Third Herd led the RIF while we searched an uninhabited area that was mostly grassland, abandoned rice paddies and small trees and hedgerows. When we came upon a lone hooch in the middle of nowhere, we cautiously walked up to it. Two men each threw a hand grenade inside. Debris from the thatched roof flew in the air and a cloud of dust rose from inside the hooch when the grenades exploded. When we checked inside it appeared to have been abandoned. We didn't find any supplies or weapons stored inside or anywhere nearby. A couple guys lit the thatched roof afire with their cigarette lighters and in a couple minutes the entire roof was burning and soon collapsed, making the hooch much less useful to the enemy.

We had been scheduled to be flown back to Patton that afternoon, but when the CO radioed the battalion command post that we had finished our RIF shortly after noon without any enemy contact or finding any signs of enemy activity. The battalion commander decided we should walk back to Patton and search additional areas on our way in. "Damn," we all thought. It was a hot, sunny afternoon and we had all worked up a sweat, humping through the boonies that morning. And then we had to walk another seven klicks back to Patton.

Vic Ortega was our point man for the right column and James "Red" Mincey was the pace man behind him. Half of the third platoon, including Rick Shields and me, were behind them while the remainder of the platoon followed Ed Leberski, the point man for the left column. We were over halfway back when we came upon two long hedgerows with a clearing in between them. The two columns began closing together while Vic Ortega and Ed Leberski slowly approached the clearing. Vic passed through first with Red following a several steps behind.

Ed Leberski suddenly stopped and yelled, "Hold up, Red!"

Red looked at Ed just before an explosion directly in front of Red hurled him to the ground. The blast sent us all instinctively to the ground.

There was only that single explosion. No gunfire or other explosions. Rick Shields, who was still acting platoon leader said, "Set up a perimeter, Hound Dog. I'll check on Red."

Doc Jackson, who had been walking behind me, had rushed forward to care for Red, who was the only man who had been wounded. With the perimeter in place, I joined Doc and Rick who were kneeling beside Red. I didn't see any major visible wounds but could see blood around Red's neck.

But Red was having serious trouble breathing and was in a desperate panic as he gasped for air. Doc checked Red for other injuries while Rick Shields tried to calm him down.

I knelt by Red's left side and lowered my head toward his and said, "Take a slow breath, Red, you'll be OK."

Red raised his left hand and I held it to give him some moral support and comfort. Red couldn't speak but kept putting his right hand by his throat, indicating he couldn't breathe, desperately hoping we could help him. Shrapnel had hit Red in the front of his neck and must have damaged his airway. Although Doc was a great medic, he didn't have any tools to open Red's airway to help him breathe. All we could do was try to keep him calm and get him to Cu Chi as soon as possible!

Bill Casey had immediately radioed for a medevac. A Huey gunship that was near our position heard the call, and the pilot radioed to ask if we wanted them to drop in and evacuate our wounded man. Casey told Doc about the nearby gunship.

Without hesitation Doc said, "Get that chopper in here now!"

I looked at Doc Jackson. I had never seen such a concerned look on his face before.

Captain Dalton had moved up into our perimeter but he stood back and let those of us in the third platoon continue to manage the scene. Doc was doing everything he could to save Red, but as the seconds passed, Red continued to frantically struggle for a breath of air while he tightly clutched my hand, frantic for help. I saw a look of desperation in Red's eyes that I had never seen before, and a look that I will never forget, while I talked to him trying to keep him calm and give him encouragement. Rick and I looked at each other helplessly but didn't say a word.

We soon heard the chopping blades as the gunship neared.

I said, "Hang in there, Red; the chopper will be here in a minute."

And it was. Someone popped smoke and the chopper landed within five minutes after Red had been hit. The gunship didn't have any litters on board, so we picked up Red and rushed him to the waiting chopper and laid him on the floor. Doc and Rick Shields hopped aboard hoping to somehow keep Red alive until they reached the 12th Evac in Cu Chi, eight miles to our southeast.

Rick yelled, "Hound Dog, you take the platoon." Which meant he wanted me to take charge.

I waved back in acknowledgement as the chopper lifted off. I knew the pilot would soon have the Huey at full throttle. Red would be at the hospital in a few minutes. As the chopper roared into the distance, I said to myself, "Hang on, Red."

We then took a few minutes to carefully search the area but found no other booby traps. The detonation sounded like another hand grenade. It appeared Vic Ortega had unknowingly tripped the wire, pulling the pin from the hand grenade, and it exploded when Red walked up to it. It was nothing sophisticated, but it had worked. It had wounded Red. Hopefully it hadn't killed him.

I talked with Ed Leberski while we searched the area. He said he had seen a reflection from something in front of Red and had yelled for him to stop, but it was too late. The grenade exploded. Ed was visibly shaken.

I put my hand on Ed's shoulder and said, "Hey, Ed, you did all you could. Don't blame yourself."

Every man in the platoon felt bad about Red being wounded and wished we could have done something to prevent it. Unfortunately, we were forced to accept that serious injury and death were the sad consequences of the war. And there was nothing that any of us could do to change that reality.

We gathered Red's gear and moved on toward Patton. I was surprised we had encountered a booby trap less than two klicks from the village of Trung Lap. Unfortunately, I was continually being reminded not to take anything for granted, and to be prepared for the worst almost anywhere. We completed the RIF that afternoon and walked through the perimeter of Patton. The men in the Third Herd were unusually quiet. We didn't know if Red was dead or alive.

An hour later Captain Dalton walked up to me near my bunker and said, "Red didn't make it. Sorry."

My heart sank. I stared into the distance for a moment, trying to comprehend what I had heard. I told the CO I would tell the men and thanked him for coming over to tell me. Captain Dalton gave me a reassuring pat on the back and walked away.

Red was only twenty years old. He had joined the Third Herd in September along with several other men. I had told Captain Branch and Captain Dalton about Red's brother dying of malaria, and they both had said they would try to get him out of the field. Unfortunately for Red, it didn't happen soon enough. I gathered the guys together. By the solemn expression on my face, they knew I had bad news.

I said, "The CO just told me Red died."

There was silence. Some of the men looked at each other and shook their heads while others dropped their heads and stared at the ground.

Someone yelled, "Those son-of-a-bitches!"

The yelling was primarily aimed at the enemy troops who planted the booby trap. But the men were also angry with the battalion CO. They knew he had made the decision for us to walk back to Patton rather than be flown back. If we had flown back to Patton, Red would still be alive.

I saw Vic Ortega turn and walk away to be by himself. Vic knew he had tripped the wire on the booby-trapped grenade. I walked over and put my hand on Vic's shoulder.

"Don't be too hard on yourself, Vic," I said,

"I know Sarge, but Red is dead because of me."

I said, "Don't feel that way Vic. The damn gooks who set the booby trap are to blame, not you."

We all knew it was nearly impossible to see trip wires and booby traps in the thick vegetation. Although none of us blamed Vic, a sense of guilt would remain with him for a long time. I took Vic off point the next day and assigned Glenn Haywood to walk point.

Doc Jackson and Rich Shields were flown back to Patton early that evening. Doc said Red died before they reached the hospital. Doc gave him mouth-to-mouth resuscitation on the way in, but they couldn't save him. Red was gone.

Rick was shaken over losing Red. He said, "Red died in my arms."

The following week was Thanksgiving. Although the sadness of Red's death remained, the rest of us were all thankful to still be alive. I thought about how random death occurred. I was walking only a few yards behind Red but I wasn't injured. Why was Red killed, not me? But what I did know, death could get any one of us on any given day. Our fate was in God's hands.

A one-day American truce was called on Thanksgiving Day giving us welcomed time off. We enjoyed a delicious turkey dinner served at Firebase Patton. Thanksgiving Day passed with guys relaxing and writing letters home. I lost a few bucks in a poker game early that afternoon.

I took time later that afternoon to write a letter to Jan Griffin. I had normally received a letter from her at least once a week since I had arrived in Vietnam, but I had only received a couple letters since early November. Jan and I hadn't made any commitments to each other before I left for Vietnam, and since she was an attractive girl, I assumed she would be asked out by other guys. That was fine; I didn't expect her to spend a year by herself waiting for me. Since I hadn't heard much from her lately, I thought she might have found someone else and had forgotten about me on the other side of the world.

I tried not to get too concerned over what Jan was doing back in Omaha. I couldn't do anything about it anyway. There weren't any pay phones next to our bunkers so I couldn't just call her. It was like most everything else in my life at that time; I had to hope and pray for the best. And besides, I still had to survive eight more months in Vietnam before I could start thinking about going home. I finished my letter to Jan and signed it, "Love and Kisses, Dick." A couple of men in the Third Herd had gotten a "Dear John" letter from their girlfriend. "Jody," was the nickname for the guy back home that hadn't been drafted and was chasing GIs' wives and girlfriends. Unfortunately, "Jody" took girls away from numerous men who were serving in Vietnam. For many GIs in Vietnam, getting letters from that special girl back home kept them going during their tour.

During the last week of November 1969, we operated out of a little patrol base several miles west of Patton. One day the third platoon went out on a short RIF by ourselves. We finished our RIF early that afternoon and stopped in a grove of trees outside a village. We planned to hold up there for a few hours and then move out to pull an ambush that night. Although the area had been relatively peaceful we set up a perimeter around the edge of the grove, and kept a few men on guard just in case.

After we settled in, most of us enjoyed a surprise experience. If there was enough water at the remote patrol bases we would hang a canvas bucket with a little showerhead on the bottom from a pole and take a quick shower; or sometimes we took turns pouring water from a five-gallon container over our heads. But that afternoon someone found a rusty bucket lying next to a well in the middle of the grove. Since none of us had taken a shower for a few days, a few men worked together to make a tripod with tree branches near the well, and then tied the rusty bucket near the top of the tripod. They attached a rope to a couple helmets and began drawing water from the well to fill the bucket. The water flowing from the holes in the bottom of the rusty bucket made a great shower. We spent the next hour taking turns keeping the water flowing while one-by-one we stripped down and took a cool shower in the middle of that grove of trees.

The causes of combat fatalities among Army troops in Vietnam are as follows: Small Arms Fire 55%; Shelling Fragments 35%; Mines and Booby Traps 7%; Other and Undetermined 3%.

➤ Corporal James "Red" Mincey was from Conway, South Carolina. He was twenty years old. Red arrived in Vietnam on September 8, 1969 and was killed by an exploding booby trap on November 21, 1969. Red's older brother John who served as a Marine had died of malaria in Vietnam in July 1968. In 1999 I contacted Red's mother and sent pictures of Red in Vietnam along with details of his death. Ironically, two weeks after I spoke with her, she passed away. It was as though she had learned how Red died and was ready to join him.

Dave Hardy (standing) and James "Red" Mincey.
The tower at Fire Support Base Patton is in the background.

Chapter 14

Christmas in Vietnam

December 1969 started on another sad note. Wop eventually got tired of taking care of the little monkey and gave it to someone back in Cu Chi. But one of the men had found a lonely young puppy during our RIF a week earlier and brought it back to become our new mascot. It was a cute little dog with a pug nose and dark brown fluffy fur. He loved to lick your face when you held him. One day shortly after the first of December, we returned to Patton and found the dog in convulsions and whining in pain. Someone found a piece of C-4 plastic explosive nearby with little teeth marks on it. The little dog must have eaten some of the C-4. We had no way to treat our suffering little friend. One of the men reluctantly fired an M-16 round into the little dog's head to put him out of his misery.

A couple of days later the Third Herd was assigned to Venice East, the small guard post south of Firebase Patton. It was a welcome relief from the hazardous daily RIFs and ambushes. It was hard for me to believe it was already December. Although some of the days and nights seemed like they would never end, in retrospect the time had gone by faster than I had imagined it would. Most importantly, I was alive. I still had a long way to go before I would be going home, but I had survived longer than some men.

The platoon also continued to undergo changes. Bob Emery had been promoted to sergeant. Mike Stark, who had been Bob's assistant machine gunner, and Doc Jackson were both reassigned back to Cu Chi, and Bill Casey moved to the CP group to become one of Captain Dalton's RTOs. Mertis Snyder became our new medic, and Larry Sutton, Doug Jansen, Hugh Hearn and Chester Sampson had been assigned to us shortly after Thanksgiving. And finally, twenty-six-year-old Second Lieutenant John Foreman arrived to become our new platoon leader. I was no longer the oldest man in the platoon. Lieutenant Foreman was from New York State and was a fairly quiet man, much different from Lieutenant Fielding. He kept a low profile while adjusting to field duty and relied on us NCOs to help him with his on-the-job-training. Several men reminded him that the duty at Venice East was far from our normal routine. I told him to enjoy it while he could.

During our second day at Venice East the focus for some of the men was women. Obviously, serving as infantrymen in Vietnam we had no social life. We were either stomping through the boonies, on an ambush or confined inside a firebase or patrol base twenty-four-hours a day. Except during our previous stand downs in Cu Chi, we normally had only a few hours at any one time to relax. Venice East was the one place where we could semi-relax and have a little fun in the field.

When the local adults and kids stopped by that morning, a couple of the guys asked for boom-boom (Vietnamese slang for sex). Most of the civilians spoke or understood little English, but they knew what boom-boom was. Two kids headed south toward the village of Bau Dieu and returned a short while later with an older woman and a young girl. The kids pointed toward the young girl and said, "Boom-boom."

I was serving as platoon sergeant because Rick Shields and Jim Overbey were both back in Cu Chi so the men asked me if they could bring the woman and younger girl into Venice East. I thought for a few seconds and then gave a hesitant "Okay" to the guys. I knew there had been women inside Venice East before. Lieutenant Foreman had been inside his bunker most of the morning reading a book but happened to step out when the woman and young girl were standing outside another bunker. He asked me what was going on. I told our new 3-6 what the men were up to, and that they had searched the woman and girl before they came inside. I said it was an unofficially condoned practice to let women come inside Venice East.

Lieutenant Foreman stood silent briefly and finally said, "All right, but you keep an eye on them."

"Yes sir," I said as the lieutenant returned to his bunker.

The men soon learned the older woman was the young girl's mother who was pimping her fourteen-year-old daughter. Some of the men were hot to trot, so to speak, and quickly negotiated a price (normally $3 to $5) with the mother and took their turn with the daughter in one of the bunkers. I didn't keep track of who shared the pleasures the young girl offered, but a few men walked around with smiles on their faces after the young girl and her mother left later that morning.

While the mother and daughter walked toward Bau Dieu I thought about how desperate that mother must have been to turn her young daughter into a prostitute. The reality was she could make much more money selling her daughter's body than she could doing anything else.

Early that afternoon a girl who looked to be in her early twenties stopped by Venice East with a thirteen-year-old girl. The older girl told the guys the young girl was *available*. Again the men asked me if they could bring the girls inside.

I sighed and said, "You guys are going to get me in trouble." I didn't know how much frolicking Lieutenant Foreman would tolerate.

"Oh, come on, Sarge," was the reply. I finally said OK and told the guys to keep a low profile and keep it quiet.

It was humorous watching some of the guys almost fall over themselves while they checked out the cute young girl, Chae, and then negotiated a price with the older girl for Chae's services. Most of those same men would have beaten the hell out of any man who would have tried to have sex with their own thirteen-year-old sister back in *the World*. But thousands of miles away in Vietnam, the drive for female companionship overcame morality issues. Many men accepted whatever was offered to them, including young teenage girls. Venereal disease (VD) was prevalent among Vietnamese prostitutes, but for infantrymen in the field, that was the least of their concerns. A shot of penicillin cured most anything a GI might pick up. VD was simply one of the hazards of the duty.

The older girl, named Sung, was attractive with long black hair. She was short and slender, like most Vietnamese women, and she spoke English fairly well. The men had told Sung I was in charge of the platoon, so she talked with me for a while that afternoon. Sung told me she and Chae lived in Saigon and had traveled to Cu Chi. That morning they had moved on to Bau Dieu where she was told some GIs up the road were looking for girls, so Sung and Chae walked to Venice East.

Late that afternoon I told the men the girls should leave. But a few minutes later, a deuce-and-a-half and a jeep stopped along the road to deliver our mail, some supplies and the evening meal. Surprisingly, I saw our CO, Captain Dalton, in the jeep. I thought, "What is he doing here?"

I turned and told the guys standing near one of the forward bunkers, "Keep the girls inside and out of sight. The CO's here!"

Lieutenant Foreman stepped out from his bunker and together we walked to the road to greet the CO. Captain Dalton had been told about Venice East but hadn't visited the compound. He had informed Lieutenant Foreman that he would stop by that afternoon. Unfortunately, our new 3-6 had not told me the CO was paying us a visit. While we stood on the road, I explained the layout of the compound to Captain Dalton and told him generally how we operated during the day and at night. The CO then wanted to walk inside and look around.

I thought, "Oh no, I'm in trouble now."

Lieutenant Foreman, who didn't know the two girls were still there, led the CO through the gate and inside Venice East. As luck would have it, Captain Dalton walked right toward the bunker the two girls were in. He kneeled down at the entrance and peeked inside. The CO spent a minute talking to the men inside while the girls lay motionless under a poncho liner inside the bunker. He then stood up and walked to the guard tower in the center of the compound. The

CO climbed the tower to check out the view and talk with one of the radar operators sitting on the platform atop the tower.

A short while later the CO decided he had seen enough and walked back to his jeep. We waved at the guys as the jeep and the deuce-and-a-half turned around and headed north towards Patton. "Whew, that was a close call," I said to myself. I knew the CO likely wouldn't have approved with us having two Vietnamese girls inside Venice East. I could have easily become Corporal Hogue that day.

But quickly, I had another problem. It would be getting dark soon. The girls would have to walk nearly a mile to Bau Dieu. I could have kicked the girls out and had them make a run for it, but they would have had to pass the ARVN compound before they entered the village. If they didn't make it to Bau Dieu before dark they would be in trouble. The men naturally wanted me to let the girls stay all night. I was reluctant because it could be my butt if the CO found out. But I also didn't want to kick them out and risk the girls getting killed if they didn't make it to Bau Dieu before dark. How would I explain that?

I finally decided to let the girls stay, but I reminded the guys we had to keep it quiet. I didn't want things to get any further out of hand than they already were. I told Bob Emery to make sure the claymores were armed and to set up the guard rotation for the night. Lieutenant Foremen had fallen asleep early and didn't know the girls were still there. I would get them out of there early the following morning.

When darkness fell we secured the perimeter and men began pulling guard duty. I peeked inside the bunker where Chae and Sung were talking with the guys while someone was fixing a place for the girls to sleep. I stepped outside and looked up at a starry sky and thought to myself, "What the hell have I let happen?" The day started simply with guys looking for girls. We then had a mother pimping her fourteen-year-old daughter who had sex with some of the guys, and later that afternoon, I had a conversation with Sung as though we were friends. And to top it off, two Vietnamese girls were spending the night inside Venice East. I chuckled to myself and shook my head in disbelief.

Later Sung stepped out from the bunker and walked up to me. She said Chae had fallen asleep. We talked for a while and then Sung put her hand on my arm and said, "I want to spend the night with you."

I was speechless. But then I thought, "How could I refuse such an offer from an attractive young woman in the middle of Vietnam?"

I put my arm around Sung and shared a few minutes of peacefulness. Sung and I then crawled inside my bunker. We lay down on my air mattress and covered ourselves with my poncho liner. While Sung snuggled close to me, I couldn't believe what was happening. We kissed while I moved one hand under her blouse and felt her warm, firm breasts as I pulled her body close to mine. As our passions quickly rose, I removed her loosely-fitting slacks and caressed her soft, warm flesh. Surprisingly, Sung whispered near my ear, "I love you, tee tee." (Tee tee is Vietnamese slang meaning a little bit).

The next morning started as normal at Venice East. I sent half the platoon out to escort the minesweeping team while the rest of us stayed at the compound to disarm the claymores and clean the place up. I told Sung that she and Chae would have to leave when the road was cleared. We all would have enjoyed having them stay longer, but I knew the girls had to leave before the old sarge got in trouble. I walked with the girls to the road a short while later and gave Sung a little hug and said good-bye when they turned and began walking toward Bau Dieu.

Later that day I talked with Willard Spivey, who had joined us in mid-October. He showed me a picture of his wife and one-year-old daughter. He was proud of them both. He said he enjoyed staying back and watching what he called the entertainment of the past day, while he remained faithful to his wife in Kentucky.

We spent three more relatively uneventful days at Venice East before we joined with the rest of our company at Patrol Base Delta. During our first night at Delta we were asked to do another first. We were to pull a company-sized ambush. We normally took twelve men on ambushes and, now and then, used a full platoon of twenty to twenty-five men. But we had never used the entire company for an ambush.

We moved fairly quickly toward the ambush site two klicks east of Delta and arrived well before dark. The company set up in a big circular perimeter near a tree line, and then moved into the site when the sun began to set. We formed a perimeter behind rice paddy dikes about sixty meters square. The site was on high ground, giving us great visibility. It looked like it would be a simple ambush. Each platoon had a designated area of responsibility where we set out our claymores and established fields of fire while the CO formed a command post in the center. We had just started guard duty when Lieutenant Foreman came over to me and said we were moving out.

I said, "What?"

The battalion commander who had planned the company-sized ambush had changed his mind. Instead, he wanted us to split up into platoon-sized ambushes. It frankly made more sense to set up three separate ambush sites, but his timing was lousy. I told Lieutenant Foreman we were asking for trouble relocating in near darkness. He didn't like it any better than I did, but we had orders to split up.

The second platoon would stay in place with Captain Dalton and his command post (CP) group while the first and third platoons moved to new sites. We quickly gathered up our claymores and gear while the men bitched and moaned about what we had to do. They knew how dangerous it was for us to be moving around in the boonies at night. It was nearly dark when we left our original ambush site and began walking 500 hundred meters north to a new site near a trail. It was completely dark when we reached our new ambush site. We set up in another rice paddy with most of the men spread along a dike, facing a rise to the north toward what we believed was the trail. We set out our claymores and settled in again.

I was sleeping between guard shifts, when someone shook me and said, "Hound Dog, there's VC out there!" I quickly grabbed a starlight scope and saw three figures walking east and away from us in the distance about 100 meters away. I almost told the men to fire some claymores, but the VC were beyond the effective range of our claymores. I whispered, "No claymores, don't fire."

We could have opened fire with our rifles and machine guns, but it would have been tough trying to hit anyone that far away in the dark. I hated to let the VC get away, but I knew we didn't have a realistic chance of getting them. In the darkness we had established our site too far away from the trail. I quickly told Lieutenant Foreman what happened, and we called in a fire mission to have several mortar rounds fired northeast of our position where we believed the trail led, hoping to nail those enemy troops.

I was on guard in one of the forward positions when daylight slowly began to appear on the eastern horizon. One of the men in the rear position crawled toward me and said there was movement to our back side. I crawled to the rear position and looked out. I could see several figures and again almost told the men to open fire. But then I recognized a GI helmet in the dim light. It must have been the first platoon. Several men were sitting up and pointing their rifles toward the moving figures in the distance.

I said, "Hold your fire! Don't shoot!" I told Bob Ryken, who had become one of our RTOs, to get on the radio and tell the first platoon to hold their fire! We were directly north of them. I knew if we could see them, they could also see us and might open fire.

Fortunately, the first platoon received Bob's message, and we didn't fire on each other. When the sun rose, we stood up and waved at men in the first platoon, wondering how we had managed to set our ambushes so close together. Somehow in the darkness, the first and third platoons had set up about 100 meters apart. If we had popped our ambush on the enemy troops walking along the trail during the night, the first platoon could have thought we were the enemy firing on them. The first platoon might have opened fire on us and we naturally would have fired back at them. It was frightening to think that we could have annihilated each other before we knew what was happening.

A few nights later most of the company set up in a circular defensive position with Captain Dalton and his CP group west of Firebase Patton. I took eleven men to set up an ambush about one klick to the northwest while half of the second platoon moved southwest to set up an ambush. We established a perimeter in a holding area surrounded by trees and hedgerows on three sides before moving to our site that was 50 meters southwest near some rice paddies. I placed our machine gun team facing east toward a small trail that was lined with hedgerows on either side. We had only been there for a few minutes when Wop began firing his M-60 down the trail. I crouched down and rushed beside Wop. Two other men on each side of Wop were firing their M-16s towards the trail.

Wop stopped firing for a few seconds and told me he had seen two gooks walking toward him as he pointed down the trail directly in front of him. "OK," I replied and patted Wop on the back.

"Open fire!" I yelled to the men on our eastern perimeter and pointed down the trail.

We covered the area to the east with M-16 fire and fired several M-79 grenades down the trail, while Wop's M-60 blasted rounds across the area. We had received only brief initial return fire that hadn't hit any of us. A minute later, RTO Bob Ryken scurried up to me and said rounds were landing near the CP group.

I immediately yelled, "Cease fire! Cease fire!" When all was quiet I asked Bob what was going on. He said the CP group radioed they were getting stray rounds from us. The CP group should have been nearly 800 meters south of us and beyond the range of the M-16, which was 500 meters. But Wop might have sprayed some M-60 rounds to the south. An M-60 machine gun round could travel up to 1,000 meters. Fortunately, we hadn't hit any of our own men.

I told Captain Dalton over the radio that we had spotted two VC on a trail. The CO wanted us to walk down the trail to conduct a search. I told him there were hedgerows on both sides of the trail, limiting our visibility. Since it was getting dark, I didn't want to walk into an ambush if the two VC were still alive or if there were others we hadn't seen. The CO reluctantly agreed. We would return to his location.

"Oh, great," I thought. "Here we go stomping around in the dark again." But I didn't have time to worry about what else might happen.

We had revealed ourselves to anyone in the area and needed to get out of there. I quickly told the men we were moving back to the CP group. I pointed straight south and told our point man Glenn Haywood that was where I wanted him to lead us. I then noticed a new guy named Ben Carlson. He hadn't been near the trail and I don't believe he had fired his M-16, but he was scared to death and wasn't moving. I shook him and said, "Hey, Carlson, we're moving out!"

He looked at me with a blank stare and then jumped up to join the rest of the men who were forming a column behind Glenn Haywood. Carlson had been carrying our starlight scope, but he walked away, leaving it on the ground. I grabbed the scope and carried it with me. I would talk with Carlson the next morning.

After I knew all the men had joined the column, I moved forward behind Haywood and helped him guide us away from the trail and trees and into an open area in the middle of some rice paddies. After we walked nearly 200 meters it was completely dark. I told Haywood to stop. I contacted Captain Dalton on the radio and asked him to call in some mortar fire along the trail hoping to hit anyone who might still be out there. We then slowly navigated our way toward the command post as mortar rounds exploded in the distance behind us. After we reached the CP group we settled in with them for the remainder of what was an uneventful night.

Early the next morning the third platoon led the company back to the trail where we had opened fire on the VC. We searched the area and found one sandal and a blood trail, but no bodies. If we had killed or wounded anyone, others must have carried them away. We walked back to Patton without finding any other enemy signs.

That evening Dennis Schultz was talking with some guys near his bunker when he started waving his arms and yelling things like, "I've got to get out of here! I know I'm going to get killed and leave Linda (his wife) and my kid alone."

Some of the guys tried to calm Schultz down, but he kept pushing them aside and continued yelling about getting killed. Schultz had arrived in country that past summer and was one of our radio/telephone operators (RTOs). Doc Snyder walked up to me and said we had better get him out of there.

Doc Snyder and Larry Sutton each grabbed Schultz by an arm and walked him to the aid station. Dennis Schultz was flown back to Cu Chi and later assigned to duty there. He never rejoined the third platoon.

Most of us didn't think about it every day, but our courage was tested when we donned our gear, slapped on our helmet and grabbed our weapon to move out on that day's mission, not knowing what our fate might be. I'm not saying men like Dennis Schultz weren't courageous, but the daily stress of combat took a toll on all of us in varying degrees. That continual stress broke Dennis Schultz that day.

That evening Lieutenant Foreman gave us the news concerning our RIF the next day. We were flying to the Ho Bo Woods to sweep through an area of suspected enemy bunker complexes, and to make things worse, the area was known to be loaded with booby traps and land mines. Although we knew the NVA and VC planted booby traps and land mines across much of South Vietnam, we were rarely told during our briefings that an area was specifically known to have booby traps and land mines.

Knowing we might encounter a land mine or booby trap most anywhere was frustrating, because we were denied the basic right of a soldier, the opportunity to fight back, because there normally were no enemy troops around when a device was detonated.

The following morning, December 17, 1969, I walked to the LZ at Patton to wait for choppers. While I checked to ensure everyone was present, I noticed our Chieu Hoi, Hue, who served as our scout, wasn't there. The Chieu Hois were given considerable latitude with their duties and often would come and go as they pleased. Hue sometimes left for a few days saying he was going to visit his family. Some of us had also noticed Hue sometimes just didn't go out with us on a RIF. We finally figured out that if Hue knew we were going into a particularly hazardous area, like the Ho Bo Woods, he would simply disappear. Knowing Hue wasn't on the LZ that morning wasn't comforting after learning his logic for not being there.

A short while later a lift of Hueys flew us to the west-central part of the Ho Bo Woods. We landed at a site that remained peaceful while we organized ourselves and headed north on the RIF led by the third platoon. We first walked through an area of mostly tall grass that had dried out after the monsoon rains had ceased. There were scattered trees and bushes in the area, but it was pretty easy walking.

We then came upon the area of suspected bunker complexes. The terrain was covered with tall grass, thick hedgerows and bushes and trees. It looked like a nearly solid eight-foot wall of vegetation with no identifiable trails into the area. It was an ideal hiding spot for enemy bunkers. We stopped and called the CO to get his approval to fire some M-79 grenades into the area hoping to detonate any booby traps that might be along our intended path. We fired nearly a dozen grenades and didn't hear any secondary explosions, Captain Dalton said, "That's enough, let's move out."

Glenn Haywood led the right column, followed by Willard Spivey, who would have a difficult time trying to count paces walking through the heavy vegetation. Bob Emery fell in behind Spivey, and I followed Bob. Wop, my machine gunner, and Hugh Hearn, Wop's assistant gunner, fell in behind me. Carl Seals led the left column that I could barely see through the trees and thick brush. We had to walk slowly and stay close together to maintain sight of each other while we wound through and around large hedgerows and trees.

We had struggled through the area for less than ten minutes when BOOM! A huge explosion in front of me shook the ground under my feet. I instinctively hit the ground and felt my heart pounding, not knowing what had happened. The explosion had made a tremendous sound that left my ears ringing. The large cloud of dirt and debris that had been thrown into the air by the force of the explosion rained down upon us. We had hit something big.

There were no more explosions or gunfire. The sudden silence was almost ghostly. My sweaty face was covered with dirt as I raised my head and looked around. I only saw Bob Emery in front of me and

Wop directly behind me. I heard someone behind me yell, "Medic!" I turned and motioned for Wop to move up toward me and told him to cover Bob and me as we moved forward to see what had happened. I stood up and walked forward beside Bob, and saw him wiping blood from a cut on his left cheek. Bob said he was OK. It appeared a piece of shrapnel must have hit him.

I said, "Let's go." Bob nodded his head and followed me.

I turned the lever on my M-16 from safety to automatic and cautiously walked forward with Bob Emery behind me. I soon found Willard Spivey. His fatigue shirt was covered with blood, as he lay motionless on the ground. I motioned for Bob to stay with Spivey, while I walked forward alone about ten feet and saw Glenn Haywood.

Most of the heavy vegetation around Haywood had been blown away by the force of the explosion, creating a clearing ten feet in diameter. Haywood sat motionless near the center of a two-foot-deep crater. I didn't know if he was dead or alive. I held my finger on the trigger of my rifle while I looked around and slowly walked toward Haywood, expecting something else to happen. I didn't know where the rest of our men were. I was on my own.

I knelt beside Haywood who was sitting upright and looking forward with a blank stare. I put my hand on his arm and he turned his head slightly and looked at me. He was alive! I then looked down and saw in shock that both of his legs had been completely blown off at his knees. There was no sign of either leg anywhere. They were completely gone! Amazingly, the shredded stumps of his legs weren't bleeding severely but were caked with blood and dirt. The heat from the explosion had partially seared some of his severed blood vessels, but he was bleeding from his hands, face and arms. Haywood's entire body was covered with a layer of dirt stirred up by the explosion.

I immediately yelled, "Medic! I need some men up here!" I needed a medic to help treat Haywood and wanted to get a defensive perimeter set up around us until we could get him out of there.

Slowly a few men began to appear as they cautiously walked forward. I was directing them to set up around me, when Carl Seals, who was slowly walking from his point position in the left column suddenly yelled, "There's another booby trap over here."

I yelled, "Don't anyone go in front of me. And watch your step."

Lieutenant Foreman, who had walked forward, then yelled, "There's a bunker just past that hedgerow!" As he pointed to the area in front of Haywood and me.

I thought, "What the hell did we get into?" Haywood and I were totally exposed, but we couldn't risk putting anyone in front of us for protection. We must have found a NVA bunker complex and were sitting in a series of booby traps or land mines. Haywood either stepped on a detonator or an NVA soldier may have detonated what was likely a land mine with a remote detonator from a nearby bunker.

Lieutenant Foreman and second platoon leader Lieutenant Kevin Higginson spread the word to watch for booby traps. I told them to set some men on line behind me for cover until we got Haywood out of there. Lieutenant Higginson directed several men forward and organized them to stand guard over Haywood and me, ready to fire at any movement. Wop had moved up with his M-60 and had a couple hundred rounds of ammunition laid out, ready to fire if needed.

Doc Morrison, our company medic, then walked up and knelt beside Haywood with a shocked look on his face when he saw Haywood's missing legs. Doc quickly opened the canvas bag containing his medical gear and pulled out bandages and large field dressings. Doc first bandaged the bloody stumps of Haywood's legs and then put a tourniquet around each thigh, while I wrapped a large field dressing around each of Haywood's hands, which were bleeding badly. The explosion had blown Haywood's fatigue pants completely off and the lower portion of his shirt had been ripped into shreds. He had been peppered with shrapnel all over his body, including his groin and abdomen, which likely had caused internal injuries we couldn't see.

It was dry and hot as hell out there, with no breeze to provide any relief. Sweat was running down my face as Doc Morrison and I bandaged Haywood's wounds. Haywood didn't say a word as we treated him, then his body began shaking uncontrollably. He was going into shock. I could tell by the look on Doc's face he was worried. I doubted Haywood even realized what had happened. His helmet was nowhere in sight, but I saw his M-16 a few feet behind him and was amazed when I picked it up. The plastic handgrips attached to the barrel had been completely blown off and the flash suppressor at the end of the rifle barrel had also been ripped off by the force of the explosion.

Only a land mine could have caused that kind of destruction. Land mines contained enough explosives to destroy or immobilize military vehicles. I was frankly amazed that Haywood was alive. I looked around the area again, but saw no sign of Haywood's legs, not even one of his boots. I kept giving Haywood words of encouragement, "Hang in there, Glenn. We'll get you out of here soon." That was what I was hoping for anyway.

After double-checking Haywood's bandages, Doc asked if I had seen his glasses. Doc's glasses had fallen off during all the commotion. We both glanced around for his glasses and then Doc said, "There they are," as he pointed over my left shoulder near a bush. Doc stood up and had taken only a couple steps, when I heard Lieutenant Foreman forcefully shout, "Stop!" Doc Morrison froze in place.

Lieutenant Foreman, who was standing behind me, pointed at Doc's feet and said, "Look, Doc, next to your right foot."

I looked toward Doc, and my heart pounded when I stood up and saw a round metal detonator within inches of Doc's right foot. Without moving his foot, Doc bent down to inspect the detonator that was barely visible amongst the grass and leaves covering the ground. It appeared to be the detonator of another land mine buried beneath the ground at Doc's feet. Doc looked at Lieutenant Foremen and calmly said, "Oh!"

Lieutenant Foreman and I looked at Doc Morrison in astonishment. We knew that if he made the wrong move, we were all were dead.

"Step back slowly, Doc," Lieutenant Foremen said as he turned and looked at me as though he wanted my assurance that he had given the right direction. I nodded my head assuredly and held my breath as Doc slowly lifted his right foot, making sure he didn't jar the detonator. Doc reached to his left and picked up his glasses from the ground and then slowly returned and knelt beside Haywood and me and breathed a huge sigh of relief.

I gave Doc Morrison a comforting pat on his shoulder and said, "Good job, Doc. Are you ready to get out of here?"

"Yes I am," He decisively replied. We both knew we had just narrowly escaped death.

I turned to Lieutenant Foreman and told him I needed two men to help carry Haywood out of there. I wanted to get away from that second land mine that was a few feet behind us.

Doc then looked at me and said, "Hound Dog, you're bleeding," and pointed toward my left ear.

I moved my hand along the side of my head and pulled it back. I saw a combination of sweat, dirt and blood. Doc took a quick look and said, "It looks like you took some shrapnel." He gave me a supportive nod and said, "You'll be OK."

Though my ears were still ringing, I hadn't realized I had been hit. I wasn't concerned about myself at that point. I wanted to get Haywood out of there before something worse happened. While we waited briefly for some men to help carry Haywood, I asked Doc if he knew anything about Spivey.

Doc hesitated a second and said, "He's dead." He had seen Doc Snyder working on Spivey on his way up, but he was getting no response. "Damn it," I said, "He's only been here two months." The force of the explosion had killed Spivey instantly and knocked him to the ground, where I had found him.

Carl Seals and Dave Hardy had cautiously walked forward to help carry Haywood. I noticed blood on Carl's fatigue shirt and asked if he was all right. He nodded his head and then leaned toward me and told me that parts of Haywood's legs fell right on him. It was Haywood's blood. Carl was visibly shaken. I put my hand on his shoulder and said, "Take it easy, you'll be fine."

Lieutenant Foreman then yelled, "They're bringing the medevac right in here."

I said, "No. We don't want to do that! What about that land mine?" As I pointed to the land mine that Lieutenant Foreman was fearlessly keeping watch over.

But it was too late. Someone *popped smoke* and one of the company RTOs was directing the pilot to the left side of the small clearing where we were sitting. I took a deep breath and hoped for the best. Doc and I leaned over Haywood to protect him from the torrent of dirt and debris that flew around as the chopper slowly dropped into the clearing and hovered a couple feet off the ground. The pilot couldn't drop any closer. The rotor blades were already clipping the tops of nearby trees.

The medic onboard the chopper handed three litters to some men and one litter was brought over near Haywood. Doc Morrison and I gently lifted Haywood and placed him on the litter. Four of us carefully watched our steps as we carried him to the waiting medevac. There was so much dirt and debris being stirred up by the swirling chopper blades I could barely keep my eyes open as I lifted the litter to the medic on board, who grabbed it and pulled Haywood onto the chopper. Men were yelling, but the roaring sound of the chopper blades swirling directly above us drowned out all other sounds as Willard Spivey's lifeless body was carried on a litter and placed aboard the chopper.

I then saw a third man being carried toward the chopper on a litter. I hadn't realized until that moment that anyone else had been seriously wounded. It was Larry Sutton, who had joined our platoon a few weeks earlier. He looked as if he was in agony. Sutton's left upper arm was covered with a large blood-soaked dressing. After Sutton was loaded aboard, the pilot revved the engine and we all protected our faces from more dirt and debris stirred up when the medevac lifted off. Amazingly, no other booby traps were detonated during the commotion of loading the wounded men.

Dave Hardy had seen the blood on the side of my face and asked me if I was OK. I said, "Yeah, I'm fine. I quickly asked Dave what he knew about Sutton. He said Sutton's left arm was badly injured by a blast of shrapnel. Dave doubted the doctors would be able to save it. I shook my head in disbelief. We were organizing to pull back when Lieutenant Foreman came up to me and told me the medevac was coming back to pick up Bob Emery and me. I asked, "What for? We can stay out here."

Lieutenant Foreman said he understood but the CO learned we had been wounded and he wanted us evacuated. I'm sure the pilot wasn't happy to get the call to drop into the Ho Bo Woods again.

We pulled back to another small clearing where the pilot dropped the chopper down long enough for Bob and me to hop aboard. Although Bob and I were willing to stay with the company and have our wounds treated later, we were frankly happy to get the hell out of there. There could easily be more casualties before the company got out of that mess we had walked into.

Bob and I squeezed on board the medevac. I was sitting on the floor with my feet hanging outside the left doorway when the pilot took off. After we were about fifty feet off the ground, the pilot veered to the left to turn south toward Cu Chi. I held on tightly to a metal pole that supported the litters to avoid sliding out of the chopper until the pilot leveled off. I slid a little further inside the chopper when we gained speed. I had survived that day on the ground; I sure didn't want to meet my death by falling out of the chopper.

Medevacs could carry up to four injured men on litters. Litters could be laid on the floor or attached to framework that held a litter midway between the floor and ceiling of the chopper. Spivey and Sutton were both lying on the floor. Haywood was suspended above Spivey and the medic on board was tending to him.

I leaned over and put my hand on Sutton's right arm and yelled, "Hang on, we'll be at the hospital in a few minutes."

He nodded his head "Yes." He was in a lot of pain from the traumatic injury to his left arm.

The pilot was flying just above treetop level for two reasons. First, Hueys could fly faster at a lower altitude. They could fly almost 100 miles per hour without a load, but with five wounded men and a medic on board, we were probably flying about 70 MPH. And second, if there were any enemy troops in our path, we would hopefully fly past them before they could spot us.

The medic focused most of his attention on Haywood while we flew towards Cu Chi, twelve miles south of the Ho Bo Woods. The medic looked at me once while he tended to Haywood and shrugged his shoulders. I assumed he didn't know if Haywood would make it. I looked at Spivey's body lying uncovered on the litter beside me. He had been a quiet but likeable man that I had just gotten to know. It was difficult to comprehend that he was dead.

I looked out over the countryside while we roared toward Cu Chi and took a moment to absorb the beautiful and peaceful view from the air. But unfortunately, right next to me was the tragic aftermath of what was really happening down there. I looked in the distance to the south and saw the big circular perimeter that surrounded Cu Chi and we were soon flying over the base camp. The pilot slowed the chopper when he neared the 12th Evac, and he gently glided us onto the landing pad outside the emergency room.

The medical staff rushed up and carried Haywood and Sutton into the emergency room. The litter holding Spivey's body was then lifted from the chopper. Bob Emery and I walked in a solemn procession behind our fallen comrade as he was carried into the hospital. I thought about Spivey's little girl who likely wouldn't understand what happened to her daddy, and his wife, who would soon endure the tragedy of the Vietnam war with the loss of her faithful husband.

When Bob and I walked into the emergency room carrying our rifles and wearing all our gear, a corpsman met us and said, "Hey, hold up guys. You can't come in here with all that stuff." Bob and I were so accustomed to carrying our rifles and ammunition we didn't think anything about it. We turned around and left our weapons, ammunition and the rest of our gear in a little storage area surrounded by a wall of sandbags outside the entrance. When we walked back into the emergency room we saw doctors and nurses feverishly working at the examination tables where Haywood and Sutton were lying. I heard Larry Sutton screaming in pain while a corpsman quickly checked Bob's and my injuries and told us to wait in a nearby room until they had cared for our seriously wounded friends.

As we waited, Bob asked, "Why don't they bomb the hell out of the Ho Bo Woods rather then send us out to get blown to pieces?"

"I don't know, Bob. This war makes less sense every day I'm here."

Although Spivey's life was tragically wasted that day, and Glenn Haywood and Larry Sutton were seriously wounded, the war would continue uninterrupted without them.

Twenty minutes later Bob and I were taken into an examination room where they treated our wounds. An X-ray revealed a single piece of shrapnel imbedded under the skin just in front of my left ear. A corpsman injected Novocain to numb the area and then he removed a quarter inch jagged piece of shrapnel. He then closed the wound with four stitches and covered it with small bandage. The corpsman put the shrapnel in a small envelope and gave it to me as my souvenir for being wounded. I was told to return in a week to have the stitches removed. As I was leaving the room, the corpsman said he would initiate the paperwork for my Purple Heart.

I said, "Okay, thanks." Until that moment, I hadn't had time to realize I had earned a Purple Heart that day.

The Purple Heart is awarded to military personnel who are wounded or killed in action. Unfortunately, Willard Spivey would never see his Purple Heart. It would be presented to his wife. I hoped Haywood and Sutton would live to receive their Purple Hearts.

The shrapnel that struck Bob Emery in his left cheek must have glanced off, because they didn't find any shrapnel in his cheek. He also received a few stitches and was soon on his way with a small bandage on his cheek. Sergeant Dave Holt met Bob and me as we left the 12th Evac. Dave had been in the Third Herd when I first arrived in country and had been rotated to the rear. He had been notified that the third platoon hit a land mine and came over to see how everyone was doing. Dave told us Haywood and Sutton were still in surgery.

Sergeant Holt had grabbed our weapons and gear from outside the emergency room and put everything in the back of his jeep. He drove Bob and me back to the Alpha Company area on the southwest side of Cu Chi. Bob and I would remain in Cu Chi until our stitches were removed. We checked our rifles in with Tom Powers and then settled into the nearby hooch that would be our home for a few days.

Most of the guys assigned to Alpha Company in the rear had served in the field for several months and had been reassigned to duty in Cu Chi. That evening I went to the club next to our company area with a few of those guys. Dave Holt bought me a fifteen-cent beer to commemorate my being wounded, while I shared the story of what had happened that day in the Ho Bo Woods.

Bob Emery stopped by the club later that night and drank a couple beers with us. There was an unwritten rule that if a man was wounded twice and survived to return to duty, they tried to reassign him to safer duty. The rationale was, if a guy had been wounded twice and survived, he shouldn't press his luck any further. Bob Emery was now in that category. I told Bob I would talk with Lieutenant Foreman about finding him safer duty. Bob told me I needn't bother, he was happy staying with his friends in the Third Herd.

I then put my hand on his shoulder and said, "Bob, think about it. You might not be so lucky next time."

The following morning I walked over to our headquarters building and asked Tom Powers if he had any news concerning Glenn Haywood and Larry Sutton. He said Haywood had survived the surgery but was in critical condition. He wouldn't be allowed visitors for a couple days. I was still amazed Haywood was alive. Larry Sutton's left arm had been severely injured but doctors were able to save the arm. He was in stable condition and was being allowed visitors. Tom had also heard the rest of the company had made it safely out of the Ho Bo woods. They found more booby traps, but the bunkers were unoccupied.

I also asked Tom about getting a new set of dog tags. I had been issued a set of metal dog tags during basic training that listed my name, service number, religion and blood type. I had worn them on a chain around my neck like everyone else, but had lost them in September. I had never been issued a new set. If you were killed in action, they would take one of your dog tags to record your identity and leave the other one on your body.

Unable to find Bob Emery after lunch, I walked to the 12th Evacuation hospital by myself to see Larry Sutton. I found him in a recovery ward with a nurse at his bedside checking the dressing that covered his left arm. Sutton smiled when he saw me. I reached out and shook his right hand. It was difficult to know what to say. I had never seen anyone who had been seriously injured. I said, "Good to see you, Larry."

He was happy to see me and asked about the other injured men. Larry remembered other men lying on litters on the medevac but didn't know who they were or how badly they had been wounded. I first told him that Bob Emery and I both received minor shrapnel wounds and would be fine. I then said that Willard Spivey had been killed instantly. Sutton was shocked. I went on to say that Haywood lost both of his legs at his knees, but was still alive.

Sutton shook his head in astonishment and said, "Maybe I was the lucky one."

I replied, "No, you weren't lucky. But you're going home alive."

While talking with Sutton he told me doctors saved his arm by taking one of his ribs to replace shattered bones in his left arm. I later shook Sutton's right hand when I left his bedside. He was evacuated from Vietnam two days later.

On Friday afternoon, December 19th, Bob Emery and I walked to the hospital to visit Glenn Haywood. We had a letter from his parents and one from his girlfriend that would, hopefully, lift his spirits. I almost didn't recognize Haywood when we walked up to his bed. He was nearly covered with bandages from his head to the stumps of what had been his legs. Both of his hands were wrapped in huge bandages that looked like white boxing gloves. Just looking at him was painful.

I stood beside his bed and quietly said, "Hey Glenn."

He slowly opened his eyes and turned his head to look at me but didn't utter a word. I said, "How are you doing?" It was a dumb question. He obviously was feeling lousy.

Haywood turned his head toward me and very quietly said, "Just let me die."

Bob and I looked at each other for an instant, not knowing what to say. Haywood was obviously in severe physical pain and emotional shock, having lost both legs, but I didn't expect to hear those words.

Bob put his hand on Haywood's shoulder and said, "Hey, man, don't talk like that. You're going to make it. You'll be back in *the World* in a few days."

Haywood looked at us with a solemn expression on his face, not saying a word. I told him we had two letters and asked if he wanted us to open them and he could read them.

He softly said, "No."

With the pain he was enduring, he was in no mood to talk. I told Haywood I would leave the letters on the bedside table and that we would stop back again to see him. As we left the ward, I asked a nurse how long he would stay in Cu Chi. She told me Haywood was in no condition to travel and would stay there for several days. I then told the nurse what he said about dying. Her reply was, "Oh, lots of guys talk like that at first. He'll feel better in a few days."

Bob and I were both overcome by what we had seen and heard. We had both seen friends seriously wounded in the field, but they were always evacuated to Cu Chi without us seeing the long-term suffering or consequences they endured. Seeing Haywood suffering in pain and then hearing him say, "Just let me die," was something neither Bob nor I were prepared for. Bob was so upset; he didn't know if he could go back to see him again. I had never seen anyone so depressed as Glenn Haywood was that day.

Several other guys also visited Haywood during the next couple days. Everyone noticed the same thing. He didn't enjoy seeing anyone. In fact, he hadn't read the letters Bob and I had left him or the other letters he had received since then. Haywood appeared to have lost his will to live. I couldn't imagine how difficult it would have been, both physically and emotionally to be in his situation, but I also knew many others had survived similar traumatic injuries and continued to lead productive lives. I hoped Haywood would give himself that chance.

The following afternoon I learned Captain Dalton had recommended me for a Bronze Star for staying with Haywood until he was evacuated, and for my leaving myself exposed to the second land mine and potential enemy fire. I thought I had simply done what was expected of me by helping a comrade who had been seriously wounded. I wasn't in Vietnam to earn medals, but I had earned a Purple Heart and Bronze Star on December 17th.

Sergeant Bob Emery and Lieutenant Higginson had also been recommended for the Bronze Star. Bob had immediately gone to the aid of Spivey. Unfortunately, it was too late. Bob and Lieutenant Higginson then organized the men to protect Haywood and me and kept everything under control while leaving themselves exposed to the second land mine and other booby traps.

It normally took several weeks to process the recommendation for a medal through Army channels. But they were trying a new process of presenting medals within days of when the action occurred. They would process the paperwork later. The next morning I shaved and found a clean pair of fatigues to make myself presentable for a General who would arrive that afternoon to present the medals. A group of men from Alpha Company gathered in formation in our company area awaiting the general's arrival.

While we waited, I asked Lieutenant Higginson what happened after I was flown out on the 17th. He said the CO reorganized the company and they cautiously swept through the enemy bunkers, but the NVA were gone. When they neared the bunkers, one of the men from the second platoon found a 105MM artillery round at his feet. It appeared to have been wired to be command detonated from a bunker because it didn't go off. Lieutenant Higginson said they pulled back and called in an air strike and destroyed most of the area before they flew back to Patton late that afternoon.

When the General arrived we were called to attention as he walked toward our formation. The ceremony began with the General standing in front of me while my citation was read as follows:

"For heroism in connection with military operations against a hostile force: Sergeant Richard F. Hogue distinguished himself by his heroic actions on 17 December 1969, while serving with Company A, 2nd Battalion, 14th Infantry in the Republic of Vietnam. While conducting reconnaissance operations Sergeant Hogue went to the aid of a seriously wounded comrade and exposed himself to potential enemy fire and detonation from a nearby land mine. Despite being wounded, Sergeant Hogue ignored his personal safety and welfare and continued to aid and comfort his wounded comrade until he was safely evacuated. Sergeant Hogue's valorous actions contributed immeasurably to the safe evacuation of the injured comrade. Sergeant Hogue's bravery and devotion to duty are in keeping with the highest traditions of the military services and reflect great credit upon himself, his unit, the 25th Infantry Division and the United States Army."

The general said, "Congratulations, Sergeant Hogue," and pinned the Bronze Star on my fatigue shirt. We shook hands and exchanged salutes. The general then moved to Bob Emery and Lieutenant Higginson and awarded each of them their Bronze Star. The general gave us a brief pep talk, telling us how grateful he was for our willingness to serve our country and thanked us for doing a great job. He then walked to his jeep and rode off down the road. The guys who were there shook our hands to congratulate us and took a few pictures.

Rick Shields returned from a week of R & R in Hawaii with his wife on December 22nd. Rick quietly listened as I told him what had happened to us on the 17th. Rick suggested some of us chip in to buy Haywood a Christmas present. Haywood's watch had been blown off his arm by the land mine, therefore we decided to get him a new one and give it to him on Christmas Day. Several of us chipped in and Rick bought a watch at the Post Exchange.

Although I had gotten to the rear the hard way, it was going to have a fringe benefit. The Bob Hope Christmas show would perform in Cu Chi on December 23rd. I would have my stitches removed on the 24th, so I would be in Cu Chi to see the show.

On December 23rd Rick Shields and I visited Haywood before we went to the Bob Hope show. We talked with a nurse before we saw Haywood. She said he had developed pneumonia and was also concerned about his emotional state. She said he had finally read a couple of the letters from his family and girlfriend, but the other letters remained unopened. The nurse said Haywood had told her he would rather die than go home without legs.

Rick and I walked in and tried to give Haywood positive encouragement, but the pain medication kept him pretty drowsy. He could barely keep his eyes open. We stayed only for a few minutes. I put my hand on Haywood's shoulder as we left and told him I would visit him in a couple days.

When Rick and I walked outside the hospital, choppers were flying in men from the field for the Bob Hope show. I had never seen that many GIs in Cu Chi. Many of them were still wearing dirty fatigues and muddy boots and had a growth of whiskers while they walked around before the show. They had flown in about half the men from Alpha Company so Rick and I joined the guys from the Third Herd.

Before the show started, I talked with Jim Overbey regarding December 17th. Jim said he helped a medic bandage Larry Sutton's seriously injured arm. After seeing several other guys in the Third Herd being wounded, Jim was getting worried about being nailed.

A stage with Christmas decorations had been built near the center of Cu Chi and hundreds of empty wooden ammunition crates were laid in rows to be used as seats. There were trucks, tanks, and APCs parked beyond the rows of ammunition crates with guys sitting all over them. There were a couple thousand men, and a few women, sitting or standing wherever they could to watch the show. Santa Claus (Chaplain Wideman) walked around wishing everyone a "Merry Christmas" while playing Christmas songs on a portable tape player.

The show began with a huge cheer when Bob Hope walked on stage and began telling his one-liners about the military and all of us serving in Vietnam. An orchestra played while a line of young girls danced and sang to the whistles and cheers of us GIs. When Connie Stevens walked on stage wearing a bright red dress, she drew a standing ovation from those of us who had briefly forgotten about the war to enjoy a brief escape from the fighting that was continuing across the surrounding countryside. There were hospital patients sitting near the stage and a couple of them joined Connie Stevens on stage in their blue pajamas to dance and sing a song with her. It was a great show that ended way too soon. I had seen Bob Hope's Christmas shows on television many times, but it was a hundred times better being there in person. I took several pictures to have a lasting memory of what was without doubt the two best hours of my tour in Vietnam.

The next day, Christmas Eve, I visited the hospital in the morning to have my stitches removed. A doctor gave me a clean bill of health and sent me on my way. I planned to wait until Christmas Day and join some of the other guys to visit Haywood and give him the watch.

It was a quiet afternoon when I walked into our hooch and found no one there. I sat down at a small table inside and thought about family and friends back home. They all knew my duties were dangerous, but I hadn't shared any information about friends being wounded or killed.

I remembered my father saying "Don't try to be a hero" as we said goodbye in Omaha. Although that was sound advice, after serving as an infantryman in Vietnam for five months I knew that on any given day any one of us may be called upon to perform acts of bravery to stay alive or to save a buddy's life. Often, being a hero was simply a part of our job.

After my close call in the Ho Bo Woods, I thought I should tell someone back in Schaller, Iowa what I was really experiencing in case I didn't survive. I wrote the following letter to Reverend Guy Nusbaum, our Presbyterian Church minister and a World War II veteran.

December 24, 1969

Dear Reverend Nusbaum,

I am writing this letter to provide details about my tour in Vietnam that I have not shared with my family. Only a few friends know any of these details so I request you keep this letter in confidence. Should I not survive my tour in Vietnam you may then share this letter with my family.

I have been serving as an infantryman since August. We have experienced enemy fire fights, have received incoming mortar fire at firebases and have encountered several booby traps. Several men in my Company have been wounded during that time and three men in my platoon have been killed in action.

I am in Cu Chi, our Division Base Camp. I received a minor shrapnel wound when a land mine detonated near me on December 17th, but I am fine. One man was killed and two men were seriously injured.

It's getting worse since the monsoon season ended. We are seeing more enemy action and encountering more booby traps.

Although I am concerned about my fate and there is certainly the possibility I could be killed any day, I try to keep a positive outlook. My fellow platoon members and I accept our daily challenges and attempted to deal with our losses.

This is obviously the most frightening and dangerous experience of my life. I ask for your thoughts and prayers for my safety.

Sincerely,
Dick Hogue

I mailed the letter and then joined several guys who had begun an early Christmas Eve celebration at the club which was decorated with a few Christmas ornaments and lights. The weather was hot and humid, eliminating the possibility of a white Christmas. But fortunately, I was in the rear so wouldn't have to pull guard or go out on an ambush on Christmas Eve.

Early that evening some of us went to the Special Services Club, where we sang Christmas songs and enjoyed Christmas goodies. When we returned to the Company area, one of the guys found some flares. The flares were foot-long silver metal tubes with a cap on the top end. You pulled the cap off which had a firing pin built into it, placed the cap over the bottom end, and then hit the bottom of the flare on something solid to fire the colored flare 100 feet into the air. We used them in the field to identify our location to other friendly troops.

Danial Heiderich (Whitey), who had stayed in the rear after the Bob Hope show to see a doctor concerning a case of gout, and a couple other guys and I fired the flares from the road in front of our hooch and celebrated Christmas Eve by lighting up the sky.

After we fired the last flare Tom Powers walked up to me. Tom put his hand on my shoulder and said, "I hate to deliver bad news on Christmas Eve, but Haywood died."

Tom had been in the headquarters building when a nurse from the 12th Evac called. She said that Haywood died from pneumonia an hour earlier. Our Christmas Eve celebration turned to silence. I looked at Whitey who was shaking his head in disbelief.

Rick Shields then walked up to the group. I told him about Haywood. We put an arm on each other's shoulder and stood there for a moment in silence. Hearing that Haywood had died was a shock, but it wasn't a total surprise. I had hoped reading the letters from his family and our visits would help him pull through his ordeal. But that wasn't to be. Christmas Eve unfortunately became another sad evening of my tour in Vietnam. Haywood became the fourth man the third platoon had lost since I had joined them.

Some of the men who had joined us on the road didn't know Haywood personally, but they each extended their condolences. Rick, Whitey and I stood in the middle of the gravel road not knowing what to say about losing another friend. Someone asked what kind of man

Haywood had been. I said he was a good man and didn't cause any problems. I went on to tell a funny story concerning him.

During a RIF we had stopped to take a break. We told Haywood, who had been walking on our right flank, to walk up on a small rise to our north and watch over the countryside to prevent anyone from sneaking up on us. Suddenly he stood up and began trotting back toward the rest of us while turning sideways and holding his arm out and firing his M-16 behind him with one hand. We thought he looked like John Wayne running and firing his rifle with one hand. Haywood said he opened fire when he saw someone moving through a hedgerow. We moved up the hill and searched the area, but didn't have any enemy contact. Haywood had scared off whoever had been out there with his gunfire. He earned the nickname "John Wayne" that day.

We all chuckled after I told the story. It helped ease the pain, a little. Some of the guys moved on to the club, but I wasn't in the mood. I walked toward the hooch and stood outside to enjoy a little peace and quiet. I felt bad that I hadn't gone to the hospital to visit Haywood on Christmas Eve. I looked skyward and saw stars shining and kept hearing Tom Powers' words, "Haywood died," over and over in my head. The good Lord had taken control of Glenn Haywood's destiny. I crawled in my bunk and fell asleep.

I slept in on Christmas morning, along with most of the other guys who had partied at the club well into the morning. I passed on breakfast to save room for a big dinner at the mess hall. I had received some Christmas cards from my family and friends, but I had told them not to send any presents. I didn't need anything. My mom had sent me some of the homemade peanut brittle she always made during the holidays, which disappeared instantly when I shared it with some of the guys.

Jan Griffin had sent me a bottle of whiskey. Unfortunately, when it arrived a couple days before Christmas, all I received was a soggy package with a broken bottle of Seagram 7 inside. I also received a letter from her. Jan apologized for not writing regularly. She had been busy studying for final exams and working extra training hours in the hospital during the past month. It was comforting to read Jan's letter.

I didn't think too much about Haywood until I thought of the watch we had bought for him as a Christmas present. Rick Shields had it wrapped in Christmas paper and we hoped it would make Christmas a little more joyful for Haywood. I walked to the PX with Rick later on Christmas morning to return the watch.

Bob Emery and Whitey joined Rick and me for Christmas dinner in the mess hall early that afternoon. Rick talked about missing his wife and family in California. Bob said his family was gathered at his mom's house in Marine City, Michigan. Whitey had a big family which was gathering at his brother's house in Oklahoma. My mom wrote in a recent letter that my two sisters were spending Christmas with them in Schaller. The Christmas dinner was great, not exactly like mom's home cooking, but pretty good for Army food in Vietnam.

With our wounds healed, Bob and I were scheduled to return to the field the day after Christmas. Whitey had been given some medication for his gout and was planning to go back out with us. Rick had been reassigned to the rear and was staying in Cu Chi. After the Christmas dinner I organized my gear, preparing to return to the field.

Late Christmas afternoon I returned to our hooch in the company area and met Sergeant Richard Benson. He was a new *shake'n bake* who had been assigned to Alpha Company. After I told Sergeant Benson about some of my experiences in the field, he was full of questions. Richard Benson and I enjoyed a couple of beers at the club that evening while I continued to answer his steady stream of questions about serving as an infantryman in Vietnam. I was more than happy to help him. Benson was a likable guy, and it appeared he would be a quick learner once he arrived in the field.

During the early afternoon of December 26, 1969, Bob Emery, Whitey and I left the comforts of Cu Chi on a convoy and returned to Firebase Patton.

➤ Corporal Willard Spivey was from Franklin, Kentucky. He was twenty years old. He arrived in Vietnam on October 13, 1969. Willard was killed instantly by a land mine explosion on December 17, 1969. He was married and had a daughter. Willard Spivey, and Larry Sutton who was seriously wounded on December 17th, grew up together, joined the Army together, arrived in Vietnam together, were both assigned to the third platoon, and ironically, were wounded the same day.

➤ Corporal Glennon Haywood was from Monroe, Louisiana. He was twenty-one years old. He arrived in Vietnam on September 1, 1969. Glennon was seriously wounded by a land mine explosion on December 17, 1969. He survived his initial injuries but died in Cu Chi on Christmas Eve.

The mortality rate for wounded military personnel reaching field hospitals during World War II was 4%. That mortality rate was reduced to 1% in Vietnam primarily because medical evaluation helicopters quickly flew injured troops to the hospital, while onboard medics provided lifesaving care during transport.

The original Purple Heart designed as the Badge of Military Merit, was established by General George Washington in 1782 in the form of a heart made of purple cloth. The current Purple Heart medal was established in 1932 with the bust of George Washington on the front to be awarded to military personnel who were wounded or killed in action. The reverse side of the heart shaped medal is inscribed: "For Military Merit."

Me standing in a bomb crater during the dry season.

Chapter 15

I Thought You Were Dead

The convoy of deuce-and-a-halfs pulled into Patton and stopped near the Alpha Company command post. Bob Emery, Whitey and I jumped down off our truck along with several other men who were returning to the field. I asked where the third platoon was located and someone pointed to the eastern perimeter and said, "They're on the east side, Hound Dog."

I waved thanks. Bob, Whitey and I walked along the perimeter road until we saw the familiar faces of the guys in the Third Herd.

I said, "Hey, what are you guys doing around here? You should be out on a RIF."

Carlton Quick walked up and told me they had gotten the day off to prepare for a special mission the next day. He said I should talk with 3-6 (Lieutenant Foremen) to get the details.

Several of the other the guys welcomed Bob and me with friendly hellos. I had seen some of them when they were in Cu Chi for the Bob Hope show but I hadn't seen the rest of the men since I was flown out of the Ho Bo Woods on December 17th. It was good to see them again.

Unfortunately, my friendly welcome back to the Third Herd was overshadowed by the sadness of losing Willard Spivey, and then Glenn Haywood on Christmas Eve. The men at Patton had received the news about Haywood the previous morning, Christmas Day. The thoughts about both men were still fresh in the minds of everyone. I told some of the guys Haywood was very depressed when I visited him in the hospital. I shared my opinion that he lost his will to live.

Lieutenant Foreman then came up and said, "Welcome back, guys," and shook our hands.

I then thanked 3-6 for having a good eye on December 17th.

Lieutenant Foreman replied, "Whew, that was a close call, I thought we were all goners."

Lieutenant Foreman had likely saved a bunch of lives when he spotted that detonator. Sometimes simply good fortune made the difference between life and death in Vietnam.

I then asked Lieutenant Foreman about our planned special mission the men are talking about. After Sergeant Jim Overbey joined us, Lieutenant Foreman began his briefing.

Lieutenant Foreman and Sergeant Overbey had been running the platoon while Bob and I were gone. With Bob Emery and me back, Jim Overbey would continue as platoon sergeant since he had seniority in country over me. Bob Emery would be the second squad leader and I would continue to lead the first squad. There were 26 men assigned to the third platoon, with Junior Houchens in Cu Chi to see a dentist about a tooth ache. Lieutenant Foreman told me the company had been given the day to prepare for a special mission called a "Bushmaster."

Lieutenant Foreman (3-6) began his briefing by saying, "We are going to be flown near the middle of the Ho Bo Woods tomorrow morning. We'll set up a remote position for two or three days."

Jim Overbey and I looked at each other without saying a word. We both knew this wouldn't be good.

3-6 said we would be supplied with materials to set up a defensive perimeter and dig in for the duration. The entire company of nearly 100 men, including our mortar platoon, would be going. One platoon would set up an ambush while the rest of the company remained inside the perimeter each night. It sounded like a pretty lousy idea to me, especially in the middle of the Ho Bo Woods.

I asked, "Who came up with this bushmaster idea?"

Lieutenant Foreman explained that companies (including Alpha Company) going into or near the Ho Bo Woods during the day routinely encountered enemy activity. Rather than pulling out before night, the brass in Cu Chi wanted a company to stay in the Ho Bo

Woods at night to set up what they termed a bushmaster in the hopes of catching the enemy off guard when they moved at night.

He then said Colonel Crutchly (the battalion commander) came to Captain Dalton with this new plan and the CO volunteered us to be the first company to set up a bushmaster.

"Maybe you can ask the CO to volunteer another company," I said jokingly. We all chuckled briefly, but none of us liked what we had been volunteered to do.

Lieutenant Foreman replied that the decision had been made so we had better get ready.

Bob and Jim walked away but Lieutenant Foreman asked me to stay with him for a minute. He said he had talked with the CO about reassigning Bob Emery because Bob had been wounded twice. The CO was willing to move Bob to the mortar platoon.

I said, "That's great. I'll tell Bob."

I walked to the next bunker and found Sergeant Emery and gave him the news from the CO.

Bob thought briefly and then said, "No, thanks. Like I told you back in Cu Chi, I'd rather stay right here with my friends."

I reminded Bob it would be a lot safer in the mortar platoon, but he again said he would stay in the Third Herd. I told Lieutenant Foreman that Bob wanted to stay with us. That was fine with him, and he would pass the word back to the CO.

I frankly was glad to have Bob stay with us. Bob was only eighteen years old, but he was a reliable man. I also admired his courage. First, he had volunteered to come to Vietnam from non-combat duty in Germany, and then he declined a transfer to safer duty in the mortar platoon. I hoped he wouldn't regret his decisions.

There had been several new men assigned to the platoon while I was in Cu Chi. Three FNGs, Allan Rader, Otis Carthage and Roger Cox had joined us. Randal Collins had been in country for a while and had been reassigned from the first platoon to the Third Herd. I introduced myself and welcomed them to the platoon. I would get to know them during the next few days.

I then gathered my squad and gave them the details about what we would be doing the following day. The first response from one of the guys was, "Oh, bullshit, Sarge," while some of the other guys chimed in with moans and groans. I smiled for an instant and then seriously told the men it was for real.

Everyone was quiet.

I told the men to double check their gear, load up extra ammunition and make sure their weapons were clean. I also reminded the guys to take their claymores, poncho liners, plenty of water and C-rations.

I said, "I'm not sure how long we'll be gone, but plan for three days. I'll be around later to check on you new guys."

Jim Overbey and I talked for a while later. He told me the third platoon was leading the RIF the day before Christmas when they ran into six VC in a tunnel complex.

Jim went on saying Hue (our Chieu Hoi) yelled for the VC to surrender but they refused and returned fire. After a brief firefight and throwing hand grenades down the tunnel, all six VC were killed. Fortunately, the Third Herd survived the day without any casualties.

Jim then said, "I'm worried about this bushmaster, Hound Dog."

I didn't like it either. We were both concerned about going out with several new guys who didn't know what they were doing.

Jim said, "They can get some of us killed, you know."

I just nodded my head "Yes" and said, "They'll have to learn awfully fast out there."

Jim and I had seen a lot during our few months together and knew the Ho Bo Woods was the most hazardous place they could send us. Although we had to accept each assignment, the stress of combat and seeing friends wounded and killed had taken an emotional toll on all of us who had survived. Maybe it was getting to be too much for Sargent Overbey. John Potts had lost it after his first and only firefight, when we were ambushed that past September and Hal Harris was killed. The stress had gotten to Dennis Schultz a couple weeks earlier. It was amazing that the constant combat exposure didn't crack more of us. We could only hope and pray we wouldn't be the next casualty. Although I was doing fine, I knew, regardless of my fate, my tour of duty in Vietnam would change me forever.

I spent time that evening with the new guys to ensure their weapons were clean and that they had plenty of ammunition, hand grenades and everything else they would need for the bushmaster. We *old timers* knew it would be a hazardous mission, but those new guys had no idea what to expect. While Jim Overbey and I could talk frankly about what might happen, I had to be careful with the new men. I wanted them to understand that the Ho Bo Woods was a dangerous area, but I also didn't want to scare them into thinking that they were all going to be killed. Those new guys really needed a month of OJT so they better understood their duties as infantrymen, but that wasn't going to happen.

After a peaceful night at Patton, I got up early the next morning, December 27, 1969, and wrote Jan Griffin a quick letter. There wouldn't be any mail service during the bushmaster. I dropped the letter in the mailbox at Patton and headed to the mess hall for breakfast.

As I was finishing my breakfast Doc Snyder walked up and told me Whitey's gout was still bothering him. Doc didn't believe Whitey needed to go back Cu Chi for further medical care, but the medication had not cured Whitey's condition. I then asked Doc whether Whitey should go on the bushmaster with us. Doc said it was up to Whitey.

We then found Whitey standing outside his bunker. I asked if he felt good enough to go out with us that day.

Without hesitation Whitey said, "Sure, I'm OK."

I looked at Doc and asked, "Are you sure it's OK with you?"

Doc said, "If he feels good enough to go, its fine with me."

I told Whitey to pack his gear.

I joined the men who were reluctantly gathered on the landing zone on the east side of Firebase Patton shortly before ten o'clock that morning, like I had done dozens of times before. I saw Chuck Merritt sitting on the ground nearby and walked over to talk with him while we waited. Chuck had become our new RTO after Dennis Schultz went to the rear. Chuck was from Runnells, Iowa, a small town southeast of Des Moines. We talked about the snowy and cold winter weather in Iowa and chuckled while enjoying the warm, sunny December morning. Chuck was normally a quiet guy who kept mostly to himself. He was the only man in the platoon who regularly read his Bible.

After relaxing for a while, we heard the choppers coming from the south. Someone popped smoke for the lead chopper and we aligned ourselves to climb aboard. We flew northwest from Patton into clear skies and bright sunshine. I expected hot and dry weather while we were out in the Woods. It had rarely rained during the past month.

Once aboard, I relaxed on the floor of the chopper. Those flights became a brief escape from the realities of the war far below. The noise from the chopper blades drowned out all other sounds, and the vibrations from the swirling blades were almost relaxing as we flew nearly one thousand feet above the ground. I enjoyed what beauty remained of the countryside that was scarred from years of exploding bombs and artillery shells and decimated by Agent Orange. As we flew toward the Ho Bo Woods I looked at the other men who were quietly enjoying the peaceful ride. Although all was quiet at that moment, I knew the dangers that lay ahead of us. I hoped we all would be able to safely board a Huey for a return trip to Firebase Patton in a few days.

We flew around for almost half an hour while Captain Dalton, who was in the lead chopper, scouted to find the location where we were supposed to set up. We were finally dropped off in the west central area of the Ho Bo Woods.

When the last lift of choppers arrived, we walked a short distance and then Captain Dalton said, "This is it, men."

The first thing we did was to cautiously sweep the area checking for booby traps and tunnels. We found none. Captain Dalton and the platoon leaders lined out a perimeter about 100 feet in diameter. The first and third platoons then identified positions to dig foxholes and assigned four or five men to each position. The second platoon would set up an ambush a few hundred meters outside the perimeter that night.

The foxholes were spaced about twenty feet apart to maintain visibility between each position after dark and to minimize the possibility of enemy troops sneaking in between foxholes. The men then began the laborious task of digging foxholes and filling sandbags that soon arrived to build a wall of protection in front of each foxhole. Our mortar platoon set up their 81MM mortar tubes near the center of the site. If necessary, they could return mortar fire much quicker than calling in artillery support from miles away. The CO also established his command post in the center of the site.

We stationed a few men around the perimeter to stand guard while everyone else dug in. If there were any VC out there, and there were, they easily could have seen or heard the choppers flying in to drop off supplies and equipment after we arrived. If they were looking for action, they would be headed our way. The tall grass, bushes and small trees limited our visibility in every direction around the perimeter. We spent a lot of time clearing as much vegetation as possible to improve our visibility.

I positioned my squad along the southern and southwest perimeter. Robert Draughn, Dave Hardy, Carlton Quick and I took a position near the center of the southern perimeter. We located an M-60 machine gun with us to cover most of the southern perimeter with machine gun fire. Bob Emery's squad was positioned to cover the northwest and northern perimeter along with Lieutenant Foreman. Jim Overbey joined three other men in a foxhole on the western perimeter. There was a pile of sandbags, rolls of chain link fence, coils of concertina wire, steel posts and tools in the center of the compound. The men took whatever they needed to set up each position.

Choppers arrived periodically, bringing in more equipment, C-rations and water. We pounded steel posts into the ground and attached sections of the chain link fence to form a six-foot-high wire wall of protection from incoming rockets or grenades in front of each foxhole. When we began stretching the coils of concertina wire around the perimeter, we found a problem. There wasn't enough concertina wire to properly encircle the entire perimeter. With the wire we had we would have to stretch it, leaving gaps in the coils and making it easier for enemy troops to sneak through.

I told Lieutenant Foreman we needed more concertina wire. He said no more materials were scheduled for delivery, but he would ask the CO about getting more concertina wire. He came by a short while later and said the CO requested more concertina wire but it wouldn't be delivered until tomorrow.

In frustration I said, "Tomorrow? We need that wire today!"

The multiple rows of concertina wire surrounding our firebases and patrol bases allowed only a few inches between the coils of concertina wire and made it nearly impossible for anyone to crawl through without getting tangled in the coils. Unfortunately, we had to settle for one row of concertina wire that was stretched so tight there were spaces more than a foot wide between many of the coils, leaving ourselves vulnerable to enemy troops possibly slipping through the wire. Fortunately, they had delivered trip flares that we could place in front of us, along with a huge supply of claymore mines. If the NVA or VC tried to sneak through the concertina wire, they would hopefully trip a flare. The NVA and VC used what were called sappers to sneak into an American position and inflict as many casualties as they could before they were likely killed themselves. It was normally a suicide mission for them, similar to the Japanese "Kamikaze" pilots diving their planes into American war ships during World War Two.

By late afternoon we were all hot, sweaty and dirty from working our butts off in the hot sun to clear some of the vegetation, dig foxholes and fill hundreds of sandbags. Finally, each position had a two-foot-high sandbag wall that curved around the front side of each foxhole, which was about two feet deep.

Jim Overbey and I took a break while we looked over the site. He had talked with the CO about looking for another site before we began setting up, but the CO wanted to stay, although it wasn't the original designated site for the bushmaster. Jim and I agreed it was a lousy spot but we had a lot of firepower. I reminded Jim it would take a lot of gooks with lots of guts to come after us.

Jim said, "Yeah, maybe so, but I can't wait to get out of here."

"Hey, we'll make it out of here," I replied knowing we might be in for a long night.

I wasn't happy to be spending the night in the Ho Bo Woods either, but I wasn't afraid. Not at that moment anyway. We put a few more men on guard as the afternoon passed. There hadn't been any sign of enemy activity but each chopper that arrived with supplies and equipment helped pinpoint our location. Late that afternoon a chopper delivered a Night Pack containing additional M-16 and M-60 ammunition, mortar rounds, claymore mines and hand grenades. Although we had lots of weapons and ammunition, my biggest concern was if the enemy happened to have a mortar tube out there, they could tear us up with a few well-placed mortar rounds. We didn't have any bunkers to scurry into for protection. Our final defensive measure was to set out claymore mines in front of each position, run the electric wires back to our foxhole and connect them to the detonators. We had five or six claymores in front of each position.

Jim Overbey and I walked around the perimeter to double check our positions and coordinate primary fields of fire between adjoining foxholes. Bushes and small hedgerows still limited the visibility for some positions, so we had two-man teams go out and chop down a few more bushes to improve their visibility. One man stood guard while the other man chopped down the bushes with a machete. The more I looked over the perimeter the more I didn't like it. At best we could only see fifteen to twenty meters in any direction. And when it was dark, we wouldn't be able to see much of anything. Finally, Jim and I decided there was nothing more we could do to prepare for the forthcoming night and began walking to our separate foxholes.

I took a couple steps and turned to Jim and asked, "Hey Jim, I haven't seen Hue, he didn't show up this morning?

"No," Jim replied, "He disappeared early this morning."

I didn't say anything and just shook my head. We both knew that Hue didn't want to spend a night in the middle of the Ho Bo Woods.

I walked back to my foxhole and opened a can of spaghetti and meatballs. Suddenly, I heard the rumbling sound of our .50-caliber machine gun firing from the northeast perimeter. I threw my half eaten can of spaghetti on the ground, grabbed my M-16 and jumped inside our foxhole. We all looked out over the perimeter with our weapons ready but saw nothing.

The firing soon stopped and someone yelled, "That was just a test fire."

The men in the mortar platoon decided to test fire the "50" and scared the hell out of everyone for nothing.

I said to the guys in our foxhole, "What the hell are those guys doing? They just told Charlie (enemy troops) where our .50-caliber machine gun was." It wasn't a smart move.

When the sun was starting to set in the western sky, I told the guys in our foxhole I was going over to talk with 3-6.

On my way, I ran into Lieutenant Higginson and his second platoon as they were leaving to set up their ambush.

As they passed by, I said, "Be careful out there guys."

I then saw Bill Casey who was in the middle of the site with the CP group checking his radio.

I said, "What do you think, Casey?"

Casey said, "I think it might be a long night, Hound Dog. Everyone in the Ho Bo Woods knows we're here."

"That's for sure. See you later, Casey."

When I reached the northern perimeter I knelt by Lieutenant Foreman who was sitting on the ground with his feet in his foxhole.

I asked 3-6 if he had set out their claymores and coordinated fields of fire. He indicated they had but he was concerned about their limited visibility.

I looked out over their perimeter and said, "You're right, but we can't do anything about it tonight."

We had a little better visibility on the south side. But after dark none of us would be able to see much out there anyway. Lieutenant Foreman shared his foxhole with Mike Myers, Bob Emery and Danial Heiderich (Whitey).

Whitey told me he was feeling better. I said, "Great," and gave him a pat on the back as I moved on.

I walked to the next foxhole where Terry Thornton, Chuck Merritt, Randal Collins and Allen Rader were located.

I asked, "Terry, you guys all set?"

Terry replied, "Yeah, we're ready, don't worry."

"Ok," I said. "See you guys in the morning."

I continued to move counterclockwise from Lieutenant Foreman's position and chatted briefly with Doc Snyder and Bob Ryken who were in a foxhole with three other men, Hugh Hearn, Roger Cox and Otis Carthage. I also stopped a minute to talk with Jim Overbey one more time before I reached my foxhole on the southern perimeter.

Carlton Quick had the M-60 resting on top of our sandbag wall. We could easily spray the area in front of our position and much of the southern perimeter with machine gun fire if we needed to. We had about 2,500 rounds of M-60 ammunition laid out and ready to fire. Robert Draughn and I had our M-16 ammunition magazines laid out in bandoleers around the foxhole and over a dozen hand grenades lay on the ground behind our foxhole. It would soon be getting dark. There wasn't anything else I could think of that we could do. We would settle in and wait to see what might happen.

Unfortunately, I had a personal problem to deal with before it was completely dark. I had felt a case of diarrhea coming on during the afternoon. I didn't think I would make it through the night without making a "Mother Nature" call. I told the guys I was going to walk toward the concertina wire to take a quick dump.

I picked up a shovel lying next to our foxhole to dig a little hole to bury my *duty*. I had grabbed a packet of toilet paper from a case of C-rations and was prepared for my personal mission.

I also told the men in the foxhole to our left that I was walking forward in between our foxholes. I quickly dug a small hole amongst the grass, dropped my pants and squatted down with my backside facing outward toward the perimeter. I had been squatted down for only a few seconds when an explosion sounded behind me and my bare butt stung as something hit it. Instinctively, I fell belly first on the ground and without hesitating began low-crawling towards our foxhole with my fatigue pants down around my knees, while the men from the foxholes on either side of me opened fire over my head.

Dave Hardy looked at me after I dove into our foxhole and said, "Are you OK?"

I said, "I think so."

My heart was pounding, and I took a deep breath while I tried to determine if I had been wounded. I quickly rubbed one hand over the cheeks of my butt. I felt no pain and saw no blood. I then pulled my pants up while Quick and Hardy sprayed M-60 rounds across the area in front of our foxhole.

I then heard "Cease fire! Cease fire!" Coming from the CP.

I tapped Quick on his shoulder and motioned to stop firing. There were no other explosions after the one that had peppered me. I looked at the foxholes on each side of us. They both gave a thumbs-up that they were OK.

Captain Dalton sent Tom Archer, one of his RTOs, over to our foxhole to learn what happened.

Tom knelt by me and said, "What the hell happened, Hound Dog?"

I told Tom that I had walked between our foxholes to take a dump and a gook must have thrown a hand grenade at me.

Tom asked, "Are you OK?"

"Yeah, I'm fine."

"OK," Tom said as he smiled, "I'll tell the CO, I hope he believes me." Tom quickly walked back to the CP (command post).

An enemy soldier must have been hiding in front of us and threw a hand grenade at me after I squatted down. Fortunately, the throw was short. I was hit only by dirt and debris blown toward me by the exploding grenade. A little longer toss and I could have been seriously wounded or killed.

"Wow," I thought. "I had been back in the field for just over one day and had come close to being killed."

I then realized my case of diarrhea had disappeared. That hand grenade must have literally scared the crap right out of me as the saying goes. After things quieted down again, the guys in the foxhole chuckled when they talked briefly about my trip near the wire.

Quick said I really looked funny crawling back with my pants down around my knees.

I said, "Yeah, I probably did. But I wasn't going to stop to pull them up. I expected more grenades."

Although I had survived my little excursion near the wire we definitely knew there were enemy troops out there. They had likely worked their way toward us that afternoon and were waiting for the cover of darkness to make a move. It remained quiet for several hours after dark while we pulled guard with two men awake at each foxhole. I had finished an hour on guard and was wrapped up in my poncho liner sleeping behind our foxhole when it sounded like all hell was breaking loose on our northern perimeter.

It started with BOOM! BOOM! Two large explosions.

There were repeated explosions and gunfire along the north and west perimeter. I grabbed my helmet and rifle and joined the three other men in our foxhole. It didn't appear we were taking any enemy fire but explosions and gunfire continued on the north and west perimeters. Gunfire then began erupting from several other positions around the perimeter. I then heard claymores being fired.

I didn't know what was happening but as a precaution I yelled, "Quick, open fire with the 60" (M-60 machine gun).

Dave Hardy fed the string of rounds into the machine gun and orange tracers glowed in the darkness while Quick sprayed hundreds of rounds back and forth along the southern perimeter. Draughn fired one of our claymore mines and I threw two hand grenades into the darkness in front of our foxhole just in case enemy sappers were trying to work their way in.

The entire perimeter soon erupted with rifle and machine gun fire. Hand grenades were flying out from every foxhole. The flurry of rifle and machine fire, combined with the hand grenade and claymore mine explosions, was as loud and continuous as I had ever heard. The flurry of action was so overwhelming I couldn't tell if it was all friendly fire or enemy fire directed back at us. I only knew that the four of us in my foxhole were uninjured. If there were enemy troops outside the perimeter, they would have to be amazingly lucky to survive the barrage of firepower we were unleashing.

Robert Draughn nervously yelled, "You guys see anything out there?"

"No, keep firing!" I yelled. I still didn't know what had initiated all the action on the northern perimeter.

I couldn't see anything to the left side of our foxhole but I sprayed several magazines of ammunition from my M-16 into bushes and tall grass anyway. I could hear the *pops* as the mortar platoon began firing outgoing rounds and could hear the explosions when the mortars landed only a short distance outside the perimeter.

After several minutes of continuous firing we heard, "Cease fire! Cease fire!" Coming from the command post.

Captain Dalton wanted everyone to stop firing to determine exactly what had happened and what we should do next. Something had obviously initiated the action on the northern perimeter, but those of us on the south side still had no idea what happened. When the firing eventually stopped, Quick, Hardy, Draughn and I huddled in our foxhole. The barrel of Quick's machine gun was smoking, so he poured lubricating oil on it to cool it down. We all strained our eyes to gaze outward over the perimeter, looking for any movement. There wasn't any moonlight making it impossible to see much of anything.

I yelled to the positions on each side of us, "Are you guys all right over there?"

"Yeah, we're fine," was the reply.

I then heard men screaming for help along the north and western perimeter. There were screams of extreme pain. Men were yelling, "Doc!"

I could hear the voices of other men who were apparently trying to aid the wounded and gain control of the situation.

I heard, "We need another medic over here, Doc Snyder is hit." Doc Snyder was the third platoon's medic.

I hesitated briefly and then told the guys, "I'm going over to help those guys."

I told Quick and Hardy to keep a close eye to the front. I stepped from the rear of our foxhole and had only taken a few steps when someone from the CP group yelled, "Don't anyone move! There's a gook inside the wire!"

I immediately stopped and kneeled down. I looked around for movement while I slowly maneuvered back toward our foxhole. Robert Draughn and I watched inward from the foxhole with our fingers on the triggers of our M-16s while Quick and Hardy watched outward along the perimeter. Although I was ready to fire at any movement, I also had to be careful not to hit any of our own men with friendly fire. Sitting in our foxhole was the most helpless and frustrating few moments of my life. Men were still screaming, but I couldn't go help them. We had to find that gook! Where the hell was he?

A minute later the bright light from a trip flare lit up the eastern perimeter. Immediately, there was machine gun and rifle fire, claymore mines detonated and hand grenades were thrown in the direction of the flare. I guessed the sapper who had been inside the wire had somehow made it to the eastern perimeter and tripped a flare trying to escape.

Robert Draught yelled, "I hope they killed the son-of-a-bitch." The firing along the eastern perimeter soon stopped. It was again relatively quiet.

Word then came from the command post that sappers attacked the northern perimeter. We were to search the area around our foxholes to ensure there weren't other sappers still alive inside the perimeter.

I told Robert Draughn I would search the area around us while he kept a watch over me.

I slowly moved from our foxhole in a low crouch toward my right with my left index finger on the trigger of my M-16. I soon met up with a guy from the first platoon who had been in the foxhole to our east. We both shook our heads "No," indicating we hadn't seen anything. When I circled to my left and toward the CP group I ran into Sam Ryan from the mortar platoon who had been searching from the center of the compound.

We knelt down for a moment and I asked what happened. He said three sappers snuck through the northern perimeter and opened up on several foxholes.

Ryan then said, "You've lost several men, Hound Dog. I think 3-6 and the guys in his foxhole are gone."

"Son-of-a-bitch!" I said in frustration, "Who else?"

Ryan didn't know who but said there're a lot of our guys down. I then asked if they needed more help over there. Ryan said, "No," then stated the CO wanted us to stay on the southern perimeter in case they launch an attack there.

Ryan said men from the CP group and the mortar platoon were aiding the injured men. The CO had also moved some men from the CP group and mortar platoon to stand guard in the foxholes on the northern perimeter where the Third Herd had suffered heavy casualties. I circled around to my left and met up with Vic Ortega who had been in the foxhole to my right.

I asked, "Are you guys all OK?"

"Yeah, we're fine, Vic replied, "What the hell happened?"

I quickly told Vic what I knew and then made it back to my foxhole without seeing anything. When I reached the foxhole Hardy immediately asked, "What did you hear?"

I said, "Sappers got through the northern perimeter and hit some of the third platoon's positions. 3-6 (Lt Forman) and the guys in his foxhole may be dead."

Quick asked, "Who was with 3-6?"

I thought for a few seconds and then my heart nearly sank when I remembered who was in 3-6's foxhole. I replied, "Whitey, Emery and Babysan (Mike Myers)."

I then told the guys there likely were several wounded and KIAs from the Third Herd but I didn't know who they were.

I walked to the foxhole to our left and told the men what had happened and to stay put. I told them to pass the word along to the position next to them. I looked at my watch after I returned to our foxhole. It was 12:30 a.m., December 28, 1969.

It remained quiet along the southern and eastern perimeter. Everyone was watching in the darkness for any signs of movement, with their weapons in their hands. I sat in the relative silence and thought about the men who were in the foxhole with Lieutenant Foreman.

"No, not those guys," I sadly thought to myself. I wondered how many of the men I had spoken with before darkness were still alive.

After a short while I heard the sound of choppers in the distance. Two Cobra gunships soon began peppering the surrounding area with rockets and machine gun fire before the medevacs came in to evacuate the wounded and dead. I had a strobe light and laid it in my upside down helmet beside our foxhole to mark the southern perimeter. Other strobe lights were set in helmets to mark each side of the perimeter, enabling the pilots to see where we were located. The Cobras circled the perimeter firing rockets and unleashing a hail of machine gun rounds into the surrounding countryside.

When the first medevac neared we heard rifle fire in the distance. Somehow enemy troops were still alive out there and were firing at the chopper. We immediately laid down a barrage of machine gun and rifle fire to protect the medevac as it descended from the south into the western perimeter. We had to protect our faces from the blowing dirt and debris when the medevac landed and then lifted off with a load of wounded men. The first medevac was followed by two more. "We must have suffered a lot of casualties," I thought.

After the last medevac disappeared into the darkness it was again quiet inside the perimeter. Robert Draughn then looked to his right and quickly raised his M-16 while saying, "Something's moving!"

I said, "Don't shoot!"

"Hey, it's Sergeant Overbey," Hardy said.

I asked, "How bad did we get hit, Jim?"

"We got the hell shot out of us," Jim replied. "3-6 and most of the guys on the north side are gone."

Bill Casey also stopped by our foxhole and said, "They're flying in more ammo. It should be here any minute."

Quick said, "We're low on M-60 ammo."

Jim said, "Everybody is getting low on ammo."

More choppers soon arrived, bringing the much-needed ammunition and also two platoons from Firebase Patton. I'm sure those reinforcements were awfully apprehensive after they were pulled from the relative comfort of Patton and told they were being dropped in the Ho Bo Woods in the middle of the night to help us.

The additional men were located around the perimeter and quickly dug small foxholes in between our existing foxholes to strengthen the entire perimeter. Additional M-60 and M-16 ammunition and hand grenades were distributed to the foxholes around the perimeter. We had fired thousands of rounds after the initial sapper attack and had been resupplied with thousands more M-60 and M-16 rounds and hundreds of hand grenades that hopefully would help us survive the remainder of what was becoming the longest night of my tour.

Every man inside that perimeter stayed on guard the rest of the night. I doubt if any of us could have slept anyway. Our strategy was to continue sporadic gunfire whether we spotted anything or not. The enemy knew where we were, but we would make it harder than hell for them to get to us.

Every few minutes, rifle or machine gun fire erupted from a foxhole. We threw out hand grenades all night long. I fired more rounds through my M-16 that night than I had during the rest of my time in Vietnam. Fortunately, our M-60 held up and fired thousands of rounds throughout the night. After what seemed like an eternity, I saw the eastern horizon begin to brighten and the sun slowly rise over our site. We stayed in our foxholes while gunships arrived to survey the surrounding countryside in the daylight.

The second platoon had safely survived their night on ambush with no enemy contact. I stood by our foxhole while they cautiously swept the perimeter looking for enemy bodies or weapons or whatever might be out there. Inside the perimeter men slowly started stepping out of their foxholes, being tentative about moving around too much or relaxing their guard. We kept one man on guard at each foxhole just in case.

I told the guys I was going over to the CP to learn more about what happened and who we lost the past night. When I walked toward the middle of the perimeter I ran into Lieutenant Larry Frank, the mortar platoon leader.

He looked at me almost in shock and said, "What are you doing here? I thought you were dead."

I said, "What?"

"I was told you were killed last night."

Lieutenant Frank said a sergeant in the third platoon had been killed last night; he had been told it was me. He told me to check with Captain Dalton, who had the names of the guys we lost.

Lieutenant Frank then said, "Sorry. But I'm glad you're alive."

"Yeah, me too," I said.

Captain Dalton had seen me talking with Lieutenant Frank. He walked up and put his hand on my shoulder.

"I have some bad news for you, Hound Dog."

I asked, "Who did we lose?"

Captain Dalton handed me a list of the men who had been killed. I slowly read their names: "John Foreman (3-6); Robert Emery; Terry Thornton; Charles Merritt; Danial Heiderich (Whitey); Allen Rader; Otis Carthage; Jr. and Roger Cox."

I couldn't believe it. I read the names a second time to be sure. I then asked about the wounded. Doc Snyder had been shot twice in the chest and Bob Ryken had a serious gunshot wound to his left leg. Randal Collins, who had been reassigned from the first platoon, had his lower left leg completely severed. And Ben Carlson, who had joined the third platoon earlier that month, had serious shrapnel wounds.

"As far as we know, the wounded men are still alive," the CO said.

I quietly stood there trying to comprehend what I had just learned when Bill Casey came up to me and put his hand on my shoulder. I looked at him and said, "I can't believe they're all gone, Casey," as tears filled my eyes. "What happened?"

Casey explained that three sappers snuck in by 3-6's position and threw satchel charges and hand grenades and fired RPGs into 3-6's foxhole and the foxholes to the west. They then opened up with AKs.

Casey hesitated for a second and then said he began walking toward the northwest perimeter carrying his M-16. He saw three men walking toward him that he first thought were GIs. But when he got closer he was face-to-face with three sappers.

I said, "You're kidding."

"No," Casey replied, "It's the God's honest truth." I shook my head in disbelief.

Casey went on saying that two sappers were each carrying an AK-47 and one had a RPG launcher. Casey then raised his arms simulating firing, and said, "I fired a burst of rounds into the sapper carrying the RPG launcher and he dropped to the ground."

Casey continued, "One sapper with an AK started moving to my left and I squeezed a burst into him that spun him completely around and into the ground."

Casey pointed a few feet away from us to where the third sapper had begun running east toward the first platoon. Casey said he turned, knelt down, and fired at his back. After the gook hit the ground Casey yelled at the men in the first platoon to finish him off.

"Damn, Casey," I said, "You saved a lot of our butts."

"Well, that's not all," Casey said, "I turned back to the first two sappers. One of them was raising his AK toward me. I put a few more rounds in him and put a couple more rounds in the other sapper to make sure they were both dead."

"You did one hell of a job, Casey," and I patted him on the back.

"Maybe so, Sarge, but it was too late for those guys in the foxholes," he said sadly. "I don't think most of them knew what hit them. They were killed before they had time to react."

We then talked about how the sappers could have crept in un-detected. We would never know for sure, but because it was so hard to see anything that past night, the sappers likely weren't spotted until it was too late.

I then asked Casey how badly Doc Snyder and Bob Ryken had been wounded. He didn't know because he hadn't seen either one of them the past night. But he had seen Randal Collins, who lost his leg. He was so scared he started hopping toward the medevac on one leg until two men came to carry him on board. Collins then yelled from the chopper, "Bring me my leg! Bring me my leg!" Someone picked up Collins' left leg that had been blown off below his knee and handed it to him before the medevac lifted off. I would never get to know Collins or the three other new men who were killed.

Casey pointed toward the western perimeter and said, "The bodies of the two gooks are still over there."

The third one, who Casey had wounded, tried to crawl out the east side. The second platoon had found his body by the wire that morning.

"I can' believe it, Casey," I said while shaking my head, "We lost half of the Third Herd last night!"

The Third Herd had arrived with twenty-five men. Eight men were dead and four more were seriously wounded. There were only thirteen of us left when the sun rose on December 28, 1969.

I walked over by Lieutenant Foreman's foxhole and saw some of the guy's gear lying nearby. I recognized Lieutenant Foreman's helmet by the purple stain on his helmet cover. We had dropped a smoke grenade down a tunnel one day and he had placed his helmet over the entrance, trying to keep the smoke from rising up out of the opening. The purple smoke had stained his camouflaged helmet cover. I picked up another helmet lying beside the foxhole. "Whitey" was written on the helmet cover. I then looked in disbelief at a bullet hole in the front of the helmet. Whitey likely never knew what hit him. Wop was sitting in the foxhole with Mike Myers. Mike had been in the foxhole with Bob, Whitey and Lieutenant Foreman. Mike was the only man to survive. He had a minor shrapnel wound in his arm but had remained with the rest of us during the night.

Mike and Wop had been close friends with Bob Emery. They were both in shock over losing their best friend. Bob and Wop had been machine gunners at the same time. Although Wop was mad as hell, he was almost ready to cry.

"Those f---ing gooks killed my friends!" Wop said in frustration. "Who had the stupid idea for this bushmaster anyway?"

I put my hand on Wop's shoulder. He looked up at me with watery eyes, not saying anything more.

Mike turned and put his face in his hands and cried. Wop put his arm around Mike while they both cried. Bob had told Wop and Mike he had turned down the reassignment to the mortar platoon. We all knew Bob's decision had cost him his life.

I continued to survey the remains of our fallen comrades. A bloody towel and fatigues covered with blood were among the remaining signs of those men I had spoken with that past evening. When I walked back by Lieutenant Foreman's foxhole I saw several trip flares lying nearby. I then walked toward the concertina wire in front of their position looking for trip flares. I found one claymore mine that hadn't been detonated and saw potholes made by exploding hand grenades. But I only saw two trip flares in front of that position. Even if other flares had been fired the empty canisters should still have been there.

I walked back toward the foxhole and saw Dave Hardy.

"Did you hear who we lost?" I asked.

He had heard but asked me to repeat their names to be sure. Hardy didn't say a word.

I then said, "I only found two trip flares out there," pointing in front of Lieutenant Foreman's foxhole. "That's where the sappers snuck through the perimeter."

For some reason they only set out two trip flares. If there had been more trip flares in front of 3-6's position, the events of that past night might have been totally different. I remembered asking Lieutenant Foreman if he had his claymores set out, and he said, "Yes." I could have kicked myself in the butt that morning for not also asking about trip flares. I have often wondered, would one more question have saved those men?

I then slowly walked toward the western perimeter and walked up to the bodies of two sappers who had killed or wounded a dozen of my friends. The dead sappers were lying face up on the ground with their black shirts and trousers covered with blood from the bullet holes made by Casey's M-16 rounds. I felt like kicking the bodies or reaching down and beating the hell out of both of them in retaliation for what they had done. But that would have been a hopeless gesture of frustration. I stared at the two bodies for a moment and walked away in silence. We had set ourselves up for a butt-kicking in the middle of Charlie's country and he had literally kicked our butts.

I then saw Hugh Hearn standing guard at the foxhole he had shared with Doc Snyder and Bob Ryken, who had been seriously wounded, and Roger Cox and Otis Carthage, who had been killed. I walked beside him and asked if he was OK.

Hugh looked at me and shook his head as he said, "I can't believe I am still here, Sarge."

I said, "We're all lucky to still be here."

Hugh said he was on guard with Roger Cox when the sappers hit the two foxholes to their right. The other three men (Snyder, Ryken and Carthage) started piling into the foxhole with their weapons. Before he knew it, he was lying on the bottom of the foxhole with the other guys on top of him. Suddenly, one of the sappers opened on their foxhole with an AK-47 hitting the other four men.

Hugh said in a quivering voice, "Those other guys took all the rounds and saved me. I didn't get hit."

I put my hand on his shoulder and said, "Hey, Doc Snyder and Ryken are still alive. Be thankful you survived."

In addition to the body of the sapper that tried to sneak back out through the eastern perimeter, the men in the second platoon found three enemy bodies along the southern perimeter. One of them was likely the son-of-a-gun who threw the hand grenade at me early that past evening. All the enemy bodies were left where they were found.

It was frustrating to think of the needless loss of life the Third Herd had suffered since I arrived. It had started with Hal Harris when we were ambushed in September and concluded with us losing eight men in a single night. Although the morning of December 28, 1969 was a terribly sad day for the thirteen members of the third platoon who survived that past night, we were all thankful to be alive. We also knew our lives would never again be the same. The enemy had killed eight of our friends and inflicted an emotional shock upon those of us who survived, so severe; it could destroy the morale of the Third Herd.

I stopped to talk with Vick Ortega, Carl Seals, Ed Leberski and the other remaining members of the third platoon as I walked back toward my foxhole on the southern perimeter. Those men were quietly milling around their foxholes trying to absorb the fact that half of the Third Herd was gone. When I asked how they were doing, they all said they were fine. But I knew they weren't doing fine. They just didn't feel like talking about it.

I then found Jim Overbey sitting on the sandbag wall in front of his foxhole staring out over the perimeter smoking a cigarette.

"Jim," I said, "Are you OK?"

He quietly said, "Not really. I knew this was going to happen. I thought for sure they would get to me."

"The rest of us were lucky," I said.

"I had to load their bodies on the choppers last night," Jim said. "I don't know if I can take any more of this."

"Hang in there, Jim," I said while I put my right hand on his shoulder. "It's been one hell of a month for us, but we have to move on."

"Maybe last night was my fault," Jim said, "I should have tried harder to get the CO to move to another site."

"Don't feel that way Jim; they could have hit us anywhere out here."

Jim then asked, "Do you know what we are going to do?"

"Not for sure. I'll go see what's going on."

I then walked toward the CP and found Captain Dalton.

I asked, "Sir, what do you want us to do?"

The CO had talked with the battalion commander. He and a General from Division Headquarters were on the way out to talk with the CO.

He concluded saying, "We'll decide what we're doing after their visit."

A lone chopper soon circled overhead and then landed near the western perimeter. Two men exited. Captain Dalton walked over and shook hands with the Battalion Commander Colonel Crutchly and the one-star General Watkins. The division commander had been informed about what happened and wanted one of his staff to fly out and talk with Captain Dalton and some men in the company.

Most of us weren't too excited to see either of those men. We knew they had played a role in sending us out on the bushmaster. General Watkins walked with Captain Dalton to talk with some of the men. When they neared our foxhole Captain Dalton stopped and introduced me to the general.

"General, this is Sergeant Hogue. He's in the third platoon."

"Good morning, Sergeant," General Watkins said as he reached out and we shook hands.

I replied with a solemn, "Good morning, sir."

The general said he was sorry to hear we lost some good men that past night. He went on to say they were going to step up our activity out there and stop those NVA bastards.

I said, "That's fine, sir, but that will be too late for the men we lost last night."

General Watkins then said, "It doesn't sound like you agree with using bushmasters."

"This whole operation was a big mistake," I replied, "We played right into Charlie's hand."

I turned and walked away. The general moved on without saying anything further to me. Captain Dalton probably didn't like my comment to the General, but it was true. We could kill every damn NVA soldier left in the country, but it wouldn't bring our eight friends back. What had been a desolate spot in the Ho Bo Woods twenty-four hours earlier had become a deathtrap for those men.

We had basically flown in and waved a big flag in front of the enemy and said, "Here we are, come get us." And they did.

After a short while Colonel Crutchly and General Watkins flew off. Captain Dalton stood in the middle of the bushmaster site and yelled, "Tear everything down. We're going back to Patton."

With a big sigh of relief, I said, "Let's get out of this hellhole."

We kept several men on guard while the rest of us began dismantling the site. When I walked in front of the sandbag wall we had built at our foxhole I noticed holes in the sandbags.

I said, "Hey guys look at these sandbags."

None of us on the southern perimeter had been wounded but those sandbags had taken some hits from shrapnel or bullets during the night.

Dave Hardy poked his finger through one of the holes and said, "Those son-of-a-bitches tried to get us, didn't they?"

I said, "It sure looks like it." I then solemnly said, "We were the lucky ones."

When we began dismantling the site we began finding dud Chinese hand grenades made with a wooden handle to throw them. They were old and had a reputation of often not detonating. Suddenly, there was an explosion on the southern perimeter.

Some of the first platoon guys were retrieving sections of concertina wire and must have shifted a dud grenade causing it to explode. Amazingly, no one was injured. We cautiously searched the entire perimeter and marked several dud grenades with sticks to be sure everyone stayed clear of them. Ironically, we found a dud grenade not far from the little hole I had dug near our foxhole early the past evening. Again, it must not have been my time to go. Although we suffered a tremendous loss, it could have been much worse if all those enemy grenades had detonated.

We gathered up the concertina wire and took down the chain link fencing and rolled it up to be hauled away. We didn't want to leave anything useful for the enemy. We piled the wire, the steel poles and anything else worthwhile in a pile to be loaded onto choppers. We worked into the afternoon emptying the dirt from the sandbags into the foxholes and tearing down everything we had worked so hard to build the previous afternoon.

As the choppers landed, we loaded up the wire and other materials and ammunition we hadn't used. We also sadly took the gear belonging to the men who had been killed or wounded and loaded the final signs of their existence onto a chopper. We threw the remaining trash, empty C-ration boxes and ammunition boxes in a pile that covered the bodies of two dead sappers.

We were all hot, dirty, hungry and tired. We had busted our butts to set up the site, none of us had gotten much sleep, and then we had been working for hours to dismantle the site. But we all kept pushing on because we wanted to get out of there. A couple of the men asked me about Jim Overbey that afternoon. They were worried about him being so quiet.

I told them, "He needs a break. He's taking this pretty hard."

After all the material and equipment had been flown out, we gathered up our personal gear and weapons and made a final sweep of the perimeter to ensure there was nothing useful left behind. We waited for over an hour for the first lift of choppers to arrive and fly out the mortar platoon and their equipment. The first and second platoons followed, and the CO's staff and the remainder of the Third Herd were the last to leave. While we waited to be flown out, Captain Dalton told his demolitions guys, Poof and Puff, to use some C-4 explosives to destroy the pile of trash that covered the two dead sappers.

I heard him say, "We will blow the trash and those two gooks straight to hell!"

When the final lift of choppers landed at about three o'clock that afternoon the fuses to the C-4 were lit. I climbed aboard the last chopper and we lifted off. We asked the pilot to circle the site until the C-4 exploded and consumed the pile of trash and the two dead bodies in a huge fiery blast, sending a huge cloud of dirt, debris and smoke into the air. The pilot turned the chopper southeast toward Firebase Patton.

The following members of the third platoon were killed during the early morning of December 28, 1969.

- Sergeant Robert Emery was from Marine City, MI. He was eighteen years old. He arrived in Vietnam on July 26, 1969. I have been in touch with his mother and sent her pictures of Bob while he was in Vietnam and shared the details surrounding his death. Robert Emery is buried in Holy Cross Cemetery in Marine City, Michigan.

- Private First Class Terry Thornton was from Tulsa, OK. He was nineteen years old. He arrived in Vietnam on July 30, 1969. He was married and had a daughter. Terry Thornton is buried in Rose Hill Cemetery in Tulsa, Oklahoma.

- Second Lieutenant John Foreman was from Manlius, NY. He was twenty-six years old. He arrived in Vietnam on November 24, 1969. He served as our platoon leader for less than one month. John Foreman is buried in Clinton, New York.

- Private First Class Charles Merritt was from Runnells, IA. He was twenty years old. He arrived in Vietnam on October 12, 1969 and served as one of our RTOs. I later learned his dad and mine had grown up together in the small southern Iowa town of Kellerton. I met with his family in 1970 and visited his grave site in a small country cemetery near Kellerton.

- Specialist Fourth Class Danial "Whitey" Heiderich was from Overbrook, OK. He was twenty years old. He arrived in Vietnam on August 27, 1969. He was a good ole boy who died too young. Danial Heiderich is buried in Leon Cemetery in Leon, Oklahoma.

➤ Private First Class Alan Rader was from Fostoria, OH. He was twenty years old. He arrived in Vietnam on December 7, 1969. Alan Rader is buried in Maple Grove Cemetery in Findlay, Ohio

➤ Private First Class Otis Carthage, Jr. was from Northport, AL. He was twenty-one years old. He arrived in Vietnam on December 9, 1969. He is buried at Oak Ridge Cemetery in Northport, Alabama.

➤ Private First Class Roger Cox was from Marietta, SC. He was twenty years old. He arrived in Vietnam on December 11, 1969.

Allen Rader, Otis Carthage, Jr. and Roger Cox joined the third platoon one week before they were killed on that fateful night.

Numerous web sites are available to view additional information regarding these men and all others killed in Vietnam.

117 members of Alpha Company, 2nd Battalion, 14th Infantry Regiment were killed in action while the unit served in Vietnam from 1966 through 1970. The loss of the eight men in Alpha Company, Third Platoon on the night of December 28, 1969, was the largest single-day casualty loss suffered by any of the five companies in the battalion during the war. As devastating as the third platoon's losses were, that night could have been much more disastrous if the NVA had a mortar tube to fire rounds in upon us. We could have been nearly annihilated because the small foxholes would have provided us little protection.

The 25th Infantry Division suffered the second highest number of casualties in Vietnam in comparison to other Army Divisions. The highest number of casualties were suffered by the 1st Calvary Division, 5,464, while the 25th Division suffered 4,561 casualties.

There were many significant American single-day casualty losses during the Vietnam War. The largest single-day casualty loss occurred on November 17, 1965 during the battle of the Ia Drang Valley near LZ Albany in central South Vietnam. A battalion of the 1st Calvary Division was ambushed by two battalions of NVA soldiers resulting in 155 American deaths and 121 wounded. The estimates of NVA casualties at LZ Albany vary, but were near 500. Analysis of many battles involving sizeable American single-day losses found that losses were often escalated by military leaders misjudging the combat capabilities of enemy forces, no or minimal enemy intelligence information and overconfident unit commanders using inappropriate military tactics.

Danial "Whitey" Heiderich cleaning his weapon at Fire Support Base Patton. A 155MM howitzer is in the distance.

In the foreground is Lieutenant John Foreman.
The first man behind John is Glenn Haywood, who died on
Christmas Eve 1969. The third man is Robert Draughn.

Chapter 16

Rebuilding the Third Herd

I normally loved flying in choppers, but the flight back to Firebase Patton the afternoon of December 28th was a depressing ride. Although it was a clear, sunny day, and the scenery of the countryside below was clearly visible, I could only think about our friends who weren't returning with us. When I had talked with every one of those men that past evening, I had expected to see them in the morning. I sat on the floor of the chopper staring into the distant countryside, sadly realizing that I would never talk with or see those eight men again. I was again reminded how precious life was and how quickly it could be taken away.

December 28, 1969 was the saddest day of my life.

After we landed at Patton I walked into the eastern perimeter of the firebase. I then walked with Captain Dalton along the interior road and began talking about Sergeant Jim Overbey. I summarized my recent conversations with Jim and told the CO that some of the other men were also concerned about Jim's emotional state. Captain Dalton told me to visit him after I settled in.

Although most of the men remaining in the Third Herd had been in country for a while and knew what they were doing, I didn't know what the CO expected from us for a while. We were again without a platoon leader and didn't have a medic. Sergeant Overbey was next in line to be acting platoon leader, but I didn't think he should stay in the field. Seeing ten friends killed and five others seriously wounded in less than two weeks had taken a serious emotional toll on Jim. He had assumed a personal guilt regarding what happened at the bushmaster; although, everyone knew there was little more any of us could have done to save our friends, Jim felt personally responsible.

When we reached our assigned bunkers, I dropped my gear outside one bunker and breathed a sigh of relief. We had all worked our butts off the past two days and had only gotten a couple of hours of sleep before the sappers hit us. We were all in need of a good night's sleep, but with so few of us remaining in the platoon, we wouldn't be getting much sleep between guard shifts. I had never seen the men as quiet while they settled in that afternoon. Obviously the loss of our friends was still sinking into everyone's mind and was taking its emotional toll as we finally had a chance to relax.

I later walked over to the Alpha Company Command Post and found Captain Dalton inside his bunker. His bunker was high enough to stand up, so I walked in and I sat on one of the two bunks inside.

The CO asked me how the guys were doing, and I replied, "Not very well. Most of those men were good friends to many of us."

The CO said he expected us to be a pretty sad group for a while. He then asked about Jim Overbey.

I told Captain Dalton that Jim had admitted to me that the past night had gotten to him. Jim had lost his self-confidence and felt guilty about losing a dozen men. I thought Jim needed a break. The CO said he hated to load everything on to me, but he agreed that it sounded like Sergeant Overbey needed a breather for a while. But the CO wanted to talk with Jim personally before he made a final decision. Captain Dalton said he would ask the battalion commander to send us to Venice East until we were assigned additional men and to give us a few days to recover.

"That would be great." I said, "We can't do much else right now."

When I stood up, Captain Dalton put his hand on my shoulder to offer a little comfort while we walked outside his bunker.

He then said, "Have Sergeant Overbey come over to talk with me."

When I returned to our bunkers, I found Jim standing outside his bunker. I told him the CO wanted to see him in half an hour and summarized my conversation with Captain Dalton.

I said, "You might get out of here, Jim."

Jim looked at me seriously and said, "I need to, Hound Dog. I'm not worth a damn out here right now."

I told the men we were probably going to Venice East for a few days. I also sensed a new feeling of uneasiness among the men that afternoon. Losing eight men in a matter of minutes made us all start thinking more about our own mortality.

When I returned from the mess hall with some chow, Jim was waiting for me near my bunker. We walked away to talk in private. Jim told me the CO was sending him back to Cu Chi. Jim then said, "I don't want to let you guys down, but I can't handle it out here, last night scared the hell out of me. I can't shake it."

I replied, "Last night scared the hell out of all of us, Jim. Some time in the rear will be good for you."

A short while later, Captain Dalton stopped by our bunkers and asked the men to gather around. He started by expressing his sorrow regarding the men we had lost. He said he had talked with the battalion CO concerning the bushmaster and that they might have miscalculated how smart "Charlie" was. He reluctantly admitted that things could have been handled differently out there. The CO then said that he was reassigning Sergeant Overbey to Alpha Company Headquarters in Cu Chi and that I would be acting platoon leader until a new 3-6 was assigned. He was also sending us to Venice East for a few days. He then asked if there were any questions.

I knew the men had a lot of questions about the bushmaster, but no one asked any. However, after losing half a platoon, some questions needed to be raised before the matter was closed.

Captain Dalton looked at me and said, "They're all yours."

I said, "Thank you, sir," before he walked away. In one day I had gone from squad leader to acting platoon leader, except I still only had three stripes on my fatigue shirt. But I was ready for the challenge. Lieutenant Fielding and Lieutenant Foreman had relied upon us NCOs during their short tours of duty with the platoon. I had often assumed much more responsibility than that of a squad leader simply because we lacked an experienced platoon leader.

Wop was standing outside our bunker when I walked up. He was normally a pretty happy-go-lucky guy, and while I didn't expect any of the guys to be too cheerful, Wop look dejected. I asked if he was OK. He said, "I'm not doing worth a damn. My best friend is dead." He was taking the loss of Bob Emery very hard.

That evening, "Top" Seavey quietly walked up to a group of us while we were standing near our bunker. Top had been in three wars and told us that the past night was the worst he had ever seen. Top expressed his personal regret about the men we lost and gave several of us reassuring pats on the back before he walked toward his bunker as darkness settled over Patton.

I took the first guard shift at our bunker, wearing my helmet and flak jacket. The firebase was quiet, giving me some peaceful moments while I scanned the darkness along the perimeter. I couldn't get thoughts of the past night out of my mind and grappled to comprehend that those eight men were truly dead. There wasn't any Army training or a handbook to prepare us for losing friends in combat. Each of us survivors would have to deal with those losses in our own way, and hopefully without an adverse emotional impact.

I also thought about the four wounded men and hoped they were all still alive. Standing in the darkness under a clear sky with stars shining above, I solemnly said a silent prayer of thankfulness for being alive and asked the Lord to be with the families of the men who were killed. I then shed a few tears for my departed friends.

After my first hour on guard I crawled into my hammock, covered myself with my poncho liner and fell asleep. We rotated guard duty at Patton through a quiet and uneventful night. The next morning we all cleaned our weapons. After firing thousands of rounds during the bushmaster, everyone's weapon needed cleaning.

Before we left for Venice East, we had one more difficult task to complete. We gathered the personal gear of the men who were killed or wounded that had been left at Patton and sat it out to be taken back to Cu Chi on the supply convoy that afternoon. The guys in the rear would sort through it and send whatever they determined to be appropriate back to the families of our eight fallen comrades and on to wherever the wounded men would be sent back in *the World*.

Captain Dalton had asked for volunteers from the other platoons to transfer to the third platoon so that all our replacements wouldn't be FNGs. Later that morning three volunteers joined the third platoon: Tom Anderson, Randy Butler and John Bergen, nicknamed Bugsy.

I knew Bugsy because of a case of VD he caught from a Vietnamese hooker a couple of months earlier, which landed him in the 12th Evac hospital in Cu Chi for two days. A few men in the company had picked up a case of VD along the way, but Bugsy was the only one whose condition couldn't be cured simply with a shot of penicillin.

After we shook hands, Bugsy told me he volunteered to join us because he wanted a Purple Heart. Since the third platoon seemed to most often be in the middle of the action, he thought he would have a better chance of earning one. He then said. "And one more thing, Hound Dog; I'll walk point for you guys."

I said, "What? Are you sure?" He said yes. I told him I would let him know. I thought to myself, "Bugsy, you crazy son-of-a-gun."

Bugsy reminded me of Lieutenant Fielding, who had nearly gotten himself killed with his gung-ho attitude. We certainly didn't want cowards in the field, but I also had to wonder a little about guys who were too gung-ho about being out there.

We later heard news regarding our four friends who had been wounded. Doc Snyder had been shot twice in the chest, but amazingly survived. Bob Ryken's left leg had been severely injured, but doctors were able to save it. Randal Collins, lost his left leg below his knee and had other shrapnel wounds and Ben Carlson had multiple shrapnel wounds. All the men were in serious but stable condition. They would all be evacuated from Vietnam when they were stable enough to travel.

That afternoon the Alpha Company supply convoy arrived from Cu Chi. Junior Houchens (Houch) rejoined us after having a tooth pulled a day earlier. A toothache had allowed him to miss the bushmaster and may have saved his life.

After the supplies were unloaded, one of the deuce-and-a-halfs stopped in front of our bunkers. The driver yelled, "Load 'em up."

After we loaded the personal gear of our deceased and wounded comrades, I threw on my backpack and climbed aboard for the short trip to Venice East. Jim Overbey joined us; however, he would continue on back to Cu Chi. Most of the men knew why Jim was being reassigned and had talked with him during the day. Although the rest of us could have argued he was getting out easy, so to speak, I think everyone knew Jim had put in his time and legitimately needed some time in the rear.

When our mail was delivered on December 30th, someone said there was a package for Lieutenant Foreman and brought it over to me. When I felt the package and shook it, I guessed it was a bottle of booze. I opened the package and sure enough, it was a bottle of Jim Beam Whiskey from Lieutenant Foreman's sister Susan. I initially considered having it sent back, but then doubted his sister cared to have the bottle returned under the circumstances. I told the guys I would keep the bottle but didn't tell them what I planned to do with it.

On New Year's Eve morning, we were up early as usual at Venice East to clear the road, and after breakfast we settled in for the day. I spent a couple of hours writing to my parents, Jan Griffin and other friends and family I had heard from recently. During the day I walked around to see how the men were doing in the peace and quiet. A few guys were writing letters, while several were catching up on their sleep. I saw Vic Ortega and Ed Leberski standing outside the front gate watching the local civilians as they passed by along the road.

I walked out to the road where we talked about the bushmaster. Vic had been in the foxhole just west of me and said he saw shadows of movement on the north side, but he didn't want to fire. He didn't know if it was our guys or the sappers. Although reliving that night was painful for all of us, we also knew that if more of us had immediately started running to the northern perimeter, we could have easily shot each other. We sadly realized the action happened so fast that none of us could have stopped it. That was frustrating for those of us who had survived.

We also talked about the general U.S. military strategy being used to fight the war. Because our personal objective was hopefully to survive each day's mission, we weren't focused on the overall military approach to fighting the war. However, it was clear from our limited perspective that we were not gaining any military advantage and that the war was far from over. Sadly, our ten friends who had been killed during the past month may have died for naught.

The three of us wandered back inside Venice East and found a few guys stirring around. Often during the day someone would be trying to organize a poker game, or guys might be out on the road hustling up some girls. Obviously, the men weren't in that kind of mood. I talked with several of the men during the afternoon and listened to their frustration about the bushmaster. We had been used as bait to draw out the enemy. Unfortunately, it resulted in the death of eight friends. It would be difficult continuing on without them.

Around four o'clock that afternoon a deuce-and-a-half with several men aboard arrived from Patton to deliver our mail, C-rations, some ammunition that we had requested, sodas and our evening meal. Shortly after the truck left I asked the men to gather around my bunker. I started by saying that the past month had probably been the toughest month of our respective lives. We would miss our friends who were gone, but we had to accept what happened and force ourselves to move on. The guys looked at me and at each other, with some saying, "Yeah," or nodding their heads.

I went on by telling the guys to keep talking to me and with each other to discuss their emotions. I also reminded them that we would go back to the Ho Bo Woods someday. We needed to be ready to deal with it. Someone asked, "When are we getting some FNGs?"

I told the men that the CO had requested nine men, including a platoon leader, a medic and two NCOs. I would talk with the CO in the morning to see what was happening.

I then said, "Guys, it's New Year's Eve. We need to pull guard tonight, but I want to pay tribute to the men we lost and celebrate a little before dark."

I reached into my backpack that was lying nearby and pulled out the fifth of Jim Beam. I reminded the guys it was the bottle that arrived for Lieutenant Foreman the day before. Rather than sending it back, I kept it to have a drink in honor of him and the other friends we lost. For the first time in two days, I heard a cheer from the men and saw smiles on their faces when I handed the bottle of Jim Beam to Junior Houchens who was standing beside me. I said, "Hey, Houch, share it with everybody else."

"Oh sure, Sarge," Houch replied, with a big smile on his face.

The men found cans of soda and poured out some of the soda and poured in some whiskey. I soon had a Beam and Coke in my hand that had been mixed for me. After a few minutes, I told the guys I wanted to make a toast. Everyone stopped talking and gathered together.

I asked the men to take a minute to pay respects to the men we had lost; Hal Harris, Red, Haywood and Spivey, and the eight men who died on December 28th. We gave them a moment of silence while we stood in the middle of Venice East with our heads bowed.

I then said, "Men, we miss each of you, and we'll never forget you. But we'll see you guys in heaven someday because we've all served our time in hell, Vietnam."

I had tears in my eyes as I raised my Beam and Coke. Someone said, "May they rest in peace."

Every man raised his can of soda, with some of them giving their own brief tribute as we shared a drink in honor of our fallen comrades. It was a much sadder moment than I had anticipated. I took a minute to dry my eyes and clear my throat before I could talk to the guys again.

We began sharing stories concerning the guys who died. Ed Leberski talked about the day Glenn Haywood earned his nickname, John Wayne, when he ran down the hill firing his rifle with one arm. The guys chuckled, "Yeah, I remember."

Other guys talked about Whitey and smiled as they recalled his stories about living in the wide-open countryside of Oklahoma. We remembered Red as the happy-go-lucky guy from South Carolina and Chuck Merritt as the quiet guy who read his Bible nearly every day. I reminded the men that many of us should be thankful that Lieutenant Foreman had spotted that land mine detonator on December 17th.

It was good to see the guys smiling as they talked about their fallen comrades. Although I commenced the tribute in a somber fashion, it became the beginning of the healing process for us. We were letting the good memories concerning those men overcome the grief and sadness we felt during the past two days. Although we had repeatedly endured the tragedy of losing friends, the camaraderie between those of us who survived grew even stronger and created a lifetime brotherhood. Whatever happened to us, individually or as a group, we would help each other overcome our losses and hopefully make it through that damned war alive. December 28th was a somber reminder of just how dangerous our duty as infantrymen really was.

It was also important for those of us who survived the night of December 28th to move on without letting that event destroy our cohesiveness as a platoon. The new men joining the platoon would be looking to us *old timers* not only to learn the routine of field duty; they would also be looking to us for emotional stability. We had taken on a new burden because every new man joining the Third Herd would likely have been told about what happened on December 28th.

Wop came up to me while I was sipping my drink and said he had been talking with some of the guys about having a memorial service for our friends we lost.

"Great idea," I said, "I'll talk to the CO."

I enjoyed one of my Crooks cigars during the late afternoon that quickly passed into evening while the sixteen guys in the Third Herd enjoyed the Jim Beam and toasted to an early Happy New Year at Venice East. Hopefully 1970 would begin better than 1969 had ended.

The men grabbed some chow along the way, and when darkness neared we closed the front gate for the night. Most of the guys quietly settled into their bunkers when we began pulling one-hour guard shifts in the tower. I took advantage of being the ranking man in the platoon and didn't pull guard duty that night. I settled into my hammock for a good night's sleep. During the night the light of a flare lit up the sky and woke me up. Startled, I stepped out of my bunker thinking the men on guard had spotted something. I yelled to the men in the tower, "What's going on?"

Mike Myers leaned over the sandbag wall and said, "Happy New Year," and pointed toward Patton to the north. He then fired a red flare over Venice East. I looked towards Patton and saw colored flares flying into the air in celebration of the new year. Several other men had been awakened and had stepped out of the bunkers anticipating that something serious was happening. I told the guys everything was OK and said, "Happy New Year."

January 1, 1970 began as a sunny morning in South Vietnam. Like the U. S. military had done on Thanksgiving and Christmas, a one-day truce was declared on New Year's Day. The men at Patton and the other patrol bases wouldn't be going out on RIFs or ambushes and could relax along with those of us at Venice East. I talked with Captain Dalton by radio later that day. He told me five new men would be arriving the following afternoon. I also asked about having a memorial service for our guys and the CO said he would work on it.

Although I knew the men could use a few days at Venice East to relax, I also knew the platoon needed to get back into the action before too long to help put the month of December in the back of everyone's mind. With five new guys arriving, we would have twenty-one men, which was as many as we had operated with on several occasions. But we needed a medic, and I hoped for a couple NCOs to help me out until a new platoon leader arrived. Just after two o'clock the following afternoon, the Cu Chi supply convoy stopped by. I walked out to the road and waved at Jim Overbey sitting in the back of one of the deuce-and-a-halves. Jim said, "Hey, Hound Dog, here's some new guys for you."

The five men walked toward me while some of the guys came out to help unload our supplies. I talked with Jim who said he was doing better. I told him it had been a few sad days for us, but the guys were slowly accepting what had happened on the 28th.

After the convoy moved on toward Patton, I motioned for the new guys to gather around me. "Welcome to the third platoon, or as we're called, the Third Herd. I'm Sergeant Hogue."

I flashed back for an instant and recalled that was similar to how Sergeant Tom Brown had welcomed me to Venice East.

I continued, "As you likely have heard, we lost a dozen men a few nights ago, including our platoon leader. So, I'm acting platoon leader, platoon sergeant and most everything else for now."

I recognized one of the new men as Sergeant Richard Benson, who I had met on Christmas Day in Cu Chi. I reached out and shook his hand and welcomed him to the platoon. I then shook hands with four PFCs, Gregory Kilgore, Greg Valdez, Pat Stone and Norm Wilson, as they introduced themselves.

I briefly explained the purpose of Venice East and our responsibilities while we were there. I also told those men that the duty there was going to be the easiest duty they would see in the field. I then smiled and said, "So don't get used to it."

I led the five new guys through the entrance and gathered the rest of the platoon for introductions. We rearranged ourselves in the bunkers to make room for the new men. The bunkers at Venice East were large and accommodated everyone with no problem.

The next day, two more men arrived. One was medic Bill Covington who didn't carry a weapon because of religious beliefs. He told us, "You take care of me, and I'll take care of you." It was that simple.

The other man was another *shake'n bake*, Sergeant Warren Hansen. I sat down with Sergeants Benson and Hansen to divide the platoon into two squads, with a mix of *old timers* and new guys in each squad. I assigned Sergeant Hansen as first squad leader, and Sergeant Benson as second squad leader.

Captain Dalton stopped by later that day and asked when we would be ready to move back to Patton. I told the CO we could move back in the morning. The CO also said he was planning an awards ceremony in a day or two, and that the chaplain was arranging a memorial service at the same time. He asked me to organize a rifle squad and said I could deliver a eulogy if I wanted to.

"That would be great," I said, "I'd like to say a few words about those guys." As we stood together on the road, the CO said he would call on the radio and let us know when to be ready to move out. He also told me a new lieutenant should be arriving in a few days.

I smiled and said, "You can just promote me if you want to."

The CO chuckled and said, "I wish it were that easy, Hound Dog," and gave me a friendly smile before he climbed into his jeep. The next day another platoon arrived to take charge of Venice East and the third platoon returned to Patton and settled into a group of bunkers along the southern perimeter.

When I talked with Captain Dalton later that afternoon, he wasn't planning to send us out on ambush that night, but he wanted us to conduct a RIF near Patton in the morning to break in the new guys. He also said the memorial service and awards ceremony was scheduled for two o'clock the following afternoon.

I had thought about who I wanted to have in the rifle squad, and one of them was Bill Casey. He had joined the Third Herd shortly after me and had been one of our RTOs until Captain Dalton asked him to be one of his RTOs in November. Casey had known the men who were killed and probably saved several lives by shooting the three sappers. He was the hero on the bushmaster and was being recommended for a Silver Star (the third highest military decoration) for his action.

When I found Casey and first told him about our New Year's tribute at Venice East, he smiled and said, "Boy, I wish I could have been there." I then asked Casey to be on the rifle squad during the memorial service. He gladly accepted.

When I returned to our bunkers, I gathered the men and told the new guys to make sure their weapons were clean and asked Sergeants Benson and Hansen to make sure their squads would be ready for a short RIF in the morning. I then asked Mike Myers, Vic Ortega, Carlton Quick, Dave Hardy, David Debiasio and Ed Leberski to stay with me. I told those men I wanted them to be in the rifle squad during the memorial service the following afternoon. I told the guys that we should take a few minutes to practice.

I asked someone to find Bill Casey and have him come over to our bunkers. After Casey arrived, the guys each grabbed a rifle. I would be in charge of the rifle squad and give the commands. The seven men lined up and I led them through the sequence of raising their weapons to *port arms* and then to their shoulder ready to fire. After a few practice runs, the men decided they were ready. We had all seen rifle squads back in *the World*, and I had conducted hours of drill and ceremony during my training. But since arriving in Vietnam, we didn't have a need for military formalities. Hopefully we would do it right during the memorial service.

After I received our RIF orders from Captain Dalton the following morning, I told Sergeants Benson and Hansen I wanted them to take charge. I would observe and take over if we ran into trouble. After the platoon walked along the path through the wire on the east side of Patton, Sergeant Hansen gave Bugsy a compass heading, and we moved out. I had taken Bugsy up on his offer to walk point. One of the new guys, Norm Wilson, walked second as our pace man and was given the distance to the first checkpoint. We walked in a single column with one man out thirty meters on each flank. Our route initially took us toward the grove of trees northeast of Patton, where the two VC had been shot out of the trees that past November. I told the new guys that although the area looked peaceful; they needed to be ready for anything at any time, just in case.

We moved through the trees and found nothing. I let the two new NCOs keep track of our route and hopefully ensure that Bugsy and Wilson kept us on course as we continued. We had walked one klick south from our second checkpoint when I sent the word forward for Bugsy to stop. I had the men circle up in a perimeter and I knelt down while motioning for Sergeant Hansen and Sergeant Benson and Bugsy and Norm Wilson to join me in the middle of our perimeter.

I said, "We're off course, guys." Quickly, Sergeants Hanson and Benson pulled out their maps, trying to pinpoint our location. Bugsy was sure he had been leading us on the correct compass heading. When I asked Wilson if he had been accurately counting his steps, he said, "Well, I think so."

"Well, have you or not?" I was familiar with the area around Patton and I knew where we were, but I was getting upset by not hearing a definite answer from Wilson. He reluctantly admitted that he might have miscounted his paces to the second checkpoint.

I laid my map on the ground to show the men what had happened. We used topographical maps that showed trails and roads, streams and rivers and identified the terrain as being rice paddies or trees or whatever it actually was. By comparing the countryside to the details on the map, I could determine where we were.

I pointed to my map and explained that we should have been moving to our third checkpoint between two clusters of trees 200 meters to our west. Wilson must have miscounted his paces to the second checkpoint and taken us too far east. I reminded the two new NCOs it was their responsibility to periodically check their maps to ensure we remained on course.

I showed Bugsy where I wanted him to lead us to get us back on the proper course.

I stood up and said, "Bugsy, let's go."

"Yes sir," he said jokingly.

Before we moved out, I told Wilson I would talk with him when we got back to Patton. I had Ed Leberski walk second and count paces the rest of the way. I knew Ed wouldn't miscount. We finished the RIF by walking through rice paddies south of Venice East and then along the road back to the firebase.

I was taking off my gear when Norm Wilson walked by. I'm sure he hoped I wouldn't notice him, but I told him to follow me as I walked away from the bunkers for a private conversation.

I said, "You know you could have gotten us in trouble out there today?"

"Yes, Sergeant."

"I know that was your first RIF, but all you had to do was to count your paces. Was that too much to ask?"

"No Sergeant."

I raised my voice and said, "Do you want to walk point tomorrow so you don't have to count paces?

"Not really, Sergeant."

"The next time you count paces you damn well better get it right. If you get the entire company lost, the CO will be on you a whole hell of a lot worse than I am. Understand?"

"Yes, Sergeant."

I told Wilson if he ever had trouble counting paces again to stop the column and talk with me. I walked away leaving Wilson standing by himself.

It was a few minutes after one o'clock when I unhooked the gear from my pistol belt and clipped the empty belt around my waist. I told Dave Hardy I was going to the CP and asked him to make sure the guys in the rifle squad were standing by near the chopper pad at the aid station by 1:45. I would meet them over there. I grabbed my helmet and headed toward the command post.

The chaplain was talking with Captain Dalton when I walked into the CP area. I said hello to Chaplain Wideman and shook his hand. The chaplain told us he had arranged the memorial service to start with the playing of the National Anthem and then opening remarks by Captain Dalton. Chaplain Wideman would then conduct a brief service. Rick Shields, who had come out to Patton for the service, and I would each deliver a brief eulogy, and then I would command the rifle squad. The service would conclude with a bugler playing Taps.

The Chaplain had printed programs for the service with a picture of the Tomb of the Unknown Soldier at Arlington Cemetery on the front. Below the picture were these words:

> *"That we here highly resolve that these dead*
> *shall not have died in vain."*
> —Lincoln's Gettysburg Address November 19, 1863

The program stated the service was being held on January 5, 1970 at Fire Support Base Patton. Willard Spivey and Glenn Haywood and the names of the eight men who were killed on December 28th, were listed along with the order of the service. The awards ceremony would follow the memorial service.

The men in the rifle squad were standing by when I arrived on the north side of the firebase. There was an open area adjacent to the chopper pad that provided ample room for the company to gather. The rest of the company had flown out early that morning for a RIF and had returned to Patton shortly after we did. The entire company soon gathered for the memorial service. I hadn't spent much time thinking about what I would say and didn't have any written notes prepared. Although delivering a eulogy would be a new and difficult experience for me, it was something I wanted to do.

An organ had been brought out for the service, and the organist played prior to the service. When two o'clock arrived, the rifle squad stood in line along the north side of the area facing south. The remainder of the company gathered in platoon formations on the east side of the area facing west.

First Sergeant Seavey called the company to attention to begin the service with the organist playing the National Anthem, while two men presented the American and Army flags that ruffled in the soft wind that flowed on that hot and sunny afternoon.

Captain Dalton then walked forward to address the company.

Captain Dalton began by saying, "Men, we're here today to pay our respects to ten members of Alpha Company, third platoon, who gave their lives for their country. I know the loss of these men has left feelings of sorrow and frustration, especially for you men in the third platoon. Unfortunately, their deaths and the deaths of thousands of other brave men are the tragic consequence of this war. I share in the sadness for their loss. We all lost ten brave comrades, but many of you have also lost ten good friends. May those men rest in peace."

Chaplain Wideman continued the service by saying a prayer for our fallen comrades and for their families back in *the World*. He then read the 23rd Psalm: "The Lord is my shepherd; I shall not want ...."

The Chaplain then talked briefly about war. He addressed the death and tragedy inflicted by the fighting and how difficult it was to understand. He said, in summary, that God allowed us the free will to create the destructive tools of war, and if we choose to use those tools to battle our fellow man, we must endure the consequences, including the loss of good friends. Although we were grieving the loss of our comrades, we would become stronger men as we ultimately moved on from that tragedy as grateful survivors.

Rick Shields then stepped forward to deliver a brief eulogy, talking about some of the men he knew best and expressing his personal sorrow over losing good friends and brave comrades with whom he had served.

I then stepped forward and read the names of the ten members of the Third Herd who were killed in December 1969:

> Second Lieutenant John Foreman
> Sergeant Robert Emery
> Specialist Forth Class Danial Heiderich (Whitey)
> Private First Class Otis Carthage, Jr.
> Private First Class Roger Cox
> Private First Class Glennon Haywood
> Private First Class Charles Merritt
> Private First Class Willard Spivey
> Private First Class Terry Thornton
> Private First Class Allan Rader

I hesitated to clear my throat before I continued. It was the most somber moment of my life. This is my recollection of what I said:

"These men were ten of the bravest men I have ever known. Glenn Haywood and Willard Spivey accepted the risks of being our point team while leading us into an area infested with booby traps and land mines on December 17th. Lieutenant Foreman saved several lives when he spotted a second land mine detonator that same day. Whitey could have stayed behind during the bushmaster because of a medical condition, but he willingly went with us. Bob Emery could have moved to the mortar platoon, but he chose to stay with his friends in the third platoon. And Terry Thornton had talked with me about re-upping to get out of field duty, but he never pursued it. Charles Merritt had a strong religious belief and read his Bible nearly every day. Three of those men joined the third platoon just days before they died. I barely knew them. Although other men will be assigned to the third platoon, these ten men will never truly be replaced. They were fellow soldiers and were our friends. These ten men are not with us here today, but they will remain in the hearts and minds of many of us forever. Although the families of these men are mourning their loss, I hope they will somehow find comfort in knowing their loved ones bravely made the ultimate sacrifice while honorably serving their country."

My voice was quivering when I concluded, and I fought back tears as I walked back to join the rifle squad.

Chaplain Wideman returned and asked that we observe a moment of silence for our fallen comrades. After the Chaplain offered the benediction, he turned toward me and nodded his head indicating we should proceed with firing the volleys.

I stepped forward and turned left, facing down the rifle squad. I cleared my throat and said, "Squad, Atten-Hut."

The squad came to attention, standing shoulder to shoulder with their rifles to their right sides. First Sergeant Seavey called the remainder of the company to attention and then gave the command, "Company, Present Arms," which was the command to salute. Each man in the company raised his right hand in a salute.

I gave a "Port Arms" command and the squad raised their rifles and held them across their chests.

"Ready." The men raised their rifles to their shoulders with the barrels pointed in the air as each man stepped forward with his left foot and turned sideways.

"Aim." The men aimed into the air to the south over Firebase Patton.

They stood ready for an instant, and I shouted, "Fire!"

The thunderous sound of seven M-16s simultaneously firing broke the silence of the moment and startled many of the men who were standing at attention.

The men in the squad kept their rifles pointed in the air, and I again shouted, "Fire!"

A second volley roared into the air.

And for the final time, I shouted, "Fire!"

The sound of the firing rifles again rang out and echoed over the firebase.

I then gave the command, "Squad, Present Arms." The men in the squad stepped back with their left foot and held their rifles vertically in front of their chests with the barrels pointed straight up. I raised my right hand to salute.

The bugler in the distance played Taps, and again, tears formed in my eyes. After the bugler finished playing Taps, I cleared my throat and gave the command, "Order Arms," the command for the rifle squad to lower their rifles to their side. The memorial service was over.

I gave the squad the unofficial command of, "OK guys, relax."

We all breathed a sigh of relief. It went just as we had practiced. I told the guys thanks and gave them pats on the back for a job well done. Our formal tribute and sad goodbye to our ten fallen comrades had been completed. Captain Dalton walked over and thanked us for doing a great job with the rifle squad.

We took a few minutes to reorganize for the awards ceremony that began with Captain Dalton speaking briefly to the company. He said he was proud of the way we had performed during the bushmaster and again expressed his sorrow for the losses we sustained. The CO then began presenting medals to several men who were lined up in front of the rest of the company. He worked his way along the line and presented each man his medal or medals. Rick Shields received a Silver Star for rescuing Lieutenant Fielding during the ambush that past November. Our Chieu Hoi, Hue, was awarded a Bronze Star for leading us back to Patrol Base Hunsley that same night.

When Captain Dalton reached me, one of his staff said, "For wounds received in action on December 17, 1969 in the Republic of Vietnam, Sergeant Richard F. Hogue is awarded the Purple Heart."

While Captain Dalton took the Purple Heart from the leather carrying case and pinned the medal on my fatigue shirt, he said, "Hound Dog, don't get any more of these."

"I'll try not to, sir." We exchanged salutes.

After the last man received his medal the company was dismissed. I took pictures of the guys in the Third Herd who received medals and hung out for a while talking with guys in the company.

The third platoon was assigned an ambush patrol that night. After getting off course during our RIF that day I wasn't sure all the new men were truly ready, but I also knew they wouldn't learn anything sitting inside their bunkers. None of us knew everything we should have when we went on our first RIF or first ambush. Every man had to learn on the job and hopefully survive through his mistakes. I told Sergeant Hansen his squad had ambush duty that night and gave him the location. Dave Hardy was in Hansen's squad, so I told Dave to keep an eye on Hansen and help with the ambush. Dave had pulled dozens of ambushes and he knew what to do out there.

The night passed with the ambush patrol not having any contact. While Sergeant Hansen and his squad stayed at Patton to catch up on their sleep, the rest of the third platoon joined the company for a RIF the next morning that would take us northeast of Patton and west of the Saigon River. We were soon aboard choppers, with several new men headed for their first RIF in the boonies. We were going to another uninhabited area near the Ho Bo Woods.

We landed in an open area on high ground. The first platoon led the RIF, with the third platoon in the middle along with Captain Dalton's CP group. The second platoon pulled up the rear. We encountered easy going through open countryside dotted with trees, bushes and hedgerows as we moved along our route. As the hot, dry morning progressed we found trails with footprints that definitely weren't made by GI boots. Although we hadn't seen any enemy troops, they had been moving through the area.

The sound of a single explosion suddenly came from the front of the columns. And then there was silence. We all kneeled down and kept a watchful eye out around us. I had been in the field long enough to know a single loud explosion was almost always a booby trap.

Tom Anderson, our RTO, was next to me listening to his radio. Tom confirmed my suspicions when he heard that the point man in the first platoon had tripped a booby trap and there were two men down. I told Sergeant Benson to move his squad forward and help the first platoon set up a perimeter for the medevac. We patiently sat in our perimeter for nearly fifteen minutes, but surprisingly, there was no medevac. We usually had a quick response from medevacs. Although we were a long way from Cu Chi, one should have arrived. I walked over to Lieutenant Mike Walsh, the first platoon leader, and asked, "What's up with the dustoff (medevac)?" He didn't know but said the CO was raising hell over the radio. Lieutenant Walsh told me his point man and pace man had been peppered with shrapnel. He said, "They'll make it if that damn chopper ever gets here."

A couple of minutes later someone *popped smoke* when they heard a chopper in the distance. After the medevac landed the two wounded men were quickly loaded on board. We slowed our pace after the first platoon hit the booby trap. There were surely more in the area. The ground was dry, and there was plenty of vegetation for concealment making the landscape ripe for setting booby traps. Even if there weren't any NVA or VC in the immediate area, the booby trap they left behind had wounded two GIs.

The afternoon got even hotter with almost no breeze to help cool us down. I could see by the expressions on the faces of some of the new guys that their butts were dragging while we continued on the RIF that would cover five more klicks (three miles). I chuckled to myself because those FNGs reminded me of my first RIF on a hot afternoon that past August when I was dragging butt and sucking down water. I had plenty of water and shared it with a couple of the new guys who had emptied their canteens and needed it much more than I did. We completed the RIF without any further incidents and were picked up by a lift of choppers later that afternoon. While we flew back to Patton, I noticed the new guys enjoying the wind blowing on them through the open doors of the Huey.

➢ *Based upon the recollections of several former members of Alpha Company, there were no further bushmasters conducted like the one we conducted in December 1969.*

Although peace talks and initial American troop withdrawals commenced in 1969, over 20,500 U.S. military personnel were killed in South Vietnam from 1969 to 1973 when the last American combat troops left South Vietnam. Lieutenant Colonel William Nolde from Mount Pleasant, MI was killed on January 27, 1973, eleven hours before the cessation of all hostilities in accordance with the Paris Peace Accords.

An estimated 8.7 million Americans served in the armed forces during the Vietnam War. While approximately 2.7 million of them served in Vietnam, less than 300,000 faced combat as infantrymen.

Memorial service rifle squad at Fire Support Base Patton on January 5, 1970. Left to right – Myself, Mike Myers, Vic Ortega, Carlton Quick, Bill Casey, Dave Hardy, David "Wop" Debiasio and Ed Leberski.

Ironically, I serve in a similar capacity as shown in the previous picture as a member of the All Veterans Honor Guard in Denver, CO. I primarily serve as the rifle squad commander while providing military honors when veterans are laid to rest at Fort Logan National Cemetery.

Chapter 17

The Ambush

Two days after the memorial service, Captain Joseph Murphy replaced Captain Dalton as the Alpha Company Commander. Senior officers felt that Captain Dalton's decision not to use the originally designated location for the bushmaster attributed to the eight American fatalities. Consequently, he was relieved as our CO.

We continued operating out of Firebase Patton in early January, when Captain Murphy brought Second Lieutenant David Phillips to our bunkers and introduced him as our new platoon leader. After Captain Murphy left I introduced Lieutenant Phillips to several men in the platoon, then told him what we had been through during the past month. I pointed out the *old timers* as men he could rely on until the rest of the new men gained more experience. With our new 3-6 on board, we had twenty-four men in the third platoon.

A short while later I heard yelling from a nearby bunker as though something serious had happened. I ran over and saw Carl Seals exiting from the bunker holding his blood-covered right hand.

I yelled, "Doc, grab your bag!"

I then asked Carl what happened. He told me that Chester Sampson was throwing his knife at a beam in the bunker and accidentally hit Carl's hand. I turned and saw Sampson standing behind me. I pointed at him and said, "I'll have a talk with you later!"

Nearly all of us carried a knife, but this was the first time anyone had been injured by one of our own knives. Carl was grimacing in pain when Doc Covington bandaged Carl's hand to control the bleeding. Doc then led him to the medical aid station.

I immediately walked off with Sampson for a little ass chewing. I started by asking, "What the hell were you doing in there?"

He explained that he had thrown his knife at a rafter and it hit Carl's hand instead. I shook my head in near disbelief.

I said, "You know, there are thousands of VC and NVA who are trying to kill us. We don't have to try to kill each other!" I was mad.

I said, "Since Carl is one of our point men, maybe you'll have to take his place."

Sampson didn't say a word. He was really a good guy and had become one of our machine gunners. I actually didn't want to reassign him, but I also didn't want to let him off the hook for what he had done. Carl was later flown back to Cu Chi for X-rays. The knife had gone completely through his hand and might have broken a bone or severed a tendon.

Lieutenant Phillips and I later decided to leave Sampson as one of our gunners to avoid having to break in a new man. I gave Sampson extra details around the firebase and made sure he knew we had let him off pretty easy. A couple of days later we received word that the knife had severed a tendon in Carl's right hand, and he couldn't move his trigger finger. He was being evacuated back to *the World* for surgery. We never saw him again.

While we continued working out of Patton for several days, I spent time with the new guys telling them about my past six months in the field and sharing some of my personal observations on the war. I had walked hundreds of miles through the rice paddies and woods of South Vietnam, flown about seventy-five air combat missions in choppers, saw many of my friends killed and wounded, slept in the rain, and literally fought for my life. And for what? Nothing had really been accomplished. When we suffered casualties, new troops arrived, and we would start all over again. Additionally, we were risking our lives for the South Vietnamese people who didn't seem to give a damn one way or the other. In fact, many of them were making money from the war and wanted to see the war continue forever.

One morning during the second week of January we were preparing to fly out of Patton for a RIF when the CO was notified of a report of VC in some hedgerows several klicks north of Patton. The entire company was choppered to the site and we organized on line in a holding position about 100 meters from the hedgerow which was approximately 50 meters long. The third platoon was in the center while the first and second platoons were on our left and right flank. The plan was for the three platoons to slowly advance toward the hedgerow while a Cobra gunship circled overhead.

Since we had not received any enemy gun fire, the CO ordered us to advance toward the hedgerow. Without communicating with the remainder of the platoon, our new 3-6 (Lieutenant Phillips) stood up and jumped over the dike we were organized behind and started walking forward expecting the rest of the platoon to follow him.

I was motioning for the rest of the third platoon to slowly move forward when 3-6 looked around and realized he was about 25 meters in front of everyone else and totally exposed to enemy troops that were believed to be near the hedgerow. He walked back and then joined the rest of the platoon as we cautiously maneuvered toward the hedgerow.

The gunship overhead spotted an enemy soldier in a tree behind the hedgerow and another one by an adjacent trail and had opened fire on both of them. Lieutenant Phillips took Chester Sampson, one of our machine gunners, and a couple other men and walked toward the trail with the remainder of the third platoon following them. Those guys opened fire and sprayed the area in front of them as they moved forward because the thick vegetation limited everyone's visibility. They soon came upon a dead VC soldier lying beside the trail.

We then heard rifle fire coming from the second platoon who were on our right. Although we weren't taking any enemy fire, we immediately took cover while surveying the area around us. RTO Tom Anderson was near me and soon told me that second platoon had radioed that they had shot another VC out of a tree. It was a young female similar to the girl that had been shot from the trees east of Patton last fall.

The company swept through the nearby area and encountered no other enemy troops. Similar to what we had encountered on previous occasions, a small number of enemy soldiers were operating in the countryside planning their next move. Fortunately, they had been killed, and most importantly, we did not sustain any losses.

We spent the remainder of that day walking southward through mostly open countryside toward Patton. We searched through a hamlet on the way but found nothing suspicious. Later we stopped in the village of Trung Lap just north of Patton while our medics treated a young boy who had cut his foot earlier that day.

After we settled into our bunkers at Patton, Lieutenant Phillips talked with me about his eagerness that morning. He smiled and said he would spend a little more time observing how we operated in the field so he wouldn't possibly get himself or any of the rest of us hurt. We continued to work as a team while the other new men gained experience one day at a time.

On January 23rd we were flown to a remote area near the Ho Bo Woods to join a mechanized unit at a hard spot, where our primary mission would be to pull nightly ambushes. The countryside was flat and covered with tall grass that had turned brown from lack of rain and thick vegetation much like I had seen before in the Ho Bo Woods. It was another desolate place, the kind the enemy liked to hide out in.

The hard spot was primitive, with one tank to provide artillery fire and three APCs, each with an M-60 and .50-caliber machine gun. Our three rifle platoons were spaced around the perimeter and assigned to foxholes with small sandbag walls in front. The mortar platoon and command post were set up near the center of the site. Our latrine was simply a small trench in the ground.

During our first afternoon at the hard spot, Captain Murphy assigned the third platoon an ambush site 500 meters south of the hard spot. Lieutenant Phillips and I both planned to go on the ambush. I would keep an eye on the new men and could take charge if necessary, if we had to pop the ambush.

They didn't fly out hot meals for us; therefore, we grabbed some chow from a case of C-rations. As the sun was starting to set, Sergeant Benson's squad gathered their gear and walked through the perimeter wire along with Lieutenant Phillips, Doc Covington and me. I wasn't comfortable going out near the Ho Bo Woods with so many new men, but the only way those men would learn about pulling ambushes was to go out on one.

We easily found the ambush site and then moved to a holding position a short distance away. As darkness neared, I put my finger to my lips and looked around at the new guys to remind them to be as quiet as possible while we moved to the ambush site. I identified three positions, with two directly behind a hedgerow, giving us visibility along the trail, and as usual, the third position to cover the rear. Sergeant Benson and I each settled in at one of the two forward positions, and Lieutenant Phillips took the rear position.

It was completely dark as we began our procedure of having two men on guard at each position. I snuggled up in my poncho liner, put on mosquito repellant, pulled my mosquito net over my head, and hoped for some sleep before I took my first hour on guard.

Carlton Quick woke me up later during the night, and whispered, "There's movement out there." I immediately sat up and Quick handed me the starlight scope. It was a clear night, and with the light from the stars and moon, I saw three people moving from left to right over 100 meters in front of us. They were too far away for us to ambush them, I radioed the command post and two other ambush patrols that we had spotted three people to our west who were moving north.

Ten minutes later we heard several explosions in the distance. We soon heard over the radio that the first platoon popped their ambush northwest of us on three NVA troops. Luckily, the first platoon sustained no casualties because claymores and hand grenades killed all three enemy troops without a firefight. The NVA had gotten by us, but the first platoon nailed them. The remainder of the night was uneventful and we safely returned to the hard spot the following morning.

We didn't go on a RIF that day, giving the men the freedom to write letters or clean their weapons, while others found a comfortable spot to catch up on their sleep. Because we didn't have enough water to spare for showers, we washed ourselves up as best we could with the available water. Some of the men had a small plastic pan they filled with water to wash with or shave. I normally pulled the liner out of my steel helmet, turned the helmet upside down and poured water in it to wash with or shave. I would set up the small mirror I carried, or held it in my right hand while I shaved with my left. Except for the fact we were engaged in armed combat, serving in the field could have been described as an extended camping trip.

For the next three nights I alternated taking Sergeant Benson's or Sergeant Hansen's squad on an ambush and leaving the remaining platoon members to guard the hard spot. We didn't spot any enemy movement during those ambushes, and for the most part, the new guys were catching on and fitting into the platoon with no major problems. Sergeant Benson was frustrated that the learning process seemed to be going slowly. I told him he would likely learn something new every day he served in Vietnam.

Most of us *old timers* talked periodically about the men we had lost during the bushmaster a month earlier. Although it became easier to talk about what had happened, the pain of losing our good friends would never go away. Some of the new guys didn't understand what we were going through, but they would someday. I knew it would only be a matter of time before we would lose more friends.

On January 27th, we were told the hard spot would be abandoned on the first of February and we would return to Firebase Patton. During a conversation that afternoon with Lieutenant Phillips and Captain Murphy, we agreed I would stay with the platoon until another NCO was ready to take over my job. I was nearly the senior NCO in the company and hoped to find safer duty in the not too distant future. I told them that Sergeant Benson appeared to be the best NCO to replace me. As an alternative, I suggested that Dave Hardy be promoted to serve as platoon sergeant. The platoon needed another NCO, so we didn't put a definite date on my reassignment, but the CO said he would get me out of field duty when he could.

After eating another meal of cold C-rations, I gathered my gear for what I hoped would be an uneventful ambush patrol. After a dozen of us including Lieutenant Phillips moved through the perimeter, Bugsy led us towards the ambush site through terrain with tall grass, scattered bushes, and hedgerows. We often had limited visibility in any direction once we left the immediate area around the hard spot. With that heavy vegetation, the enemy could often move about without detection. After we reached the ambush site we stopped while Lieutenant Phillips looked around, and then asked me what I thought.

I said, "We can't set up here."

It was a wide-open spot with no concealment or protection for us to set the ambush. The nights had been clear, and there had been a nearly full moon the past evening. Enemy troops could easily spot us if we set up there. I told Lieutenant Phillips I had noticed a better site about 100 meters back down the trail. We still had enough daylight if we hurried back and set up there.

Lieutenant Phillips agreed that we should find another site. I motioned to the men that we were turning around and told Bugsy to lead us back. I followed Bugsy and told him to stop when we arrived at the site I had recalled. There were dirt mounds and bushes on the west side of the trail that we could use for concealment. It wasn't an ideal location, but it was too late to look elsewhere.

I quickly designated positions for the men to settle into as the sun began setting. I had originally planned to take the rear position, but changed my mind and set up in the left forward position along the trail. I set Sergeant Benson in the right forward position while Lieutenant Phillips settled into the rear. I was with Bugsy, Greg Valdez and Doug Jansen. While we settled in we began setting out our claymores, I told Bugsy and Jansen, "Go ahead," while Valdez and I stood guard.

The two men walked forward and placed their claymores facing the trail. When Bugsy stood up and began to walk back toward me, I started walking out to set up my claymore. I had taken only a few steps when I heard a seemingly muffled explosion. It was different from any other explosion I had heard in Vietnam. I immediately felt a terrific force and a blast of heat from the explosion, and in what seemed like slow motion, I fell backwards onto the ground.

I lay on my back, dazed, not sure what had happened. But I knew something was seriously wrong. I felt the startling feeling of both numbness and pain throughout my body. My ears were ringing, but I could hear other men screaming in pain and someone yelling, "Doc!"

I slowly raised my head in an effort to see what had happened to me. What I saw scared the hell out of me. All I could see was blood squirting out of my lower left leg with every beat of my pounding heart. My first frightening thought was, "I'm going to bleed to death!"

I yelled, "Doc, I need help!"

I laid down and looked up to the darkening sky overhead and silently said, "Lord, don't let me die this way."

The first man to come to my aid was Greg Valdez who had not previously seen anyone seriously wounded. Valdez knelt beside me and was stunned when he saw my mangled left leg and then slowly said, "Jesus Christ." Those weren't encouraging words for me.

I shouted, "Stop the bleeding!"

Valdez opened the field dressing he carried and placed it over the gushing wound in my leg. He then took the towel he had around his neck and tightly wrapped it around my left leg. I was relieved not to see any more squirting blood. I hoped and prayed that the bleeding could be controlled long enough to get me back to Cu Chi alive.

There was commotion and shouting voices all around me. Men were screaming in pain and I heard Lieutenant Phillips yell, "One man at each position stand guard!"

"That's good, 3-6," I thought to myself.

While some men stood guard, others helped Doc Covington attend to other wounded men. There had been only a single explosion and we weren't taking any enemy fire. I knew we had hit another booby trap and shrapnel had wounded several of us. One man continued to scream in pain as Doc Covington knelt beside me.

I tried to sit up but Doc put his hand on my shoulder and said, "Lie down, Hound Dog." Doc looked at my left leg and quickly pulled a large field dressing from his bag and tightly wrapped it around my leg.

I grabbed Doc's arm and asked, "Is the bleeding stopped?
Doc replied, "It's under control, you'll make it."
I breathed a sigh of relief. I then asked Doc, "Who's screaming?"
"It's Sergeant Benson."
I rested my head on the ground and thought, "Damn, he just got here."

Doc gave Valdez another bandage to wrap around my right hand that had been hit with shrapnel and was covered with blood. I also told Doc Covington my right foot hurt. Doc checked my foot and said there were shrapnel holes in my boot, but saw only a little blood. He wanted to leave my foot alone because my boot and sock were likely controlling the bleeding. I just nodded my head, indicating I understood.

The combined sensations of pain, warmth and numbness engulfed my left leg while I lay on the ground. I told myself, "It's gone." My right hand and right foot both hurt like hell, but all I wanted to do was stay alive long enough to get back to the 12th Evac in Cu Chi. Before Doc moved on to check the other wounded men he asked if I wanted some morphine.

"Yeah, Doc," I said. I was feeling more pain than I had ever felt in my life.

Doc gave Greg Valdez a morphine tube and said, "Just stick it in his arm."

Morphine came in little disposable tubes (like a tube of glue) with a needle on the end. You stuck the needle into someone and squeezed the tube. Valdez had never given anyone a morphine shot before.

I told him, "Just, stick it in my arm."

Valdez stuck the needle into my upper left arm. I didn't feel anything with all the other pain I was experiencing. Mike Myers kneeled beside me and handed me my glasses that he had found on the ground nearby. Surprisingly, they were still in one piece. Mike then put his hand on my shoulder and said, "Hang in there, Hound Dog. We'll get you out of here in a few minutes."

"I'm trying; but it hurts like hell, Mike."

I was awfully thirsty, and I asked Mike for a drink of water. I knew we weren't supposed to give an injured man water, but he found a canteen and gave me a sip of water anyway. I said, "Thanks."

Mike told me it looked like Bugsy had tripped the booby trap a few feet to my right. The explosion must have blown shrapnel to the sides rather than straight up. Greg Kilgore and Norm Wilson had been peppered with shrapnel but were not too seriously injured. Bugsy and I had been more seriously wounded, and Sergeant Richard Benson had been critically wounded in his left arm, left leg and abdomen. I continued to hear Benson's screams of pain while we waited for a medevac. The Third Herd was still recovering from the loss of half of our men a month earlier, but again, in an instant, five more of us were down.

Tom Anderson, our RTO, had called for a medevac immediately after the booby trap detonated. I hoped and prayed it would be there soon. I was totally at the mercy of the good Lord. If the enemy attacked us, I was a goner. And if a medevac didn't get there pretty soon I might be a goner anyway. I knew the bandages on my left leg wouldn't control the bleeding forever.

To my great relief, I soon heard the most beautiful sound in the world – the distant sound of rotor blades chopping their way through the evening air. Someone popped smoke to identify our position, and I heard Anderson talking on the radio to guide the pilot into our location.

As the chopper neared, Lieutenant Phillips came over to me and said, "They don't have enough litters for everyone. Can you walk?"

If I hadn't been in so much pain, I might have laughed.

I said, "You're kidding me?" He walked away without saying another word.

My initial fears of bleeding to death began to subside as the chopper neared. Although we were fifteen miles north of Cu Chi, the medevac had arrived in what seemed to be only a matter of minutes after the booby trap detonated. But I wasn't out of there yet. They still had to land the chopper, get us loaded aboard and get out of there before *Charlie* had a chance to ruin the rescue.

Mike Myers leaned over and put his arms around my head to protect me from the dirt and debris stirred up by the chopper while it descended onto the trail in the front of our ambush site. Two men ran to the chopper and pulled the litters off. One of the new guys, Pat Stone, placed a litter on the ground beside me. Doug Jansen helped Mike Myers and Greg Valdez cautiously lift me on to the litter with Mike saying, "Be careful with his leg!"

Doug and Mike carried me to the waiting medevac and my litter was locked in place on the floor of the chopper. Three of the other wounded men were lying on litters loaded above and beside me. Norm Wilson was able to walk to the chopper with help and sat on the floor. I lay on the litter with the noise of the chopper blades drowning out all other sounds.

I thought, "Let's get out of here."

The pilot soon revved the engine and slowly lifted the chopper off the ground. I looked over my shoulder and glanced out the open door and saw the remaining seven men starting to pack up all the gear. Since the site had obviously been revealed to the enemy, they needed to get out of there. They could set up another ambush site, but with only seven men, they were vulnerable. I assumed they would try to move back to the hard spot. Ready or not, Lieutenant Phillips was fully in charge of the Third Herd.

A brief moment of sadness hit me as I lay on the litter. I might never see any of those men again. Guys I had fought with in the field and had fun with back at Cu Chi were quickly being left behind as the chopper roared through the evening sky over South Vietnam.

The medic on board checked on each of us while we flew along, making sure our bandages were secure and asking if we were OK for the moment. I told him my body hurt like hell, but there was nothing more he could do for me. I didn't hear any more screams from Sergeant Benson. I hoped he was still alive. I was grateful to have gotten off the ground and that we would be at the 12th Evac within minutes.

As we flew above the countryside, I thought about the thousands of wounded men in previous wars who died or suffered for days before being evacuated. I had helped carry several of my buddies to a waiting medevac after they were wounded, and most of them survived because of the prompt medical attention they received. I hoped that chopper would be the salvation for Sergeant Benson and the rest of us lying there, clinging to our lives.

The morphine seemed to be having little effect. My left leg began throbbing in pain and my right hand and foot continued to hurt terribly. But all that was bearable. I knew I would soon be receiving medical attention from a host of doctors and nurses. Unless some new complication set in, I started to believe I was going to live.

I looked at the bandage on my right hand and noticed my watch was still attached to my wrist and was still running. It was 7:00 p.m.

I lifted my head and saw the outline of the perimeter bunkers as we neared Cu Chi. I could see a few dim lights as we flew overhead and neared the 12th Evac landing pad. I remembered my previous flight in a medevac a month earlier. I had easily walked off the chopper after it landed at the hospital. However, I wasn't going to be as fortunate the second time.

Nearly 8,000 American women served in Vietnam, most as military nurses. Several women were wounded and eight nurses died in Vietnam. One nurse was killed by hostile fire. Army Lieutenant Sharon Lane was killed during a rocket attack at Chu Lai on June 8, 1969.

South Vietnam was divided into 44 provinces, similar to county designations in most U.S. states. Alpha Company primarily operated in the Binh Duong, province that generally encircled the Cu Chi area northwest of Saigon. Army casualties suffered in the Binh Duong province during the war (2,742) were the second highest number of Army casualties suffered in any other South Vietnamese province.

Chapter 18

Doc, Save My Leg

———————— ~~~~~~ ————————

After we touched down on the hospital landing pad, medical personnel rushed to the chopper and carried us into the emergency room and placed us on examination tables that were aligned near the center of the room. Doctors and nurses immediately surrounded me and began cutting off my fatigues while they examined me to determine the location and the extent of my injuries. I felt a surge of pain and gritted my teeth when they cut the boot off my right foot. The medical staff also removed some of the bandages Doc Covington had put on my wounds. I couldn't see what they were doing with my legs, but one doctor was concentrating solely on my left leg to control the bleeding. I didn't ask any questions. I hoped that by some miracle my leg could be saved.

A nurse asked my name, rank and service number as she documented my personal information and recorded details the medical staff was telling her about my injuries. I heard doctors and nurses shouting orders and asking for help as a flurry of activity continued while they aided the five of us. Sergeant Benson periodically screamed in agony as another team of medical personnel attended to his serious injuries. I heard nothing from the other three wounded men as bustling activity continued in the emergency room. I endured surges of extreme pain while the medical staff continued to examine and bandage my injuries.

A nurse injected a needle into my left arm and started an IV of ringer's lactate while another nurse put a new dressing on my right hand. After several minutes, most of the medical staff stepped away. I slowly lifted my head to look at myself and realized I was completely naked. A nurse asked if I wanted a towel placed over me. I told her I really didn't care. Lying there naked was the least of my concerns. She did lay a towel over my waist. I softly said, "Thanks."

Soon afterward a chaplain stopped by and asked if I would like him to say a prayer for me. I said, "Yes," whereupon he quietly said a brief prayer for me. I don't remember what he said, but it was comforting knowing he was praying for us five wounded men.

A doctor walked to my side and introduced himself as Dr. Sullivan. He told me they would first take X-rays and then I would be taken into surgery. He also said my left leg was seriously injured, and then put his hand on my left shoulder and said, "I don't know if we can save it."

I nodded my head indicating I understood before he walked away.

The doctor's words confirmed what I had feared from the moment I first saw blood gushing from my left leg. I raised my head one more time, realizing that I wasn't just having a bad dream. I saw my entire left leg wrapped with dressing and gauze. My right foot looked like one huge bandage. I also moved the tips of my right fingers that were sticking out of another large bandage to make sure all five were still attached. They were.

Two corpsmen soon wheeled me toward the X-ray room. I waited a while because Richard Benson was given first priority among the five of us. Although I was conscious while they took a series of X-rays, I was in a daze, only partially comprehending what was going on. The sedation medication they had given me in preparation for surgery was taking its effect. I was eventually wheeled into the operating room and gently placed upon an operating table. While the medical staff scurried around, I struggled to remember what had happened that evening.

We were establishing an ambush like I had done dozens of times previously. Suddenly, an explosion knocked me to the ground, and I was quickly fighting for my life. There would be no more firefights, no more booby traps and no more ambushes for me. From that night forward, my challenges would be significantly different than I had ever imagined, and might be as difficult, if not more so, than any of the challenges I had experienced during the past six months in Vietnam.

Dr. Sullivan approached the operating table and told me they were ready to administer the anesthetic. I reached up and touched his arm with my left hand and said, "Doc, save my leg."

He said he would do the best he could. I began counting. "1, 2 …" Everything went black.

When I first opened my eyes after the surgery I was so groggy I didn't comprehend anything that was happening around me. I heard muffled sounds of the medical personnel talking and walking around me and sensed them touching me periodically. Although I felt considerable pain, I also felt continued numbness throughout most of my body while I drifted in and out of consciousness. It was like I was dreaming and had no control over what was happening. Sometime later I was wheeled into a recovery ward and carefully lifted onto a bed. My left leg felt totally numb. I was too weak and groggy to lift my head to look and see if I had one leg or two.

No one spoke to me primarily because I wasn't alert enough to hold a conversation. I spent most of that night sleeping, but woke up periodically because of the severe pain and general discomfort.

When I woke up the following morning, I gradually began to feel more alert and also felt a lot more pain. I slowly sat up enough to glance down at the foot of my bed. I was stunned when I saw only my right foot sticking up from under the sheet. My left leg was gone. I didn't know where they had amputated it; I only saw that the sheet was lying flat where my left foot would have been. Although I knew there was little chance of saving my leg, I was still shocked to see that it truly was gone. I had often thought about being killed in Vietnam, but surprisingly, I hadn't thought about losing one of my legs.

A nurse stopped by to check on me and asked how I was doing. I told her I felt pretty lousy. She brought me some cereal and juice for breakfast, but I wasn't hungry. I just sipped some juice through a straw.

Some time later another nurse walked up to my bed, followed by Dr. Sullivan. He explained that the bones, nerves and blood vessels in my left leg had been so severely damaged by shrapnel it was impossible to save my lower leg. My leg was amputated four inches below my knee. He showed me an X-ray of my left leg taken before I went into surgery. A section of the bones below my knee had been completely shattered. Only a few bone chips were visible on the X-ray.

Dr. Sullivan went on saying shrapnel had broken bones in my right foot and my right thumb had been broken. He had also removed pieces of shrapnel from my right hip. With all the pain I had experienced elsewhere, I hadn't realized my hip had been injured. My right eardrum had also been broken by the concussion. Although I had sustained life-threatening injuries, he believed I would fully recover. The doctor concluded by telling me that I had lost considerable blood. They had used three units of ringer's lactate and two units of blood during surgery.

I wasn't alert enough to ask questions. The news was so overwhelming it was all I could do just to comprehend what had happened to me. After Dr. Sullivan left, the nurse told me I would be leaving Vietnam in a couple of days and would be flown to Japan, where I would stay for several days before I would be flown back to *the World*.

After the nurse left I took a moment to look at my mangled body. My left leg was gone below the knee. A huge dressing covered my left knee and severed limb. My right foot was bandaged, and a splint wrapped with gauze extended to just below my right knee. A large bandage was taped over my right hip. And there was a big dressing wrapped over my entire right hand, with only the tips of my fingers sticking out. Fortunately, I was left-handed.

Later that morning someone brought me a small bag with my personal belongings including my wallet, my watch and my glasses. I was happy to see my wallet again. I didn't have much money in it, but all the addresses for my family and friends were in there. I hoped to write a few letters soon to let family and friends know more concerning what happened and how I was doing.

A nurse told me a telegram had been sent to my parents, but she didn't know how long it would take to be delivered. I wondered how

Mom and Dad would take the news. At least I was alive. I knew whenever the telegram did reach my folks; the news would quickly spread all over town. I asked a nurse for a sheet of paper and a pen to write a letter to my folks. I knew they would be anxious to hear from me personally. I wrote the letter as follows in shaky handwriting:

---

28 Jan

Hi

You probably heard what happened, <u>don't worry</u>. I will be all right. We hit a booby trap and five of us were wounded. They had to amputate my left leg below the knee. Besides that, I wasn't hit too badly. Now don't worry, I will be ok. I'm going to Japan in a couple days. I will be there awhile and then come home. They say I will walk OK again but will take a while. Don't worry, I will be home safe soon.

Love Dick

Shortly after I had finished the letter to my folks, three men entered the ward. They were awarding Purple Hearts. Getting another Purple Heart had been the farthest thing from my mind. When the group reached my bed, a colonel asked my name to confirm they had the right man. Another man read the citation:

"This is to certify that the President of the United States has awarded the Purple Heart, first Oak Leaf Cluster (meaning second Purple Heart), established by General George Washington at Newburgh, New York, August 7, 1782, to: Sergeant Richard F. Hogue, United States Army for wounds received in action January 27, 1970, Republic of Vietnam. Given under my hand in the city of Washington this 28th day of January 1970."

The colonel handed me the citation and the Purple Heart medal in a blue leather-covered case. He shook my left hand and wished me well. The men then moved along to award Purple Hearts to several other men on the ward. With much less fanfare than was associated with my first Purple Heart, I was holding my second. My injury in December was little more than a scratch. But when I was wounded on January 27th, I could have died. Upon reflection, my first Purple Heart was easily earned, but the second one definitely wasn't worth it.

In addition to the pain I felt, I was also very uncomfortable. I could only lie on my back. It was too painful to try rolling to one side or the other. I was able to fall asleep periodically, and when I was awake, I watched the activity on the ward to pass the time. The ward was nothing more than a steel Quonset-hut type building with a row of hospital beds aligned along each side. Fortunately, it was air-conditioned.

Most of the other men on the ward also appeared to be seriously wounded. For the most part, we were a pretty quiet bunch. If the rest of the men felt like I did, I knew they weren't in a talkative mood. I tried to look around and see if any of the other guys from the Third Herd were on the ward, but I didn't recognize anyone.

To my surprise, I saw familiar faces early that afternoon. Vic Ortega, Dave Hardy, Ed Leberski, Mike Myers, Bill Casey and David Debiasio were walking toward my bed along with Rick Shields and Jim Overbey. It was great to see those guys again. I shook their hands with my uninjured left hand while they gathered around my bed.

I smiled for the first time since I had been wounded. I summarized what Dr. Sullivan had told me. My left leg was amputated below the knee, but my other wounds should heal with no major problems. I talked about the past night with the guys who were on the ambush with me. Mike Myers said after the medevac flew off, they quickly packed up and cautiously walked in the darkness and met up with a squad from second platoon who had set up an ambush closer to the hard spot. They all returned to the hard spot early that morning.

Before those men were flown back to visit me that morning, the company had returned to our ambush site to be sure no gear had been left behind. It appeared the booby trap was a mortar round, or possibly a 105MM artillery shell. Either way, I was lucky to be alive.

I then asked the guys how they got to Cu Chi. Bill Casey said he told Captain Murphy some of them wanted to see me before I was evacuated, and the CO had a chopper flown out to bring them in. Seeing my friends one more time was a great boost to my morale. I couldn't remember any time in the past when they let men fly back to Cu Chi to see someone who had been seriously wounded. We normally just loaded men aboard a medevac and never saw them again.

I asked the guys what they knew about the four other guys who had been wounded. They thought everyone would be OK, except Benson. Sergeant Benson's left leg was amputated above his knee, his left arm was badly mangled and he had serious internal injuries. He was in critical condition after going into cardiac arrest three times during the past night and wasn't allowed visitors.

Those men made me feel very special by coming back to visit me. After going through hours of hell the past night, flying those men in to see me was the best thing anyone could have done for me. Amazingly, I felt little pain from my injuries while they were there.

The camaraderie and friendship that had developed among all of us was special because we had fought for our lives together. Although I knew I might never see some of those men again, I also knew I would never forget them. Each of those men said, in their own way, they were sorry I had been wounded and hated to see me leaving that way. Jim Overbey was very quiet that day. Seeing me lying in the hospital bed was difficult for him.

I shared a good-bye with a handshake or gentle hug with each of my friends before they left and we exchanged best wishes, knowing we were moving our separate ways to fight totally separate battles. I said, "You guys be careful out there without me. I'll keep in touch."

Dave Hardy said, "Let me know where you end up back in *the World*. I'll look you up someday."

Soon after the guys left, a hospital corpsman came by and asked if I was ready for a sponge bath.

I hadn't had a shower in over a week and likely had some aged dirt on me that hadn't been cleaned off during my surgery. The corpsman first washed my face and then shaved me. I hadn't shaved for a couple of days and was in need of one, at least by Army standards. The corpsman then helped me to wash the rest of my body that wasn't covered with dressings. Although that sponge bath was difficult, because most every movement was painful, I felt refreshed after we had finished.

A short while later I had more visitors. Captain Branch, my former CO and Lieutenant Donaldson, my former platoon leader, stopped by. A few minutes later, second platoon leader Lieutenant Higginson came in followed by Chuck Gorman, our former RTO, and Ken Hungate, an RTO in the CP group. I didn't know where all those guys had come from, but I was happy to see them. They were all naturally concerned about me and quietly listened while I explained my injuries and what I knew about my prognosis.

Lieutenant Higginson said he hated hearing about me being wounded so badly, but he could tell by the expression on my face that I was relieved to be going home. I told those men that I never expected to end up like I was, but fortunately I wasn't lying in the morgue. I had to accept my fate and was thankful to be alive. Those men stayed for a while and then we shared good-byes and best wishes.

Although it had been great for those guys to come by to see me, it was sad to see them go. During the past six months those men entered my life and we had put our lives on the line for each other without limitations. Accordingly, we formed a friendship and comradeship, more special than any relationship we had formed with anyone in the past. Suddenly, those men would no longer be a part of my daily life. In an instant on January 27th I had become a short-timer; my fighting days were over.

I fell asleep later that afternoon and woke up when they served the evening meal. I still wasn't very hungry, but a few bites of food did hit the spot. A young nurse who introduced herself as Maggie stopped by early that evening to tell me that unless complications arose, I would be flown to Saigon the next day, and then on to Japan to continue my recovery. I had looked forward to leaving Vietnam almost from the first day I had arrived, but I hadn't planned on leaving flat on my back.

However, after seeing twelve of my friends killed in action, I knew I was fortunate. The hours after being wounded had been the most traumatic hours of my life. Although physically and emotionally, I would never be the same, I was anxious to leave Vietnam. Lying in bed and sleeping whenever I chose was a huge contrast to the past six months. But nearly getting killed was an awfully hard way to get some bed rest. I awoke again later that night when most of the lights were turned off. It was quiet while most men slept, but I stayed awake wondering what would happen to me and how losing my leg would impact my life. Maggie and another nurse were catching up on paperwork. When Maggie saw me stirring, she walked over to see if I needed anything. I said I was fine, just concerned about my future.

Maggie pulled up a chair and began talking with me. It wasn't a nurse-to-patient conversation; rather, it was a young woman talking with a concerned GI. She asked me about myself and what I had been doing during my time in Vietnam. I told Maggie I was from Iowa and briefly summarized my experiences stomping through rice paddies and the Ho Bo Woods and seeing twelve friends killed.

Maggie (Army 1st Lieutenant Margaret Mackaben) told me she had worked in the emergency room for the first few months of her tour, but enjoyed the less challenging pace since being transferred to the recovery ward for the remainder of her tour that would be ending in August. Maggie said the most difficult part of her job was never knowing what happened to her patients after they left the 12th Evac.

Maggie asked how I was dealing with losing my leg. I told her I had accepted what happened and was thankful to be alive. "That's great," Maggie replied with a smile and then offered her insight into my future. She thought I would be in Japan for a week or two and then be flown back to *the World*. I would likely end up at Fitzsimons Army Hospital in Colorado.

Maggie said I would be fitted with a prosthesis (artificial limb), to enable me to walk again. She encouragingly told me I should be able to lead a nearly normal life. Maggie spent about 10 minutes talking with me and then said she should check on other patients. Maggie gave me a quick kiss on my cheek before she walked away.

Maggie's sincere words helped to relieve my concerns and made me feel more secure about my future. That conversation was the best medicine she could have given me. Maggie's comforting words helped me get through my long and slow recovery. Although there was a lot of uncertainty in front of me, I anticipated it wouldn't be any worse than what I had experienced during the past day and a half.

I awoke the morning of January 29th to the sounds of the staff on the ward. The lights were on and the nurses were checking patients and dispensing medications while others served breakfast. Maggie stopped by before she went off duty and gave me her best wishes. I thanked her for taking good care of me and said good-bye.

While I lay in bed that morning I wondered if my parents had received the Army's telegram, and if so, how they were dealing with it.

(The following occurred in Schaller, Iowa on January 29, 1970.)

It was a typical cold winter day with snow on the ground. Dad was out of town making deliveries all day. Like most small towns, Schaller didn't have a Western Union office, but there was a telegraph machine at the Central Popcorn Company. When the office staff arrived on the morning of January 29th, the following telegram was there:

WESTERN UNION
TELEGRAM

W. P. MARSHALL, President

Paid from Washington D.C. Jan. 28, 1970   10:37 P.M.

Mr. & Mrs. Charles Hogue
Schaller, Iowa

Secretary of the Army has asked me to inform you that your son Sgt.
Richard F. Hogue was wounded in action in Vietnam on 27 Jan. 1970 by
fragments while establishing a night defensive position when a booby trap
detonated. He received traumatic amputation on the left leg below the knee
and wounds to the right hand, right foot and flank.

Please be assured that the best medical facilities and doctors have been made
available and every measure is being taken to aid him. He is
hospitalized in Vietnam. Address mail to him at the hospital mail section
APO San Francisco 96381. You will be provided progress reports and kept
informed of any significant change in his condition.

Kenneth Wickham, Major General USA

Because everyone in the office knew my family and me they were
stunned when they read the telegram. The staff discussed how they
should deliver the news because they assumed my mother would be
home alone.

Jim "Ham" Currie, who was a member of our Presbyterian
Church, said he would deliver the telegram. He found our minister,
Reverend Nusbaum, to go with him to deliver the telegram to my
mother. Around ten o'clock that morning Ham Currie and Reverend
Nusbaum stopped in front of our house and walked up to the door.
When my mother answered the door, she knew they were delivering
bad news.

Knowing Mom's first thought would be that I had been killed, the
first thing Ham said was, "He's alive."

They gave my mother the telegram and quietly stood with her
while she read the shocking message. She started crying, partially in
grief that I had been seriously wounded and partially in relief I was
still alive. Although my parents knew I was facing combat in Vietnam,
that telegram was naturally very disturbing.

Ham Currie called the plant where Dad worked and explained what had happened. They would try to contact Dad somewhere along his delivery route. Mom then called my sister Marilyn in Sioux City and delivered the news. Marilyn later drove to Schaller to be with Mom.

Mom called my sister Jan and other relatives and friends to tell them the news concerning me. My granddad walked over to be with Mom after she had called him. After many people around Schaller heard the news, they called, and some stopped by the house to see if there was anything they could do.

Mom later called my girlfriend Jan Griffin in Omaha to deliver the news that I had been wounded. Ironically, Jan had received a letter from me recently saying that I was doing fine.

They hadn't been able to contact my dad during the day; he pulled up in his truck late that afternoon not knowing I had been wounded. When he walked into the house Mom immediately told him what had happened to me and handed Dad the telegram.

The word of my being seriously wounded again brought the war close to Schaller and created more worries for the families of several hometown men who were still in Vietnam. My parents spent the next several days worrying about me while awaiting more news regarding my condition. Fortunately, they had the support of family members and many friends.

During the early afternoon of January 29th at the 12th Evac in Cu Chi, they prepared to move those of us who were stable enough to leave. I had been lying naked under my sheet the entire time, so a corpsman helped me through the painful task of putting on a pair of blue hospital pajamas. Almost any movement hurt. I was then placed on a litter and taken from the ward to a waiting bus. We were then driven to the airfield and loaded onto a C-123 twin-engine transport plane designed to carry litters on both sides of the main cabin.

The men walked slowly while they carried us on board and then gently laid each litter onto the brackets that held the litters in place during the flight. They thoughtfully didn't want to create any more pain for our already aching bodies. Once we were secured on board, the engines roared as we rolled down the runway and lifted off from Cu Chi and turned southeast towards Saigon.

I had experienced many long days and nights trying to survive in the boonies during the past six months. There were many times when I thought my tour in Vietnam would never end. But when we lifted off that afternoon I remembered my arrival in Cu Chi like it had been last week. My tour of duty in Vietnam was nearly finished. We flew over the rice paddies and hills below where other men were still exposed to firefights and booby traps. I wondered, "How many more men would lose their lives or limbs before the war was over?"

It was a short flight to Saigon about twenty-five miles southeast of Cu Chi. The pilot made his approach and a smooth landing at Tan Son Nhut Air Base. We were again loaded onto a bus and transported to a hospital holding ward where I would spend the night. I would fly on to Japan the next morning. I was beat and in pain after I was helped from the litter onto a bed. My whole body ached from the vibrations and bumps during the trip. I obviously had little endurance.

After I settled into my home for the night, a nurse came by to check on me. She gave me a shot of medication to ease my pain that was getting worse and also gave me a penicillin pill. All of us who had been seriously wounded were given penicillin for several days to combat infection from the rusty shrapnel, dirt and debris that had pelted our bodies. After they brought my evening meal, I nibbled on a few bites of food but left most of it on the plate. I didn't feel like eating. Later they offered me the choice of a beer or soda. I normally wouldn't have passed up an offer of a beer, but I felt so bad, a beer didn't sound good. I asked for a 7-Up and slowly sipped it through a straw.

For the first time since I had been wounded I was dejected. Physically, I felt lousy, and emotionally, I was completely alone. Bugsy and some of the other injured men from the Third Herd might have been somewhere on the ward, but I hadn't seen any of them during the day. All my other Army friends were back in Cu Chi or out in the field, and I was still a long way from my family and friends back in *the World*.

Emotionally, leaving Vietnam was nearly as difficult as leaving home that past summer. I had to make another sad emotional transition as I left very special friends behind in Vietnam, not knowing whether I would ever see any of those guys again.

Physically, I actually felt worse that night at Tan Son Nhut than I had the previous night in Cu Chi. I was dead tired but couldn't fall asleep. I couldn't find a comfortable position for long and nearly any movement continued to be painful. And the wound in my right hip started to become, literally, a pain in the butt. If I happened to turn toward my right side, the pain was severe. I took several short naps during that long and uncomfortable night.

The hustle and bustle started early the next morning as the hospital staff prepared us for our scheduled nine o'clock flight to Japan. I finally felt a little better. Some of the severe pain I suffered the past night had subsided, but it was still very painful to move any of my injured limbs. I was hungry enough to eat some breakfast along with taking my early morning dose of medication. And I was also surprisingly in better spirits knowing I was leaving Vietnam in an hour or so. That would lift anyone's spirits.

They again started the ritual of moving each of us onto a litter and loading us on a bus that carried us to a large Air Force C-141 transport plane. It took maybe an hour to load us on board and to make sure dozens of us wounded GIs were secured for the flight to Japan.

After the four jet engines started to whine we were soon headed down the Ton Son Nhut runway and lifted off from South Vietnam. It was a remarkable feeling, knowing I no longer had to worry about serving in combat. During the past six months I had grown accustomed to being exposed to the hazards of war and accepted the consequences of serving as an infantryman, including the possibility of death. I was still amazed how most of us had accepted our combat duty. We were expected to perform like men, while most of us were still boys. We got up every morning, put on our gear, grabbed our weapons and, in a fashion, went to work. However, we had the most dangerous job in the world and never knew if we would live through the day.

But that was all being left behind while the plane rose skyward, leaving Vietnam in the distance. Although I was leaving seriously injured, I felt as though the burden I had been carrying for the past six months had been lifted from my shoulders. After the plane leveled off, the nurses came around to check on us patients. I told a nurse that except for some pain, I was doing well considering my injuries. I later settled into a reasonably comfortable position and fell asleep.

The six-hour flight to Japan was uneventful, although it was a challenge to pee into a little disposable urinal since I only had the use of one hand. I ate a little lunch, but for most of the flight I watched the nursing staff take care of the patients and slept.

The pilot then announced we were on our final approach into Japan. After the plane landed and the doors opened, I felt something I hadn't felt in a very long time: cold air. I had expected it to be warm in Japan, similar to what it had been in Vietnam, but I was wrong.

I was glad I had a blanket over me when they carried me from the plane that afternoon. It wasn't a freezing cold like I had often experienced in Iowa, but it was cold enough to be a bit of a shock to my body until I was inside the warm bus. After another short ride, we were carried through the cold air and into the 106th General Hospital. I was placed on a wheeled cart and rolled down a long corridor and into a ward that held a dozen men. After being assisted into a bed, I put the small bag containing my wallet, shaving gear and a pen and paper I had been given before I left Vietnam on a bedside stand. I was settled in.

I looked around to check out my new home. There were windows behind a row of six beds on each side of the ward with men lying in them, looking much like me, covered with huge white dressings. I saw several other men with limbs missing; two men had lost both of their legs. Every patient basically looked in relatively bad shape. It appeared that we had all been wounded in Vietnam and were recuperating until becoming stable enough to be flown back to *the World*.

After crossing nearly 3,000 miles of ocean that day and being a little closer to *the World* I felt pretty good. It still hurt when I moved, but I didn't have constant pain like I had during my first couple of days and nights. After the evening meal I settled in and finally got a decent night's sleep.

The next morning, I encountered a new experience associated with what I anticipated would be a long hospitalization. I had used a urinal several times the past couple of days but hadn't had a "BM." After breakfast it was time. A nurse knew it would be too difficult and too painful for me to move to a toilet. She handed me a bedpan and then pulled the curtain around my bed to give me some privacy. I pulled myself up with my left arm using a bar that hung over the center of my bed. After some painful maneuvering, I scooted my butt onto the cold, metal pan. Getting on was tough, but getting off without creating a mess was an even greater trick. As the days passed, we chuckled at each other when we called for a bedpan, knowing what a struggle it was to use. I couldn't wait to be able to use a regular toilet again. Even those smelly out houses in Vietnam were better than using a bedpan.

My next experience was to be taken in a wheelchair to physical therapy (PT). I thought after nearly being killed and losing one leg, I would be able to relax for a few days. But no, they wanted me to start exercising to help the healing process and prevent my muscles from degenerating too much. After the therapist helped me onto a padded table, he had me lift small cloth bags filled with metal pellets with my arms and legs. My right foot didn't hurt too much when I lifted the weight with my leg, but it was painful when I lifted a pellet-filled bag with my right hand. I could lift my left thigh with little pain, but when I tried to bend my left knee, and my stump, as I had learned to call it, it hurt like hell.

After spending thirty minutes with the physical therapist, he wheeled me back to the ward. Later that morning a doctor told me I would be going into surgery the following morning to ensure all the shrapnel and debris had been removed from my left leg and to further close the wound with stitches. I wasn't looking forward to another operation but I wasn't given a choice.

That afternoon a corporal stopped by and asked me if there was anyone I wanted to call back in *the World*. They would arrange for calls through the Military Affiliate Radio System (MARS). MARS would transmit a signal from Japan to a radio operator in the United States, who would contact our desired party by telephone to communicate with us. They would coordinate in advance with the calling party for a time to call and then bring a mobile phone to us at the designated time for our call. The calls were normally made during the mornings in Japan when it was the previous evening back in *the World*.

My folks were the first ones I wanted to call. I knew they would be relieved to talk with me and hear how I was doing. I also listed my sister Marilyn, girlfriend Jan, and college buddy Paul Alesch as people I would like to talk to. I was excited about being able to talk with my folks and others back home during the next few days.

I hadn't done much the past couple of days except travel, but the time had passed quickly. I kept wondering what the guys in the Third Herd were doing and how Lieutenant Phillips was adjusting without me. I hoped every man I knew in Vietnam would eventually make it safely home, but I also knew that was a long shot. Between December 17, 1969 and January 27, 1970, the Third Herd lost twenty men. Ten were killed and ten had been seriously wounded, including me.

A nurse woke me up early the next morning for my eight o'clock surgery. I'm not sure how long I was in surgery, but I woke up sometime later feeling groggy and my left leg ached. After an hour in the recovery room, I was taken back to my bed on the ward.

After I settled into my bed they attached a harness around my left knee and attached a cable from the harness to a weight suspended from a pulley at the far end of my bed. The weight kept traction on the skin they had saved around my stump and would keep the skin from shrinking upwards. I was told they were able to save enough skin to form a flap over the end of my stump that would heal and become durable enough to hold up when walking on an artificial leg.

That harness soon became another discomfort and further limited my movement.

Later that day I got some bad news. The practice for those who had amputations was to leave an area around the amputation site open for several days to allow any infection to drain out. A nurse or corpsman would come around twice daily to change the dressing over that open wound. I had seen the staff changing the dressings on other men the previous day and listened to them moan and sometimes scream in agony when they removed the old dressing from their raw open wounds. I didn't realize I would be in store for that same treatment.

I was fortunate though. I had only a small opening near the end of my stump. Changing my dressing would be less painful than for those men who had nearly the entire end of their stumps open because doctors weren't able to save natural skin. Those men would require skin grafts from other parts of their body to cover their stumps.

Late that afternoon I experienced my first dressing change. After watching the other men, I knew it was an experience to prepare for. I began by putting a washcloth in my mouth to prevent breaking a tooth when I gritted my teeth. I then grabbed the crossbar over the bed with my left hand and tightly held on for the oncoming pain. I almost felt sorry for the hospital staff who had to change our dressings. They knew how much pain they were inflicting, yet they knew it was something that had to be done.

The corpsmen unhooked the traction from my left leg and removed the harness. That felt great. He then started removing the heavy dressing covering my stump. I felt no pain at first. But when he removed the layers of gauze closer and closer to my open wound, I first felt some tingling and then a little pain, and then it hurt like hell! I gritted my teeth and quietly moaned while gripping the wooden bar with all my might during the excruciating pain while the final few layers of gauze were removed from the exposed tender nerves. They had moistened the dressing closest to the open wound with saline to make it easier to remove, but it still hurt terribly. I breathed a sigh of relief when the corpsman said he was finished.

Putting on the new dressing wasn't as painful. It hurt, but I knew the worst was over until the next change. Enduring those dressing changes were definitely the worst pain I had ever felt in my life. It was worse than the pain I endured when I was first wounded. After experiencing all that pain with my first dressing change, I definitely felt sorry for those men with large open wounds on their stumps who literally screamed in agony during each dressing change. A nurse told me they would reduce the number of dressing changes in a few days and allow my stump to heal if there were no signs of infection.

During the morning of my third day in Japan a mobile telephone was wheeled near my bed. My parents had been reached. I had to say "Over" at the end of each of my statements so the radio operator could switch the controls enabling me to hear the other person when they talked. Mom had a list of questions including, "Could I sleep? Did I have my glasses? How was my hand? How long would I be in Japan?"

We talked for several minutes, and I reassured her I was doing fine. I told her I would let her know when I would be leaving Japan and where I would be hospitalized in the United States. I then briefly talked with my dad who wished me the best and hoped I wasn't in too much pain. Our conversation was slow because each transmission took a few seconds to travel halfway around the world through the airways. But it was great to talk with my folks again. I knew they also felt much better after hearing my voice.

With each passing day, I began to feel a little better and was able to do a few more exercises as I continued with physical therapy each morning. But it was still too painful to lie on my right side because of the wound on my hip. One afternoon my doctor cut off the large bandage that covered my right hand and removed the stitches that had closed two wounds between my fingers and several stitches below my right thumb. A corpsman then put a plaster cast on my hand that extended to just below my elbow because shrapnel had broken the bone at the base of my thumb.

The days in Japan were wearisome. I was confined to my bed with the traction attached to my left leg except when I went to PT. I spent a great deal of time writing to my family, Jan Griffin and many friends to make sure they knew I had been wounded and to let them know I was doing fine under the circumstances. When one of my calls back to *the World* was arranged, a phone was brought to my bed. I talked with my sister Marilyn and she sent her love and best wishes. Jan Griffin was glad to hear from me and she passed along the best wishes from the Wayne State gang. Paul Alesch said he had received my first Purple Heart and the Bronze Star I had sent to him a few weeks earlier. I had sent the medals to Paul rather than to my parents to avoid having to explain the events of December 17th to them.

One morning I felt the sensation of the toes on my left foot itching. I wanted to scratch them, except they weren't there. A nurse smiled when I told her about the sensations. They were phantom feelings caused by the nerves that formerly went down to my foot. Although they were severed, my brain sensed those nerves were sending feelings from my toes. She said I would continue to have those sensations and that the severed nerves would also cause periodic phantom pains in my stump for the rest of my life.

One afternoon I was surprised when John Bergen (Bugsy) rolled up to my bed in a wheelchair. He had somehow tracked me down. We smiled and shook hands. It was good to see a familiar face. He had been peppered with a lot of shrapnel, but it didn't hit anything vital. His doctor told him he would be flying back to *the World* in a couple days, but it would be a couple months before he could do much again.

I said, "Well, you got your Purple Heart."

"Yeah, I sure did," Bugsy said with a little smile. "That sure was a stupid wish." Bugsy shook his head as we both chuckled.

The only remembrance Bugsy had about the booby trap was walking back from the trail and being surrounded by a huge explosion that threw him to the ground. He hadn't found any of the other guys who had been wounded and knew nothing about their condition. We talked for a while and then wished each other well and shook hands before Bugsy wheeled himself back to his ward. I never saw Bugsy again.

Almost every day a few men on the ward left for the United States, and others moved into the vacated beds. Although I had left the war 3,000 miles behind me, seeing seriously wounded men arriving every day reminded me of the battles that continued in Vietnam.

After several days of painful dressing changes on my stump, my doctor said he believed the risk of infection was over. From then on they changed the dressing only once a day while the wound began to heal. With each passing day, movements became less painful and I was able to partially turn on my left side to sleep. Some days it felt like my butt was totally numb after lying on it all the time. Unfortunately, my left leg was still attached to that uncomfortable traction that was nearly enough to drive me crazy.

After eight days in Japan my doctor told me my injuries had stabilized enough for me to be flown back to the U.S. My orders hadn't been finalized, but he believed I would be going to Fitzsimons Army Hospital in Aurora, Colorado, just like nurse Maggie told me. I was able to place a call to my folks the following morning and told them I would arrive in Colorado in a few days.

Two days later it was my turn to hit the road, so to speak, and catch a flight back to *the World*. I had never imagined flying back to *the World* lying on a litter, but it was a lot better than going home in a coffin.

After we lifted off, I continued to think about my friends in the Third Herd and the thousands of other men who were still fighting for their lives. Although I was seriously wounded, I would soon be safely back in *the World*. A month ago, *the World* seemed so far away. Gradually, Vietnam was becoming a faraway place.

Late morning on February 13, 1970 I arrived at Buckley Air National Guard Base in Aurora, Colorado. I wondered what was in store for me in Colorado.

Approximately 300,000 American service members were wounded in Vietnam. 75,000 service members were permanently disabled by their injuries. 5,283 suffered single limb amputations and 1,082 suffered multiple limb amputations.

The 12th Evacuation Hospital at Cu Chi was a 400-bed facility serving the area around Cu Chi and also served areas surrounding Tay Ninh and the U.S. Dau Tieng base camp to the west. A staff of approximately 30 doctors, 60 nurses and many corpsmen and support staff operated the hospital. During January through November 1970 3,373 GIs wounded in action were admitted. The 12th Evac closed in December 1970.

I have reconnected with nurse Maggie, Army 1st Lieutenant Margaret Mackaben, who had cared for me at the 12th Evacuation Hospital in Cu Chi.

In February 2015 I visited with Richard Benson (Sgt. Benson who was also seriously wounded on January 27, 1970) during a business trip. Richard had a list of personnel who had been assigned to the 12th Evac during the 1969-70 time frame because he was interested in connecting with any of the hospital staff who had cared for him.

When I scanned the list of names, I saw "Maggie Mackaben." I only remembered her as Maggie, so I noted her name. I later found an email address for Margaret Mackaben and contacted her. After exchanging some details regarding my stay at the 12th Evac, I knew she was nurse Maggie. Truly an amazing experience.

After leaving Vietnam in August 1970 Maggie continued her military nursing career until she resigned her commission as Captain Mackaben in 1973 when she married. She continued her nursing career in the private sector, including several years at a Veterans Affairs Medical Center (VAMC) in South Carolina. Maggie is retired and volunteers for the United Services Organization and the VAMC.

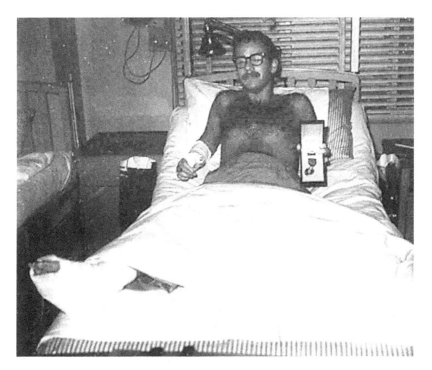

Pictured in Japan a few days after I was wounded.

Chapter 19

Fitz

It was a short bus ride to Fitzsimons Army Hospital in Aurora, Colorado, an eastern suburb of Denver. Four of us were wheeled into the large hospital on carts and lined up in a corridor while a clerk took our medical records and checked us in. I was anxious to get settled in, but it was another one of those Army drills of hurry up and wait. After almost an hour of waiting, the clerk returned, and I was taken to Ward 5-East, a men's orthopedic ward. I was wheeled down a long corridor and then we stopped by a bed in the middle of the large ward. With some help I slid from the litter onto the bed.

Ward 5-East (5-East) was divided into sections, with twelve men in two rows of beds in each section. Again, I saw men with missing limbs and others with dressings covering their multiple injuries received in Vietnam. The man in the bed directly across from me slid off his bed into a wheelchair and rolled over to say hello. He had no option but to use a wheelchair, because both of his legs were missing.

"Hi, I'm Gale Bertrand."

I reached out with my left hand and shook his hand.

"I'm Dick Hogue."

Gale told me he had lost his legs when two enemy hand grenades exploded almost at his feet. He was lucky to be alive. Gale briefly explained how things functioned around the ward and introduced me to a couple of men in other nearby beds. Susie, a young nurse then stopped by to take my vital signs and check my injuries and dressings. She said a doctor would visit me the next morning.

I asked Susie if I could make a phone call. She brought a phone and connected it to a phone jack near my bed so I could call my folks. It was midafternoon on Friday, February 13th. My mother had been anxiously awaiting my call and was happy to hear I was safely in Colorado. Mom, Dad and hometown friend Dennis Christiansen would start out early the following morning and arrive in Colorado that afternoon.

I also called Jan Griffin in Omaha. It was great to hear her voice again. She was also glad I had finally made it back to the States and was anxious to see me. I told Jan my parents were driving out that weekend, but I recommended she not rush out to see me until I was feeling better and could leave the hospital. I asked her to call some of my Wayne State buddies to let them know where I was.

Later that afternoon a corpsman brought a wheelchair to my bed that was designed for patients who only had the use of their left arm. Most wheelchairs had a metal ring attached to each wheel to navigate. But with my right hand in a cast, I couldn't grip the metal ring on the right wheel very well. That wheelchair had the normal metal ring for the left wheel, but it also had a second ring adjacent to it attached to an axle that ran to the right wheel. I was shown how to grasp the two metal rings with my left hand to turn both wheels. After I slid into the chair I wheeled around the ward, and after a few zig-zags I was able to go where I wanted most of the time. I used that time to check out 5-East. I found the restroom at the rear of the ward with running hot and cold water and real flush toilets.

"Welcome back to *the World*," I thought.

Near the front of the ward was the nurses' station and patient treatment rooms. Along the main corridor leading into the ward were private rooms occupied by officers and higher-ranking enlisted men. Rank had its privileges, even in a military hospital. There was also a balcony we could go out onto when the weather was nice to get some fresh air and view the mountains to the west. President Eisenhower had spent time on that balcony after he suffered a heart attack while in Colorado and was hospitalized at Fitzsimons in 1955.

Most of the terminology I had learned up to that point in my Army career was associated with the infantry and combat duty in Vietnam. But for the past couple of weeks I had learned new termi-nology associated with hospitals and medical care. I had a below the knee (BK) amputation; thereby making me a "BK" amputee. An "AK" was no longer a Russian made enemy rifle, but was an "above the knee" amputation. The men and women who assisted the doctors and nurses weren't called "medics," they were "corpsmen." They didn't serve meals in a "mess hall," the hospital had a "dining hall." The medical term for what remained of my left leg was "residual limb," but it was normally called a "stump." And I quickly learned that Fitzsimons Army Hospital was simply called "Fitz." The list of new terminology grew every day for a while.

That evening I wrote a few short letters to friends letting them know where I was. I was then reminded of another reality of *the World*. I had to pay postage. After a relatively good night's sleep, I woke on Saturday morning when they delivered breakfast. I hadn't paid too much attention to the food while I was in Japan, mainly because I often wasn't hungry. But I was regaining an appetite. The food at Fitz tasted pretty good, a heck of a lot better than C-rations.

After breakfast a corpsman brought me a pan of warm water to wash up and shave. I had just finished shaving when a man stopped by my bed and introduced himself as Dr. Marti, an Army captain, who would be my doctor. He asked a few questions while he looked at my medical records and then took a few minutes to examine my injuries to ensure I was being properly cared for. He said a cast would be put on my right foot in a couple days after he viewed my X-rays. He would also develop a long-term treatment plan for me after he had an opportunity to examine me further. After my right foot and right hand healed, he could also determine the extent of any muscle or nerve damage and whether it could be corrected by rehabilitation or require surgery.

I then asked Dr. Marti how long he thought my recovery would take. He believed it would be at least six months. He explained it would be a few months before I could be fitted with a prosthesis and that I wouldn't be discharged until the medical staff had done everything they could for me, and I could walk again.

When I looked at myself I knew I had a long way to go before I would be anywhere close to normal. But as bad as it looked, I had been fortunate. Gale Bertrand was one of several double amputees on the ward. He had an AK and BK amputation. One man had lost one leg and one arm, and another man had lost one arm, one leg and his testicles. Several of the patients could get out of bed and move around in wheelchairs while others were confined to bed.

I wondered how other men on 5-East were dealing with the emotional impact of their devastating physical injuries. Although most of them appeared to be in relatively good spirits, I wasn't sure if I would have a very positive outlook if I were lying in bed after losing both legs or an arm. It appeared that most of us would likely endure extensive rehabilitation and additional surgeries before we would be discharged. We also had the dual challenge of dealing with the emotional impact of sustaining serious injuries, in addition to living with our harrowing combat experiences in Vietnam.

A self-diagnosis of my emotional state was that I was stable. I had accepted the loss of my left leg and the extent of my other injuries soon after Dr. Sullivan had talked with me at my bedside at the 12th Evac in Cu Chi. And being a half of a world away from South Vietnam made it easier to accept the loss of my good friends.

Another thought that remained on my mind was the fact that I was no longer serving in combat. Although that was good, just as I had to adjust to the hostile combat environment after arriving in Vietnam, I was again adjusting to not carrying my M-16, ammunition and hand grenades and not worrying about enemy soldiers trying to kill me every day. It may sound strange, but I had to readjust during my return to the peacefulness and security I could again enjoy.

While I waited for my folks after lunch, I wrote a letter to Rick Shields and Dave Hardy in Vietnam, telling them I was in Colorado. I asked them to let me know how things were going with the Third Herd. It was a strange feeling to be back on the opposite side of the world from the men who had been such a big part of my life for the past six months.

Around three o'clock that afternoon, I looked up and saw a nurse leading my parents and Dennis Christensen toward my bed. I smiled and raised my broken right hand to wave at them. Mom almost ran to my bed and gave me a big hug while tears filled her eyes. I reached out with my left hand to shake my dad's hand while he greeted me with a big smile. I didn't notice at the time, but Mom later told me my dad cried when he first saw me. She said it was the first time she had seen him cry. Fortunately, they were tears of joy. Dennis stood at the foot of my bed while my folks hugged me.

He then moved closer and said, "Hey, guy, great to see you." We shook hands and shared a hug.

I didn't realize how much I had missed my parents until I saw them that day. Vietnam slipped a little farther to the back of my mind. My mother sat down in a chair next to my bed, but Dad wanted to stand for a while. He had been sitting for nearly 700 miles.

I was bombarded with questions concerning how I was feeling, the extent of my injuries and what they were doing to treat me. My parents were obviously most concerned about the loss of my left leg. I told them I would eventually be fitted with an artificial leg (prosthesis) enabling me to walk again. I was fortunate to still have my knee making it easier to walk than someone with an AK amputation.

Dennis was on leave before reporting for duty in Belgium. I was glad he took some of his precious leave days to visit me. His twin brother Dean was still doing fine at Fort Ord, California.

While we talked, Mom handed me a plastic bag of homemade chocolate chip cookies. I quickly took a couple and gobbled them down. She also had several cards and letters people had given her to deliver. I enjoyed reading the get-well wishes and expressions of thankfulness that my injuries had not been even more serious. My mom said the phone had nearly rung off the wall the past two weeks with people calling to share their concerns and asking about my progress.

After I talked with Dennis and my parents into the evening hours, they spent the night at a nearby hotel, and returned to see me early Sunday morning. My parents were naturally happy to see me, but were shocked when I told them some of the realities of my duty in Vietnam that I hadn't previously shared with them. They were even more thankful I was alive after learning twelve men in my platoon were killed while I was there.

My parents felt much better after seeing I wasn't suffering extreme pain and learning I should be able to lead a fairly normal life. Late Sunday afternoon I slid off my bed and wheeled myself down the corridor to the elevator where I shared hugs and good-byes with my parents and Dennis. The elevator door slowly closed. I was on my own again.

The following week Dr. Marti examined me and put a walking cast on my right foot. He also removed the stitches from the wound in my right hip that would leave a nasty looking six-inch scar for the rest of my life. I then started a twice-a-day physical therapy (PT) regimen designed to maintain my existing strength and to rebuild strength in my left thigh before I was fitted with a prosthesis.

I soon learned my way around the hospital, which was on a square-mile Army post. The eight-story main hospital building contained patient wards, operating rooms and other medical facilities. Fitz was one of the largest military hospitals in the country and provided medical care for men who had been wounded in Vietnam, in addition to caring for active duty and retired military personnel and their families. There was a post office and a small post exchange (PX) on the first floor of the main hospital and a larger PX, Commissary (grocery store), movie theater, NCO and Officer's Clubs, bowling alley and administrative offices and maintenance facilities located elsewhere on the post.

I soon got to know several of the men on the ward and spent time with them shooting the bull or playing cards. The man in the bed to my right was Don Chilson. He and his twin brother had both been drafted, and his brother Ron had been sent to Vietnam. Because it was the Army's policy not to allow brothers to serve simultaneously in Vietnam, Don had been stationed at Fort Riley, Kansas. Ironically, Don broke his hip when he accidentally fell from a bridge. His brother Ron had survived his tour in Vietnam to that point without a scratch.

I also met Rodney Wunschel who was from Ida Grove, Iowa, which was twenty miles southwest of Schaller. We learned we both knew a few people from each other's hometown and quickly developed an "Iowa" connection. An exploding RPG had seriously wounded Rodney in June 1969, and forced the amputation of his left arm above his elbow and resulted in multiple other injuries.

One evening shortly after I arrived at Fitz, two girls visited Don Chilson. While the girls were visiting, I boldly wheeled over to Don's bed and said hello. One of the girls was his cousin Vicki McKee. She hadn't visited Don before that evening, but said she would stop by again and gladly take us off-post when we were able, since none of us had a car. Most of us on 5-East were in the early stages of recovery and weren't allowed to leave the hospital until our doctor determined we were well enough to do so. But eventually, we would receive our doctor's blessing to go off-post during the evenings or weekends.

During my first few weeks at Fitz I received a couple of hundred cards and letters. I returned to my bed on several days to find a big stack of mail lying on it. Some of the other patients were amazed.

"Where are all of those cards coming from?" Gale Bertrand asked one day. He then laughed and said, "There can't be that many people out there who like you."

I received cards or letters from what seemed like nearly every family that lived in or around Schaller. I also heard from relatives I hadn't seen in years and friends I had nearly forgotten. I appreciated everyone's expressions of concern and their best wishes for my recovery. Like Gale had joked with me, I didn't realize there were so many people who cared about my welfare. I also received letters from guys in the Third Herd and opened them with hesitation; hoping for good news, but also knowing the news could be bad. Fortunately, all my friends I had left behind in the Third Herd were alive. I learned that Lieutenant Fielding, former third platoon leader, had recovered from his injuries received that past November, and had voluntarily returned to Vietnam. He was serving as the first platoon leader in Alpha Company.

I continued to encounter new events during my first month at Fitz. After the cast on my right hand was removed they discovered two problems. The shrapnel had severed nerves in my hand and left numbness in my ring finger and little finger, and the underside of my right thumb was completely numb. I felt no pain when they poked my thumb with a needle. Dr. Marti said the nerves would partially heal and I would regain some feeling; however, that would take years.

The more serious problem was that I could not move or control the tip of my right thumb. When I tried to grip something, the tip of my right thumb would bend backwards. Dr. Marti believed shrapnel may have severed the tendon leading to my thumb. I worked with a physical therapist daily for two weeks hoping to regain movement. When I tried to move my thumb, I felt the tendon move near my wrist but the tip of my right thumb didn't budge. Finally, Dr. Marti was certain the tendon leading to the tip of my right thumb had been completely severed. It would have to be repaired surgically.

Around the first of March Dr. Marti also ordered a pylon to be placed on my left leg. A pylon was a plaster cast molded over my left stump and continued six inches above my knee. Built into the plaster was a connecting device that enabled them to attach a metal pipe with an artificial foot on the far end. With the pylon, I could walk to rebuild strength in both legs.

After the plaster dried, a pipe was cut to the proper length and a shoe was put on the foot. I was anxious to try walking again. But that was difficult. I still had the cast on my right leg, and the pylon didn't allow any flexibility in my left knee. It was painful at first, but after a few days walking in the parallel bars, I graduated to walking with crutches. It was slow progress, but each day I became more proficient.

Although I certainly wasn't happy about losing my left leg, being around other men who had similar and often more traumatic injuries, helped me emotionally. Periodically sharing *war stories* about our respective tours in Vietnam and telling each other how we were injured kept many guys from feeling self-pity or becoming depressed. All I had to do was remember my twelve friends in the third platoon who died to realize how fortunate I really was.

During the second week of March, I was transferred from 5-East to the outlying Ward 502. Ward 502, or 502 as we called it, was a two-story World War II era building 100 yards west of the main hospital. It housed over sixty patients. When a patient's medical condition improved, he was transferred to 502, to free up bed space on 5-East for the new patients who arrived almost daily. Eventually each man completed his rehabilitation and was discharged from Fitz, and then, either returned to duty status or was medically retired from the service depending upon the severity of his injuries.

During that same time period, the cast on my right leg was removed, making it much easier to walk. The shrapnel wounds had left a large scar across the top of my right foot and other scars near my ankle. I could move all my toes, but the shrapnel had severed nerves leaving most of the topside of my foot totally numb. Although the numbness felt strange, it didn't affect my ability to walk. Within a few days I was walking using only a cane. Although it was far from walking normally, I felt like I had been given newfound freedom.

While our injuries healed and we became more mobile, many of us patients pursued our liberty again. Don Chilson's cousin Vicki drove Don, Gale, Rodney and me to the mountains west of Denver one Saturday. I was amazed by the beauty and vastness of the Rocky Mountains and clear blue skies. It was great to have her to help us get out and about, because getting around wasn't an easy task. Guys were either in a wheelchair or using crutches and moving pretty slowly. Although for most of us it was a challenge just getting into and out of a car, getting out into the world again was a great emotional boost.

I was scheduled for surgery to accomplish a tendon transplant on my right hand the third week of March. Dr. Marti said tendons acted like a rubber band when severed, and the tendon had likely retracted into my forearm. A hand specialist would assist him to make an incision on my right thumb and wrist until he found my severed tendon. They would then pull the tendon back toward my hand and then take a section of an unused tendon from my forearm and graft it onto the severed tendon and reconnect it to the tip of my thumb.

On March 17th, I was transferred back to 5-East, and I was wheeled into the operating room the following morning for my third surgery in less than two months. I awoke in the recovery room feeling lousy, with my right hand in pain. I slowly regained my senses and was returned to 5-East later that afternoon. My hand then started to throb and hurt like hell. I tried to sleep that evening, but the pain kept me awake most of the night. The following morning Dr. Marti stopped by to see me.

I said, "My hand really hurt last night. What did you do to me?"

Dr. Marti then told me they grafted in an unused tendon to attach to my thumb. A large dressing around my hand and forearm held a splint in place. He said everything went well and I should regain movement in my right thumb.

After a couple of days, the pain and discomfort subsided and I was back to my two-a-day PT visits. A week after the surgery on my hand, the stitches were removed, and Dr. Marti explained the scars from the incisions made during the surgery. One incision went from the tip of my thumb down to my wrist looking for the severed tendon. They didn't find it. A second incision was made from the base of my hand going three inches up the underside of my arm until they found the retracted severed tendon. Three little incisions across my forearm were made to remove an unused tendon, which was then attached to my severed tendon and finally reconnected to the tip of my thumb using a thin wire. The end of that wire protruded through my thumbnail. It seemed pretty amazing to me. After the stitches were removed, a plaster cast was placed on my hand and forearm to keep my thumb immobile for the next month.

I had been talking with Jan Griffin about once a week after arriving at Fitz. She was planning to fly to Denver and visit me over Easter weekend, which was the last weekend of March. When I asked Dr. Marti for a weekend pass he asked me if I had been home yet. I told him no. Rather than issuing me a weekend pass, he gave me two weeks' leave, starting March 27th. He asked me to see him that morning to check my hand before I left.

I called Jan and told her to cancel her plans to come to Colorado. I then called my parents and told them to get ready; their son was finally coming home. I would spend Friday night in Omaha and drive with Jan to Schaller on Saturday. I made plane reservations on a United flight leaving Denver at three o'clock Friday afternoon. I also called my Wayne State friend Paul Alesch and told him to plan a party because I was arriving in Omaha around five o'clock Friday evening.

After completing my physical therapy Friday morning, I found Dr. Marti who wanted to check my thumb to ensure I had good circulation. He then wanted to remove the little piece of wire that was protruding from my thumbnail. He found a pair of tweezers, and like doctors normally say, he said, "This will just hurt a little bit."

I smiled and said, "Yeah, right, Doc."

He clamped onto the wire with the tweezers and pulled the wire out through my thumbnail. Surprisingly, it did hurt only a little bit. I had learned to walk fairly comfortably with the aid of my pylon and I often walked without crutches. But Dr. Marti recommended I take my crutches in case I had any problems while I was on leave.

I quickly changed from my hospital pajamas into civilian clothes since we weren't required to wear a military uniform when we traveled. I then walked to the nurses' station and it took them forever to check me out on leave.

I walked out of the hospital that afternoon looking for the cab I had called to take me to the airport, but there was no cab in site. About ten minutes later a corpsman who knew me saw me waiting and offered me a ride. After he dropped me off by the United entrance I walked as fast as I could to the ticket counter. The ticket agent requested an electric cart when she saw my crutches, because I only had a few minutes to catch my flight. I was soon whisking down the long concourse toward the gate.

However, when I arrived at the gate the plane was being pushed away from the terminal. "Damn," I said, "I missed the plane."

Fortunately, there was a compassionate staff working that day after they learned I had been seriously wounded in Vietnam. They returned the plane to the gate allowing me to board. Within a few minutes we lifted off into the skies over Colorado and turned east toward Omaha.

After we arrived at the gate at Eppley Field in Omaha, I slowly exited the plane and walked into the terminal. I smiled when I saw Jan waving at me. We greeted each other with a kiss and long hug.

She said, "Welcome home, Dick. You look great."

I smiled and replied, "I do?"

Jan saw the cast on my right hand and I told her about the pylon on my left leg. I explained what I had been going through at Fitz as we walked out to her car and while Jan drove us across town to Paul and Jane's Alesch's apartment where some of the Wayne State gang had gathered to welcome me home. I anxiously walked to the apartment door and heard the noise from my friends inside.

I didn't knock; I opened the door and yelled, "You guys can't have a party without me!"

The cheers went up, and I was mobbed with hugs and kisses and handshakes. Naturally, Paul and Jane were there along with several Wayne State friends and their wives or girlfriends. I was soon laughing and chatting with the old gang and answering their many questions. Everyone was interested in how I was able to walk and were astonished when I showed them the pipe attached to the plaster pylon.

A short while later Paul asked for everyone's attention. Paul went on, "Sergeant Hogue, for wounds received in action, I present you a Purple Heart. For bravery in action, I present you a Bronze Star."

I had forgotten about the two medals I had sent to Paul for safekeeping in January. The gang gathered around to see the medals and then quietly listened while I described the events of December 17th when the land mine killed Willard Spivey and then Glenn Haywood dying on Christmas Eve.

Jan and I enjoyed the evening together while I soaked in the pleasure of seeing her and my good friends. Only a few months earlier, I had wondered whether I would ever see them again. After experiencing some of the lowest emotional times of my life in Vietnam, I was beginning to experience much better good times seeing good friends again.

Jan and I slept in at her apartment Saturday morning and then headed toward Schaller shortly after noon. I sat behind the wheel of Jan's Chevy II and drove a car for the first time in eight months. When I drove over the little rise on the south edge of Schaller and saw the familiar rows of houses, I felt an unbelievable sensation of happiness.

I stopped in front of my parents' house and saw my sister Jan who had just arrived home from college. She welcomed me with a big hug. Mom and Dad walked from the house and greeted all of us with big smiles on their faces. They remembered my being confined to a wheelchair when they visited me at Fitz six weeks earlier and were amazed to see me walking toward them.

After enjoying some great home-cooked food with my family, Jan Griffin and I went downtown to the VFW hall where many folks were enjoying a delicious steak meal. When we entered the hall, I was swarmed with welcome home hugs and handshakes. People were amazed to see me in relative good physical condition.

Several people stopped by during that evening to say hello as the word spread around town that I was home. Everyone was amazed to see me walking. After six long months in Vietnam and two months in the hospital, it was wonderful being with Jan and relaxing with old friends while I answered questions regarding my tour in Vietnam.

On Monday evening during my second week at home, I went out with my buddy John McDonough, and good friend Ron Holstein who had served in Vietnam in 1966. We went to Carl and Dorothy Borger's place, a little bar and restaurant in Galva, another small town seven miles west of Schaller.

I went to the restroom during the evening and when I took a step to leave the restroom I heard a *cracking* sound from my pylon. I stopped and shifted my weight to my right leg until I could determine what was wrong. I leaned down and felt the pipe connection to the pylon was loose. When I moved it, the pipe came off in my hand.

I yelled, "Help!"

John and Ron rushed through the door and were stunned as I stood there on my right leg while holding the pipe in my left hand. After the guys helped me back to a barstool I looked at the pipe and saw the connection attaching the pipe to the pylon had broken. After everyone understood what had happened, we all had a good laugh about my leg falling off in the restroom. John and Ron helped me into the house later that night and I slept on the living room couch.

The following morning Dad took the pipe and broken connection downtown to Glenn Woodke's Machine Shop. Glenn couldn't salvage the connection but used a torch and brazed another adaptor to the pipe that worked out well. I was again happily back on my *two* feet. I stopped by that afternoon to thank Glenn for fixing my broken leg.

He laughed while he told me that he had fixed almost everything over the years, but it was the first time he ever welded someone's leg back together. Glenn was a member of the VFW's Hup-Tu Squad. He asked me if I could attend their annual dinner the following Sunday evening as their special guest. I gladly accepted his invitation.

I also made a trip to Omaha near the end of my second week of leave to see Jan and to enjoy more time with some of the Wayne State gang. Jan had graduated from nursing school and was working at a hospital in Omaha. Although we both enjoyed being together, I had been gone for most of the past two years and would be in Colorado for several more months. We both acknowledged it was difficult trying to maintain a long-distance relationship, but we agreed to keep in touch with each other, and would see what happened after I was discharged from the hospital. We were both comfortable with letting our causal relationship continue with no commitments or restrictions. Jan and I shared a hug and kiss when I left to return to Schaller Friday morning to spend my final weekend of leave.

That Sunday evening the members of the Hup-Tu Squad and their wives warmly greeted me when I arrived at the VFW Hall. After enjoying a great steak meal, I used a slide projector to show the group some of my pictures from Vietnam, while many of the men recounted some of their own experiences when they were in the service many years earlier. I described the event or men in each picture, but it was difficult when pictures of Whitey, Bob Emery or other men who had been killed popped up on the screen, and I explained how each of those men had been killed. Although I answered lots of questions, many of those men and women quietly watched and listened as I described the grim realities of the war in Vietnam.

Monday morning, April 13th I drove with my folks to Sioux City to catch a noon Ozark Air Lines flight to Denver. As we gained altitude and turned west toward Colorado, I lay back in my seat and thought about how great it had been to be home the past two weeks. I had never received that much attention in my life. I was truly thankful to have been from the small town of Schaller, Iowa, which had so many caring people. The war in Vietnam was unpopular with some Americans and many GIs were welcomed home by people spitting on them or yelling obscenities. I couldn't imagine how fellow Americans could be intentionally cruel to men who were just doing what Uncle Sam asked them to do – serve their country.

After I checked back in at Fitz I found Dr. Marti. He had a good laugh when I told him the connection on the pylon broke, and my dad took it to a welder's shop to repair it.

Shortly after I returned from leave I received a letter from Rick Shields in Vietnam. He was doing fine, but he had bad news. Rick wrote, "On April 1 (1970) Lieutenant Fielding was killed instantly by an exploding booby trap."

I couldn't believe it. I read Rick's words again. That gung-ho son-of-a-gun had voluntarily returned to Vietnam after his wounds healed, and it cost him his life. Sadly, it must have been his destiny. He had arrived back in country a few days before I was evacuated, but I didn't see him. I unexpectedly had to deal with losing another friend in Vietnam. Ironically, Lieutenant Fielding had been a patient at Fitz after he was wounded that past November.

Rick said the rest of the guys in the Third Herd were doing fine, and he enclosed a picture that made me laugh but also nearly made me cry. It was a picture of me stark naked, taking a shower with water flowing from the rusty bucket in the middle of the grove of trees that past November. Rick said he found the picture when going through Terry Thornton's personal gear after he was killed on December 28th. Rick obviously didn't think Terry's family would appreciate a naked picture of the old Hound Dog. I chuckled to myself as I looked at that picture and wondered why he had taken it, unbeknownst to me. But then I sadly thought about Terry being killed one month later.

After the cast was removed from my right hand the first week of May, Dr. Marti asked me to move the tip of my thumb. It moved! It felt stiff, and there was some pain, but I could move it. I continued PT and regained partial movement of my right thumb without discomfort. Although I would have permanent limited flexibility of my thumb, my right hand looked normal except for the scars.

The following week Dr. Marti had my pylon removed to examine a deep scar on the front of my stump. Dr. Marti believed the scar would be problematic when I was fitted for my prosthesis. He determined that a *revision* was required to cut out the deep scar and re-close the wound to leave a smoother scar. He would simply revise the shape of my stump; therefore, the procedure was called a *revision*.

Without the pylon I couldn't walk. I either moved around on crutches or rolled around in a wheelchair. It was a little disappointing to lose my mobility, but I accepted it as part of my recovery. I knew it wouldn't be forever, and I also reminded myself I was still one of the more fortunate ones. The double amputees, like my friend Gale Bertrand faced significantly more difficult challenges than I did.

Now and then one of the men who had lost one leg would fall when he got up from bed. Simply from habit, he would try to take a step with that missing leg and fall to the floor. Just like phantom feelings gave us the sensation that our missing limbs were there, when those men were still half asleep, they sometimes forgot they had lost a leg. Unfortunately, those men were quickly brought back to reality as they were lying in pain after hitting the floor.

There was one advantage to not having a cast on my right arm and the pylon on my left stump: I could finally easily take a shower. It was nearly impossible to take a shower with both the pylon and the cast.

I washed myself with a washcloth as best I could. After my cast was removed from my arm, I would sometimes put a plastic bag over the pylon and wrap tape tightly around my leg to keep it dry while I took a shower. But now, without the pylon and the cast, showers were much easier. Except I had to take a shower while standing on one leg; something I would have to do for the rest of my life.

Early on the morning of May 12th I was prepared for surgery. After I was wheeled into the operating room and a nurse readied a tourniquet around my left thigh, Dr. Marti walked to my side and asked the anesthesiologist to put me to sleep. I slowly woke up in the recovery room with pain in my left leg. That was my fourth surgery since I had been wounded and I hoped it would be my last. That afternoon I was back in my bed on 5-East.

Don Chilson had told his cousin, Vicki McKee, I was having surgery. She visited me the evening after my surgery. I had gotten to know Vicki when she had taken a group of us out a couple times. While she visited me that night, I asked her if she would like to go out sometime. She said, "Yes." And gave me her phone number. I told her I would call her when I was able to get up and around again.

There were no surgery complications so I was transferred back to 502 two days later. Most of the men I had originally met while on 5-East were gradually being transferred to 502. Don Chilson's cast had been removed from his hip, and he was allowed to walk with crutches. Gale Bertrand faced a skin graft on his AK amputation, but he had been sent to 502 until they performed the surgery. My fellow Iowan, Rodney Wunschel and other newfound friends eventually joined me as fellow patients on 502 to continue their recovery.

Each ward at Fitz had a ward master, whose job it was to keep the patients in line, so to speak. They usually held the rank of E-7s, Sergeants First Class, and they enforced the rules of living on the ward. They made sure that we didn't let our hair get too shaggy and they also dealt with administrative matters involving the patients. The ward master on 502 was Sergeant First Class David Alderson. He was a big, bald-headed guy with a gruff personality. If he didn't like something, he yelled at us. Although Sergeant Alderson had a gruff exterior he was really a good guy once you got to know him.

While the ward master was the enforcer, like Top was in Vietnam, many of the doctors were young captains or majors who were more interested in practicing medicine than following military protocol. They didn't ask us to call them "Sir" and didn't expect a salute when we met them outdoors. In fact, the doctors sometimes got into trouble for wearing their hair too long or not following the Army's rules.

Although my first few weeks of hospitalization had often been agonizing and monotonous, my life at Fitz eventually became more comfortable and was far from my past Army life. Although most of us had suffered traumatic injuries, we enjoyed a relatively soft military life while we continued on our respective roads to recovery.

Each weekday morning at 502 began with a 7:30 roll call. We were then mostly on our own, but were expected to stay on the hospital grounds during the day to attend PT sessions and any appointments with doctors or other hospital staff. We wore blue military hospital pajamas while we were on post to identify us as patients. Those blue pajamas weren't very attractive, but they gave us certain benefits, like not having to pay to see a movie at the Post Theater and going directly to the front of the line when we went to the dining hall. We could check out after four o'clock each weekday afternoon and stay out all night as long as we were at roll call the following morning. On weekends we could check out from Friday afternoon until 7:30 Monday morning.

Many evenings we just stayed at 502, playing cards or writing letters, and as the weather warmed, we would sit outside on a deck and enjoy the evening air while we chatted with each other. A couple times we disobeyed the rules regarding not having alcohol on the ward. One of the guys would drive to the NCO Club and buy some beer and put it in a cooler. After dark someone would take the cooler to the rear of the ward and we would quietly sit on the back porch enjoying a cold beer or two. Fortunately, we were never busted.

I called Vicki McKee during the first week in June and asked her for a date. I didn't have a car, but she was more than willing to pick me up. We went to the drive-in theater near Fitz on our first date. One weekend shortly thereafter Vicki and I visited her parents, Glen and Thelma, at their Rocky Mountain home in Estes Park, Colorado. Glen had served as a Navy Seabee during World War II. Although Glen cussed when he criticized President Nixon and Congress for the way they were handling the war in Vietnam, he had a lot of respect for us guys who fought over there. Although we were a generation apart, I felt an immediate camaraderie with Glen as a fellow veteran.

As time passed, Vicki often joined me and some of my fellow patients when we went out on evenings or during the weekends. One of our favorite outings was going to Central City, an old mining town in the mountains west of Denver that was mostly gift shops, restaurants, and bars. Our favorite place was the "Gilded Garter," a honky-tonk bar with a band playing lively old-time songs with the crowd often singing along. We always drew lots of attention when we arrived with guys in wheelchairs or others on crutches with a missing leg. We appreciated the sincerity of many strangers who generously bought us a round of drinks when they learned we had been wounded in Vietnam.

It was amazing how a group of men who had been seriously wounded while experiencing harrowing combat in Vietnam could relatively quickly rebound and get out into the world to enjoy themselves. We encouraged guys to get out of the ward to enjoy themselves and would help each other as needed to navigate during our outings. For the guys in wheelchairs, we would often need to assist in and out of restrooms, because handicapped accessible restrooms were rarely available at that time. Over time our injuries healed and many of us who had lost one or both legs were fitted with a prosthesis greatly improving our mobility.

The Army also took us on outings periodically. We went to a horse racetrack in Denver one afternoon, and Don, Rodney and I pooled our money and actually came out ahead. We also went to Mile High Stadium and watched the Denver Zephyrs, a minor league baseball team. One night an American Legion post invited us as their guests for a steak dinner.

Having friends and relatives make a special effort to visit me lifted my spirits, and being able to get away from the hospital with them helped me realize that I would be able to continue with a near normal life despite my injuries. I began to look forward with anticipation to my discharge from the hospital and moving on with my life.

After the surgery on my stump, I had to wait a few weeks while they attempted to reduce the size of my stump by keeping an elastic wrap tightly bound around it. Forcing my stump to shrink before I was fitted for my prosthesis would minimize further shrinkage after I began to walk. If my stump shrank too much after I was fitted with my prosthesis, it wouldn't fit properly and I would soon require a new one. Although my stump would continue to slowly shrink for years, my first prosthesis would cost the Army approximately $1,000. They wanted to get as much life out of it as they could before I would need a new one. I watched some of the other guys begin to walk with their "new leg(s)," while I patiently waited for my stump to shrink so that I too could start walking again.

There was a small recreation area on the first floor of 502 with a television, a bumper pool table, games, playing cards, and magazines we could read. One day near the end of June, I picked up an Army Times Magazine that was lying on a table. The Army Times listed the names of Army personnel recently killed in Vietnam in each edition. I often checked those lists, knowing I still had many friends serving there, but hoping not to see a name I recognized. I scanned down the list and read "William A. Branch, Capt., June 6, 1970."

I was stunned and read the name again. It was Captain Branch, my former company commander. He had visited me in the hospital in Cu Chi, and I could clearly remember him walking out with Lieutenant Donaldson and turning to wave good-bye. He was a great guy. Sadly, he was gone. I sat there for a few minutes and quietly mourned the loss of yet another comrade. I wondered how many more friends I might lose before they all completed their tours in Vietnam.

A couple of days later a sergeant in a Class-A Army uniform walked toward my bed and said, "Hey, Hound Dog."

The nickname "Hound Dog" hadn't caught on around Fitz, therefore I was surprised to hear someone calling me by that name. In amazement I realized it was Dave Hardy from the third platoon. We both smiled and shared a handshake and hug.

On his way home to Wisconsin, he had stopped in Denver to see his brother and wanted to see me too. Dave fortunately had completed his tour in Vietnam without being wounded. Although it was great to see one of the Third Herd again, we solemnly talked for a moment regarding Captain Branch being killed. Dave said the chopper Captain Branch was riding on was shot down, and he and another man were killed. Dave also told me that no one in the Third Herd had been killed after I left, but my good friend Rick Shields had been sent back to the field and was wounded for a second time, fortunately his injuries weren't serious.

I felt a special bond with Dave Hardy. He had been a great help to me during my first few weeks in the field and ultimately became a good friend. The comradeship that existed between us in Vietnam continued after Dave's brother drove us to his house in Denver, and Dave and I talked and relaxed that afternoon. Dave said after I left Vietnam, they stopped rotating men from the field to the rear because there weren't enough replacement troops arriving in country. Dave and most of the men who were in the third platoon when I left had to stay in the field for nearly their entire tour.

Dave and I went out that night and we ended up at a little bar with some of the guys from Fitz. Dave and I shared a few war stories, and everyone laughed when Dave talked about the first time I jumped out of a Huey and fell on my face.

Dave later stood up, put his hand on my shoulder and said, "And Sergeant Hogue was the best platoon sergeant we ever had." And raised his glass to toast me. I laughed and said, "Sit down, Hardy. You've had too much to drink."

On the first of July, Dr. Marti told me it was time to be fitted for my new leg. The Army contracted with private prosthetic firms referred to as *limb shops* to make the new arms and legs for the patients at Fitz. I was sent to Kliber Limb Shop in east Denver. The first step in making my prosthesis was to take a plaster mold of my stump. Al Kliber pressed on the plaster as it dried to form a mold exactly the shape of my stump. The mold would be used to build a socket at the top of the prosthesis for my stump to comfortably fit into. Al also took measurements of my stump, measured my height and the approximate distance from the end of my stump to the floor and began constructing my new tailor-made leg.

A couple of days later I returned after Al had made my socket out of a hard plastic material that was temporarily set onto a small block of wood. A pipe was attached to the block, with a series of adjustment bolts used to make refinements and alignments to design my permanent prosthesis. On the far end of the pipe was an artificial foot. It was a weird looking contraption.

Al gave me a heavy wool stump sock that I easily pulled over my stump to provide a cushion between it and the hard socket, and to make a snug fit. A thick foam pad was also molded to fit into the bottom of the socket to provide additional comfort and support. I stood up and slipped my stump into the socket while standing between parallel bars. I slowly shifted my weight to my left leg. It hurt like hell.

I said, "I can't walk on this thing?"

Al said, "Don't worry, it'll feel better in time."

A small harness slipped over my knee and was held in place with a Velcro strap that wrapped around my leg to hold the socket on. I slowly took a few painful steps holding onto the parallel bars. When I identified pressure points in the socket that caused pain, Al sanded down those areas to relieve the discomfort and more evenly distribute my weight. I continued to walk between the parallel bars for nearly an hour, while Al made adjustments to the length of the pipe and adjusted the alignment of the foot to eventually give me a comfortable stride.

A few days later my new leg was ready. The block of wood and pipe had been replaced by a solid piece of willow wood that had been contoured similar to the size of my right leg. Willow wood was used because it had the best combination of strength and weight for artificial legs. Oak was strong but was too heavy. Pine was lightweight but was too weak. The willow wood was covered with a cloth material which was then coated with a flesh-toned liquid plastic. It didn't quite look like the real thing, but I took it. I slipped into the leg and walked between the parallel bars. After Al sanded down a couple of pressure points in the socket, my new leg gradually became comfortable.

I wasn't able to put all my weight on my left leg, not so much because of the discomfort, but because it felt like my left knee would collapse. Al said that feeling would disappear as I regained strength in my thigh as I continued to walk. After some final adjustments, I was happily on my way back to Fitz with my new leg, knowing it would be a while before I would be comfortably strolling down the sidewalks.

During the next few days, the physical therapists worked with me while I walked between parallel bars, and then graduated to walking with crutches. The PT staff showed me how to navigate up and down stairs and helped me walk along inclines and declines, which wasn't easy. Although the artificial foot had some flexibility, there was little ankle movement. Walking on anything other than a flat surface was a challenge. I worked diligently and progressed each day, gaining confidence in my ability to walk again. I still could only comfortably take a few steps without crutches, but I was happy. I was walking and getting closer to being on my own.

Mom called during the first week of July and asked if I could come home for Pop Corn Days. The Chamber of Commerce wanted me to be the Grand Marshal in the Saturday morning parade.

I said, "Sure, if that's what they want."

Mom also said Dad had bought me a 1964 Pontiac. I would fly back home and then drive my car back to Fitz. I flew to Sioux City on Friday July 17th and Mom picked me up at the airport that afternoon.

One of the first things I did when I got home was check out my car. It was a light blue four-door full-sized Pontiac and it was in great shape. The second thing I did was to find my Class-A uniform to wear during the parade. I had purchased the colorful ribbons that represented the medals I had been awarded and attached them to my uniform. When I left for Vietnam I had only been awarded the National Defense Service Ribbon – it was awarded to everyone who joined the service. However, after six months in Vietnam I had three rows of ribbons representing my two Purple Hearts, Bronze Star, two Army Commendation Medals, three Air Medals, Vietnam Campaign and Service Medals and a Good Conduct medal. I also pinned on my silver and blue Combat Infantryman's Badge above the rows of brightly colored ribbons. I was ready to proudly lead the Saturday morning Pop Corn Day parade.

My sister Jan was again home from college for the summer. I gave her a hug when she came home later that afternoon. After bringing my parents and sister up-to-date on my recovery, I took a spin around town in my new car and then stopped downtown.

I walked along Main Street using my crutches and was greeted with smiles, hugs and handshakes by almost everyone I saw. I soon became the main attraction as people walked up to welcome me home, happy to see me doing so well.

Early that evening, I moved on to Marlys and Kenny Kroese's house where I knew a party was in progress. I was immediately greeted with more hugs and handshakes as I walked into their house. Marlys welcomed me with a big hug. She then said, "Follow me; I have a surprise for you."

When we reached the back yard, Marlys pointed and said, "Look who's here."

It was my draftee buddy Allan Schwab. I knew he had received an early out from the Army to finish college, but we hadn't seen each other since returning to *the World*. We shook hands, and I shared a group hug with Allan and his wife Vicki. We briefly talked about our respective tours in Vietnam, but mostly we were happy to have survived and talked about how glad we were to be moving on.

Later that evening, Allan wanted a partner to play yard darts. He yelled, "Hey, Hogue, get rid of those crutches and come out here."

With some encouragement, I left my crutches behind and cautiously walked out on the lawn and began playing. I was a little unsure of myself at first and thought for sure I was going down a couple times. Playing yard darts with Allan and standing unassisted on my own two feet again was a tremendous confidence builder and another literal step forward in my recovery that I had been waiting for months to do.

I was up bright and early on Saturday morning to shave and shower and then put on my Army uniform. I hadn't worn that uniform in almost a year, but it fit fine. I walked outside and saw a red convertible waiting for me on the street in front of our house.

Each year the Chamber of Commerce selected an individual or sometimes a married couple as the Grand Marshal(s) to lead the Pop Corn Day parade. Vietnam had been on the minds of many people around Schaller with about twenty men from the community having served or still serving there. They wanted to give me a special welcome home by honoring me as the Grand Marshal.

I sat on the back of the convertible as we drove to the starting point of the parade route, where I saw the Hup-Tu Squad. Glenn Woodke, my leg repairman came up and shook my hand.

Several other guys I had known all my life and who had served in Vietnam, walked over to say hello and shake my hand. It was wonderful seeing those men again and briefly sharing our new-found camaraderie as Vietnam veterans. Promptly at ten o'clock, the Hup-Tu Squad led the parade, with Glenn Woodke calling the cadence, "Hup, Two, Three, Four." Keeping the men in step while they carried their rifles and the American and VFW flags that ruffled in the breeze.

I followed the squad in the convertible, riding along the parade route waving and smiling to the crowd of people who waved back or stood up and clapped their hands as I passed by. I felt a sense of pride I had never felt before while listening to the applause and cheers from those watching the parade. I felt the tremendous sense of caring and love that hundreds of people along the parade route were expressing.

One year earlier I said good-bye to my family and friends during the Pop Corn Day weekend when I left for Vietnam. But during a beautiful sunny morning on July 18, 1970, I received an unbelievable hero's welcome home from those same people. Honoring me as the

Grand Marshal was the greatest tribute I could have received from my life-long friends and made me the happiest and most grateful person in Schaller, Iowa that morning. I was truly thankful to have survived my tour of duty as an infantryman in Vietnam and to be able to return to the peaceful and friendly surroundings I had known all my life.

Although I was moving on with a positive perspective about myself, I also knew my life had changed forever, because:

"For those who have fought for it,
life has a meaning others will never know."

- ➢ First Lieutenant Craig Fielding was from Salt Lake City, UT. Craig was my platoon leader who was wounded on November 6, 1969. Lieutenant Fielding voluntarily returned to Vietnam on January 21, 1970 to again serve as an infantry platoon leader. On April 1, 1970, Lieutenant Fielding was killed by an exploding booby trap. He was twenty years old and is buried in Wasatch Lawn Memorial Park, Salt Lake City, Utah (see picture on page 374).

- ➢ Captain William Branch was from Fitzgerald, GA. Captain Branch was my company commander during the late summer and fall of 1969. He was killed when the helicopter he was riding in was shot down on June 6, 1970, ten days prior to the end of his second tour. He was twenty-eight years old. Alpha Company members have been in touch with his daughter Jennifer, who was two years old when her father died. William Branch is buried at Fort Benning, Georgia. A street in his hometown of Belleville, NJ was renamed William A Branch Way. To view pictures of William Branch and read his story visit:
  http://www.virtualwall.org/db/BranchWA01a.htm

➤ Fighting for their lives took a tremendous emotional toll on many Vietnam veterans. Some of those men returned home feeling bitter, resentful or withdrawn. Rodney Wunschel, my friend and fellow patient at Fitzsimons Army Hospital, committed suicide in 1991 after the Desert Storm conflict erupted. He was forty-two years old. His mother later told me Rodney never fully accepted the physical and emotional trauma he endured associated with his service in Vietnam. The Desert Storm conflict created a flashback he couldn't tolerate. Rodney hanged himself. He left a wife and one stepchild.

➤ Former girlfriend Jan Griffin (Bowman) died in 2016, one year after retiring from a nursing career in Washington state.

The Vietnam War cost the American taxpayers an estimated $111 billion. Over 1,600 Americans remain missing in action in Vietnam.

Fitzsimons Army Hospital (known as Fitzsimons Army Medical Center after 1974) opened in 1918. The eight-story main hospital building was constructed in 1941, and at that time, was the largest structure in Colorado. Fitz closed in 1999. The grounds have been redeveloped for civilian use as the Anschutz Medical Campus and the Fitzsimons Life Science District. Also, on the site is the Rocky Mountain Regional Veterans Affairs Medical Center.

A night out from Fitz.
Left to right – Myself, Don Chilson and Rodney Wunschel.

Chapter 20

My War, Was It Worth It?

In early August 1970 Dr. Marti determined I had fully recovered from my injuries and there was no further medical care warranted. I could walk comfortably with my prosthesis without a cane. Although the injuries to my right hand and right foot were healed, I would have permanent numbness because of severed nerves. After a thorough examination by the doctors on the Medical Evaluation Board I was determined eligible for medical retirement from the Army.

It would take approximately six weeks to process my retirement documents through Army channels. I could remain as a patient at Fitz or go home on convalescent leave to await my retirement. Although I had developed many good friendships and a unique sense of comradery with many of my fellow patients at Fitz, I was ready to go home and resume my civilian life. It had been just over two years since I left home to join the Army, and I was prepared to say goodbye to my relatively brief but very eventful military career. I was discharged from Fitzsimons Army Hospital on August 28, 1970 and headed east toward Iowa. I officially remained in the Army until I was medically retired on October 6, 1970.

After spending a few days with my parents in Schaller, I left for what I felt was a well-deserved vacation. I flew to Los Angeles and spent several days with my good friend and comrade Rick Shields who was attending college. I then flew to San Francisco and enjoyed a fun weekend camping at Yosemite National Park with my home-town buddy Dean Christiansen, who was serving at nearby Fort Ord. I then flew to Reno and stayed with Dean's older brother Floyd and wife Ruth where Dean joined us on the weekends. My vacation that I had planned for two weeks extended to a month. Having no short-term commitments, I relaxed and enjoyed my newfound freedom away from the Army.

Soon after returning home I learned that a local businessman, Don Pyle was looking for a bookkeeper. I had known Don since I was a kid, and after a brief conversation he offered me the job. Finally, that desk job the Army declined to give me.

While at Fitz and continuing when I returned home I was able to put the traumatic experiences I endured in Vietnam and sadness of losing good friends behind me. It wasn't as though I purposefully blocked those memories from my mind because I wanted to forget; rather, I chose to move on with my life with my military experience as a part of my background, that I obviously would never forget. I wasn't bitter about losing my leg and I didn't hold resentment against the Army or the Government about fighting a war which many Americans objected to and others avidly protested.

I established a mostly positive attitude the day after I was wounded and lying in bed at the 12th Evac hospital in Cu Chi. No, I wasn't one of the lucky ones, I was one of the nearly 5,300 American servicemen who lost one limb in Vietnam. Although I certainly wasn't happy about losing my left leg, I was fortunate. I came home alive. I thank God to this day for my survival.

After retiring from the Army, I continued on, enjoying my mostly carefree life with family and friends and having a comfortable income from my new job and Veterans Administration disability compensation to truly enjoy myself for the first time in my life. I shared fun times with several hometown buddies, many who also had served in Vietnam and were readjusting to the peace and harmony of *the World*.

While some Vietnam veterans didn't feel welcome at veteran's organizations because older veterans felt, "You guys lost the war," I fortunately felt nothing but a sense of pride and camaraderie at my hometown VFW Post.

Although I was comfortable discussing my Vietnam experience, I didn't get into intense conversations or debates regarding the politics surrounding the war. I was in a small Midwestern town where most people had conservative political views and few people openly expressed opposition to the war. However, there had been anti-war protests at the University of Iowa and near the State Capital in Des Moines.

Unfortunately, many war protesters took their frustration out on returning GIs, indifferent to their sacrifices, and left emotional scars for some Vietnam veterans to this day. Another focus of some protests was the military draft, where many draft eligible men burned their draft cards as a gesture of defiance. Over 1.7 million men were drafted during the Vietnam Era; with the vast majority serving in the Army (the Marine Corps drafted 42,000). An estimated 650,000 draftees served in Vietnam and nearly 18,000 draftees were killed. However, it is further estimated that 30,000 to 50,000 American males over the age of 18 dodged the draft by moving to Canada or other countries during the war.

I say to those draft dodgers, "Shame on you!" You disgraced yourselves by abandoning your country while over 9 million loyal Americans served our nation during the Vietnam Era, with nearly three million serving *in-country* and over 58,000 Americans sacrificing their lives in Vietnam. While many Americans had their rationale for opposing the war, all American men had the obligation to honor the call to duty. And then in 1977, President Carter dishonored all of us who served in the armed forces by pardoning the draft dodgers.

While anti-war demonstrations dominated the news as the war continued, there were less publicized demonstrations supporting the war and U.S. troops occurring simultaneously. Although the demonstrations ceased when America negotiated a peace settlement and withdrew from Vietnam in 1973, strong emotions about America's involvement exist to this day. It took years for many Americans to quell their emotions enabling discussions about the war in a civil manner.

In April 1971, I moved to Colorado and continued dating Vicki McKee who I had met while a patient at Fitz. We were later engaged and married in 1972. We had one son, Benjamin, born in 1979. However, our marriage did not last and we divorced in 1982.

Dozens of movies and television programs have portrayed the war from differing views. The first *Vietnam* movie I saw was *Platoon*, directed by Oliver Stone and based upon his experience serving in Vietnam. Also disclosed were the struggles of many veterans after receiving an often-hostile welcome home from their fellow Americans. The movie was disappointing for me because it focused on American infantrymen drinking and using drugs in the field or in-fighting within a platoon, Vietnamese civilians being killed by American troops and one platoon member purposefully shooting another in battle. While I would not deny that some of those incidents may have occurred during the war, those events were likely included in the movie for sensationalism, and certainly were not the norm.

Because the vast majority of those who viewed that movie didn't serve in Vietnam, they could have assumed that movie's portrayal was accurate. Based upon my experience, the movie *Platoon* was not an accurate portrayal of the war because of the anti-war sentiments depicted. However, Stone illustrated an accurate portrayal of the futility of the war, which I did experience.

I served in Vietnam for six months. The U.S. military had no more control over the countryside northwest of Cu Chi on the day I left than we did on the day I arrived in the field. Twelve men in the Third Herd were killed and many others were seriously wounded during those six months, including myself, with no military advantage gained. What began as a military war became a *political* war orchestrated from the White House that altered the military strategies into what became a futile endeavor.

Ho Chi Minh, North Vietnam's President, warned the French during the First Indochina War (1946-1954), "You can kill ten of my men for every one I kill of yours, but even at those odds, you will lose and I will win." In reality, NVA and VC casualties were approximately twenty times more than American casualties during our war in Vietnam, and they continued to fight.

After the war, American's learned more about how the war was conducted and the politics that guided the war. For some their opinions softened, while for others, their disagreement with the war became even more intense. People read about the war and viewed movies or television programs which not only portrayed graphic combat actions, but portrayed the impact upon families of GI's who were killed in Vietnam and the struggles many veterans experienced after returning from an unpopular war, and often, receiving an unfriendly welcome home from their fellow Americans.

While many Americans continued to believe that the United States should not have gone to war in Vietnam, over time, many Americans separated their views about the war versus the warrior. Vietnam veterans were no longer viewed as "Baby Killers." Despite the well-publicized My Lai massacre in 1968 where over 400 unarmed civilians were killed by U.S. Army soldiers, most Americans understood that in the vast majority of situations, Vietnamese civilians became un-intentional casualties of the war because they were living in a combat zone, just as had occurred in wars throughout history.

The number of American casualties in Vietnam listed on the Vietnam Memorial in Washington, DC as of May 2014 is 58,300; approximately 10,800 are considered non-combat deaths. Although the remains of over 1,000 Americans have been found in Vietnam and identified since the war's end, there are approximately 1,600 GIs that are unaccounted for and are listed as missing in action.

NVA and VC deaths are estimated to have been 1.1 million, while Vietnamese civilian deaths are broadly estimated at 195,000 to 430,000 South Vietnamese and 50,000 to 65,000 North Vietnamese. While it is believed that many of the North Vietnamese civilian deaths resulted from American bombing in the North, the number of South Vietnamese civilian deaths caused by American munitions is much less certain.

The NVA and more so the VC forcefully recruited South Viet-namese civilians to join their fight or to support their cause by hiding weapons or supplies in their homes or elsewhere in the small villages and hamlets scattered across the countryside. Those who refused were often killed. It is believed that the NVA and VC killed approximately 164,000 South Vietnamese civilians between 1954 and 1975.

Army of the Republic of Vietnam (ARVN) losses are estimated between 219,000 and 313,000. Casualties suffered by seven other countries who participated in the war alongside America (Cambodia,

Laos, Thailand, Australia, New Zealand, Philippines and South Korea) were over 7,000. China and North Korea provided troops in support of North Vietnam and also suffered casualties. The estimates of total Vietnamese military and civilian casualties during the war vary widely with some estimates exceeding three million.

Additionally, nearly 19 million gallons of Agent Orange chemical defoliant were sprayed over 10% of South Vietnam's countryside during the war. While the medical effects of exposure to the chemical were not publicized during the war, they were ultimately acknowledged by the Department of Veterans Affairs (VA) with health care and other benefits provided to thousands of Vietnam veterans or their families because of illnesses or death related to Agent Orange exposure.

Vietnam's government has also claimed that over 400,000 civilians have died or were medically impacted by Agent Orange which entered their water supply and food sources. The U.S. and other countries have contributed millions of dollars towards Agent Orange clean-up efforts in Vietnam and medical care for those affected.

After the war thousands of Vietnamese civilians were killed or otherwise died during attempts to escape from the former South Vietnam on foot or by boat. It is estimated that over 200,000 Vietnamese *boat people* died at sea and possibly over one million civilians were killed during the political violence created by the Communist takeover.

The Vietnamese government reports that since the end of the war, 40,000 civilians have been killed and thousands more injured by exploding booby-traps, bombs and other unexploded ordnance that remains across much of the former South Vietnamese countryside.

America lost over 405,000 service members (and 1,700 civilians) during World War Two (WWII), while German and Japanese combined military and civilian casualties are estimated between eight and nine million. Russian losses totaled over 20 million. Total casualties for all countries involved in WWII, including civilians, is estimated to be over 60 million.

An estimated 673,000 Americans were wounded in WWII while 303,000 were wounded in Vietnam. WWII cost America nearly $300 billion while the Vietnam War cost approximately $111 billion. The cost of the wars being fought in the Middle East is estimated to be $4.4 trillion since the 9/11 attacks on America. The 2016 Department of Veterans Affairs budget is $168 billion. Accordingly, the cost of America's wars continues to increase to pay for veterans' entitlements.

Regardless of how Americans view the cost of a war, the question remains, "Was it worth it?" While most Americans might agree WWII was worth it, would the Germans, Japanese or Russians agree?

The number of American service members killed in all wars going back to World War One is approximately 700,000. Was it worth it?

Weekly American casualty rates ranged between 200 and 300 during the height of the Vietnam War. The highest weekly American casualty total was 543 during the third week of February 1968. In addition to the weekly causality figures that were often announced on television newscasts, the outcome of three major battles in Vietnam turned even more Americans against the war.

First, on January 31, 1968 enemy forces attacked more than 100 cities across South Vietnam during the *Tet Offensive* associated with the Vietnamese New Year. Nearly 80,000 enemy forces launched major battles against ARVN and U.S. troops at South Vietnamese cities and U.S. military bases for nearly one month. Enemy casualties were estimated at 50% of their forces while America lost 2,500 servicemen.

While *Tet 1968* was considered an overwhelming U.S. military victory, it had the opposite psychological impact. The NVA and VC amassed a major force to launch attacks across South Vietnam without advance knowledge by U.S. forces. They truly surprised America's military leaders. Many U.S. military and political leaders became more convinced the war had become a futile effort and there was no decisive military objective to win the war. As a result, *Tet 1968* became the beginning of the end of America's involvement in the Vietnam War.

Second, during late January through early April 1968 the *siege of Khe Sanh* occurred when at least 20,000 NVA troops attempted to overtake the Marine outpost fourteen miles south of the Demilitarized Zone manned by 5,600 U.S. Marines. While NVA losses are broadly estimated to have been 10,000 to 15,000, America lost 205 Marines with over 800 wounded. Although some American military leaders in Vietnam believed the outpost continued to have tactical value, American commanding General Creighton Abrams ordered that Khe Sanh be abandoned in July 1968.

And third, in May 1969 American GIs battled for ten days for the heavily enemy fortified Hill 937, referred to as *Hamburger Hill*. Over 600 NVA bodies were found when the GIs reached the summit and many more NVA soldiers were killed by bombs and air strikes in the surrounding countryside while trying to escape the U.S. attack. Although 72 Americans were killed and 372 were wounded during that battle, the U.S. military abandoned the Hill within two weeks as it was determined to have no strategic value. Ironically, the NVA reoccupied Hill 937 three weeks later without a fight from U.S. forces.

After news was publicized about those significant battles and the considerable number of U.S. casualties, many Americans, and specifically those who actively protested the war, became even more enraged about the continuing American casualties and an indecisive military strategy. As a direct result, to hold down casualties, General Abrams discontinued a policy of *maximum pressure* against the North Vietnamese to one of *protective reaction* for troops threatened with combat action. Certainly not an approach to winning the war.

America had become so polarized about Vietnam by the late nineteen sixties that trying to promote any positive political notion about continuing the war had lost credibility. By 1970 an increasing majority of Americans considered our involvement in Vietnam a mistake. Anti-war demonstrations which began in the mid-1960s increased with up to 100,000 protesters marching on Washington, DC and other cities to demonstrate opposition to the war, often in violent fashion.

One of the most tragic events occurred on May 4, 1970 during an anti-war protest by students at Kent State University in Kent, OH. Ohio National Guardsmen fired 67 rounds at the students, killing four and wounding nine others. Sadly, Americans were killing Americans because of their opposition to the war.

Many war proponents continued to argue the "Domino" theory, meaning as one country fell to communism other nearby countries would follow. That theory was primarily based upon the fall of eastern European countries to communist Soviet Union control after WWII. Although military advisors continued to advise President Nixon the war should be continued, the President had campaigned prior to his election to end the war in Vietnam. And with the continued public sentiment to get out of Vietnam, the President pursued his plan.

President Nixon had a two-phased plan whereby American forces would gradually withdraw (and the Army of the Republic of Vietnam (ARVNs) would assume a greater fighting role) while peace discussions would continue with the North Vietnamese. While the President's *Vietnamization* plan was initiated shortly after he took office in January 1969, the plan was not fully executed until January 1973.

Friends have told me that after I left in January 1970, Alpha Company began working more with the ARVNs, anticipating they would take over the fight as U.S. troops withdrew. However, that transition proved difficult because many ARVN units lacked discipline and effective leadership. Mike Walsh (first platoon leader) relayed his ARVN experience in mid-1970. After settling in on an ambush with a group of ARVNs he smelled cigarette smoke and then heard music. He first suspected it was enemy troops, but then discovered the ARVNs were smoking and playing music on a radio at their ambush site.

Peace negotiations with North Vietnam were painstakingly slow. While U.S. troop reductions continued, the President increased bombing along the Ho Chi Minh Trail and ordered bombing of North Vietnam for the first time in an effort to stimulate North Vietnam toward a peace agreement. Unfortunately, over 20,000 Americans died in Vietnam between January 1969 and January 1973 when the Paris Peace Accords were executed, ending U.S. combat involvement in Vietnam and the North agreeing to release American prisoners of war.

The last American combat forces left Vietnam on March 29, 1973 except for a few civilians and Marines who guarded U.S. installations near Saigon. However, the communists soon violated the cease-fire agreement and by early 1974 full-scale war had resumed in South Vietnam. Although the Nixon Administration had agreed to provide American airpower if needed in defense of South Vietnam, Congress did not authorize funds to provide such support because of the robust public opposition to America reengaging in the war in any manner.

At the end of 1974, South Vietnamese authorities reported that 80,000 of their soldiers and civilians had been killed in fighting during the year. NVA forces using Russian tanks and artillery advanced south while the ARVNs were ill-equipped and often unwilling to defend their country. Many ARVN soldiers threw down their weapons and deserted.

As the NVA pushed into South Vietnam in 1975 ARVN units withdrew in a near panic and fled further south while the NVA took control of northern cities. With ARVN defenses collapsed, the NVA launched a rocket attack at Saigon's Tan Son Nhut airport on April 30, 1975 killing two U.S. Marines, the last two Americans to die in Vietnam during the war. The last of the Marines who had been guarding the American Embassy flew off to a waiting Navy ship later that morning.

Later that day North Vietnamese troops gained control of Saigon and NVA tanks stormed through the gates of the Presidential Palace and forced South Vietnam's unconditional surrender from Mr. Duong Van Minh, President of the Republic of Vietnam (South Vietnam).

American troop strength and casualties (deaths) in Vietnam

Year	Troop Strength*	U.S. Fatalities**
1960	900	5
1961	3,200	16
1962	11,300	53
1963	16,300	122
1964	23,300	216

American troop strength and casualties (deaths) in Vietnam

Year	Troop Strength*	U.S. Fatalities**
1965	184,300	1,978
1966	385,300	6,350
1967	485,600	11,363
1968	536,100	16,899
1969	475,200	11,780
1970	334,600	6,173
1971	156,800	2,414
1972	24,200	759
1973	(Jan) 23,700 (Dec) 50	168

*Data from the American War Library
**Data from the Defense Casualty Analysis System

NVA tank crashing through a gate at the
Presidential Palace in Saigon on April 30, 1975.

It is the view of many Americans that the U.S. *lost* the Vietnam War. However, war is not a game. Although victors are often proclaimed there are no true *winners* of any war. It is estimated that 1.1 million NVA and VC troops were killed. Additionally, several hundred thousand Vietnamese civilians died during the war. Those individuals and their families certainly were not *winners*.

After American combat forces withdrew from Vietnam in March 1973, the continued battle to defend South Vietnam was left to ARVN forces. While American military and political leaders proclaimed the ARVNs were capable of defending the South, in reality they were not prepared to fight the NVA and VC who had mounted a formidable well equipped force after the U.S. exited Vietnam.

To worsen matters, the U.S. Congress reduced American military aid to South Vietnam in 1974. Subsequently, the South was unable to adequately support or equip the ARVNs, resulting in soldiers abandoning tanks and artillery guns because they were no longer operational. Some units actually ran out of ammunition.

The ARVN's defense of South Vietnam ultimately failed when NVA troops overran Saigon and forced South Vietnam's surrender in 1975, two years after American forces left Vietnam. America negotiated a peaceful withdrawal from Vietnam in 1973. If a nation was to be declared the *loser*, it would be South Vietnam in 1975.

With that brief summary of the war, I return to the question, "Was it worth it?" Each reader will have an answer based upon his or her view of the war. The following is my two-part answer.

First, the Vietnam War was financially costly, but more importantly over 58,000 American lives were lost and 75,000 Americans were permanently disabled. The purpose of America's commitment was to halt the spread of Communism and to preserve South Vietnamese human rights. With the exception of the fall of South Vietnam to the communist North in 1975 and Laos becoming communist that same year, Communism has not spread to any other country (the domino theory) since the war. While the matter has been debated, it is theorized that America's involvement in Korea and over 10-year commitment in Vietnam stopped the spread of communism into other countries.

What if the U.S. hadn't gone to war in Vietnam? The communists North would have most certainly overtaken South Vietnam, but would Communism have overtaken other countries? What would have happened if Communism had taken over other countries? Would America have become involved in a war elsewhere to stop the spread of Communism? What would have been the cost of such a war? It didn't happen, and therefore we will never know the American impact, or worldwide impact, if we had not gone to war in Vietnam.

While many American's quickly say "No," the war wasn't worth it, if individuals would consider the possible consequences of our not fighting in Vietnam, they might not so easily reach that conclusion.

Secondly, I address the "was it worth it" question from my personal perspective. I was drafted into the U.S. Army and sustained multiple injuries including the loss of my left leg below the knee when I was wounded while serving as an infantry platoon sergeant in Vietnam. Accordingly, most people would conclude that I would say "No; the war was not worth it."

Before entering the Army, I was a *follower* with little self-confidence. However, after completing military training, I gained the needed self-confidence to become a leader. After being assigned as a squad leader and later platoon sergeant in Vietnam, my self-confidence grew while my leadership skills improved as I took charge during daily operations and numerous combat actions where lives were on the line. After we lost twelve members of our platoon, including our platoon leader, in December 1969 our company commander assigned me as acting third platoon leader until a new platoon leader was assigned.

Another test for me was being seriously wounded on January 27, 1970. My previous thoughts about my survival primarily related to the possibility of being killed. I hadn't often thought about losing a limb. From the moment in my hospital bed when I knew my leg was gone and learned the extent of my other injuries, rather than becoming depressed, I was truly thankful to have survived my tour in Vietnam. If I had to lose my left leg to make it home alive, I accepted that fate.

While I was certainly dependent upon the skills of doctors and nurses to care for my injuries, I knew that my emotional recovery would depend upon maintaining a positive attitude and my ability to move on from the most challenging physical and emotional experience of my life. Recovering from my injuries and literally learning to walk again was a dramatic confidence builder for me.

As I moved on with my life, the self-confidence I gained in the Army and the leadership skills I gained through my experiences in Vietnam benefited me greatly. I have repeatedly used my self-confidence to face difficult professional and personal challenges. My leadership skills were repeatedly recognized as I progressed through my civilian career by being selected for management and supervisory positions.

After becoming active as a member of the Disabled American Veterans (DAV), my leadership skills were recognized when I was elected as Chapter Commander five years after I join the organization. In 1978 I became a volunteer firefighter and within two years I was elected as a lieutenant. I soon progressed through the ranks and became the Fire Chief in 1983.

And once again, my leadership skills were recognized when I was elected as the DAV Department of Colorado Commander (state commander) in May 2015. Truly a great honor.

I have been walking with an artificial leg for over 46 years, and frankly can't remember what it was like walking on two natural legs. I can bowl, play golf, ride a bicycle, hike in the Colorado mountains, and I also snow skied for several years.

Although a day rarely passes that I don't think about my time in Vietnam and the men with whom I served, I am able to live my life without those memories being a distraction and preventing me from living a relatively normal life. That being said, I will never forget the men with whom I served in Vietnam, especially the fourteen friends, who became like brothers, and who died there.

So, my personal answer to the question "Was it worth it," or "Was my involvement worth it?" My answer is "Yes."

I can't imagine what my life would have been like if I had not served as an infantryman in Vietnam. Being a disabled combat veteran has been a hugely important part of my life and has provided me with tremendously valuable experiences. My military service was a positive life changing experience.

My military service was the most demanding physical and emotional experience of my life, and I continue to endure periodic pain and discomfort from my injuries. However, by confronting and overcoming the challenges associated with military service I have learned who I am. I am a better man because I gained self-confidence and leadership skills that have benefited me to this day.

I have shared my military experience by speaking before hundreds of school-aged and college students and before civic, church and veterans' organizations. I have also spoken at Memorial Day and Veterans Day ceremonies and at the dedication of veterans' monuments. I continue to share my experiences whenever I am given the opportunity.

During some of those speaking opportunities I offer a tribute to my friends who were killed in Vietnam with my portrayal of The American Fighting Man. My portrayal begins:

"The average American fighting man is 20 years old. He is a short-haired, tight-muscled kid, who under normal circumstances, some might consider to still be a boy. Although he isn't old enough to buy a beer, he's old enough to die for his country. He is a man like 20-year-old James Mincey (Red), an easygoing guy from South Carolina. Red was walking a few yards in front of me one hot and humid afternoon in Vietnam, when he was wounded by an exploding booby trap. I helped our medic Doc Jackson treat Red's injuries and I held Red's hand to comfort him until we loaded him aboard a helicopter a few minutes later. Unfortunately, Private First Class James Mincey died on that chopper, before he reached the hospital."

I then share portrayals of other friends in the third platoon who were killed in action. However, I often must stop briefly to compose myself while I talk about those men, because the pain of losing those friends hurts as much today as it did the day they died and brings tears to my eyes and a quivering voice while I tell the story of their deaths.

Although it is often difficult, I willingly share my experience because I believe it is extremely important that all Americans understand what is asked of our fellow Americans when we send them into combat.

One of my great honors has been to serve on the All Veterans Honor Guard since 2013, providing military honors to deceased veterans when they are laid to rest at Fort Logan National Cemetery in Denver, CO. I have been active in veterans' organizations for over 40 years and continue to receive incredible satisfaction by supporting programs and activities which assist veterans and their families.

If I had not served as an infantryman in Vietnam and if I had not been seriously wounded, I would not have encountered the many experiences which have become such an important part of my life. Obviously, I would not have become an author by writing and publishing my first book entitled *We Were The Third Herd* and this book. I have the utmost pride in my military service and am proud to be a Vietnam veteran.

➤ The two U.S. Marines killed during the NAV rocket attack at Tan Son Nhut airport on April 30, 1975 were eighteen-year-old Lance Corporal Darwin Judge from Marshalltown, Iowa and twenty-one-year-old Corporal Charles McMahon, Jr. from Woburn, Massachusetts. Sadly, two Marine pilots were also killed that day when their helicopter crashed at sea while attempting to return to a U.S. aircraft carrier.

NOTE: The statistical information cited in this chapter was primarily obtained from Wickipedia.org, National Archives data and History.com. While some statistics varied, I cited what I believe are the most accurate data.

As the Vietnamization program was implemented, American troop reductions continued and many units changed their area of operations. In some cases GIs were assigned to other units. Alpha company joined other units in Cambodia searching for enemy sanctuaries and captured tons of supplies, weapons and ammunition. By December 1970, elements of the 25th Infantry Division began redeployment to their headquarters at Scholfield Barracks in Hawaii. On December 8, 1970 the 2nd Battalion, 14th Infantry Regiment (including Alpha Company) left Vietnam. All 25th Division units left Vietnam by May 1971.

After the fall of Saigon in 1975, North and South Vietnam were unified under communist control to form the Socialist Republic of Vietnam. Saigon was renamed Ho Chi Minh City in July 1976. An estimated 1 to 2.5 million South Vietnamese citizens, mostly former ARVN soldiers, government workers and civilians sympathetic to South Vietnam's war effort, were imprisoned in "Reeducation Camps." They were tortured, malnourished, forced into hard labor and many were executed. As many as 200,000 prisoners died while confined for up to 17 years.

Phnom Penh, the capital of Cambodia, fell to the communist Khmer Rouge in April 1975. In 1978 Vietnam invaded Cambodia and ousted the Khmer Rouge in the Cambodian–Vietnamese War. A new government was installed led by Khmer Rouge defectors who killed thousands and enslaved thousands more. In response, China invaded Vietnam in 1979. The two countries fought a brief border war, known as the Sino-Vietnamese War.

From 1978 to 1979, some 450,000 ethnic Chinese left Vietnam by boat as refugees or were expelled back to China.

Since that time Vietnam has been at peace. The Socialist Republic of Vietnam maintains an active duty military force of approximately 412,000. In addition to ground forces, they have a few hundred military aircraft and a very small number of naval vessels.

Chapter 21

Return to Vietnam – 2013

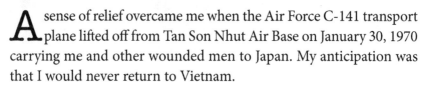

A sense of relief overcame me when the Air Force C-141 transport plane lifted off from Tan Son Nhut Air Base on January 30, 1970 carrying me and other wounded men to Japan. My anticipation was that I would never return to Vietnam.

For many years after returning home I lost contact with the men I had served with. That didn't happen purposefully; rather, I was busy with my family life, personal activities and pursuit of my career as a federal employee. However, almost daily I thought about those men, the experiences we shared, and the friends we lost.

As years passed, I began searching for some of the guys I had served with in Vietnam. Maybe it was nostalgia as I aged, but I developed the desire to reconnect with the men who had helped me survive. Over time I located several men, and some of them had also reached out and contacted other members of the Third Herd and Alpha Company.

During the early 1980s, I met my current wife Marilyn. We began dating in 1983, and we were married in 1986. She believed the first three years of a relationship are just infatuation, and after that time, it can become true love. And it did. We have been married for 34 years and have enjoyed the pleasures of marriage, shared travels around the world and experienced both good and bad times with our three sons and eleven grandchildren.

In 1999 I accepted an early retirement from the federal service. One of my intentions was to continue the pursuit of publishing my first book about my military experience that I had begun in 1983.

Armed with a new computer with internet capability, I expanded my efforts by drafting chapters and conducting online research for details relating to the war. I consulted with several of my comrades to help me remember names and places and details of some of the events we shared so many years previously.

During conversations with those guys I reached two distinct conclusions. First, we were all impacted by our experience in Vietnam. Some of us were changed physically because of our injuries, but we all were changed emotionally by the shocking events we endured, most specifically the brutality of war and the loss of good friends who were killed in action. You can't take young men who had lived in the peacefulness of America and send them into brutal combat without anticipating an emotional change. Yes, we were forever changed.

What was also amazing, although it had been over thirty years since I had seen those men, we carried on conversations like we had never been apart. We laughed about the fun times we shared and had serious conversations about the bad times and friends we lost many years ago. Although we likely didn't realize this until possibly years after returning from Vietnam, we lost our innocence and much of our youth in Vietnam.

Secondly, several of those men continued to have significant emotional trauma and have been diagnosed with Post Traumatic Stress Disorder (PTSD), which for some has caused severe distractions in their lives to this day. Some turned to drugs or alcohol in an attempt to erase their memories or ease the pain, while most ultimately sought consoling with the VA or other support groups. Although most of those men are willing to discuss our mutual experiences and their personal feelings, many of those same men are reluctant to talk about the war with their friends or family members. For some, the war happened in their past and that is where they have chosen to leave it.

One man who has struggled emotionally with his experience was fellow NCO Jim Overbey. He never recovered from the events of December 28, 1969 when we lost half of the third platoon. Jim feels partially responsible for those losses, although many of us have told him none of us could have prevented the tragedy of that night. Jim used alcohol for years to deal with his emotions and continues to deal with medical and emotional issues with daily prescription medications.

However, for all of us, the most troubling memories are those of our friends who died in Vietnam. While some of us will share our fond memories of those men, it remains a difficult conversation and stirs sad emotions regarding men who became like brothers to us all.

My writing cumulated in May 2003 by publishing the memoirs of my tour in Vietnam entitled *We Were The Third Herd*, the nickname for our third platoon. Later that summer eight former Third Herd members and four other members of Alpha Company held a reunion in Salt Lake City as guests of the family of Lieutenant Craig Fielding, our former third platoon leader who was killed on April 1, 1970. Also in attendance was Jennifer Denard, daughter of our company commander Captain William Branch who was killed on June 6, 1970. Jennifer was only two years old at the time of her father's death.

Members of the Third Herd and other members of Alpha Company
are pictured in 2003 at the gravesite of Lieutenant Craig Fielding in
Salt Lake City. Left to right: Mike Myers, Steve Robinson, Chuck Gorman,
myself, Rick Olsen (1st platoon) Sid Morrison (company medic)
Charlie Norton (battalion commander), Mike Stark,
Bill Albert (2nd platoon)), Bill Casey, David Phillips, Rick Shields.

Talking and spending time with friends who had risked our lives together was extremely fulfilling for me and I believe brought a sense of solace to some of the men who may have been struggling with their experience. Although we had signed up to serve our country and defend the flag while we were in Vietnam, in reality our priority was to take care of each other and hopefully ensure our mutual survival.

Reuniting not only to share war stories but to discuss how we had moved on after the war and sharing pictures of our kids and grandkids, helped all of us heal to a degree, and it was gratifying to see that most of us had moved on to lead productive and successful lives. Although many of us had less hair, and what was left was turning gray, we were for the most part the same guys who had served together in combat many years ago.

The emotions associated with our experiences became evident during our Salt Lake City reunion when we conducted a memorial service for the friends we lost at Lieutenant Craig Fielding's gravesite. I led the service by talking about our time together and struggled while talking about the men we lost. Several of the men shared in reading the names of our friends who were killed in action while we were in Vietnam.

As it happened, when Bob Emery's name was to be read, it was Mike Myers turn to read the name. He broke down and couldn't say Bob's name. Rick Shield who was standing next to Mike, put his hand on Mike's shoulder and read Bob Emery's name. Mike and Bob had been close friends and they had been in the same foxhole on December 28, 1969 when Bob and seven other members of the third platoon were killed by enemy sappers.

Publishing my first book was one of the greatest experiences of my life because it resulted in events that I could never have imagined. I connected with family members and friends of comrades who were killed in action and reconnected with many of the men with whom I had served. I have reunited with some of my comrades during travels across the country and many of us have gathered for periodic reunions to renew friendships and share stories of days long gone by.

As diplomatic relations between the United States and Vietnam improved over the years many Americans, including Vietnam veterans, began traveling there to see the country where that controversial war occurred at the cost of over 58,000 American lives. While I had considered going back to Vietnam and had opportunities to go with other Vietnam veterans, it was not a priority for me. I chose to visit other parts of the world, with my wife Marilyn, traveling to the Caribbean, Mexico, Europe, Alaska and several trips to Hawaii.

In early 2013 Chuck Gorman, a fellow third platoon member, said he and his brother Dan, who had also served in Vietnam, were planning a trip to Vietnam. They were coordinating with a travel company to develop a tour, primarily in the south-central part of the former South Vietnam where we had served. After reviewing the itinerary, I decided it was time to return to see villages and countryside where I had served 44 years earlier. We would leave on November 1, 2013 for our adventure back to the place that had changed my life forever.

When I told friends and family members about my planned trip to Vietnam, a frequent response was; "That should bring closure for you."

However, my response, which most people didn't seem to understand, was that I wasn't looking for closure. While many people may seek closure regarding a sad event or traumatic experience in their lives, I don't want to close my Vietnam experience. I have fully accepted that experience and what happened to me and the unfortunate fate of my friends who were killed in action. I hold no resentment toward my former enemies and was not returning to Vietnam to make peace with myself. That experience is what made me the man I am today, and I am prepared to take the memories of that time to my grave.

While there would certainly be emotions associated with visiting locations where friends were wounded or killed or being near where I was seriously wounded, I finally wanted to see what Vietnam looks like today, what the villages and countryside look like and to see how the people are living today in comparison to 44 years prior. Although most Vietnam veterans I talked with about my planned trip indicated they had no desire to return, I was ready to go.

Upon confirming the reservation for Marilyn and me we received information regarding what to expect in Vietnam, do's and don'ts while there and also information regarding vaccinations and medical related matters to plan for.

One bit of information of particular interest to me stated that when visiting the Vietnamese countryside to stay with the group and your guide to prevent people from getting lost. However, visitors were encouraged not to venture into areas not known to be safe to prevent the possibility of accidentally detonating what we called a booby trap, or as they are called today improvised electronic device (IED).

Unexploded bombs and booby-traps across Vietnam's countryside have injured or killed an estimated forty thousand Vietnamese civilians over the years. Having been wounded twice by booby-traps during my tour in Vietnam, I certainly didn't want that to happen again.

With our bags packed, Marilyn and I left our home in Littleton, CO early on the morning of November 1, 2013 for our flight to Los Angeles International Airport (LAX) where we would join others who would be traveling with us to Vietnam.

After claiming our baggage, we met up with Chuck Gorman and his wife Cherie and learned the airport was on lock down after a Transportation Security Administration employee had been shot and killed in a nearby terminal. We sat on a curbside bench much of that afternoon. After a long day, our group boarded our China Air flight and lifted off from LAX at 12:30 a.m. on November 2, 2013 for a fourteen-hour flight to Taipei, on the island of Taiwan. The plane was a Boeing 747 packed with 400 passengers.

We arrived at Taiwan Taoyuan International Airport in Taipei at approximately 6:00 a.m. on November 3rd, because we lost one day when crossing the International Dateline in the Pacific Ocean. We then boarded our three-hour China Air flight from Taipei to Vietnam, which was nothing after our fourteen hours flying over the Pacific.

The plane was less than half full, giving us the luxury of stretching out and moving around as we chose. As we neared the eastern coast of Vietnam the four of us Vietnam veterans moved to the right side of the plane to view the countryside. I saw mostly lush green vegetation with sporadic roads and small homes. In what appeared to be small cities, there were large warehouse type buildings and clusters of other buildings, which were likely small businesses and shops.

I was looking for scars of the war, craters created from the thousands of exploding bombs and artillery rounds. Although it had been forty years since America withdrew from Vietnam, it was still amazing to see how the landscape had healed itself. There was no visible evidence from the air that there had ever been a war in Vietnam.

We arrived at Ton Son Nhut International Airport at 10:30 a.m. on November 3rd. As the plane rolled toward the terminal we saw Huey helicopters in the distance which were near what was the former Ton Son Nhut Air Base used by American forces during the war and was the target of major enemy attacks during the 1968 Tet Offensive.

The international terminal where we deplaned was constructed in 2007 and looked similar to most U.S. airports. My arrival in Vietnam that day was in stark contrast to my arrival at Cam Ranh Bay in 1969. Back then I anticipated considerable danger and uncertainty as I entered the war, but on this day, I anticipated a pleasant journey while revisiting the country in a peaceful setting.

After we gathered our baggage and checked through customs, we found our bus with our tour guide Viet Nguyen, a 47-year-old Vietnamese native. We later learned that in Vietnam the family name is first and the given name is last, in America he would be Nguyen (pronounced "When") Viet. He asked that we just call him Viet.

While we traveled from the airport Viet identified historic buildings and locations, some of which we would visit later during our tour. The city had been known as Saigon until North Vietnam overtook South Vietnam. In 1976 the city was renamed Ho Chi Minh City in honor of the Communist revolutionary leader. However, many of the local citizens still referred to the city as Saigon; accordingly, I will refer to the city as Saigon during the remainder of the book. Saigon, which had a population of less than 3 million at the end of the war in 1975, had grown to a population of over 9 million.

We later arrived at our hotel, which ironically was named Grand Hotel Saigon. While a short nap would have been great after our long trip, we were advised not to sleep until that evening, making it easier to adjust to the time change. There is a fourteen-hour time difference between Colorado and Vietnam (10:00 a.m. in Colorado is 12 midnight in Vietnam, the beginning of a new day.

After settling into our room, Marilyn and I ventured into the city by walking south and finding the Saigon River, which I had seen during some of our patrols northeast of Cu Chi. The river as it flowed through Saigon and into the South China Sea was huge, similar to the Mississippi River as it flows through New Orleans.

My wife Marilyn near the Saigon River. We enjoyed a dinner cruise on the boat in the background during our last night in Vietnam.

Early that evening we met the three other members of our tour group. They were John and Donna Thalacker and Andreas Otto. Viet then led the group a few blocks to the Rex Hotel where we gathered on a rooftop lounge for cocktails and conversation while we enjoyed the beautiful city view.

While sipping cocktails, our guide Viet gave us the lay of the land and rules we should follow. One important rule was don't drink the water; however, Viet would advise us if it was safe to have a soda or drink with ice. Safe bottled water would be provided on the bus each day. That evening most of us had a drink with ice after Viet said it was safe to do so. While we were gathered, we introduced ourselves.

Chuck and Cherie Gorman were both retired schoolteachers from Plattsmouth, Nebraska.

Jeff and John Gorman, Chuck and Cherie's sons, were both married with children. Jeff lived in Denver and John lived in Lincoln, Nebraska.

Dan Gorman and Audrey Caine were from Minnesota. Dan had served in Vietnam in 1968. He was a truck driver and had driven on some of the same roads we would be traveling on during our tour.

Tom Graeve was a friend of Chuck and Cherie from Nebraska who had served as an Army infantryman in Vietnam in 1967-68. He had retired as the Chief of the Omaha Fire Department.

John and Donna Thalacker were from Iowa and spent winters in Florida. John had served with the 25th Division in Vietnam and was a retired prison warden. Donna was a retired Navy Captain.

Andreas Otto worked for a newspaper in Germany. He was visiting Vietnam to gather information for a research project.

And then there was my wife Marilyn and me. Marilyn is a native Coloradan while I am a native Iowan but have lived in Colorado since 1971. We are both retired federal employees. Because I was wearing shorts and members of the group noticed my prosthesis, I shared the story of losing my leg while serving in Vietnam. After an enjoyable dinner and cocktails, we returned to our hotel for a good night's sleep.

During our ventures into the city, we gained the unique experience of crossing streets through the maze of passing scooters and motorcycles, because the majority of intersections didn't have a traffic light. After a couple of days, we became accustomed to crossing the streets while the cyclists would yield or swerve around. We also learned not to stop walking, but keep moving until we had crossed the street.

Most streets in Saigon were two lanes in each direction. However, most people drove scooters or small motorcycles and weaved through the streets not staying in any particular traffic lane. It was amazing how well the traffic flowed with thousands of scooters and motorcycles traveling on the streets. Although there were some cars and a few busses, pickups or larger trucks, some people loaded boxes, crates, lumber or whatever they needed to transport onto their scooters or motorcycles. There were sometimes up to four people on one motorcycle.

Because there were no American type freeways in Vietnam, traffic was often congested on two-lane roads and smaller city streets. Travelers were normally going to or from work or on shopping excursions. Adding to the congestion were many people traveling from surrounding small towns to conduct their business.

Over 90% of the vehicles registered in Vietnam are scooters or motorcycles. A government decree requires that all riders wear a helmet. Surprisingly, I saw only two accidents during our travels.

On Monday November 4th, we boarded our air conditioned 26 passenger bus about 8:00 a.m. with our first stop planned for Cu Chi. Leaving Saigon we traveled west on Highway 1, a two lane and sometimes four lane paved road with small buildings, stores and homes scattered along the roadside. Most buildings were one- or two- story wood framed or masonry structures and many in need of maintenance.

We traveled about an hour until we reached Cu Chi's War museum about 25 miles northwest of Saigon. The museum naturally contained pictures, weapons and many other relics from the war, bringing back many memories for us Vietnam veterans.

Vietnam veterans in our group with a Huey at the Cu Chi War Museum.
Left to right, John Thalacker, Tom Graeve, Dan Gorman,
Chuck Gorman and myself.

We continued through Cu Chi that had grown from a small town during the war to a city of 75,000 people. We turned west and drove along the southern perimeter of what had been the 25th Division Base Camp where I was hospitalized at the 12th Evacuation hospital after being wounded in January 1970. Before we left for our trip, I jokingly told people I was going back to Vietnam to look for my leg. However, I didn't get the chance. We couldn't access the former base camp site because it was a Vietnamese military installation.

There were trees and thick vegetation along the former perimeter of the base camp much different from when the vegetation was cleared during the war to provide visibility over the surrounding countryside.

From Cu Chi we ventured west to Trung Lap that I remembered as a small village north of Firebase Patton accessible only by a gravel road identified as 7 Alpha from the south and dirt trails from other directions. Trung Lap had become a small town covering a couple square miles accessible by paved roads with small shops and primitive homes where some people operated businesses with their wares scattered in their front yard.

When we reached 7 Alpha, now a paved two-lane road, we turned south toward the site of former Firebase Patton that Chuck and I had often called our home during the war. Chuck had kept a map of the area, and working with Viet using GPS, we stopped at what we believed was the site of our former battalion firebase.

As I walked around I saw no resemblance of what had been Fire Support Base Patton. I had hoped to see the remains of bunkers or other remnants of the firebase. But disappointingly, there was nothing. An irrigation canal ran through the former site and there was a cluster of small buildings nearby. The only familiar sites were the surrounding rice paddies and scattered trees just like there had been 44 years ago.

We then rode south on 7 Alpha a short distance and stopped at what we believed was the site guard post Venice East. Nothing remained of the former Venice East. We walked across open grassland and up a small rise alongside a drainage canal about 100 yards east of the road from where we could see for miles around. As I stood there I thought back to the days when the third platoon walked across that same countryside and remembered firefights that occurred or booby traps we encountered not far from where I was standing. The peacefulness that morning was almost eerie as I overlooked the lush green countryside.

Me at the site of former Fire Support Base Patton, November 4, 2013.

We learned later by talking with Viet, after communist North Vietnam took control of South Vietnam and the countries united into the Socialist Republic of Vietnam, the government slowly demolished and removed most evidence of American military presence. Therefore, today places like Firebase Patton only exist in the minds of those of us who served there and with pictures taken so many years ago.

After a lunch of Vietnamese food at a restaurant surrounded by beautiful gardens near the Saigon River, we traveled through portions of the Ho Bo Woods en route to the Cu Chi tunnels. While we walked a short distance to the tunnels, it was a strange feeling to again see the trees and thick vegetation that we encountered there during the war, while remembering friends I lost likely not far from where we were.

Entrances to tunnels were concealed during the war, making them extremely difficult for us GIs to find. Construction of the tunnel systems around Cu Chi began in the 1940s and covered hundreds of square miles. However, entrances to the site we visited had been cleared, enabling us to see how the tunnels had been constructed. Some tunnel systems went down three levels. The first level was six to eight feet underground and then subsequent levels were constructed another six to eight feet further underground.

Some tunnel systems included rooms used to provide medical care, for sleeping areas or a command post. The tunnels were an ingenious system used throughout much of the countryside. Although thousands of American bombs were dropped attempting to destroy those tunnels, they remained an effective tactical system throughout the war.

One by one, we walked down a few steps and entered the first level of one of the tunnels. I had to bend over at my waist to navigate through the tunnel that was arched at the top and about three feet high and two feet wide. My shoulders repeatedly rubbed along the sides until I reached an opening leading into a large room. From there you could go into the lower levels or to the exit. Marilyn and I didn't go into the lower levels because tunnels became smaller and were wet.

Some of the group continued on and came out with mud on their hands and knees because they had to crawl through the lowest level. Most NVA and VC soldiers were smaller than most of us, making it easier for them to navigate through those tunnels.

Although we were only about thirty miles northwest of Saigon, it took over an hour to return to our hotel that afternoon because of the congested traffic. That evening Viet guided the group a few blocks to the Bitexco Financial Tower, a 68-story high-rise that opened in 2010. We rode up two separate elevators to reach the 52nd floor of what was a beautifully designed and as modern of a building you might see in America. We then gathered in a lounge for a drink while we enjoyed a spectacular view of the nighttime Saigon skyline.

What was truly unique about the downtown Saigon experience was that mixed in amongst modern high rises, were small one to three story buildings where people lived and operated small stores and literally cooked their meals on the sidewalks using a small stove. In addition to the street vendors who were always trying to sell us something, there were some people simply begging for money.

As we observed while driving around Saigon and by talking with our guide Viet, most Vietnamese people in Saigon lived in apartments or what we call condominiums. We saw one area along a canal that fed into the Saigon River with plywood shacks built next to each other where people lived. We saw very few single-family homes owned by the *wealthy* according to our guide Viet. Although Vietnam has made significant advances to improve the quality of life for its citizens, most are far behind the standard of living we enjoy. The per capita income in Vietnam is approximately $2,000 annually.

Tuesday, November 5th, we checked out of our plush hotel in Saigon because we were on our way to Tay Ninh City (Tay Ninh) where we would spend that night. We boarded our bus and rode northwest approximately sixty miles through the Vietnamese countryside toward Nui Ba Den, the Black Virgin Mountain that I often saw in the distance while I served in Vietnam. The mountain is about six miles northwest of Tay Ninh which is near Vietnam's western border with Cambodia.

As we traveled through the small towns and countryside, I noticed both differences and similarities from 44 years ago. Many people still lived in very small homes, but most homes now had electricity. Surprisingly, we could see a big screen television in some of those primitive homes. We actually saw a man performing dental work in front of his home. We would periodically see a large newer home that our guide Viet said was likely owned by a local landowner.

There was no running water in homes during the war, but today there were aluminum tanks on the rooftops or on a nearby tower. Water is pumped into the tank from a nearby well and gravity supplies water into the home. We also noticed cows and water buffalo still being used to pull a wagon or cart of supplies or crops. However, there were also a few tractors pulling farming equipment or a wagon and trucks transporting crops or other items to their destination.

It was rice harvest time in Vietnam, and just like I had seen during the war, we saw large piles of rice that had been transported from the paddies to be placed in large bags for transport to market. It appeared that rice harvesting was still a labor-intensive process.

Nui Ba Den that we could see from miles away as we approached was used by both military forces during the war. The U.S. operated a communications base at its top while enemy troops controlled the bottom of the mountain and used tunnels and caves honeycombed in the mountain for storage and housing troops. The U.S. communications base was attacked twice in 1968, killing 29 American servicemen.

After arrival at the mountain we rode up on a gondola that carried us approximately one third of the way up the 3,300-foot mountain to a beautiful temple representing Buddhism and Taoism religions built into the side of the mountain surrounded by dense trees and lavish green vegetation. Mid-sized monkeys scampered outside, and we could see for miles from that site across the mostly flat surrounding countryside. We were told we were seeing Cambodia in the distance to the west. It was a unique experience to actually stand on the mountain that I had often seen in the distance so many years ago.

Nui Ba Din in the distance looking west.

Exterior view of the temple on Nui Ba Din.

It was then off to Tay Ninh where we visited a Cao Dai Temple and quietly observed a noon-time service with about 200 worshipers sitting on the floor wearing white robes. It was a huge and beautifully adorned temple both inside and outside. Outside along the curbside were hundreds of pairs of shoes left by those who had entered the temple.

Worshipers at the Cao Dai Temple in Tay Ninh.

We then had an unanticipated lunch-time experience. Viet said we were eating at the Quan Ngoc Tuyet Asian restaurant in Tay Ninh which was owned by a former female Viet Cong soldier. Some of us Vietnam veterans looked at each other wondering how we would deal with that experience.

Upon our arrival we were escorted to a private room, and after a short while, a variety of Vietnamese food was served. Oriental food is not my favorite, so when Vietnamese food was my only choice, I didn't have a hearty meal, but Marilyn loved it. But that was fine because I returned home not gaining any weight as often happens on vacations.

As most of the group was finishing their lunch, Viet escorted the owner, Ms. Tuyet, the former Viet Cong soldier into the room. Members of the group stood up and shook her hand as she walked around the table to greet us.

Then, with little hesitation, one by one, each of us Vietnam veterans approached our former enemy, and stood by her with our arms around each other while someone took a picture. It was definitely an unexpected moment for me that I will never forget. As we Vietnam veterans discussed over a beer later during our trip, combatants on both sides were just doing their jobs in support of their country. The war had ended forty years earlier; we need not be enemies forever.

Me with former Viet Cong soldier Ms. Tuyet in Tay Ninh.
The raised hand was her way of saluting us.

After that very unique lunch-time experience we traveled past a border station between Vietnam and Cambodia, then continued on to visit what had been the South Central Department Viet Cong Base. The complex consisted of several masonry buildings and defensive positions outside and long concrete trenches that were used to find cover from American bombings.

We all took our daily malaria pill and were using insect repellant when we were in the countryside. As we walked through the grounds of that VC base camp with thick vegetation, several of us guys commented that the mosquitoes were out there in mass that afternoon just like they were during the war.

Our group at a trail bridge at the site of the former VC base camp.

That evening we returned to Tay Ninh and checked into our hotel that was considerably less extravagant than the Grand Hotel Saigon. Our room was very small, the television didn't work and while the air conditioner blasted like a small jet engine it gave us little relief from the heat. But at least I wasn't sleeping in the rain with mosquitoes flying around my head as I experienced during my tour in Vietnam.

However, we did encounter a pleasant surprise (at least for me) when we arrived at Uncle Dave's Pizza Bistro and Grill that evening. The owner Dave had served as a U.S. Marine in Vietnam during the war. He later married a Vietnamese native and had been living in Tay Ninh since that time.

Most of us enjoyed a cold beer for starters and then some of us shared pizzas while others enjoyed burgers and fries that reminded us of good old American food. The food was delicious, but we were told the menu changed almost daily depending upon the availability of food.

On November 6th we headed mostly east from Tay Ninh on a paved road that turned into a rough gravel road and led us into the remote countryside. There were scattered hamlets, water buffalo grazing alongside the roads, with few vehicles or people to be seen.

We finally stopped along a huge berm, and when we walked to the top we saw the Dau Tieng Reservoir, a 100 thousand square mile reservoir constructed years after the war for flood control and irrigation. Vietnam's government allows no boats on the reservoir and no commercial or private development is allowed near the shores.

Our tour then took us to the Dau Tieng district south of the reservoir where the 25th Division's 2nd Brigade Dau Tieng Base Camp was located during the war. The base camp had been the site of a two-day battle in February 1969 when a large contingent of NVA soldiers attacked the base. Although the enemy troops were ultimately repelled, 21 American soldiers were killed and over 70 were wounded. Enemy losses were estimated at nearly 200.

All that remained of the approximate two square mile base camp was a quarter mile section of the former runway. The blacktop runway was badly deteriorated with dirt exposed in many places and the remaining asphalt cracked and crumbling. I had never been at that base during the war; however, some of the other guys had been there so that stop returned special memories of long ago for them. While standing on that abandoned runway, my wife Marilyn said she could picture the planes landing and taking off from that base camp during the war.

That day we also saw rubber plantations covering thousands of acres, most owned by the Michelin Rubber Company. Rubber trees actually produce latex that is drained from each tree and collected in a small container attached to the tree. The latex is refined into rubber.

Enemy Troops often operated within some of the rubber plantations and there were numerous encounters with U.S. forces in those areas during the war. Many of those rubber plantations remained in operation during the war, in fact, it is believed that Michelin paid the Viet Cong to keep their plantations in operation. Our next stop was special for Chuck Gorman and me at one of those rubber plantations.

Captain William Branch was our company commander when I arrived in country and continued until he was reassigned to our battalion headquarters. He gathered intelligence information regarding enemy activities while flying over the countryside on aerial observations in helicopters. On June 6, 1970 the four-passenger OH-6A chopper he was flying on was shot down in a rubber plantation south of the Dau Tieng Base Camp. Captain Branch and Captain William Byrd were killed by enemy troops after the chopper crashed. The pilot survived and safely walked to the Dau Tieng Base Camp to alert officials of the incident which enabled the recovery of the two Captain's bodies.

Chuck and I knew Captain Branch well. He was a great company commander and an even better man. Chuck had map coordinates of the crash site and worked with Viet using GPS to find the site.

There were scattered houses and other buildings in the area adjacent to the grove of rubber trees. We walked a short distance into the trees and then stopped. Chuck had told Jennifer Denard of our planned return to Vietnam and our desire to find the site where her father had died. She had given Chuck a letter to read at the site. Jen has devoted much of her life paying tribute to her father.

The group gathered around Chuck as he read Jen's letter addressed to her dad saying how much she still loved him and expressing her tremendous respect she continues to have for him as her father and for his military service and sacrifice. With teary eyes and in a slightly quivering voice, I asked that we five Vietnam veterans stand in line to render a hand salute in honor of our fallen comrade Captain William Branch. While it was obviously a very solemn time for Chuck Gorman and me it was also a tremendously special experience to return to that site and pay my respects to a good friend.

We continued east toward Ben Cat where there had been a U.S. Special Forces Base Camp. The surrounding area was referred to as the Iron Triangle during the war that was heavily infiltrated by enemy soldiers and was the site of many significant battles. We stopped at a large memorial dedicated to the Viet Cong (VC) troops who had been killed during a month-long series of battles for control of the Iron Triangle area, termed by the U.S. as Operation Cedar Falls in January 1967.

Us Vietnam veterans honoring Captain Branch
with a salute at the site where his chopper was shot down.

The plaque near the memorial entrance stated that 2,000 American servicemen had been killed during those battles. We veterans knew that wasn't a true statement. Tom Graeve, one of our group, had served in that same area in 1968 and did some on-line research that evening. He found that American losses during Operation Cedar Falls were 72, while VC losses were estimated to have been 750.

Late that afternoon we checked into our hotel in Bien Hoa that was a clean and modern hotel where we enjoyed a delicious evening meal with the group.

During our tour some members of our group experienced indigestion for a day or two. In Mexico it is called Montezuma's revenge, in Vietnam they call it Ho Chi Minh's revenge. Viet said some tourists get sick because local water is often used to prepare food and a bug can be picked up from the food even if you didn't drink the water.

On Thursday, November 7th we walked outside to board the bus and found a site that brought memories for us Vietnam Veterans, rain.

We had planned our trip for November to avoid the daily monsoon rains and also avoid the even hotter weather experienced in January and February. A light shower continued throughout much of that day. The weather during most of our time in Vietnam was sunny, with the daytime temperatures in the low 90s and very humid.

Our tour continued through the city of Bien Hoa and a stop at the former U.S. Air Force Base there. We were allowed to walk onto the site, in the rain, where nothing remained except portions of the abandoned runway. We then stopped near the entrance to the former Army Base Camp at Long Binh but weren't allowed to enter because the site was under control of Vietnam's military. The base had been the site of the Long Binh jail or LBJ as it was often called. The jail housed American servicemen who had been convicted of crimes in Vietnam.

We then continued on toward Vung Tau, an eastern coastal resort city on the South China Sea. While touring that day, we noticed that in front of many of the nicer homes that had a stone or metal fence and an entrance gate in front, there were statues for either a dog or a lion on pillars located on each side of the entrance to the home. Viet told us that the residents believed that those statues protected their property. We also saw children near schools each day. Interestingly, the students all wore black trousers, white shirts and a bright red neck scarf.

Vung Tau is a city of approximately 323,000 inhabitants and serves as a resort destination for area citizens and tourists to enjoy the beaches and many nice hotels and restaurants. During the war, the U.S. military operated a rest and relaxation (R&R) center there; so our first stop after arriving in the city was at that R&R center that remains today as a hotel.

During our stop at the R&R center we were greeted by several street vendors offering souvenirs, clothing, books, or trinkets for tourists to purchase. Those street vendors were very persistent in trying to make a sale because they knew once someone walked away, their opportunity for a sale was over. One of those vendors, a woman likely in her late 30s, made a connection with my wife Marilyn, and although Marilyn surprisingly didn't buy anything, that woman apparently believed Marilyn would eventually make a purchase. As we traveled toward our hotel, Marilyn looked out the window in amazement and saw that woman riding alongside the bus on her scooter waving at Marilyn.

When we arrived at the Sammy Hotel, a lovely hotel directly across the street from a beach on the South China Sea, that Vietnamese woman was waving at us from a nearby side street because she wasn't allowed to make sales on the hotel property. Marilyn couldn't resist walking over to the woman and gave her $20 for risking her life driving through the local traffic to keep pace with our bus. In return, the young woman gave Marilyn a pretty laced fan.

Some of us walked to the beach after we checked into the hotel. There were large waves coming in generated by a typhoon that had caused considerable destruction and loss of life in the Philippines which were about 1,000 miles east of Vietnam. We had learned about the typhoon and our guide Viet was concerned that the storm would continue toward us and possibly disrupt our flight home in two days. Some businesses located directly on the beach had placed rows of sandbags as protection from the potential oncoming storm.

Although I had arrived in country during the war at Cam Ranh Bay, located on the coast north of Vung Tau, I don't recall seeing the beach and South China Sea back then. It therefore was an amazing site for me as Marilyn and I strolled along the beach looking out over the South China Sea a half a world away from home. We gathered a few seashells as souvenirs of our walk on the beach that day.

We were again up early to eat breakfast before we headed out to tour Vung Tau on Friday, November 8th. Our first stop was at a former retreat for the South Vietnamese President. The building had not been used as a retreat for years and was a museum filled with beautiful furniture and priceless artifacts from a ship that had sunk in the South China Sea. The former retreat was on a hillside providing a beautiful view to the east of the nearby harbor and the South China Sea. Surprisingly, the retreat was guarded by a little elderly man with no weapon.

Marilyn and I on the beach of the South China Sea.

We then rode a gondola to a hill overlooking the city that offered a tremendous view of Vung Tau and the South China Sea in the distance. At a park there was a small zoo, small ponds and waterfalls, a huge white Buddha statue, and a 100-foot tall metal American radar tower used during the war. We then visited a large cave on another hill above the city that had been used by the enemy during the war as living quarters and to store weapons and supplies.

After our Vung Tau tour that morning we enjoyed lunch at David's "Italian" restaurant offering an open view of the large ships and small fishing boats in the harbor directly across the street.

After lunch we were in for a special experience which was on our tour schedule but would be a first-time experience for all of us. Rather than riding the bus back to Saigon we would be taking a hydrofoil cruise on the Saigon River. Our luggage would be taken by our bus driver to our hotel in Saigon.

Hydrofoil boats look similar to a small ferry-type boat used to carry passengers. But they use a unique technology whereby as speed is gained, two hydrofoils (that look like skis) lift the boat's hull out of the water, decreasing drag and thus allowing for even greater speed.

Hydrofoils can reach speeds of up to 70 MPH, but we would be traveling about 50 MPH. Our trip to Saigon would be about an hour via the South China Sea at Vung Tau then traveling northwest on the Saigon River.

We boarded the hydrofoil along with about 80 other passengers and settled into comfortable seats near the front of the boat. We slowly left the dock but as we continued across the bay of the South China Sea towards the Saigon River, we gained speed and felt the hull of the boat rise out of the water. The boat was literally skiing on the water.

The Saigon River was more than one half mile wide as it met the sea and narrowed slightly as we skied towards Saigon, with the river remaining about a quarter mile wide as it flowed through Saigon. The ride was smooth considering our speed with vibrations felt from the roaring engine and hydrofoils skimming over the water. Some of us walked around during the cruise and Marilyn and I and Chuck and Cherie found an open hatch where we enjoyed the view over the water and the lush green vegetation along the distant shoreline. While that hydrofoil ride was exciting for us tourists, for the many local civilians riding with us, it was just a mode of transportation to or from work.

Although we encountered a few large transport ships and barges, many small fishing boats, and met several other hydrofoils as we sped toward Saigon, the vastness of the river made it easy for our pilot to navigate. As we slowed when we neared the dock near downtown Saigon, the craft lowered itself into the water meaning the end of a unique and exciting return to Saigon. After we disembarked, Viet led the group on the three-block walk to our luxurious Grand Hotel Saigon.

Saturday November 9th was our final full day in Vietnam with a tour of Saigon planned. The weather remained a concern as the typhoon was moving toward Vietnam, but the location and time of its arrival remained uncertain. Viet would monitor the weather and flight impacts because we were scheduled to fly out late the following afternoon. Fortunately, the weather remained pleasant with no rain in Saigon.

Our tour of Saigon began with a stop at the Colonial Saigon Post Office constructed by the French in the early 20th century. The French control of Vietnam began in the 19th century and continued into the early 1950s. France controlled Laos, Cambodia and Vietnam, collectively called French Indochina. Accordingly, French architecture is seen in many buildings constructed during that time period. We also toured the nearby Notre Dame Cathedral with a beautiful interior.

Interior of the post office with Ho Chi Minh's picture in the distance.

Our next stop was the Presidential Palace where NVA troops crashed the gates on April 30, 1975 forcing President Minh of the Republic of South Vietnam to surrender (see picture on page 364).

Because the palace is a big tourist attraction, we encountered a huge crowd as we passed through the gates and walked across the beautifully landscaped courtyard toward the palace entrance. The palace had been used by South Vietnam's President to conduct governmental business and manage the war. It was the site where American military leaders met with President Minh during that time.

The palace was also the family's living quarters, like the White House in Washington, DC. There were many meeting rooms, dining rooms and other rooms used to greet dignitaries. There was a basement communications center used during the war and a helicopter landing pad on the roof. It was an amazing place to visit because so much of the history relating to the war occurred there. One of the NVA tanks that crashed the gates remains on display adjacent to the courtyard.

Our group at one of the two front gates to the Presidential Place in the background.

There was considerable upheaval in South Vietnam when it was overtaken by Communist control in 1975. Land and businesses were seized, with former North Vietnamese military officials receiving much of the confiscated property. The new government (Socialist Republic of Vietnam) took control of most of the commerce, leaving most Vietnamese citizens very oppressed.

However, beginning in the 1990s Vietnam opened trade relations with many countries, including the United States, which improved the economic conditions for many of its citizens. Tourism is now a big business with nearly eight million tourists visiting the country in 2014. Religious freedoms have been granted with numerous religions, including Christianity, practiced. There are also human rights limitations such as punishment of anyone who openly criticizes the government, and private ownership of weapons is prohibited.

The availability of adequate health care remains a concern, with malnutrition and high infant mortality rates in many provinces. The lack of clean water promotes typhoid and cholera, while tuberculosis and malaria continue to plague much of the country.

Despite the numerous socialist controls in place, we were all pleasantly surprise how friendly most Vietnamese civilians were to us. Most people we interacted with spoke English and assisted us during our visit. It also appeared that everyone freely traveled about the cities and countryside without limitations.

After leaving the Presidential Palace, we visited a site that returned memories for all of us. We saw the memorial in tribute to the Buddhist monk Thich Quanag Duc who set himself afire in 1963 in protest of the government's persecution of Buddhists. The monument is in a small park adjacent to the street where the monk set himself afire.

Marilyn and I at the Buddhist Monk's Memorial in Saigon.

For lunch that day Viet took us to a PHO restaurant (PHO meaning soup and pronounced "*Fa*") where President Clinton had eaten lunch during his visit in November 2000. We ate in the same second floor room where President Clinton did. There was a picture of him enjoying his lunch and a sign on the wall with the restaurant's circular logo that read, "PHO 2000, Lunch for the President." That was certainly a unique experience but I didn't enjoy the PHO, although Marilyn loved it.

After lunch we went to Chinatown, yes, there is a Chinatown in Saigon. It looked similar to Chinatowns in other cities with small crowded streets and many small shops and restaurants.

Walking along the sidewalks in Chinatown, and in most other Vietnamese cities, was a challenge because there were scooters and motorcycles parked on the sidewalks, often leaving only a small path to walk through. I had seen a few parking lots with hundreds of scooters and motorcycles, but for the most part, the sidewalks were their parking lots, with store owners often collecting a fee for the privilege.

Most of us noticed in most major cities in Vietnam the utility wires were strung between poles above ground. We often saw a huge bundle of wires where hundreds of utility wires converged into what looked like a huge beehive.

Our next stop was at the War Remnants Museum containing, just as the name implied, exhibits of the war. The museum operated by the Vietnamese Communist Government was opened in 1975 as the *Exhibition House for U.S. and Puppet Crimes* (puppet meaning the South Vietnamese Government). The exhibition was not the first of its kind for the North Vietnamese, but rather followed a tradition of such exhibitions exposing what they believed to be American war crimes. In 1990, the name changed to Exhibition House for Crimes of War and Aggression, then in 1995, following the normalization of diplomatic relations with the United States, the museum's title became the *War Remnants Museum*.

Although the museum's name had been changed, the exhibition portrayed the war from Vietnam's point of view as our enemy. There were graphic pictures accompanied by texts in English, Vietnamese and Japanese, covering the effects of Agent Orange defoliant on citizens, the use of napalm and phosphorus bombs, and war atrocities such as the My Lai massacre. There were pictures of towns destroyed by American bombs with the account of the numbers of civilians killed or wounded.

The following statement issued in 1967 was on display:

"The United States bears responsibility for the use of force in Vietnam, and has therefore, committed a crime of aggression, a crime against peace. In subjecting the civilian populations and civilian targets of the D.R.V.N. (North Vietnam) to an intense and systematic bombardment, the U.S.A. has committed a crime of war. This is on the part of the U.S. armed forces, utilization or testing of weapons prohibited by the laws of war (cluster bombs, napalm, phosphorus bombs, combat gasses, toxic chemicals). The prisoners of war captured by the U.S. armed forces are subjected to treatments prohibited by the laws of war. The U.S. armed forces subject the civilian populations to inhuman treatments prohibited by international law. The U.S.A. is guilty of genocide against the Vietnamese people."

I would not assert that American actions during the war did not cause hardship for many Vietnamese civilians; however, and unfortunately, the weapons of war used by all combatants, in any war, causes unintended consequences for innocent civilians living in a war zone. The majority of actions initiated by American forces during the war, were not intended to cause injury or death for the civilian population.

The museum went to great lengths to portray the U.S. armed forces as the *bad guys* while there were no exhibits depicting any of the atrocities committed by the NVA and VC against their own population both during the war and thereafter, causing thousands of deaths.

As we had seen at the memorial near Ben Cat where American losses were exaggerated, the War Remnants Museum also offered a very *slanted* view about America's involvement in the war, and unfortunately, for the thousands of people from around the world who visit that museum, and who know no differently, they leave with that slanted perception. The museum visit resulted in considerable discussion amongst our group and a sense of frustration and a bit of anger for us Vietnam veterans.

Interestingly, in America we refer to the war as the *Vietnam* War; however, in Vietnam the war is referred to as the *American* War.

That evening we walked two blocks south and boarded a dinner cruise boat that journeyed us on the Saigon River while we enjoyed our meal and entertainment of dancing girls in traditional Vietnamese costumes that followed. It was a very pleasant evening as we talked about our experiences the past week while enjoying the view of downtown Saigon from the river.

After dinner the men decided it was time for a *guy's* night out. There was no objection from the women as they were tired and ready to relax in their rooms. Jeff and John Gorman, Chuck's sons, had spent time during the late evenings checking local venues, while we older folks were sleeping. Jeff and John suggested we go to a little bar two blocks north of the hotel called the "Bier Garden."

We eight guys ordered a round of beers, with some drinking Ba, Ba, Ba (333) beer brewed in Vietnam while others chose Tiger beer brewed in Singapore. American beers such as Coors, Miller or Budweiser weren't available in Vietnam. We enjoyed a couple of beers while we discussed the many sites we had visited, and for us Vietnam vets, we talked about some of the memories the tour had brought back for us. It obviously had been an incredible week for each of us.

Something most noticeable to us veterans was that the former fire bases and base camps had been demolished and removed from the countryside. With the exception of portions of some runways, the buildings, bunkers and other structures were gone. There must have been a tremendous desire by the communist government to remove visible signs that America's military existed in Vietnam. It had to have taken years and hundreds of thousands of man-hours to remove almost everything America's military had constructed during the war. That evening was our way of commemorating the past week and a final time to relax together before we headed back to *the World*.

Sunday morning, November 10th, our last day in Vietnam began with several of us having breakfast together at the hotel that offered a buffet style breakfast with most anything you might want. Walking out of the dining room I saw a Christmas tree that had been set up in the corridor. Apparently Christmas was celebrated by Christians in Vietnam, but a fully decorated tree on November 10th seemed a bit early.

We weren't scheduled to leave for the airport until midafternoon, so Marilyn felt the need for one more shopping venture. There were many places to shop in Saigon including street vendors, gift and souvenir shops, and then there were some lavish stores where you could spend considerable amounts for more elegant items. Most businesses accepted American dollars and Vietnamese "Dongs" (VND) The exchange rate was 21,080 VND to one U.S. dollar.

Marilyn and I visited several stores where she purchased more souvenirs and I bought a t-shirt, which I found after arriving home was too small. A large or x-large size shirt in Vietnam is not the same as those sizes are in the U.S. After a couple hours I had experienced enough shopping and was ready to head back to the hotel. We happened to pass by the Bier Garden, so naturally, we stopped in and enjoyed a cold Tiger beer after our shopping excursion.

Marilyn had become quite popular with the street vendors who regularly gathered near our hotel in Saigon. Marilyn rarely would say "*No*" to a street vendor. While most of us purchased a book or a souvenir from one of those street vendors, during our last two days in Saigon, the vendors near our hotel would nearly swarm Marilyn when they saw her. She borrowed money from me but she still left Vietnam totally broke helping to support those street vendors while buying books, wallets, sunglasses and other souvenirs.

Our guide Viet reported that the typhoon had lost much of its power while passing over the South China Sea and was expected to hit

Vietnam's coast north of Saigon likely on Monday. So that afternoon we arrived at Tan Son Nhut Airport to board our flight back to *the World*.

As our plane lifted off from Tan Son Nhut Airport late that afternoon I was slightly saddened that our tour of Vietnam was over, but I was extremely happy that I had made the trip. My return to Vietnam was the greatest experience of my life. To return to the country and to walk upon some of the same ground that I had fought on 44 years prior was an extraordinary experience. Just like I couldn't truly imagine what it would be like to serve as an infantryman in Vietnam before I arrived, I couldn't truly imagine what it would be like to return to Vietnam until I completed our tour.

We had a brief layover at Taipei to transfer to the plane taking us to Los Angeles. Ironically, by the clock, we arrived in Los Angeles *before* we left Taipei because we crossed back over the International Date Line and gained back the day we had lost traveling to Vietnam. We departed Taipei at approximately 11:50 p.m. on November 10th and landed at LAX at approximately 7:15 p.m. the same day.

With both my initial tour in Vietnam and my return visit, my actual experience was much different than I had imagined. My war-time experience was worse than anticipated, not because I lost my leg, but sadly, I lost fourteen good friends. Fortunately, my return trip to Vietnam was better than anticipated, and I am thankful to have had the opportunity to return to the place that changed my life forever. It was a wonderful trip for both Marilyn and me.

My Final Thoughts

In an email from Victor Ortega, my friend and fellow member of the third platoon, he commented "For only the dead is the war truly over." A very simple but true statement.

Although I served only six months in Vietnam, those memories will remain with me forever. And while those memories are not seriously troubling for me, they remain for some veterans of all wars, memories that haunt them for decades. Hearing the word "Vietnam" can send a tingle through my spine to this day. So my advice to my fellow veterans is, "Let it out." Don't carry the burden of holding those emotions inside yourself. While it may be difficult, share your experiences and feelings with family members or friends, it should provide terrific therapy.

My wife Marilyn has commented that she notices that beginning in the fall of each year I imbibe more than normal when I recall the dates of my most disturbing experiences in Vietnam, including September 16th when Hal Harris was killed while leading our ambush patrol, November 21st when James "Red" Mincey was killed by a booby-trapped hand grenade, December 17th when Willard Spivey was killed and I was wounded by the exploding land mine in the Ho Bo Woods, Christmas Eve when Glen Haywood died, December 28th when we lost nearly one half of the third platoon, and of course, January 27th when I was seriously wounded.

I am not saying my conduct is appropriate and I also don't claim that I have a good excuse to drink more than normal. But yes, maybe that's how I deal with that time of each year as I remember the traumatic events that I experienced so many years ago. However, with certainty, the most extraordinary experience of my life in Vietnam changed me forever both emotionally and physically.

But fortunately, I annually move through that time of year and continue on without more serious ramifications. However, my behavior proves the long-standing adage that no one leaves military service unchanged, some more than others. And that is why a unique bond of comradeship exists among America's veterans, a bond that only veterans truly understand.

I conclude by saying to all my fellow American military veterans, "Thank you for your service."

About 60% of Vietnam's population of over 90 million were born after 1973 when American combat troops left the country, and therefore have no personal memory of the war. One lasting effect of the war is the large number of older Vietnamese women who never married because of the significant number of Vietnamese males who were killed during the war.

Although we saw few signs of the war remaining in southern portions of Vietnam, in the northern areas around Hanoi there are remains of U.S. aircraft on display that were shot down during the war. Some sections of the countryside remain pock marked with bomb craters, some of which have been transformed into ponds to raise fish.

While we felt warmly received by the Vietnamese civilians in southern Vietnam, those who have traveled to the former North Vietnam say they were not always as well received by those civilians. Many Vietnamese civilians living in northern Vietnam have retained more conservative Asian traditions, while citizens in the south have adopted more progressive and modern views and welcome all tourists. A divide still exists between many citizens living in northern vs southern Vietnam because of lingering differences about the war.

Another distinct observation during our visit, was the complete lack of public acknowledgement of those who served in the Army of the Republic of South Vietnam (ARVNs) who possibly suffered over 300,000 casualties while defending South Vietnam. Vietnam's government does not believe those individuals warrant recognition.

Tourism is a significant component of the modern Vietnamese economy. Vietnam's National Administration of Tourism is following a long-term plan to diversify the tourism industry, which brings needed foreign exchange into the country. From an insignificant number of visitors in the early 1990s, tourist arrivals in the country have leaped from around 2 million in 2003 to 7.8 million in 2014. In tandem with these growing numbers, facilities for visitors are constantly improving. New hotels are opening, appealing to both luxury and budget travelers. The popularity of the country's battlefields and other places associated with war, such as the Cu Chi Tunnels northwest of Saigon, reflect a growing niche market in Vietnam's tourism.

Epilogue

During the second week of September 2015, fifteen members of Alpha Company who served together in Vietnam gathered for a reunion in Estes Park, CO, along with several wives and special others. We greeted each other with hugs and handshakes and laughed at how the years had changed us physically. However, amazingly we shared war stories, viewed pictures of us when we were all slim and fit, and shared our life's experiences since the war as though we had never been apart.

The bonds of brotherhood that had been formed in Vietnam remained as we enjoyed time together in the scenic and peaceful beauty of the Rocky Mountains with deer and elk wandering near our lodge. I could sense the mutual respect shown amongst us, sometimes with comments about an individual's actions during a specific combat event, but most often with the sincere tone of individual or small group conversations displaying recognition of our mutual combat experiences and sacrifices. We all shared one other common thought; thankfulness that we survived our time in Vietnam.

And while our wives and special others often gathered separately while us veterans shared our stories, they too bonded knowing that having a long-term relationship with a Vietnam veteran is not always easy, and that compromises and understanding are needed to maintain those relationships. I know every Vietnam veteran greatly appreciates the support of their spouse and special others for their love and support over the years.

I remained in contact with many of my former comrades and found that most of them are doing well and remember me as Hound Dog. Below is a brief update on those men.

- Richard Benson, Sergeant, wounded on January 27, 1970. He is a retired Congressional aide and lives in Connecticut.

- Bill Casey, RTO, is retired and lives in South Carolina.
- Steve Donaldson, third platoon leader, retired from the Army as a Lieutenant Colonel in 1990 and lives in Virginia.
- Chuck Gorman, RTO, is a retired teacher in Nebraska.
- David Hardy, rifleman, is retired and lives in Wisconsin.
- Kevin Higginson, second platoon leader, is a retired New York State police officer.
- Junior Houchens (Houch), rifleman, is retired and lives in Kentucky.
- Ed Leberski, rifleman, is a retired electrician in Pennsylvania.
- Sidney "Doc" Morrison, company medic, is a retired teacher in California.
- Mike Myers (Babysan), rifleman, is retired and lives in Idaho.
- Victor Ortega, rifleman, is a retired carpenter living in Oregon.
- Jim Overbey, Sergeant, lives in Kentucky; however, he continues to deal with PTSD that has impacted his quality of life.
- Dave Phillips, third platoon leader, retired from AT&T and lives in Indiana.
- Bob Ryken, our RTO seriously wounded on December 28, 1969, is a retired federal employee living in California.
- Carl Seals, rifleman, is a retired truck driver living in Oregon.
- Rick Shields, Staff Sergeant, is a retired police officer in California.
- Mertis "Doc" Snyder, third platoon medic wounded on December 28, 1969, is a retired truck driver in Pennsylvania.
- Michael Stark, assistant gunner and gunner, retired telephone company employee in Wisconsin.
- Mike Walsh, first platoon leader, is a retired marketing executive for a pharmaceutical manufacturer living in New Jersey.

Eight former members of the Third Herd are known to have passed away since safely returning from Vietnam:

- Dennis Schultz. RTO, died in 1982 (cause unknown).
- Carlton Quick, rifleman, died in 1983 of a heart attack in Griffin, Georgia.
- John Bergen (Bugsy), rifleman, died in 1983 (cause unknown).
- Robert Draughn, rifleman, died in 1993 (cause unknown).
- Verney Prettyhip (Chief), rifleman, died in 1985 (cause unknown).
- Larry "Doc" Jackson retired from the Navy and died in 2006 of cancer related to exposure to Agent Orange in Vietnam.
- Larry Sutton, rifleman, wounded on December 17, 1969, died in 2011 of complications from diabetes related to exposure to Agent Orange in Vietnam.
- David Debiasio (Wop), machine gunner, was a retired Florida State employee. He died of cancer in 2012 related to exposure to Agent Orange in Vietnam.

To gain further information regarding the men in Alpha Company and to view additional pictures please visit the following web site:
http://www.i-kirk.info/2nd14th/index.html

I thank Kirk Ramsey, former member of Alpha Company, for maintaining that site.

Some Vietnam veterans have chosen to use their experience as an excuse for failure. Fortunately, I chose to use my experience as a learning event to help me successfully progress through my life. I was proud to honorably serve my country in the armed forces, and I hold my head high when I say, "I'm a Vietnam veteran."

I fought for my life in Vietnam and endured the tragedy of seeing friends die in what became a futile military effort. However, I believe the greatest tragedy of the Vietnam War was that our country allowed nearly three million Americans to serve in a politically manipulated war that proved to be unsuccessful. America should have learned from the lessons of Vietnam, and those lessons should never have been forgotten. However again, American forces have fought in Afghanistan and Iraqi far longer that we fought in Vietnam, with no definitive plan for success. Philosopher and novelist George Santayana said, "Those who cannot remember the past are condemned to repeat it."

"No people who have ever lived have fought harder,
paid a higher price for freedom, or done more
to advance the dignity of man than Americans."
—Ronald Reagan, 40th U.S. President

GOD BLESS AMERICA

Let every nation know, whether
it wishes us well or ill, that we
shall pay any price, bear any
burden, meet any hardship,
support any friend, and oppose
any foe to assure the survival
and the success of liberty.

—John Fitzgerald Kennedy
35th President of the United States

Glossary

AFB – Air Force Base.

APC – Armored Personnel Carrier – heavy track-driven vehicle used to transport troops in the battlefield.

AIT – Advanced Infantry Training – training to become an infantryman.

AK-47 or **AK** – Russian made rifle used by enemy troops in Vietnam.

AK (Fitz chapter) – Above the knee amputation.

ARVN – Army of the Republic of South Vietnam – supported the South Vietnamese cause and American troops.

ARVNs – General term referring to ARVN troops.

AWOL – Absent Without Leave.

BK – Below the knee amputation.

CIB – Combat Infantryman Badge.

CO – Commanding Officer.

CP – Command Post – The location of the unit commander and his staff.

CP Group – Men assigned to the unit commander or a general referral to the unit commander and his staff.

C-4 – White plastic clay-like explosive.

Deuce-and-a-half – 2 ½ ton triple axel military cargo truck.

DMZ – Demilitarized Zone – the boundary between North and South Vietnam.

Dustoff – Nickname for medical evacuation helicopter.

E-1, E-2, etc. – The pay grade for enlisted military personnel - E-1 is the pay grade for a private, E-5 is the pay grade for a sergeant.

FNG – F---ing New Guy – slang term meaning a person who recently arrived in Vietnam.

GI – Government Issue – slang term for military personnel or relating to the military (GI haircut).

Gook – Derogatory slang for Asian – normally used when referring to enemy troops in Vietnam.

Gunship – term referring to aircraft (a plane or helicopter) armed with guns and rockets primarily used to attack ground targets.

H & I – Harassment and Interdiction mortar or artillery fire.

Hard Spot – A short-term defensive position normally consisting of a perimeter of foxholes (no bunkers or other fortifications).

Hooch - Slang term for a hut or small house inhabited by Vietnamese civilians. Also slang term for small GI living quarters.

Huey – Nickname for the Bell UH-1 utility and medical evacuation helicopter – originally designated as HU-1, hence nickname huey.

KIA – Killed in Action.

Klick – One kilometer – one klick = 1,000 meters or .6 miles.

LAW – Light Anti-Tank Weapon.

LAX – Los Angeles International Airport

LZ – Landing Zone – area designated for helicopters to drop off troops.

M-16 – American rifle primarily used in Vietnam.

M-60 – American machine gun primarily used in Vietnam.

M-79 – American grenade launcher used in Vietnam.

Medevac – Abbreviated term for Medical Evacuation Helicopter.

MM – Millimeter – referring to size of artillery or mortar rounds.

MOS – Military Occupational Specialty – 11B/Bravo was the MOS Light Weapons Infantryman.

MPC – Military Payment Certificate – paper money used in lieu of American dollars in Vietnam.

NCO – Non-commissioned Officer (Sergeant, Staff Sergeant, etc.).

NVA – North Vietnamese Army – enemy troops.

OD – Olive Drab (green) – the color of Army fatigues and most Army vehicles.

OCS – Officer Candidate School – training to become a military officer.

OJT – On-the-Job-Training.

PFC – Private First Class – pay grade E-3.

PX – Post Exchange – similar to a department store.

PT – Physical Training (physical therapy Chapters 18 & 19).

PZ – Pick-up Zone – area designated for helicopters to pick up troops.

RIF – Reconnaissance in Force – military term meaning a patrol.

RPG – Rocket-Propelled Grenade – enemy B-40 rocket.

R & R – Rest and Relaxation.

RTO – Radio-Telephone Operator – the man who carried the radio and handled radio communications.

Spec 4 – Specialist Fourth Class – pay grade E-4.

VC – Viet Cong – slang for Vietnamese Communist – enemy troops.

3-6 – Radio call sign for the third platoon leader – often became his nickname.

12th Evac – 12th Evacuation Hospital in Cu Chi.

Bibliography

The following were sources of reference in writing *A Soldier's Story: Forever Changed*.

The Vietnam Experience, Boston Publishing Company, 1982, fifteen volume series detailing the Vietnam War.

The Illustrated History of the Vietnam War, Chris McNab & Andy Wiest, Thunder Bay Press, 2000, a history of the Vietnam War.

The Vietnam War Almanac, Harry G. Summers Jr., Presidio Press, 1999, analysis and reference source for the Vietnam War.

One More Mission, Oliver L. North and David Roth, Zondervan Publishing House/Harper Collins 1993, assessment of American Involvement in the Vietnam War.

Dirty Little Secrets of the Vietnam War, James F. Dunnigan and Albert A. Nofi, Thomas Dunne Books, 1999, military information you're not supposed to know.

The ARMY, Army Historical Foundation, Hugh Lauter Levin Associates, Inc., 2001, history of the Army.

United States Military Almanac, Walt Lang, Salamander Books Limited, 1998, a chronological compendium of American history.

Schaller Centennial, History Book Committee, 1983, history of Schaller, Iowa.

Wikipedia, the free encyclopedia.

Vietnam, Michael Maclear, Black Dog & Leventhal Publishers, 2003, A complete photographic history.

Other information was obtained from numerous Internet sites regarding general military information, the 25th Infantry Division, Vietnam and the Vietnam War.

Richlyn Publishing
Order Form

To order copies of *A Soldier's Story: Forever Changed* copy this form and complete the following information:

*Number of Copies	Price	Total*
_____	$16.95	$ _____

Shipping and
Handling: $ _____ $ _____

1 Book $4.00
2-3 Books $5.25
4-5 Books $7.50   Total Amount: $ _____

*For orders in Colorado add 5% sales tax

(Enclose check or money order for the total amount
payable to Richard Hogue.)

* For large orders, email for pricing to: richlyn2@msn.com

NAME: _____

ADDRESS: _____

CITY: _____STATE/ZIP: _____

PHONE: _____
Email: _____   Information provided will be
maintained in strict privacy.

Mail to: Richard Hogue
                  12045 W Brandt Pl
                  Littleton, CO 80127- 4572

Orders will be shipped by regular mail book rate
within three business days of receipt of order.

Ebook versions are available at: amazon.com/dp/B01N5P064Q

Books make excellent gifts that can last forever.

CPSIA information can be obtained
at www.ICGtesting.com
Printed in the USA
FSHW011530080321
79035FS